Of War and Men

Of War and Men

World War II in the Lives of Fathers and Their Families

Ralph LaRossa

The University of Chicago Press
Chicago and London

Ralph LaRossa is professor of sociology at Georgia State University. He has written extensively on the topic of fathers and families, and is the author of *The Modernization of Fatherhood: A Social and Political History*, which is also published by the University of Chicago Press.

The University of Chicago Press, Chicago 60637
The University of Chicago Press, Ltd., London
© 2011 by The University of Chicago
All rights reserved. Published 2011
Printed in the United States of America

20 19 18 17 16 15 14 13 12 11   1 2 3 4 5

ISBN-13: 978-0-226-46742-9
ISBN-13: 978-0-226-46743-6
ISBN-10: 0-226-46742-2
ISBN-10: 0-226-46743-0

Library of Congress Cataloging-in-Publication Data

LaRossa, Ralph.
    Of war and men : World War II in the lives of fathers and their families / Ralph LaRossa.
        p. cm.
    Includes bibliographical references and index.
    ISBN-13: 978-0-226-46742-9 (cloth : alk. paper)
    ISBN-10: 0-226-46742-2 (cloth : alk. paper)
    ISBN-13: 978-0-226-46743-6 (pbk. : alk. paper)
    ISBN-10: 0-226-46743-0 (pbk. : alk. paper) 1. Fatherhood—Social aspects—United States. 2. Fatherhood—United States—History—20th century. 3. War and families—United States—History—20th century. 4. Soldiers—Family relationships—United States—History—20th century. 5. World War, 1939–1945—Social aspects—United States. I. Title.
    HQ756 .L375 2011
    306.874'2—dc22

                                                    2010049631

♾ The paper used in this publication meets the minimum requirements of the American National Standard for Information Sciences—Permanence of Paper for Printed Library Materials, ANSI Z39.48-1992.

With love and with gratitude to

Joseph G. LaRossa
Frances M. LaRossa
George A. Mulligan
Marie M. Mulligan

One does not *erase* the effects of war.
Its impact on society goes too deep for that.

Winifred Rand, Mary E. Sweeny, and E. Lee Vincent,
Growth and Development of the Young Child (1946)

CONTENTS

PART IV

ACKNOWLEDGMENTS

I recall the day when I discovered my father's World War II memorabilia in the attic of our home. I was just a kid at the time. At first, I did not know what to make of the items. There was not a lot there. An olive-colored waistcoat with insignia. A flat rectangular hat. A silk handkerchief embossed with a map.

I put on the hat to see how it fit and stared for a moment at the handkerchief. The map on the silk seemed especially odd, with lines going this way and that. It was not like any map or handkerchief I had seen before. I do not know what I did immediately after finding these items, but I do remember having a conversation with my parents about the war soon thereafter.

My dad, I learned, was in the army air corps and served as a radioman on B-series bombers. My mom was employed for a while in a Brooklyn factory that manufactured gyroscopes for planes and ships. Her work attire included a plastic cap that she wore to keep her hair from falling into the mechanisms. She held on to the cap after the war, and it now hangs on a wall by my desk at home. I do not know what became of my dad's uniform and map.

Writing this book has brought me closer to my parents in ways that I had not anticipated. It also has made me feel a tremendous sense of loss. There are so many questions about their experiences during and after the war that I never thought to ask them when I was younger, and that I want so much to ask now, but cannot. My father and mother passed away before this project was conceived.

There is really nothing that I could say here, or anywhere else, that could adequately express my appreciation to my parents for all they did for me. Although their names do not appear on the cover of the book, their influence is evident in its pages and in everything I do.

While working on this project, I thought a great deal about my sons, Adam and Brian, not only because I wanted to share with them what I was assimilating, but also because, with each passing day, I further realized just how much they have taught me and how their presence has been such a positive force in my life. I never asked Adam and Brian to read any part of the book in advance, preferring instead to wait until it was finished before I shared it with them, but their influence is also evident in its pages and in everything I do.

The one person I did call upon to read countless drafts, and to whom I talked about the book endlessly, is Maureen. She and I have been best friends, and more, for more than forty years, and I look forward to being with her for decades to come. We have raised two kids together; played and worked together; laughed and cried together; even, long ago, stared death in the face together. Maur's constructive feedback has made this an infinitely better work, and her love has sustained me throughout. It is a book that, in some ways, is as much hers as it is mine. Thanks "Kid." We did it again.

I never would have been able to complete this project without the generous support received from the College of Arts and Sciences and the Department of Sociology at Georgia State University. Dean Lauren Adamson, Associate Dean Mary Ann Romski, and Department Chair Donald Reitzes repeatedly have done whatever they could to make it possible for me to research and write, and for that I am extremely grateful. The administrative staff of the Department of Sociology has also been enormously helpful. Selma Alston, Dracy Blackwell, Brian Buckwald, Eric Johnson, and Quanda Miller have all been generous with their time. Selma Alston, who has been the department's Business Manager for many years, deserves special recognition. She has provided assistance in numerous ways while I have been at Georgia State.

Several individuals read drafts of chapters and offered valuable comments. They include Charles Jaret, Marie Mulligan, Donald Reitzes, Wendy Simonds, Griff Tester, Frank Whittington, Adia Harvey Wingfield, Saori Yasumoto, and, last but not least, Pam Regus, who, toward the end, read the entire book.

I am fortunate to have received help from graduate students who, sometimes working with me as my research assistants, tracked down and retrieved sources, or, in a few cases, simply brought relevant items to my attention. Several of them have earned their Ph.D.s and gone on to pursue academic careers of their own. For their varied contributions to the project, I thank

Angela Anderson, Christina Barmon, Roni Bell, Alexis Bender, Jeanna Boyd, Elizabeth Cavalier, Jennifer Chandler, Regina Davis-Sowers, April Ferguson, Amanda Jungels, Wei Li, Gail Markle, Amy Novak, Bobby Jo Otto, Amy Palder, Pam Regus, Cynthia Sinha, Elroi Windsor, and Saori Yasumoto. Faculty members and family members who provided sources and offered leads include Elisabeth Burgess, Phillip Davis, Charles Jaret, Jung Ha Kim, Anthony Maniscalco, Marie Mulligan, Paula Stephan, and Adia Harvey Wingfield.

I am especially appreciative for the materials that I was able to obtain from the following libraries: the Rare Book and Manuscript Library at Columbia University, which houses the Rose Franzblau Papers; the George Arents Research Library at Syracuse University, which houses the Benjamin Spock Papers; the Manuscript Division of the Library of Congress, which houses the American Gold Star Mothers Papers; the National Archives and Records Administration, which houses documents pertaining to the 1940 Selective Service Act and the 1943 Senate Hearings on the Drafting of Fathers; the Auburn Avenue Research Library on African American Culture and History, which houses issues of the *Chicago Defender*; and the Georgia State University Library, which houses many of the secondary sources upon which I have relied and also processed a number of interlibrary loan requests.

I am indebted as well to the Henry A. Murray Research Center Archive at Harvard University, which houses the interview transcripts and survey files for "Patterns of Child Rearing," a project conducted by Robert Sears, Eleanor Maccoby, and Harry Levin in 1951–52, and "Identification and Child Rearing," a project conducted by Robert Sears, Lucy Rau, and Richard Alpert in 1958. I especially appreciate the help I received from Archival Operations Manager Sonia Barbosa, who was kind enough to grant my request to use these data. I appreciate as well the individuals at the archive who copied the files and sent them to me.

A section of the book includes an excerpt from "'Until the Ball Glows in the Twilight': Fatherhood, Baseball, and the Game of Playing Catch," a chapter published in *Situated Fathering: A Focus on Physical and Social Spaces*. I am grateful to Rowman and Littlefield Publishers for allowing me to retain the copyright to the chapter, which facilitated my being able to incorporate it here. Other sections of the book include excerpts from my 2004 article, "The Culture of Fatherhood in the Fifties: A Closer Look," published in the *Journal of Family History*. I am grateful to Sage Publications for granting me permission to reprint the excerpts.

This is the second book that I have published with the University of Chicago Press and the second opportunity I have had to work with Executive

Editor Doug Mitchell, who, as before, saw value in the book when it was only in the prospectus stage. His enthusiasm for the project and his patience and unequivocal support when I told him that I needed a little more time to do justice to the subject further motivated me to write the best book I could. I also want to acknowledge the wonderful assistance that I received from Tim McGovern, who provided guidance on matters pertaining to logistics, permissions, digital files, and so forth. I want to recognize as well Nicholas Murray for his outstanding copyediting, Bonny McLaughlin for her excellent indexing, and Katherine Frentzel and Robert Hunt and their teams for their skillful production efforts. Finally, I want especially to thank the two anonymous reviewers for the Press whose detailed comments helped me to hone the book.

Ralph LaRossa

This is a book about warfare and its myriad effects. Specifically, it is a story about America's fathers and their families in the throes and aftermath of World War II, covering the period from 1941 to 1960—from the attack on Pearl Harbor to the election of John F. Kennedy.

My original motivation for embarking on the project is that I wanted to pick up where a prior project had left off. I felt a certain amount of ambivalence, similar to the experience of being wrapped up in a movie and hating to see it end, when I completed a historical study of fatherhood in the early twentieth century that had taken me years to research and write. Although I was excited to bring the study to a close, there was a part of me that wanted it to continue. I was curious about what happened next.

In the earlier project, I documented the history of fatherhood from colonial times to the Great Depression, with special emphasis on the 1920s and 1930s, two decades that scholars refer to as the machine age because of the technological advances that were made at the time.[1] It was during the machine age that many of the expectations that we currently apply to fathers became institutionalized. It was then that child-rearing experts actively promoted the idea that, besides being economic providers, fathers should also be their children's pals and male role models. Some experts also believed that fathers should be involved in the routine aspects of child care (e.g., diapering); but when it came to these activities, most assumed that men would serve as women's "helpers" or "stand-ins." This is not to say that men did little or no child care. A number of fathers, in fact, did quite a bit. But the nitty-gritty aspects of parenting were thought to be mainly the mother's job.[2]

The idea that fathers should be more than breadwinners was not an entirely new concept. In one form or another, it had been around since at least the nineteenth century.³ But during the machine age a combination of economic and cultural events worked to fuse a set of expectations—about more than just breadwinning—into a stereotype that, starting with the middle class and later spreading to other groups, became America's notion of what a "good" father was.

What made the fusion all the more intriguing were the paradoxical features beneath it. For at the same time that fathers were being told to be more central in their children's lives, they also had to deal with the burdensome consequences of the Great Depression. Men who lost their jobs or were forced to take significant cuts in pay frequently became so demoralized that they withdrew from their families. Ironically, the challenge to men's breadwinning status did not negate but helped to accentuate and legitimate other paternal expectations. If fathers could not financially support their wives and children, or could not support them as well as they had before, they could at least take comfort from the fact that there were alternative roles that people would honor. One measure of this dynamic was the growing popularity of Father's Day in the 1930s.⁴

The *modernization of fatherhood*, as I have referred to the process, proceeded apace during the Great Depression. With each passing year, the expectations for fathers to be more involved with family life increased. With each passing year, men's importance in child rearing was further acknowledged and acclaimed. What happened, however, when America entered World War II and the Great Depression came to an end? Did the modernization of fatherhood speed up? Did it slow? Did it stop? These are the questions that I wanted to be able to answer.

The deeper I got into the project, the more it became apparent that the story involved much more than this. I began to realize that, contrary to what some have implied, World War II was not a circumscribed event that momentarily interrupted the course on which fatherhood had been before. Rather, it was a social and political tidal wave whose impact on fathers and their families was profound. The key to appreciating this is not to presuppose what fatherhood was like in the 1950s and retrospectively wonder how it was affected by the war, but to begin with the war itself and prospectively examine how it affected society in general, of which fatherhood is a part. This alternative perspective underscores the importance of context and brings into view a host of war-related effects that are often excluded from scholarly and popular accounts of fatherhood but routinely included in basic historical works.⁵

Consider, first, people's reactions to the attack on Pearl Harbor on December 7, 1941. Besides prompting Congress to declare war on Japan, the bombardment heightened the level of fear and xenophobia in America and led to an increase in racial profiling. Anyone—or anything—associated with Japan was considered suspect. Japanese American fathers were especially vulnerable, but individuals mistakenly thought to be of Japanese descent (e.g., Chinese Americans and Korean Americans) were singled out, too. Because America was at war not only with Japan but also with Germany and Italy, people's animosities were directed to German Americans and Italian Americans as well, though to a much lesser extent than was true for Asian Americans. Many fathers and their families never recovered, financially or otherwise, from the prejudice and discrimination.

Men with children who were conceived on or before December 7, 1941, were at first exempted from the draft. Thousands of fathers, however, were already in uniform on the day of the attack, and others enlisted soon thereafter, in some cases taking the oath alongside their sons. After a year and a half of war, with no end to the hostilities in sight, the military recommended that the exemption for fathers be lifted. America's casualty figures were severe; more "bodies," as one general put it, were needed on the front lines. Congressional Hearings to debate the exemption were held in the spring and summer of 1943. The Pentagon and White House argued in favor of a fatherhood draft; others, including some members of Congress, spoke out against it. Opponents believed that fathers were too important to be separated from their children. Ultimately, the White House and Pentagon prevailed, and six million fathers, who previously had been shielded from the draft, became potential recruits.

World War II took men out of the home for months and made it difficult for fathers to stay connected to their daughters and sons. Letters back and forth were numerous but not enough to bridge the geographic divide. The battles in Europe and the Pacific were horrific. More than four hundred thousand American soldiers were killed (considering battle deaths and other deaths). Children were forced to grow up without fathers. Parents grieved the loss of their sons.[6]

When the war ended, the troops returned in phases, depending on, among other things, how long they were overseas and whether they had been assigned to a combat unit. Though it may be hard to believe now, there were few welcome-home parades for the sixteen million who served. Also, as the stories of wartime duty began to be told, it became apparent that the vast majority of soldiers did not fire a weapon, nor were they fired upon, which was a letdown for those who wanted their kinfolk to be heroes. One man, who was eleven years old when his father came home, said, "I was disappointed to learn that, after everything the rest of us went through so he could go off to war, he never even got shot at. I felt cheated."[7]

Of the eight hundred thousand or so men who did see combat, many came through the experience basically intact. Others, however, bore wounds, physical, psychological, or both, that would remain with them until the end of their days. For these men, reestablishing ties with their families was especially difficult; for a number of them, the fractured relationships were never again made whole.

World War II generated the social and political chemistry that led to both the Korean War and the Cold War, which generated further conflicts down the line (e.g., the Vietnam War and the student protest movement in the 1960s). World War II resulted in the Servicemen's Readjustment Act of 1944, or G.I. Bill, which created opportunities for millions of veterans to obtain advanced educations and affordable mortgages. The war also gave millions of women the chance to work outside the home (in munitions factories and elsewhere) and, though many of these women were fired from these jobs once the war was over, the fact that they were able to hold their own in male-dominated environments was not forgotten. Gender equality in the workplace would become a central plank in the postwar women's rights movement and a key element in the national conversation about men's roles as fathers in the 1950s and after.

Blacks were systematically blocked from enlisting in the military; and when they were allowed to join, they often were channeled into nonfighting roles and units. Many in the black community saw combat as a rite that would eventually undermine America's racist policies. They believed that segregation could not continue after those discriminated against showed a readiness to defend the country. When black fathers and sons eventually were given the opportunity to join the battle, they served with distinction, both in Europe and the Pacific. Although the war did not put an end to prejudice and discrimination, it did lead to the *de jure* desegregation of the armed forces (in 1948, with the signing of Presidential Executive Order 9981) and helped to invigorate the black civil rights movement. The 1954 *Brown v. Board of Education* Supreme Court ruling was a product of World War II. So was the 1955–56 Montgomery, Alabama bus boycott (along with other demonstrations). These strides toward freedom gave many in the country a reason for hope, but they also subjected black families to a backlash from white supremacists. Fathers and mothers, and sons and daughters were verbally and physically threatened; their homes and places of worship firebombed.[8]

Scientific discoveries made during World War II led to advances in communication and travel. The war also launched the atomic age and demonstrated that humans had it within their power to destroy not just a city or region but the entire planet. Everyone had reason to be scared. Youngsters, who might otherwise feel secure, feared for their safety and turned to their fathers and mothers for assurance, which—given the state of the world— was not always easy to provide.

The strong postwar economy made it possible for Americans to purchase cars and other big-ticket items that they could not have afforded in prior times. The war contributed to suburbanization, which provided larger homes and yards where fathers and their families could enact domestic ideals. Suburbanization also contributed to the growth of Little League baseball, with men serving as coaches and mentors. Little League baseball, in turn, refashioned the game of playing catch into a symbol of paternal love.

Television was to the post–World War II era what radio was to the machine age. Between 1950 and 1960 the proportion of American households with a television set rose from below one in ten to nearly nine in ten. Fathers were central characters in a number of television shows, including not only the ones that often are recalled (e.g., *Leave It to Beaver* and *Father Knows Best*) but also others that were very popular at the time but are rarely talked about today (e.g., *Make Room for Daddy* and *The Rifleman*). The shows broadcast images of fathers that, though fictitious, were used by children to judge their own fathers and families. The lives of most kids did not match the television "ideal." None of the shows, for example, seriously addressed domestic battering and abuse, yet we know that violence toward women and children was common. The disappointment in not having TV-like childhoods would remain in the minds of some, not only as they were growing up, but also later when they became adults. The memories that baby boomers have about families in the postwar era are a product of these contradictions.

Television also figured significantly in the 1960 presidential election, in which John F. Kennedy and Richard M. Nixon squared off. One of the closest political contests in U.S. history may very well have been decided by who looked more attractive on TV. But other variables may also have played a part, among them the candidates' service in World War II (which allowed one nominee to argue, during a high point in the Cold War, that he knew from experience what war was all about), and a fatherhood factor (which brought to bear the love of a man for his son and his family, and the attention that another man gave to his baby girl). The election, on some level, was about war and about fatherhood, and it signaled (to quote from the inaugural address) the ascension of a generation that had been "tempered by war," but also "disciplined by . . . peace"—a generation that soon would steer the country through the challenges that lay ahead.

The story I am about to relate begins with America's entry into the war and proceeds chronologically from there. The book is divided into thirteen chapters grouped into four parts. Part 1 covers the war, and part 2 talks about what happened in its immediate wake. Part 3 discusses events that began to take shape in the late 1940s and early 1950s, and part 4 mainly discusses what transpired between 1955 and 1960. In the epilogue, I return to the question of the war's impact and outline several connections between yesterday and today.

As I did with the study of fatherhood in the machine age, I rely on a rich set of materials to ground the story, including magazine articles, newspaper reports, child-rearing manuals, advertisements, posters, comic strips, radio and television shows, public and private records, advice-seeking letters to various experts, family correspondence, interviews with fathers and mothers, and a host of secondary sources. Also, as before, I pay close attention to periodic shifts and fluctuations. Doing so enables me to uncover patterns that other historical works have tended to overlook—patterns that indicate that fatherhood between 1945 and 1960 (also known as "the fifties") is best understood not as a single moment but as a complex of phases.[9] Fatherhood in the late 1940s was different from fatherhood in the early 1950s, which was different from fatherhood in the late 1950s. Thus, a parenting manual published in 1946 (e.g., Benjamin Spock's first edition of *The Common Sense Book of Baby and Child Care*) cannot be construed to represent the philosophy of childrearing in 1960. Nor can a parenting manual published in 1957 (when Spock's second edition came out) be assumed to represent the philosophy of childrearing in 1951. Noteworthy, too, is that when all three phases are closely examined, the phase that is the most traditional, with the greatest emphasis given to differences between fatherhood and motherhood, is not the first but the last. Fatherhood in America did not become more modern in the fifties; it actually became less so. The modernization of fatherhood that had begun in the prewar era was reversed.

The postwar pattern—the *traditionalization of fatherhood*—was a departure from prewar trends, but it ironically would help to spark a social movement in the 1960s, 1970s, and 1980s that demanded greater father involvement. A key component of the movement was the effort on the part of the children of the fifties to convince everyone, including themselves, that they were *not* like their parents (i.e., not the traditional folks they thought their parents were).

As laudable as increased father involvement is as a goal, sometimes people's recollections have gotten a bit strange. So as to cognitively distance themselves from their parents, children of the fifties periodically have taken an extreme position and spoken not just of their fathers but of *all* of the men in their fathers' generation—as *totally* uninvolved in the lives of their children. This exaggerated or hyperbolic narrative often has been used to explain why the sons of the fifties purportedly have had a difficult time knowing how to be fathers themselves. The basic claim is that yesterday's fathers were inadequate guides.

"What does it mean to be a father?" asked two dads who grew up in the fifties. "Men of our parents' generation gave this question little serious consideration." Having been raised by men who, they implied, *never* earnestly contemplated what being a father meant, the dads were in a quandary about what to do. How were they supposed to know how to "shape" their definitions of fatherhood? "We could look to the past," the dads hypothesized. "But, for the most part, we are not supposed to be like our own fathers, nor do we wish it."[10] Similarly, another dad who grew up in the fifties insisted, "The men of my father's generation didn't consciously consider that they were missing anything by being less than present in the lives of their children. . . . Men believed [then] that their *only* role was to provide."[11]

A cursory examination of the evidence on fatherhood in the postwar era may lead one to believe that these statements are correct: men in the fifties were uniformly deplorable dads. Careful study, however, indicates more variety than these hyperbolic narratives allow. The absence of nationwide surveys on fatherhood in the postwar era may make it difficult to know for sure the amount of time that men spent with their children and, equally if not more important, what the quality of their interactions were.[12] Nonetheless, there is more than enough information at various archives and in the public domain to challenge popular lore. Yesterday's fathers, taken as a whole, may not have been as involved in child care as women were, but they also, in general, were not as aloof as they often have been characterized. Take, for example, the following cases.

A father of a baby girl penned a letter in the late 1940s to Rose Franzblau, a clinical psychologist and syndicated advice columnist for the *New York Post*, and stated that when his daughter came home from the hospital "she was only a little thing" and that she was prone to cry. "Those first 3 or 4 months," he said, " . . . I can't remember a time when wee [*sic*] were able to sit down together to enjoy a meal. I never went to 'Fathers' School,' but I learned fast how to diaper, bathe, feed and burp that little one. . . . [A]t night and week-ends I performed maybe 75% of the services which the little ones demanded."[13]

Another father wrote around the same time to Franzblau to report that he had sole responsibility for his and his ex-wife's four-and-a-half-year-old son. He said that over the past two years he had run into difficulty keeping a job and was sometimes homeless, and that, at the moment, he was paying $15 a week to a family to take in the child. Although he was currently employed, he yearned to do more. "My son . . . has never had a stable life and I want to do something good for him. . . . Right now we have nowhere to live. Nowhere to call home." He implied that his friends thought he should place his son up for adoption—something he was unwilling to do. "I can't give up the baby," he wrote. "He [is] so adorable."[14]

Even in the late fifties, when expectations for fathers were very traditional, there were men who were actively engaged in their children's lives. A father who was interviewed in 1958 described the bedtime routine of his three small children (a baby plus a two-year-old and four-year-old) and offered insight into a man who appeared to relish being a dad.

> When it gets around seven-thirty, either I or my wife put the baby to bed . . . around eight o'clock, I give the [two-year-old] girl—start her in the bath, and when I've got her all in, then I go get [the four-year-old]. [. . .] I dry her and dress her, and by that time my wife's through with the dishes, and she will help with her if she's—if our little girl is trying to float, like she usually is, gets her hair wet, then my wife has to dry her hair. [. . .] Then I get [the boy] out, and we usually roughhouse a bit while I'm drying him off [. . .] and then, by then, it's our girl's turn to brush her teeth, so I give her the toothbrush, and she won't let me help her, she brushes her own teeth, and I take him into the bedroom, and get him dressed . . . and then, she goes to bed with a little hassle, and my wife's working on her . . . and then, [the boy] gets one "carry," I mean, he gets to go to bed once, and get up once . . . and that's—so I put him to bed, and we talk a while, while my wife's getting the little girl to bed, and then he—then we go to the living room and he won't come till I sit down and pick up the paper, so he can interrupt me! (laughs) . . . that's part of the game! So, I pick up the paper, and I don't even start to read it, 'cause I know he's the—he creeps down the hall like a commando, and then he waits till it's all quiet—and we never let this go on more than three or four minutes, and he jumps out "Ready!" . . . so then depending on how gay a mood we're in, I either say "O.K., give your mother a goodnight kiss," and I carry him to bed . . .

and every night [. . .] he wants to be carried a different way—some nights I hold him by the feet and he puts his hands on my feet, and we go down the hall that way, and sometimes it's piggyback, and sometimes it's over the head and upside down, or sideways.[15]

Not every father in the fifties exhibited the level of child care that these men did. They are, in some ways, unusual. But theirs are not the only stories of men trying to be the best caregivers they could be. To say that yesterday's fathers *never* thought about what it meant to be a father or that they believed that their responsibility to their families was *only* to provide economically is absurd.

How and why these historical narratives became such a central feature of fatherhood discourse in America is an interesting question all by itself. One thing is clear: they are not new. Over the past one hundred years, if not before, similar kinds of narratives have been regularly put forth.[16] In the fifties, when men supposedly never gave any thought to what being a father meant, pundits spoke of how different fathers "today" were from fathers "then." An article in the *New York Times Magazine* in 1953 proclaimed, "In the past twenty-five or thirty years a radical and inevitable change has taken place in father's role in the family, radical in the degree of change, inevitable after the shifts in the roles of mother and child. Advised, often demanded by experts in the field of family living, the change for the most part has been a healthy one, based on father's mature willingness to share more of family life, including routine chores and day-to-day details of child-rearing."[17] Likewise, an article in *Parents Magazine* in 1957 said, "More and more, today's fathers are trying to . . . give definition to their roles by including themselves in as many facets of family life as possible, and particularly in the lives of their children."[18]

Another thing is that the narratives clearly have consequences. Some men have been inspired by the invidious comparisons with the past and dedicated themselves to being the kind of dads that previous generations of fathers allegedly "never were." For these men, negative anecdotes about yesterday's fathers have had a compensatory effect, fueling their commitment to be the best dads ever.[19]

Other men, however, may knowingly or subconsciously use the narratives as a license *not* to be as involved with their children as much as they could. The myth that yesterday's fathers did next to nothing makes it possible for today's fathers to receive accolades for not doing much. A father holding an infant in public, for example, can instantaneously—and without any further proof—be thought of as "a good dad." Declared one man, recalling just such an incident when he was out and about with his twenty-month-old, "The handy thing about being a father is that the historic standard is so pitifully low."[20] However "handy" this proposition may be, if we look to the past and carefully examine the evidence, we find that men's level of involvement with children was not as low as some suppose.[21]

Two concepts are germane to the history of fatherhood that I present here, and they are important to define. One is the *culture of fatherhood*; the other is the *conduct of fatherhood*.[22]

The culture of fatherhood, as I conceptualize it, refers to the webs of meaning and interpretive practices pertaining to fatherhood, and includes the language that is used to describe fatherhood, as well as the array of symbols, rules, values, repertoires of knowledge, and rituals pertaining to men's relationship with children. Embodied in form, the culture of fatherhood is displayed in cultural objects like magazine articles, newspaper reports, child-rearing manuals, and so forth—that is, in much of the material discussed above.

Understanding the culture of fatherhood requires that we scrutinize not only cultural objects, but also the individuals who create the objects and those who receive and interpret them. The creation and reception process also must be seen as occurring in a larger context. Cultural objects produced and valued during an economic depression or a war, for example, may not be produced and valued thereafter.[23]

Culture itself is also multifaceted and fragmented, in that any number of people can contribute to an ideological mosaic, and all of them do not necessarily speak in one voice. Inconsistencies in textual materials can frequently be discerned within a single sentence, and the simplest of ideas can be interpreted in a variety of ways. Culture thus is best conceptualized in the plural—*cultures of fatherhoods*—though to continue in this vein throughout the book would be stylistically awkward.

Given that there are multiple cultures of fatherhood, it is essential to study the intricate relations among the different forms. These relations, like the relations among multiple cultures of masculinity, are likely to be configured in terms of dominance, disadvantage, and alliance. Politics thus is undeniably central to the social construction of fatherhood cultures, which is to say that power and resources shape how paternal cultures are constructed and displayed, with dividends accorded to the men who embrace the ideal and penalties levied against the men who do not.[24] For example, during World War II a "hard" or more forceful image of fatherhood (e.g., the father as protector) was elevated in importance, while other images (e.g., the father as playmate) were emphasized less. To be in the fight was to reside at the pinnacle of fatherhood. To be on the sidelines (even if in the military) or to serve in a supportive capacity on the home front (working in a munitions factory) was to occupy a lower rung on the fatherhood ladder.[25]

Whereas the culture of fatherhood refers to fatherhood in mind, the conduct of fatherhood refers to fatherhood in action. Basically, the conduct of fatherhood constitutes the routine activities of men when they are trying to act "fatherly." One may argue that the difference between the culture and conduct of fatherhood is only semantic and that the two essentially are the same. To a certain degree, this is true. After all, what is the difference between a *representation* of a man holding an infant (e.g., in a drawing or photograph) and the *act* of holding an infant? Are not both symbolic? Are not both cultural?

Where one stands on the culture/conduct issue comes down to whether one believes there is merit in separating attitudes from behaviors. I happen to believe there is. While I recognize that much of the activity we observe is linked to ideations, I also find it helpful to ask whether attitudes and behaviors are in sync.[26] *Leave It to Beaver* may offer insights into how the television industry chose to portray fathers in the fifties, but it cannot be used as a measure of how postwar fathers, in fact, conducted themselves. As one historian wryly noted, "Contrary to popular opinion, *Leave It to Beaver* was not a documentary"[27]

Many of the materials upon which I rely may appear to be more indicative of culture than of conduct. A letter to a psychologist is not so much a description of an incident (or incidents) as it is an *inscription* of what the writer selectively saw and chose to put into words. The same might be said of an interview transcript or a quantitative survey. Neither is an unadulterated account.[28] Even so, it is not my intention to speak only about culture. Although I devote significant attention to the culture of fatherhood, when it seems reasonable and appropriate, I infer men's behavior through a careful examination of the materials I have gathered. In this way, I hope to convey accurately the daily lives of fathers and their families during and after the war.

What follows is predicated on the assumption that an important goal in any historical project is to understand how social and political circumstances make a difference in people's lives, and how individual and collective actions alter historical events.[29] The most obvious impact of World War II

was the carnage it produced. The war also created a state of fear, tore families apart, forced many to make do with less, and demolished hopes and
dreams. At the same time, the war liberated countries, brought people together, initiated a period of abundance, and laid siege to the foundation of
racial apartheid.

It is important to acknowledge explicitly that the war did not affect everyone in the same way. Apart from the fact that being on the winning or losing side made an enormous difference, the experience of the war varied by
gender, nationality, race, social class, family situation, whether one was in
the military, whether one had seen combat, and the nature of one's relationship to the casualties. It also varied by age. The year that a person was born
dictated whether he or she experienced World War II and its aftermath as an
older or younger adult, or as an older or younger child. The age variations
in meanings attached to the war were considerable.[30]

Middle-aged and older Americans were more likely to remember World
War I and to know firsthand what it was like to live through the Great Depression. Although probably not in the military themselves during World
War II, they had an intimate feel for the war because their children and
grandchildren were the ones who did the fighting and dying.

Those in their late teens or early twenties were in a different situation.
They were the most likely to be drafted; the most likely, if married, to be
at the early stages of their marital careers; and the most likely, if they had
children, to be fathers and mothers of infants and toddlers. This is the group
that suffered the most casualties in the war. This is the group that we generally think of (and regularly honor) when we talk of the "World War II
generation."

Preschool and school-aged children constituted another group. They
were the "children of the war," who did not go overseas but whose fathers,
grandfathers, brothers, and uncles did, and whose most vivid memories of
childhood included saying goodbye to loved ones, caring for the wounded,
and burying the dead. They entered high school and young adulthood in
the fifties, and were at the forefront of the era's youth culture. They were the
first to embrace rock and roll and were the twenty-to-thirty-year-olds who
participated in the 1950s black civil rights movement.

The last group was primarily made up of those who were born soon after
the war ended and who constituted the first cohorts of the postwar baby
boom. They did not directly experience the war, but they did "collectively
remember" it through the tales their parents told and through a variety of
TV and film accounts that they absorbed. This group entered high school
and young adulthood in the 1960s and were the ones who most directly ex-

perienced the Vietnam War—as soldiers, friends of soldiers, or protestors. It is from this group that the post-fifties women's movement and late-twentieth-century new fatherhood movement (calling for men to be more actively involved in children's lives) got most of its strength. These are the parents and grandparents of the children who grew up in the Internet age.

Finally, it is important to appreciate that although the effects of the war may seem predictable in hindsight, by no means were they anticipated from the start. Any number of outcomes may have developed, depending not only on the results of this or that battle or this or that economic/techno-logical development, but also on the choices that individuals and groups made. (Contingency—the possibility that something might or might not occur—was always in play.)[31] The story that follows thus acknowledges the large-scale events that shaped people's lives during and after the war, but it also recognizes the individual and group decisions that helped to set some of these events in motion.

PART ONE

Attacked

Pearl Harbor is located on the Hawaiian Island of Oahu. In December 1941 it was a major base for the U.S. Pacific fleet, and housed not only servicemen and servicewomen but also, in some cases, their families. Japanese fighter aircraft attacked the base at 7:55 on a Sunday morning. The bombardment lasted for more than two hours. Almost the entire Pacific fleet was destroyed; more than three hundred U.S. aircraft were demolished or crippled. Casualties on the American side added up to 2,403 killed and 1,178 wounded. Japan lost twenty-nine of its 350 planes.[1]

The attack had come as a complete surprise. Sailors fired back at the planes as best they could, but there was not much they could do; the Japanese held the advantage. Servicemen who happened to be home had to choose between protecting their loved ones and defending the base. One sailor recalled trying to get his wife and child to safety and, with the benefit of hindsight, was able see a bit of humor amid the shock. "When we're almost to the car, my wife says, 'The baby doesn't have any diapers! Get some!' . . . Bear in mind that this is Armageddon, the end of the world, and my wife has me chasing diapers!"[2] Local residents were caught in the crossfire as well. A Hawaiian father reported that he "drove his family into the sugarcane fields above the harbor, where they hid among the tall cane stalks."[3]

As news of the attack spread throughout the United States, Americans absorbed the terrible truth that the country was at war. A ten-year-old boy saw his father weeping in front of the radio: "Dad was bent over, his head in his hands . . . his shoulders were faintly shaking as the announcer rattled on." Some parents took their anger out on their children—screaming at them, even striking them. Others vented their fury at the Japanese. One man, visibly drunk, kept repeating, "I'm gonna get me a machine gun and kill every one of those slant eyed sons-of-bitches I can find."[4]

Although Pearl Harbor precipitated America's formal entrance into World War II, the social reality of the conflict gripped the country long before the attack, particularly after Germany invaded Poland in September 1939. Believing that the aggression overseas would continue unabated, President Franklin Delano Roosevelt had taken steps to prepare the United States for battle. Coastal installations were placed on high alert.[5] Factories were built, industries were retooled, and new military gear was ordered. All the while, newspapers printed daily reports of war, while letters from family members in Europe described "the ominous drone of German bombers, [and] the fire and rubble of the Blitz." For some, the anxiety over what lay ahead was too much to bear. A twenty-three-year-old farmer in Monmouth, New Jersey, shot and killed himself—after scribbling a note saying he did not want to be drafted.[6]

Fear became a central element in America's collective consciousness and altered the shape and tenor of people's lives. Even advertisements projected alarm. Seventeen months before the Japanese attack, the Bell Aircraft Corporation published an ad that showed a father and son looking across a tarmac where several U.S. fighter planes were lined up. The father, with his hand on the shoulder of the boy, counsels, "Remember Lincoln's words, my son: 'The progress of our arms, upon which all else chiefly depends[,]' [is] the keynote to the Nation's future."[7] Fourteen months before the attack, the Lehigh Portland Cement Company declared, "Hurry! Hurry! America's call is urgent for more armament, more tools for its manufacturers, more facilities for making both." By "speeding up [their] construction" with "Lehigh Early Strength Cement," the builders would be "speeding up the first lines of defense."[8] Nine months before, the New England Mutual Life Insurance Company equated buying a life insurance policy with creating a "Defense Committee of One." Said a man pictured in the ad, "Although our defense program is much smaller than the Government's, they're a lot alike. Both are aimed at the same thing—protection now and independence in the future. Both are important—to neglect either would leave us open to the worries and hazards of the unprepared."[9] And just five months before, the White Motor Company, manufacturer of trucks and buses, assured people, "America is secure against any wave of the future pounding at her shores . . . as long as there are men and machines to build America's ramparts stronger, faster and better."[10]

After Pearl Harbor, the tone of advertising changed. The actions of the Japanese, coupled with the early success of German submarines (in the first three months of 1942, German U-boats patrolling off the East Coast sank 216 ships) heightened people's sense that the United States was vulnerable.[11] America's industries responded in kind. A March advertisement for Warner and Swasey Turret Lathes began, "Did you ever face the sobering thought that your country may not win this war?"[12] Another Warner and Swasey ad showed a youngster left homeless by the bombing raids in Europe. "It *can* happen here. If workmen in the machine shops of now-conquered countries had worked harder and longer *in time*, there would have been enough planes and guns to beat off the Nazi raiders who bombed this pitiable little child."[13] In yet another ad, the company cautioned,

"Pearl Harbor is inviolate"—yet it was attacked

"Singapore is impregnable"—but it fell.

"America and Britain control the seas"—yet Nazis sink tankers in sight of New York; the Japs shell California.

"Our Navy can repel any invasion"—but now the Axis Navy outnumbers ours.

We lull ourselves to sleep with things we want to believe, and while we sleep our enemies close in from either side. . . . The enemy who will take [our comfortable lives] *all* away is closing in.[14]

In April 1943 the Magazine Publishers of America ran an advertisement that proclaimed "every civilian" to be "a fighter." The MPA's forecast of what would happen if the United States lost the war was clearly intended to scare: "If they win . . . only our dead are free. These are our enemies. They have only one idea—to kill, and kill, and kill, until they conquer the world. Then, by the whip, the sword and gallows, they will rule. . . . Make no mistake about it—you cannot think of this as other wars. You cannot regard your foe this time simply as people with the wrong idea. This time you win—or die."[15]

In the summer of 1943 the United Gas Pipe Line Company followed with an ad that included photos of two boys—one in Nazi youth garb, the other in a Boy Scout uniform—and asked, "Which will Johnny be?" The answer provided for the reader: "Without question, no red-blooded, freedom-loving American father or mother would want Johnny to be like that misguided, regimented Nazi lad. America's sons have a priceless heritage of Freedom that no fuehrer-trained, goose-stepping Nazi youth can understand or enjoy."[16]

In communicating alarm, the advertisements paled in comparison to the venomous illustrations and texts in war propaganda posters. In these, the enemies of the United States were routinely portrayed as "murderers" and "rapists" bent on crushing everything people in America held dear. (The opposing side's characterizations of Americans could be equally raw.) Because Japan had directly attacked the United States, and because of the xenophobia toward Eastern cultures, the posters tended to single out the Japanese more than the Germans—or the Italians, with whom America also was at war (until September 1943, when Italy surrendered). "Remember Pearl Harbor" became a rallying call. The emphasis of the posters, however, did not necessarily reflect the perceptions of all individuals or groups. Jewish American soldiers tended to focus on battling Germany because of the Nazis' anti-Semitic persecutions.[17]

Accounts of captured U.S. soldiers being harmed also fueled people's rage. One poster—which displayed the newspaper headline, "5200 Yank Prisoners Killed by Jap Torture in Philippines; Cruel 'March of Death' Described"—encouraged Americans to "Stay on the Job Until Every Murdering Jap is Wiped Out!" Even more incendiary was a full-color illustration of a Japanese soldier, with sharpened teeth and dark complexion, grabbing a light-skinned woman by the mouth and holding a knife to her throat. "Keep This Horror From *Your* Home," men in the United States were told.[18]

Another reason why the Japanese were especially targeted is that they were perceived as manifestly different from America's other enemies. As one woman put it, whereas German soldiers were recognized as "fathers/sons/brothers," the Japanese were stereotyped as "family-less" and as "unspeakably evil, vicious, and subhuman."[19]

The Japanese started to come to the United States in significant numbers in the early 1900s, in response to the jobs that had become available to them after the Chinese Exclusion Act of 1882 (which restricted how many Chinese could enter the country).[20] At the time of the attack on Pearl Harbor, approximately 127,000 Japanese Americans lived in the United States. Of these, 93,000 resided in California, while another 19,000 lived in Oregon and Washington.[21] The population included both those born in Japan (*Issei*, the first generation) and those born in the United States (*Nisei*, the second generation, and *Sansei*, the third generation). Some *Issei* were naturalized U.S. citizens. All *Nisei* and *Sansei* were U.S. citizens by birth.

Once word of the attack hit the U.S. mainland, the lives of Japanese American men, women, and children—citizens and noncitizens alike—took a dramatic turn. One man recalled, "Well, one hour after Pearl Harbor, I was very, you know, this innocent kid that opens the door. And this is one hour after Pearl Harbor now and here two big white gentlemen would say, 'We're the FBI, where is Mr. Jimmie Raisaku Fujii?' And I say, 'Oh, Dad's here some-where.' And I get him and they took him. I didn't see him after that for three-and-a-half years."[22] Another remembered how his father was escorted away: "He was taken without any explaining. He was taken right away. The men from the FBI or police station came. . . . They told my father to get [his] suitcase and toothbrush and so forth. He didn't understand why he had to do that, but anyway without reason, he was taken."[23] Yet another talked of how his father and several other men were jailed after a family celebration:

> On the evening of December 7, 1941, my father was at a wedding. He was dressed in a tuxedo. When the reception was over, the FBI agents were wait-ing. They rounded up at least a dozen wedding guests and took 'em to county jail. For a few days we didn't know what happened. We heard nothing. When we found out, my mother, my sister, and myself went to jail. I can still re-member waiting in the lobby. When my father walked through the door, my mother was so humiliated. She didn't say anything. She cried. He was in prisoner's clothing, with a denim jacket and a number on the back.[24]

One Japanese child, coming home to an empty house, initially believed— or *wanted* to believe—that his father had been called upon to serve as an interpreter.

> My mother and I were not home that evening. . . . When we came home, they had ransacked the apartment, taken a lot of things, and left the door open, unlocked. . . . At the time we thought it was because he spoke English well and because he was quite prominent in the community, that they probably needed him for some interpreting or some darn thing like that. Never, you know, realizing that he was going to be interned.[25]

Although the attack on Pearl Harbor was something of a surprise, the possibility that Japan and the United States would be adversaries some day had been on people's minds for years. (Some categorize Japan's invasion of China in 1937, rather than Germany's invasion of Poland in 1939, as "the first battle of World War II.")[26] A San Francisco man, who had come to the United States in 1923 and who had "never dreamt there could be [a] war between Japan and the United States" (he said it would be "like ants pok-ing an elephant"), talked of receiving letters from his father in Japan who warned of a "great tragedy" and how his father implored him to bring his family back to his home country. But the man decided to remain, figuring that since his two sons were *Nisei* citizens of the United States, they would be safer in California if a war were to break out. He said that he "trust[ed] the United States" to "protect" his "two boys."[27] In another case, a father was said to have destroyed many of his personal belongings the day after the attack in an effort to play down his connection to Japan. "Dad got scared and started to burn all the books, Japanese books. He was panicking; he said to get everything out—all the records—and we just built a bonfire, busted everything, you know. When you panic and you don't know what's going to happen, I think you do these things without thinking."[28]

Hatred toward the Japanese was widespread and intense. Japanese parents were fired from their jobs.[29] Hospitals turned away Japanese needing treatment.[30] Japanese children were scorned and ridiculed at school. People were denounced as "dirty Japs" or "dirty yellow Japs" or "little slant-eyed bastards." Signs outside restaurants and other establishments read "No Dogs or Japs Allowed." Comic books and movies included Japanese stereotypes. Toys and other items stamped "made in Japan" were destroyed or thrown away.[31]

Not everyone in the United States displayed bigotry. One father and mother, after hearing their daughter sing an offensive limerick, sat her down and told her, "Japanese children were loved by their parents just as [she] was by them." Theirs was not the predominant attitude, however. By and large, the war tended to magnify an attitude of "us" versus "them."[32]

What to *do* with Japanese Americans was bandied back and forth. The U.S. government was not satisfied with the curfews that had been imposed and the detention of "suspicious" individuals.[33] On February 19, 1942, President Roosevelt issued Executive Order 9066, which restricted where residents could live. Although the order did not refer to any particular group, it clearly was directed at Japanese Americans residing in the Pacific Coastal Zone (i.e., California, Oregon, and Washington State). One month later, on March 18, 1942, FDR signed Executive Order 9102, which established the War Relocation Authority. This order, which was implemented throughout the spring, authorized the incarceration of thousands of Japanese in what were euphemistically called "assembly centers" or "relocation centers," situated mainly in California, Idaho, Wyoming, Utah, Arizona, Colorado, and Arkansas. (Military installations throughout the country also were used in some capacity.) Ultimately, more than 110,000 were exiled.[34]

In some instances, only certain members of a family were required to leave. Fathers might be carted away, while their wives and children remained behind. One man recalled the date he was woken up in the middle of the night and imprisoned. It was his daughter's birthday—February 21, 1942—two days following the circulation of Executive Order 9066. After a month and a half of being detained in the local jail, he was shipped off to Montana. His family came to the station to say goodbye. As he boarded the train, his daughters yelled out, "Papa, Papa." Years later, he could "still hear the ring of their crying."[35]

Fathers maintained contact with their families through letters, which allowed them to experience their children's growth and development from afar. While on a driving trip with his mother, a three-year-old boy recognized a turn in the road and said that he had passed the same place before—only with his father. The mother used the occasion to let her husband know that his children remembered him: "They mention you in that way often. Since they saw you leave with the authorities, they say that you are with men who look like the mailman. A few days ago they wanted me to call you over the phone and ask you to return. I had to tell them you were so far away, I couldn't reach you."[36]

The father was in the Lordsburg, New Mexico, camp. He had been there since March 1942. In May 1942, mother and children were incarcerated, too, but they were sent to the Colorado River camp near Poston, Arizona. The couple continued to correspond. "Masahiro is being registered today in the nursery school which is just across the road from us. Misao is still too young to go. . . . Masahiro has his grief when his playmates say, 'My daddy came back. You're [sic] daddy isn't coming back.' Then I'd have to tell him you will return—some day." In July 1943, after a number of appeals, the father was permitted to join his family in Poston.[37]

Even for families that were together, life in the camps could be hard. Children were especially affected by what they saw. "I was about three and a half years old then, when my father, who refused to accept our imprisonment quietly, was arrested by the soldiers and taken from the camp," recalled one former detainee. Charged with instigating a riot, the father and a friend were hauled off to jail.

> I watched as they took them away, handcuffed and shackled. That night was terrifying. All night long, the searchlights swept the camp, and bands of men could be heard running past our barracks, shouting angrily. We had no idea what happened to my father, and at one point in the night I sneaked out to try to find him. . . . I remember telling my mother that they were going to shoot him, because it seemed to me that was what they did with those guns when they took you away from the camp.[38]

Some children were never reunited with their fathers: "Dad was gone, and we just heard from him a little. We have a few letters from him. And you know, I have no feeling if I look at them now." Moved from camp to camp, the father suffered a series of strokes: "I think he died in Bismarck, North Dakota. It's really kind of sad if you think about it, that I don't know where he died."[39]

Japanese immigrants and their families were not the only ones imprisoned. German nationals were also arrested and placed in custody, though in smaller numbers. Whereas the U.S. government often thought of *Issei*, *Nisei*, and *Sansei* as an undifferentiated group, its focus on the German community tended to be on German nationals.[40]

Soon after Germany attacked Poland in September 1939, President Roosevelt instructed the Justice Department "to arrest and detain those persons that they deemed dangerous 'in the event of war, invasion, or insurrection in and of a foreign enemy.'" The FBI "was given the responsibility of compiling reports on potential sympathizers with the Nazi cause, including those capable of initiating or assuming leadership roles in a public uprising."[41] Animosity toward Germans living in the United States continued to build over the next two years. The day after Pearl Harbor, a number of German resident aliens deemed to be threats (based on lists already compiled) were rounded up.[42]

As with Japanese Americans, men generally were the ones who were forcibly incarcerated, while the women and children accompanying or following the men to the camps were called "voluntary" prisoners.[43] Those who were not interned often had to contend with glares and taunts from neighbors and strangers. One Texas women, pregnant with her first child, could not contain her revulsion in a letter that she wrote to her husband, who recently had been sent overseas: "Sometimes there is so much hate in my soul against the Germans that I can't take it in. I loathe every butcher and baker and hausfrau. And I hope that when the Russians get to Germany they kill every man, woman and child as wantonly as they have been taught to by those Teutonic fiends. Hope they torture them too."[44] In self-defense, German Americans often hid or de-emphasized their ethnicity, by "passing" as another nationality (e.g., Swiss) and by not speaking German in public or even at home. Said one father to his children: "Don't dare tell anyone you are German. *Never.*"[45]

Because America also was at war with Italy, Italian Americans were targeted, too. Thousands were brought in for questioning. Others were forced to move out of homes in designated restricted areas. The number of Italians jailed or sent to the camps was low compared to the number of Japanese and Germans.[46] The experience of being singled out, however, was searing. A son recalled, "My dad was picked up at the produce market on Saturday morning; it was raining. When the two men from the FBI and my dad came in the front door my sister and I were there to greet them. We were scared stiff." A daughter remembered the moment that she and her family were forced to move from their home, and how much it hurt her father. "He said, 'All the work that I did in the house,' 'cause he built it. 'This land we have here, all this, and I'm going to have to move and I didn't do anything. I don't know whether I can ever come back.'. . . . He was crying." The father had lived in the United States since 1902, but was evicted from the dwelling that he had constructed because he was not an American citizen. "He was working night and day and he just didn't have time to study," the daughter explained.[47]

The U.S. government had considered instituting a wholesale roundup of Italian Americans on the scale of what was done to Japanese Americans, but the logistics of corralling such a large and diverse population was daunting. It thus "settled for relocating 10,000 alien resident Italians living on the West Coast away from the waterfront, which was designated a prohibited zone as a result of the Pearl Harbor bombing. Over 50,000 more Italian Americans in California lived under curfew."[48]

The war had a devastating effect on a number of Italian Americans. Homes were routinely searched. Mere possession of Italian-language news-papers and letters could be enough to raise the suspicions of authorities. Shortwave radios were confiscated, the "threat" being that they could be used to listen to broadcasts from overseas. Oddly enough, "although there was no formal policy regarding Italian or any other enemy alien language usage, the FBI—and by extension the government—viewed the use and pro-motion of the Italian language whether in the home, in print, on the air-waves or within organized settings as evidence of potential disloyalty . . ."[49] Close to six hundred thousand nonresident Italian Americans were obliged to register with the government and carry with them at all times a "Certifi-cate of Identification," purportedly for their own "protection."[50] The suicide rate in Italian neighborhoods increased. One sixty-five-year-old man threw himself in front of a train. Another purchased $4,500 in defense bonds—prior to killing himself.[51]

Other groups also found themselves subjected to greater scrutiny, though they were not identified as "official" enemies of the United States. Jewish Americans, for example, were sometimes blamed for the war. A 1942 survey of war rumors in Boston uncovered a range of anti-Semitic at-titudes. Respondents said that Jews had "brought on [the] war as part of an international plot" and had "blackmailed Roosevelt into getting [the country] into [the] war." Others charged that Jewish doctors were doing whatever they could to get Jewish men categorized as IV-F (not qualified for military service). Jewish businessmen were accused of being "profiteers."[52] All this was happening as news of Nazi-manufactured Jewish death camps filtered out from Europe, and Jewish refugees were being turned away from American ports.[53]

After the Japanese were moved to noncoastal regions of California, public officials and the press, along with many others, transferred their anxiety to Mexican Americans (despite the fact that thousands of Mexican Americans and other Hispanics were serving in the military). Unreasonable fear "eventually led to public hysteria over an alleged Mexican American crime wave."[54] A Mexican American woman who lived in San Antonio during the war recalled the difficulty that her father had in finding work. Mexican American children, witnessing what had happened to Japanese Americans, wondered whether the government was going to do the same thing to them and their families.[55] Puerto Ricans in New York were vilified as well.[56]

Not just the Japanese but also other Asians were subject to attack. One Chinese father was "dragged out of his truck and beaten by police until," according to his son, "'they were sure he wasn't Japanese American.'"[57] Another was repeatedly reported to the police by neighbors who "insist[ed] that he was a using a secret radio transmitter to communicate with enemy agents." Reacting to the negative ethnic profiling, some Asians wore badges and posted banners outside their shops to declare that they were *not* Japanese.[58]

What made the plight of the Chinese particularly incongruous was that China was an ally of the United States. Publishing mogul Henry R. Luce, born to Presbyterian missionary parents stationed in China, was bothered that the Japanese and the Chinese sometimes were mistaken for one another, and decided to use his considerable resources to "dispel" the "confusion." Fifteen days after the attack on Pearl Harbor, two of the magazines he controlled, *Life* and *Time*, published articles on "How to Tell Japs from the Chinese" and "How to Tell Your Friends from the Japs."[59] Reported *Life*: "In the first discharge of emotions touched off by the Japanese assaults on their nation, U.S. citizens have been demonstrating a distressing ignorance on the delicate question of how to tell a Chinese from a Jap. Innocent victims in cities all over the country are many of the 75,000 U.S. Chinese, whose homeland is our staunch ally."[60] Using side-by-side photographs and relying on ethnic stereotypes, the articles endeavored to contrast the physical characteristics and demeanor of the Japanese and Chinese. Japanese facial expressions were said to be "positive, dogmatic, arrogant"; Chinese expressions, "placid, kindly, open." Japanese were "nervous in conversations" and "laugh[ed] loudly at the wrong time." Chinese were "not as hairy as Japanese" and "seldom gr[e]w an impressive mustache."[61] Japanese showed the "humorless intensity of ruthless mystics." Chinese exhibited the "rational calm of tolerant realists."[62]

The Chinese were not the only Asians singled out; Koreans were, too. A Korean woman, who lived on a farm in California with her husband and children, recalled that people "just assumed that all Orientals were Japanese" and reported that, even after the Japanese were sent to the camps, non-Japanese Asians still were worried: "They were afraid to go out at night; many were even beaten during the day. Their cars were wrecked. The tires were slashed, the radios and batteries removed. Some [of my] friends driving on the highways were stopped and their cars were overturned. It was a bad time for all of us." She did, however, recall one act of kindness:

> The day of Pearl Harbor, . . . I stopped by the Nixon's grocery store to buy something. I left my one-year-old son, Tony, in the truck, thinking I'd be back in two minutes. I was surprised to see the room full of people who stared at me with hateful expressions. One man said, "There's one of them damned Japs now. What's she doing here?" Mrs. Hannah Nixon came over to me and said to her friends, "Shame on you, all of you. You have known Mrs. Lee for years. You know she's not Japanese, and even if she were, she is not to blame for what happened at Pearl Harbor! This is a time to remember your religion and practice it."[63]

Unfortunately, the kindness the mother received in the store was overshadowed by what she witnessed when she went outside: three teenage boys standing ready to pummel her son. "Does it take three of you to beat up a one-year-old baby?" she shouted.[64]

TWO

"The Bodies That We Need"

September 15, 1943. A storm is off the Florida coast and moving rapidly toward New England. Winds are predicted to reach as high as sixty miles per hour. Towns and cities in its path will experience gusts, but inland communities will be only mildly affected. Still, for many, it is going to be a soggy day.[1]

On a September morning in 1943, Americans would have been happy to leap out of bed and worry only about whether their galoshes and umbrellas would keep them dry. But they were nearly two years into a war, and the news from the battlefield was grim. Huge losses and demoralizing setbacks had created a solemn state of affairs. To have any chance at winning, the United States needed more men at the front.[2] The bleakest reports were coming from an area in and around the Italian town of Salerno. American and British ships in the Mediterranean had launched a "full-scale invasion of continental Europe," with the purpose of reclaiming territory held by Germany. It was assumed that the beach assault "would be a quick success."

The Allies had reason to be optimistic. Italy, which had been fighting alongside Germany, had surrendered on September 8, and the German soldiers defending the region numbered 20,000, compared to the 100,000 British and 69,000 American forces. The British and American battle plans, however, were seriously flawed, and German resistance was fierce. Said one account of the action, "Allied troops were pinned to the beach by murderous fire. Many had been put ashore at the wrong place, and officers desperately pored over out-of-date maps trying to get themselves oriented. The British, assigned the north sector of the twenty-mile stretch of beach, found themselves ten miles from the nearest Americans to the south, and the Germans soon filled the gap." Although the Allies would eventually be victorious, the Battle of Salerno emboldened German Chancellor Adolf Hitler and his generals: "What was expected to be a triumphal march north through a beaten Italy became a slogging, tortuous, year-long campaign that repeatedly stalled and finally sputtered to a stop just north of Florence." In time, 350,000 Allied lives would be lost.[3]

Americans thus awoke on September 15 to a war unlike the one they might have imagined even twenty-four hours before. "Gravity of position at Salerno ends 'It's all over now' talk," declared the *New York Times*.[4] It was clear, the paper reported in a related piece, that the hardest battles were still ahead.[5] Bulletins from other reaches of the war offered little solace. The United Press chronicled a battle in the upper part of the Kurile Islands (some eleven hundred miles north of Tokyo) that was "the hottest, deadliest and costliest aerial action of the North Pacific to date." In an engagement reportedly lasting only fifty-two minutes, twenty U.S. bombers "plunged at deck level into a hell of ack-ack and a swirl of flames, pitting themselves against a swarm of Zeros and Nakijimas over Paramushiru and Shimushu." The anti-aircraft fire was intense and described by the pilots as "the heaviest and most accurate" ever encountered. Though the U.S. forces inflicted heavy damage (a number of Japanese warships and cargo vessels were sunk or set ablaze, and thirteen enemy planes were destroyed), the Americans, in the words of one officer, "lacked fighter support and . . . had too few bombers to afford the mutual support comparable to the thousand-plane raids over Europe." Only ten U.S. aircraft were able to make it back, and most "were badly shot up and carrying dead and wounded crewmen."[6]

These reports and others would weigh heavily on a debate that was about to begin at ten o'clock in the morning on September 15 in room 357 of the U.S. Senate Office Building in Washington, D.C.[7] At that hour, the Senate Committee on Military Affairs was to hold public hearings on Senate Bill 763, which, if passed, would shield certain fathers from military service. In technical terms, S. 763, as it was called, was "a bill exempting certain married men who [had] children from liability under the Selective Training and Service Act of 1940."[8]

As to why such a bill was being discussed in the first place, it is important to know that in July 1941—five months before the attack on Pearl Harbor—local draft boards had been instructed to "reconsider the case of all married men or men with minor children who [had] been place[d] in Class I-A" (meaning they were available for military service) and to withhold their induction while their classification was being reconsidered.[9] Then, in April 1942—four months after the attack—the director of the selective service system ordered that "registrants with one or more dependents" be classified as either III-A or III-B. Being classified as III-A meant that a father was not "engaged in any activity either essential to the war production program or essential to the support of the war effort"; III-B, on the other hand, meant that he was engaged in such activity. Fathers classified as III-A were to be exempt from the draft until October 1, 1943, at which time they would be reclassified as I-A, provided all eligible single men had been inducted. Because they were engaged in war production work, fathers classified as III-B could continue to be protected from the draft. The exemption applied only to those men with children who had been conceived on or before December 7, 1941. If a man's first child was conceived after that date, he still could be called up.[10]

It was the October 1, 1943, target date that got Congress thinking in earnest about whether post–Pearl Harbor fathers should be drafted. Had the time come to press these fathers into military service? Should certain men with dependent children continue to be held in reserve until all eligible single men had been drafted, or should they be put at the top of the list along with others? Given the growing need for more troops, could the country afford not to draft all able-bodied dads?

The key word here is *draft*. Men with dependent children were not absent from the military. Hundreds of thousands of fathers, in fact, were already in uniform. Some, as already indicated, were post–Pearl Harbor fathers who had been drafted. Some were career soldiers who had been in the service for years. Others had volunteered in the early stages of the war, having been caught up in the patriotic fervor that immediately followed the Pearl Harbor attack and President Franklin D. Roosevelt's call to arms ("Yesterday, . . . a date which will live in infamy . . .").[11] But, again, until 1943, one group of fathers had been placed in a special category that excluded them from *involuntary* service.[12] Proponents of the bill wanted married men with dependent children conceived on or before December 7 to be permanently exempt. The War Department, on the other hand, wanted a larger pool from which to select. It was estimated that there were six million fathers in America who would be eligible for service if the bill exempting them failed.[13]

The sponsor of S. 763 was Montana Senator Burton K. Wheeler, who was an outspoken critic of Roosevelt's policies and had opposed America's involvement in the war from the start. Wheeler introduced the bill not because he wanted to undercut the war effort (or so he implied) but because he believed that drafting more fathers would lead to higher rates of juvenile delinquency, destroy the sanctity of the family, and generally "undermine the American way of life."[14] To his way of thinking, married men with dependent children were too valuable on the home front to be shipped off to the battlefield. The senator was not alone in this belief. A Gallup poll, conducted in fall 1943, found that a majority of Americans did not want fathers to be called up.[15]

That so many citizens would be opposed to the idea of men with dependent children being drafted should not have come as a surprise. Gaining momentum before the war was a new fatherhood movement that emphasized the value of men in children's lives. Beginning in the early 1900s and accelerating in the 1930s, the movement was reflected in both popular culture and everyday conduct. Family-oriented periodicals increasingly included articles on the joys and responsibilities of fatherhood. In the decade before the war, more popular magazine articles were published about fatherhood than about motherhood. Parenting manuals also were calling for men to be more involved in raising children.[16]

The military's position on drafting fathers, while at odds with the polls, was equally heartfelt. With the nation in a fight for its life, drafting fathers was seen as an unfortunate necessity—but a necessity just the same. General Joseph E. McNarney, army deputy chief of staff, who was the first to testify, stated that, although Japan and Germany had suffered bruising defeats, they had "instituted the most vigorous measures to mobilize their available military manpower." He went on to say, "The fact that our enemies, after staggering loss in men and materials and the industrial losses resulting from our bombing offensives, cannot only maintain the armies with which they started the war but actually increase them is proof of the opposition still to be overcome."[17]

Asked later whether he felt that passing the bill would interfere with the military's needs, McNarney expressed the War Department's (and the president's) view on the matter in the starkest possible terms. It all came down to the arithmetic of war: "The military requirements of the Army are for a certain number of men who are physically fit to carry out the duties to which they will be assigned. If the men are single or if the men are fathers is really immaterial. It is the men, *it is the bodies that we need.*"[18]

Through six days of testimony that September, fathers' contributions to the war effort and to the home front were keenly assessed. Questions of competency, courage, and national loyalty were all factored into the equations on both sides. At one point, Senator Wheeler asked General McNarney "whether or not fathers, married men with children, make as good soldiers as does the single man." Wheeler's question was prompted by his feeling "that if a man has three or four children at home that have to be taken care of in some institution and his wife has to go to work, he is going to be worried about his wife and children." The general resolutely answered, "Naturally. Every man worries about his family. It might make him fight all the harder, too." Asked about his experience with fathers who were soldiers, McNarney added, "We have a considerable number of married men in the Army now, but they are all under the age of 38 and they are as a rule the younger married men. They make good soldiers." (This was not a precise statement. Some married men in the service were older.) What about the morale of the people at home? If fathers were to be drafted, would it not be negatively affected? General McNarney agreed that it was crucial that the morale of the people at home be kept high, but offered in response—as his "personal opinion"—that "there is a very large class of people in the United States composed of mothers, sisters, sweethearts, sons, and daughters, if you will, of people who are now in the Army, and their morale is also important, and if any one class is exempted from serving, either in the Army or in essential industry, what about the morale of those people whose boys are overseas?"[19]

Undersecretary of War Robert P. Patterson, who also testified before the committee, talked in personal terms as well: "I have just returned from the Pacific front. I saw thousands of our brave men doing their duty overseas. I saw the wounded in the hospitals. I saw the lonely graves in the jungles. We have pledged those men and the men fighting on other fronts the full resources of the Nation to support them. We must not fail to send them the reinforcements of men and of munitions they stand in need of." He prefaced these remarks with a comparison that could only be interpreted as a criticism of the existing policy: "*No other nation at war excuses fathers merely as fathers.*"[20]

Another reason that the War Department was pushing to draft fathers is that it wanted to increase the pressure on men to work in the defense industry. Patterson told the senators, "The only deferment from military service should be occupational deferment." He predicted, "With no other ground of deferment recognized, many of the fathers of military age now engaged in unessential activities would be prompted to go to munitions plants, and a large part of our present shortage of manpower in those plants would be relieved. The gain in output of munitions would be large."[21]

Whether the contributions of fathers could be measured only in terms of soldiering or war-factory work was a sensitive issue. Wheeler challenged Patterson on the matter:

> I don't think you want to let it stand that 6,000,000 married men with children haven't been doing their part in the war. . . . I say to you that those 6,000,000 fathers in this country are as patriotic as you or I, and as much interested in winning the war as you or I am. It isn't a question of these married men trying to get away from doing their part in the winning of the war. That isn't the question at all. They are just as patriotic and just as willing to do their part as anybody else."[22]

Wheeler here was echoing a position that others had taken. The role that fathers were playing in jobs deemed essential was, for some, the more important question. New York City Mayor Fiorello LaGuardia appeared before the committee to report worker shortages that, in his estimation, threatened the health and well-being of the city's residents. LaGuardia maintained that the same situation existed "in every large city, or every city"; it was "just a matter of proportion." He then noted that "certain departments, or certain functions of local government, are absolutely indispensable to the prosecution of the war. Police, fire, water, sanitation, including sewage disposal and street cleaning, hospitals and health care are indispensable. . . . We have reached the point where, if there is any further impairment, there will be a breakdown in local government."[23] In addition to pleading with the Selective Service System to provide "an itemized list of essential employment, such as they [had] given to industry" ("I beg on bended knees"), LaGuardia also recommended that men between the ages of thirty-eight and forty-five as well as those who were younger be subject to the draft. The older men could be furloughed *on the condition* that they would replace the younger men (serving as city police officers, firefighters, sanitation workers, etc.) who had been called to duty.[24]

Throughout the hearings, the question also was raised as to whether other categories of men, besides fathers, could be drafted. Senator Wheeling asked Presidential Advisor Bernard M. Baruch if some of the three million men who were IV-F (not qualified for military service) might have been misclassified. "When you see a married man with children going in and being taken in, when a boy, many of them, are exempted as not physically fit for the Army, and then you see them playing football or baseball or something of the kind, does that, in your judgment, create a good sentiment in the

United States of America?" Baruch replied, "Not when you see people physically fit except for a punctured eardrum being exempted and playing baseball." Wheeler shot back, "Well that is what is happening." Wheeler also wondered about single older men who, though they may not be suitable for combat, could be enlisted to perform some of the essential services that single younger men were carrying out. Once free of these jobs, the younger men could be drafted, thus reducing the number of fathers who would be called up.[25]

And then there was the color line. What about drafting African Americans and other minorities? The basic answer from the military was no; white soldiers were preferred. Interestingly (but in a racist society, not surprisingly), the military's exclusionary position on the matter came only minutes after a question about whether the standards for induction in the armed forces could be "lowered."[26] "I can readily understand how a man would not want Negro troops, he would prefer to have white troops rather than Negro troops," Wheeler declared. "I can understand where he would rather have men of the most intelligent group that he could possibly find rather than have some of the people that were illiterate and whose standards were not up to par," he further argued, seemingly unaware of (or not caring about) the bigotry in his remarks. "I can understand [also] where he would not want to take aliens who did not speak the best English in the world, that is natural, but on the other hand he ought to think in terms of not breaking up American homes."[27]

America's racial apartheid hung like a cloud over the room. For years, civil rights leaders had decried the country's refusal to allow black soldiers to fight. Black units were mobilized during the Revolutionary War, Civil War, and World War I, and they had performed courageously in combat. In each war, the hope they embraced was that, by demonstrating their willingness to risk their lives in defense of liberty, they and other minorities would be accepted as equals. They believed that by honorably serving, they could force the federal government to outlaw segregation in the military as well as in other areas of social life. Thus, with America embroiled in World War II and with "the game" on the line, the question of whether and in what capacity black men in general (and black fathers in particular) should be allowed to serve in the armed forces became the focus of the debate.

Given that troop numbers were the real crux of the hearings, it probably was inevitable that the use of black soldiers would be brought into the discussion. A former officer in the 370th Infantry Regiment, a black unit, wrote to Wheeler, expressing his view on the matter:

A news item in the September 11 edition of the *Afro-American* attracted my attention, in fact, aroused my indignation, and I clipped it out and am sending it to you, hoping that you will be interested (I'm sure you will). It concerns the Three Hundred and Sixty-sixth and Three Hundred and Seventy-second Infantry, which have been in training for more than 2½ years, and are ready for combat duty, but haven't been assigned to any. It occurs to me that there could be no talk of manpower shortage and drafting fathers for lack of it, when there are highly trained men ready for combat duty standing idle. It seems to me rather foolish to drain men from defense plants where they are needed, only to train them for soldier jobs which they are not allowed to fill. I realize it would be an honor for these men to go overseas and fight for their country, but I must say that it is their undeniable right to have this honor. Furthermore, it is not justifiable to delay the progress of an Allied victory by withholding from duty colored divisions (that have shown their worth in World War No. 1) because of the prejudiced viewpoint of their being commanded by their own color. Incidentally, I am sure that this will make them twice as dangerous to the enemies of democracy.[28]

Blacks eventually were pressed into combat, although, as before, they almost always fought in segregated units (not uncommonly with white officers in command). The most famous of the units was the Tuskegee Airmen, fighter pilots who chalked up significant victories. Their heroics, however, represent only a fraction of what the black community contributed to the war effort. (The men of the 370th, for example, eventually got to see combat in Europe.) By 1945, more than 1.1 million black Americans were in uniform, half of them serving overseas.[29] Thousands of others were employed in munitions plants, shipyards, and so on. In contrast, only 3,640 black soldiers were in the army in 1939, while even fewer served in the navy where, as a matter of policy, they were relegated to subordinate roles (e.g., working in the galleys). Prior to June 1941, when FDR issued Executive Order 8802 banning employment discrimination on the basis of race, creed, color, or national origins in the defense industry, blacks were prevented from working for companies that were gearing up for war.[30]

As for the so-called aliens, who, in Wheeler's words, "did not speak the best English in the world," the military eventually would allow members of other minority groups to serve, but it did so begrudgingly. After the attack on Pearl Harbor, Japanese Americans immediately were lumped with "the enemy," and many were incarcerated (see chapter 1). In early 1942, American soldiers of Japanese descent were drummed out of the armed forces and American-born Japanese Americans were reclassified as IV-C ("alien").

Not until January 1943 were Japanese Americans given the opportunity, once again, to volunteer for military service, and they were not subject to the draft until January 1944.[31] Italian Americans, Hispanic Americans, and Native Americans, among others, also had to confront exclusionary policies, though nothing like what Japanese Americans experienced. When finally called upon, these groups all served with distinction.

The hearings ended on September 23, 1943. After all was said and done, Wheeler's bill failed to pass. Regardless of their value at home, fathers were needed more overseas. The war would go on for another two years, and, as predicted, the toughest clashes still lay ahead.[32]

THREE

The Fog and the Sun

Goodbyes can be difficult under any circumstance, but they are often agonizing in a time of war. Just the thought that their fathers might be drafted was enough to terrify some. One seven-year-old girl cried herself to sleep each night because she was afraid her father would be sent overseas, and never mentioned it to anyone because she was "too scared to talk about it."[1]

When the moment came for a father to leave, the sorrow often heightened. An eight-year-old boy in a family of seven children, ages nine years to two months, was "ill from grief" on the day that his father left. "We'll get along, somehow," said the soldier's wife.[2] Years later, a daughter recalled the pain of seeing her father getting ready to go: "Mom began to cry as she and Dad packed his things; she didn't stop crying for what seemed like forever. I asked Dad when he would be home and for the first time in my life I saw tears in his eyes as he answered he didn't know."[3]

Time did not necessarily reduce the pain. A mother, whose husband had been overseas for months, tried to comfort her young son by telling him that his father was not the only one who had to serve, that thousands of fathers were fighting. "And thousands of them will get killed too," the boy replied.[4]

For some, saying goodbye *once* was more than enough. A group of fathers who were offered the opportunity of a three-day Easter delay chose not to accept it because they already had bid farewell to their loved ones and did not want to go through "the heart-tugging ordeal again."[5] In actuality, there was no tried-and-true method to ease the parting. Some soldiers "developed their own psychology as to the easiest way to say 'au revoir.'" Most, it was reported, preferred to do it in private (e.g., at home).[6] Not everyone was given that choice, however. When the men in one Virginia community left as a unit (in early 1941), "most of the town seemed to turn out for the sendoff."

As the new recruits struggled to say goodbye at the train station, many were near tears, but not one cried for fear "that they would shame themselves and their friends." Maintaining emotional control may have been perceived as the "manly" thing to do. Nevertheless, it was hard.[7]

Children could be reasonably comfortable with the idea of their fathers leaving, regardless of where or when the last hug occurred, provided they thought that their dads would be returning soon. This was more likely when a father was heading to basic training for several months and might be offered a brief leave to be with his family before being shipped out, but things could get more tense when a father's unit was ordered to the front. Then, *how* the goodbyes were performed might make little difference. One six-year-old refused to leave his house to go to school after his father departed for overseas: "I'm going to stay here until Daddy comes home."[8]

The new draft guidelines for fathers stepped up the search for draft evaders. One individual who had been avoiding service said that "he did not think he could eat Army food and so would be under a handicap if he were to be inducted." Another, it was discovered, had listed his horse as a dependent: "Of course, she's a dependent. The oats she eats keep me broke."[9] More serious was the case of a young father who killed himself by jumping off a New Jersey cliff. In a suicide note, he said that he was concerned about what would happen to his wife and three-week-old daughter if he were drafted.[10]

Stories like these were not typical, however. The chairman of a local draft board in New York reported that, as far as he could tell, fathers "seem[ed] perfectly willing to go," and that the men who had come before him offered little resistance. "We find them remarkably cooperative," he added. One of the first fathers to be processed under the new regulations—a thirty-five-year-old man who had been married for three years and who had a fourteen-month-old son—said he "[didn't] mind going at all." He interjected, "My wife is working and she will be able to make arrangements for the care of the baby."[11] Some draft boards "leaned over backwards" to offer deferments to fathers who were willing to leave nonessential employment and work in war factories, but many men "declared they would rather be drafted so that on the termination of the war they might return to their old jobs."[12]

How many children a father had was not necessarily factored in—either by the draft boards or by the men themselves. A father with seven children and an eighth on the way was ordered to report in January 1944. A man with fourteen children volunteered, along with his seventeen-year-old son, the following March. A Michigan farmer and father of thirteen entered in May, joining his oldest son, who already was serving.[13]

That men with large families were being called to active duty, however, did not sit well with everyone. A woman who had two sons in the service and said she "kn[ew] how *hard* it was to see them go" wrote to President Franklin D. Roosevelt to say that she "was deeply moved" by a newspaper article, which she had enclosed, announcing that a New Hampshire man with nine children had recently been drafted. "I am pleading with you, dear President, to release this poor father and let him go home to his children. They need him, I'm sure." She then advised that married men without children be drafted instead and, as a way of assisting in such an effort, provided the names of two men who did not have any children and who were said (in another newspaper article, which she also enclosed) to be seeking divorces.[14] Other solutions were proposed as well. One ten-year-old, who could accept the fact that her father was going to be sent to war, penned a letter to FDR to suggest that fathers be drafted in a particular order—namely, alphabetically. Expecting a personal reply, she included her address, phone number, and family name, which just so happened to begin with the letter W.[15]

During World War II, Americans may not have been able to rely on television to tell them what was happening in the world, but they certainly were not unaware. Nor were they residing in a proverbial vacuum, where the hostilities "over there" had little to do with life "over here." Local newspapers, radio reports, and newsreels covered major military encounters, while the topic of the war permeated family discourse.[16]

Front page headlines provide but a glimpse of the kinds of stories that Americans were confronted with every day. Battle after battle after battle. Who could ignore what was going on?

JAPANESE POUNDED IN LUZON, WARSHIPS CHASED; RUSSIANS ROUT NAZI ARMIES ON MOSCOW FRONT; HOUSE GETS BILL TO REGISTER ALL MEN 18 TO 64 (December 13, 1941).[17]

TOBRUK FALLS, AXIS CLAIMS 25,000 PRISONERS; GERMANS DRIVE WEDGE INTO SEVASTOPOL LINES; JAPANESE ASHORE ON KISKA IN THE ALEUTIANS (June 22, 1942).[18]

U.S. FORCE WINS BEACHES ON MARSHALLS ATOLL; BATTLES RAGE ON FIRST JAPANESE SOIL INVADED; ALLIES ATTACK BELOW ROME; RUSSIANS ADVANCE (February 2, 1944).[19]

ALLIED ARMIES LAND IN FRANCE IN THE HAVRE-CHERBOURG AREA; GREAT INVASION IS UNDER WAY (June 6, 1944).[20]

U.S. MARINES STORM ASHORE ON IWO ISLAND; 509 PLANES, 36 SHIPS SMASHED IN TOKYO BLOW; BRITISH AT EDGE OF GOCH; PATTON STRIKES AGAIN (February 19, 1945).[21]

OKINAWA IS OURS AFTER 82 DAYS; 45,029 U.S. CASUALTIES, FOE'S 94,401; GEN. STILWELL HEADS 10TH ARMY (June 22, 1945).[22]

The headlines, to be sure, helped to bring home the war, but what made the war even more paramount in people's minds was that so many men and women were serving. In this as in every other war, the political was personal. Thus, for individuals and families, the question was not simply "Who's fighting whom?" but "Did anyone we know die today?"

When the marines landed on the Japanese island of Iwo Jima and engaged in a brutal battle for territory, the activities of the troops participating in the invasion were followed closely by the folks at home. People's anxiety understandably was high. "Daily editions during the week of February 19 brought battle accounts within twenty-four hours of actual time," wrote James Bradley, whose father was a medic and one of the six marines in the now-famous photo of the raising of the U.S. flag atop Mount Suribachi. "Papers told the story in bold headlines, pages of background stories, and numerous maps and diagrams."[23]

Private First Class Bill Madden, who was wounded in the assault, described to his father what it was like to be on the island. ("I read once that a Dad likes to get mail addressed just to him sometimes, so if you can stand lefthand writing this is for you.") He also mourned for the men who were lost and for the many others whose torsos and limbs were shattered. And he wondered what it all meant.

I'll tell you a few things about Iwo. . . . I was in the 1st wave of troops to land, but a wave of armored tanks landed 2 minutes earlier. This would have been swell if there hadn't been a 15 ft. embankment of loose sand in my sector. The tanks didn't get off the beach, & you can imagine the trouble we had! The Nips pattern-shelled the beach with mortars, cross fired it with pill-boxes, block houses, & individual nambu & heavy machine-guns. They had the beach mined too, & I saw plenty of Marines die before they got over the first bank. . . . After the first bank of sand there were two more and just as well defended. I got my first Nip on the second bank. He raised up to throw another grenade & I shot him in the neck with an armor piercing shell. You can imagine what was left of him! . . . You know our casualties were given at 4,000 dead & 16,000 wounded. Well 2,000 more died of wounds & several thousand men are crippled for life. Do you think that rock was worth those men's lives, Dad??[24]

Of all the battles in World War II, perhaps the one that was the most anticipated was the Allied invasion of France, on the beaches of Normandy, June 6, 1944—D-Day, as it has come to be called.[25] In the attack on Iwo Jima, no advance warning was given to those in the United States.[26] With the Normandy assault, the U.S. administration had signaled its intention to free Western Europe at least a year and a half before, and in the months and days preceding the invasion, reports about the buildup were thick. What was not telegraphed, of course, was the exact point of the invasion; that piece of important information was a closely guarded secret.[27]

Radio bulletins in the early morning hours of June 6 announced that the operation had begun. Bells were rung across the country. People flocked to places of worship and stood in silence, in large and small groups, to somberly ponder the significance of the assault.[28] Some preferred to note the occasion by themselves. One boy, nine years old, hearing about it on the radio and knowing that his father was among those involved, "went down to the garden, hoisted the American flag, placed it in its stand and stood at salute."[29]

In the evening, President Roosevelt spoke to the nation and offered an "invasion prayer," asking God to look favorably upon Allied soldiers, particularly those whose lives would be sacrificed.

Our sons, pride of our nation, this day have set upon a mighty endeavor, a struggle to preserve our Republic, our religion and our civilization, and to set free a suffering humanity. Lead them straight and true; give strength to their arms, stoutness to their hearts, steadfastness in their faith. . . . Their road will be long and hard. For the enemy is strong. He may hurl back our forces. Success may not come with rushing speed, but we shall return again and again; and we know that by Thy grace, and by the righteousness of our cause, our sons will triumph. They will be sore tired, by night and by day, without rest—until the victory is won. The darkness will be rent by noise and flame. Men's souls will be shaken with the violence of war. . . . Some will never return. Embrace these, Father, and receive them, Thy heroic servants, into Thy kingdom. And for us at home—fathers, mothers, children, wives, sisters and brothers of brave men overseas, whose thoughts and prayers are ever with them—help us, Almighty God, to rededicate ourselves in renewed faith in Thee in this hour of great sacrifice.[30]

The invasion, itself, was indeed "hard." The weather over Normandy was exceptionally cloudy and caused some paratroopers to miss their drop zone. (Because of the poor conditions, the invasion had been delayed twenty-four hours.) The military's glider planes, if they were able to survive the anti-aircraft fire, were frequently ripped apart when they sailed into trees and hedgerows that were taller than the pre-invasion surveillance had indicated. A number of the amphibious landing crafts dropped their ramps prematurely, requiring the troops aboard to rush headlong into water that was above their heads. With all the equipment on their backs, the men could not float or swim, and many drowned. Passing crafts could not stop to offer assistance; in fact, they had been ordered not to stop. Units that made it ashore were cut to pieces by a murderous hail of machine-gun fire. The almost constant bombardment of the Germans' defenses in the days preceding the invasion had failed to destroy the heavily fortified gun placements.[31] As if on cue, the fog of war—the inevitable uncertainty of battle—had visited itself upon the advancing forces. In the end, the invasion succeeded because of the multitude on the beaches. The Germans could mow down only so many "bodies."[32]

In the rural town of Bedford, Virginia, interest in D-Day was especially intense. Forty of Bedford's "boys," all members of a local National Guard unit, were known to have been in training for the assault, and townspeople were anxious to learn whether the soldiers were safe. "Was the Bedford unit among the first to hit the beaches? Were any of the boys killed?" Viola Parker was awakened in the early morning hours with the news that the invasion had begun. She and her husband, Earl, had been married for two years and were the parents of a baby girl, born four weeks after Earl had shipped out. Although Earl had not seen his daughter, he did have photos of her, which he carried around and proudly displayed. On a British transport heading for the landing zone, Earl told his buddies that "he would not mind dying if he could only see her just once." He never got that chance. Though Viola did not know it at the time, Earl was in the initial wave at Normandy. She eventually received word, via telegram, that her husband was "missing in action." She later discovered that he was "hit by a mortar shell" during the assault and that his body was "washed out into the English Channel, never to be found."[33]

Bedford suffered more losses, per capita, on D-Day than any other town in the United States. Twenty-two of the forty Virginia men, all members of

Company A of the 116th Infantry Regiment, were killed on Omaha Beach, where some of the heaviest fighting occurred. Earl Parker was the only dad in the Bedford group, but he certainly was not the only dad affected. A sister of one of the fallen recalled years later, "I can still see my father now, standing on the street corner, just hoping to see one of the survivors . . . [and] find out exactly what happened."[34]

One activity that defined life during the war was the exchange of letters between soldiers and their families. Indeed, without these chronicles, we would not know as much as we do today about World War II. Not an hour went by when someone somewhere was not writing about the war and about what it meant to her or him. Family members, via dispatches, strove to create a sense of affinity across a geographic divide. "Today [June 6, 1944] we have lived history," wrote a wife to her husband assigned to the headquarters of the Allied Expeditionary Force. "We are part of something tremendous."[35] Said another, more immediately and more anxiously,

> 6:45 a.m. The phone just rang about ten minutes ago. It was your mother. She told me the Invasion had started. I just put on the radio and this time it's real. I don't quite know what to say, Sweetheart. It goes without saying that I feel very nervous and very afraid. I do feel though, that you weren't in this first wave. I hope and pray, Darling, that if I am right you will never have to go in. I suppose I want too much. . . . Georgie [the couple's fifteenth-month-old son] just woke up so I'll have to go get him. I love you, Sweetheart, and I'll always love you. I miss you terribly and I'll pray for you night and day. Georgie is saying "Da-da" as loud as he can. Come back to us, Darling.[36]

The emotional connection through letters was felt on both sides. Whatever the date, whatever the battle, soldiers relished the opportunity to read, and often share, family news. While it is certainly true that in the middle of fighting, the most salient role was that of "warrior"—or of "brother in arms" ("We were a mutual survival society" is how one veteran put it)—within the periphery of war (which could include plenty of idle time and, for some, little or no combat), being a father, husband, and son continued to be central. In this respect, letters to home—but especially *from* home—had a tremendous effect on a soldier's well-being.[37]

Military personnel received tons of mail—by some estimates about fourteen items per week. In turn, soldiers would send mail—in some cases, as often as every day.[38] For wives and children, the act of sending and the delight in receiving letters helped to keep the memory of fathers alive.[39] Children might ask their dads the simplest of questions ("Do you live in a house?") or share the simplest of news ("I've been outside playing with my tank").[40] Wives reported the mundane ("I cleaned the cellar") as well as the melancholic ("Sonny . . . was killed in a plane crash").[41]

The letters that often generated the most excitement were the birth announcements. "We have a lovely son, dearest," wrote one wife. "I've only had one glimpse of him, but he's got the things we need to make a perfect baby." She then went on to describe "the whole tale" of her labor and delivery.[42] Another reported the birth of a boy who, the father was told, looked and acted just like him:

> Your wish has come true, dear, and you are now the proud daddy to the most handsome son ever. He is really a beauty and is the perfect image of you. He weighs 8 pounds 10 ounces, your laughing eyes, the tiniest nose ever, a small bud-like mouth and the chubbiest cheeks. He even has your hair, Darling. When I look at our son, Harvey Joel, I see you precious. The folks are simply wild over him. . . . Your son certainly has a way with women—takes after his dad even in this respect. He's really a fine boy and good, too. I shall take good care of him for you, precious, and I know that he shall love his daddy just as much as I do—and that's so very much. Your picture is there right beside his crib.[43]

What was it like to get these announcements? Walter Schuette penned a letter to his baby daughter to tell her of his reaction to hearing that she had been born. "You will never know the joy I knew when I received word that you had arrived," he exclaimed. "Suddenly *the sun shone through the fog*. The mud paths seemed paved with gold. The boys thought I had gone stir crazy or maybe slap happy. I guess I was a little daft."[44]

George Rarey wrote a letter as well to share his reaction and that of his fellow soldiers upon learning that he was a father. (Rarey had just returned from a combat mission.) He, too, now viewed the world more luminously.

> All the boys in the squadron went wild. Oh its [sic] wonderful! I had saved my tobacco ration for the last two weeks & had obtained a box of good American cigars—Old Doc Finn trotted out two quarts of Black and White from his medicine chest and we all toasted the fine new son and his beautiful Mother. Old Bill is proud and almost as excited as I am. . . . I'm anxious to know all the details—I figure Damon was born on the 19th—I wonder what he weighs and all about him. Tell him that he has the proudest, happiest and luckiest

Pop in the whole world. Junie if this letter makes no sense forget it—I'm sort of delirious—Today everything is special—The iron hut looks like a castle— The low hanging overcast outside is the most beautiful kind of blue I've ever seen—I'm a father—I have a son! . . . What a ridiculous and worthless thing a war is in the light of such a wonderful event. That there will be no war for Damon!—Junie, isn't there anything I can do to help out—[45]

One does get a sense from these and other accounts that news of a birth could trigger a communal response and was perceived by soldiers as a joy to be embraced in concert: "Sergeant Jones . . . got a . . . letter [and] came up . . . with this picture of his new baby that had just been born in the States. We passed this picture from one foxhole to another until it was rumpled. For about three days and three nights all we seemed to talk about was Jones's baby, as though it was ours. I mean it seemed like such a funny thing to be happening."[46]

Although becoming a father was clearly a special moment, hearing about what older children were up to could be precious, too. One soldier received a letter from his ten-year-old daughter who wanted to cut off her pigtails because the boys in her class were yanking them, and her grandmother found them difficult to braid. Besides, all of her friends were getting hair-dos. "Granny won't let me unless you say ok," the young girl wrote, "so I hope you say ok." The squad members sat around and debated what should be advised. Said one soldier to the father, "Oh, no. Don't let her. Keep her a kid as long as you can."[47]

Men also talked among themselves about how their children would view them when they got home. After all, they had been away for a while. The worry was that "their kids would slam the door and run to mother shouting, 'There's a strange man outside!'" They also engaged in broader discussions about how they would be viewed by the people in their communities. What would folks say to them? Would neighbors and friends who had grown tired of the war call them "suckers"? What about "the new generation"? Would "the teenagers . . . look at their war tired brothers and fathers and speak of [them] as [they] once spoke of the men of the last war"? In other words, speak badly.[48]

How much soldier-fathers shared in the lives of their children—how much they knew about their kids' daily activities—was largely in the hands of their families. One man said after the war that his wife made a sincere effort, while he was away, to incorporate him into the social world of father-hood. "To accomplish this," he said, "she did much more than inform me of the day-to-day progress from the time of our baby's birth. She did much

more than send me snapshots at different stages of development with de-
lightful penciled notes on the back, such as: 'This is her well-fed contented
smile.' . . . Far more important [than these updates] for my education as a
parent were the references to my own future part in things." He offered the
following as an example:

> On one occasion my wife wrote me that Judy seemed to enjoy her grand-
> father's voice, and that this was a sure sign she would welcome mine. "Ba-
> bies," she said, "evidently like women's voices for reassurance, and men's
> voices for fun." At the time I read her letters I tended to be skeptical, sup-
> posing that she was sending these pages and pages of air mail either to build
> up my morale or satisfy my male ego. But now that Judy and I are well ac-
> quainted and our early evening playtime together is a period neither of us
> can bear to miss, and since she unmistakably knows me and enjoys me and
> depends on me, I see that my wife knew what she was talking about, and also
> what she was doing.[49]

Needless to say, family members could only do so much to bring a sense
of "home" to a soldier stationed overseas. Many things happened while
fathers were away. During the time one man was gone, his parents passed
away, and his wife gave birth to twin boys. (He would not meet the sons
until they were twenty-six months old.) One of his other kids started school.
Another came down with scarlet fever. His wife bought a new house. When
he returned, the town he once knew, as he put it, "was filled with strangers."
The same perhaps could have been said about his family.[50]

Those on the home front also could feel a sense of loss because family
members were overseas. Not just the daughters and sons of soldiers but also
their fathers and mothers had to accept the fact that holidays and other special occasions would have to be celebrated with loved ones away. Wrote one
soldier to his father in 1944, "HAPPY BIRTHDAY!!! . . . This is the first—and
last, I hope—time that I've missed being home for your birthday. In 1945
we'll go fishing TOGETHER on your birthday. At present you are right in the
prime of your life, with many more happy birthdays ahead of you." The
soldier and his dad never did go on that fishing trip. Eleven months later,
while the son was in combat in Germany, the father passed away.[51]

Thus, on a number of levels, the war disconnected men from their children and their partners. But the war created kinship bonds as well. This
was especially true for the fathers and sons who were—or had been—in
the military. Serving together in the armed forces created a shared reference

point that allowed generations of warriors to relate as they could not have otherwise.

A World War I veteran, for example, expressed his hopes and concerns for his son, who was about to go overseas. Having been in combat himself, he knew what was on the horizon.

> Well, I figure you're off on the Great Adventure. There will be many disagreeable experiences; soul searching experiences; tragic experiences; uplifting experiences. You will see examples of selfishness and selflessness that will stir you tremendously. I have no doubt that you will develop the same respect that I have for the Infantry, the Gol-Darned Infantry, and the same awesome regard for the Medics. I have no fears for you; you will do well. You have the finest spirit of any one I know of. I wish I could go FOR you, or at least WITH you, but this is your war.[52]

Another father who endeavored to bond with his son in wartime was the renowned General George S. Patton Jr. On D-Day, the troops he commanded were deployed in Dover (the port in England that was closest to France) to deceive the Germans into thinking that the main attack would come at Calais rather than Normandy. Not being in the fight—which bothered him to no end—and having time on his hands, Patton took the opportunity to write to his son who, in 1944, was enrolled at West Point. Besides giving other pieces of advice, Patton spoke of what he thought it took to win in a war: "Cowards are those who let their timidity get the better of their manhood. You will never do that because of your blood lines on both sides. . . . To be a successful soldier you must know history. Read it objectively. . . . Weapons change but man who uses the[m] changes not at all. To win battles you do not beat weapons you beat the soul of man of the enemy man [sic]."[53]

Finally, there was the father, an army colonel, whose connection to his son in war arose from a sense of competition and evolved into something macabre. The colonel had been in the service for thirty-nine years and was scheduled to retire in a few months. Although he had served in both World Wars, he always had a desk job. His son was an air corps pilot who had seen a fair amount of action and "was gloating over his combat successes." To be able "hold his own with his son in the postwar years," the colonel told a fellow officer and "old Army friend" that he "wanted at least one shot at the enemy before he was forced out of uniform." Soon after, he was granted his wish:

In a pouring rain, he was escorted to the front and slithered into a fox-hole. . . . As dawn broke, the rain let up and the sun came up. . . . He cleared his glasses and peered out front, and for an instant the sun glistened on something metallic. The Colonel had spotted his German. . . . He settled down to waiting. Throughout the day the enemy sniper would stick his head up a few inches, then jerk it down again. But the Colonel was patient; he had waited thirty-nine years for this. Then his chance came. . . . The Colonel nuzzled his cheek against the stock of his [Springfield] '03 [rifle], squinted down the sights at the gray-green tunic, and gently squeezed the trigger.

Later on, the colonel got another opportunity to fire. Again, he hugged a weapon; again, he took a life. With two recorded kills, the father felt he "now could match stories with his pilot son."[54]

FOUR

"Giving It the Best They've Got"

Before the war, fathers were judged by how well they provided for their families economically and whether they were playmates and companions to their children. Fathers also were expected to be models of "manhood," but, in the 1920s and 1930s, this typically meant teaching sons how to play sports and to be risk-takers, and impressing upon daughters, if only by example, the qualities to look for in a husband. World War II reinforced another image of fatherhood, namely, the *father as protector*.[1]

Certain kinds of protecting were thought to be particularly noble, creating a system of stratification in which some fathers were ranked higher than others. Fathers in the military, and especially those overseas, were valued, while fathers who saw combat were revered (particularly if they had been wounded in battle). Fathers who were awarded medals for bravery were highly regarded. Fathers killed in action, however, were the most respected of all. As one soldier, who fought in the Iwo Jima campaign, put it, "The real heroes . . . are the guys who didn't come back."[2]

Fathers who had children in the armed forces were also appreciated. Having a child stationed overseas reflected well on a man. A child assigned to a fighting unit—whether it be in the army, air corps, navy, or Marine Corps—further increased the esteem in which a soldier's father might be held. And if a child died in defense of the country, the father of that child was elevated to the rank of the virtuous. (The mother of the child would be, too. More will be said about this in a moment.)

Next in the system of stratification were fathers who could claim to be warriors on the home front—men employed in the arms industry and those whose jobs could be linked to the war machine. Farmers could fall into this category, too.

Some men were married to women who took over the jobs that soldiers once held and who, by doing so, were keeping the economy going. The men who helped to sustain the women in these endeavors, emotionally or otherwise, were perceived to be contributing to the war effort, as were the "Rosie-the-Riveter" husbands—men married to (or, in some way, linked to) the women working in munitions plants and so forth. The women workers, in these cases, were thought to deserve a fair share of the country's admiration, but evidence indicates that their partners were recognized, too.[3] Consider, for example, an advertisement for the American Mutual Insurance Company, which depicted a father wearing an apron and stooping down to sweep up a broken dish. The fact that the father was in attire that would be considered "feminine" is remarkable but not unusual. Photos and illustrations of dads in aprons in the 1940s and 1950s tended to poke fun at men's housekeeping skills. What is unusual is that this particular father was being *praised* for doing a "woman's job." Here was a man who was ready to step in to support America's military mission.[4]

There was another way to be honored while working in industry, even if on the surface that industry appeared to have nothing to do with the war. Corporations routinely attempted to lift their status by linking their products and services to America's protection. If a corporation was successful in making such a link, the nobility it claimed could be also claimed by its workers. The Dixie-Vortex Company, manufacturers of paper drinking cups and water dispensers, argued that its products cut down on "colds, influenza, and trench mouth," allegedly the "most prevalent of lay-off illnesses." ("Small wonder, then, that you'll find Dixie Cups at industry's drinking founts . . . [and] aboard Navy's ships and at Army stations.")[5] The American Thermos Bottle Company, which made vacuum bottles and metal lunch kits, pitched the idea that "the man with the lunch kit and the man with the gun are equally vital to America's war effort." This analogy allowed the company to claim, "Thermos protects the health of the men whose work protects America."[6]

Then there were fathers who did whatever they could to support the troops, even if what they did seemed minor compared to what others were doing, and who embraced the principle that they—along with the men "above them"—were true patriots. Being a civil defense volunteer, purchasing war bonds, using the "right" products and services, strictly adhering to the government's policy on rationing—all were ways to show that one was a guardian of the nation and a person of good will and integrity. Buying batteries that lasted longer, cars that conserved gas, and tires that kept their treads also demonstrated that one knew what it took to a win the war.[7]

Life insurance companies frequently promoted the idea that buying their policies protected men's families and, by extension, the United States. The Mutual Life Insurance Company showed a father directing traffic while wearing a civil defense band on his arm. "No uniform for Dad in this war," read the ad. "Only double work and strain to keep the family going, to man the civil defense—to send a son away with a smile. For you, Dad, it's all work and sacrifice without a shred of glory." (But, of course, one unmistakable purpose behind the ad was to bestow glory on the dad.) The company then made its pitch: " 'To keep the family going' . . . that means tomorrow, Dad, as well as today. . . . Let the Mutual Life representative in your community explain our 4 new 'war economy' policies to help make your premium dollar buy more family security. Remember, premium dollars are patriotic dollars, too."[8]

Yet another way to be seen as contributing to the war effort was to serve as a surrogate father for a child whose father was overseas. In 1942, the Child Study Association of America, in collaboration with the Committee for the Care of Children in Wartime, reported that significant numbers of children whose fathers were in the military and whose mothers worked in factories were being left unattended when they were not in school. " 'Door key' children," explained the president of the committee, "are those who wear the key around their neck and go home after school to play without adult supervision in an empty house or flat, a health and fire hazard." Day care centers and cooperative "babysitting" clubs helped some, but there still were "war job 'orphans' " who were not being genuinely cared for around the clock.[9] In some families, grandparents filled the gap: "My granddaddy took over for my Daddy in many ways," said one daughter. "He read the funny papers to me, . . . took me to the park and movies, and bought me a cherry smash . . . after church. . . . [And] he would sing me to sleep at night with 'You Are My Sunshine.' "[10] Other men—uncles, cousins, and neighborhood dads—also were asked to "stretch" their caregiving: "If you want to do something worth-while try this," suggested one author. "Let your child invite Jimmy or Jane whose father is overseas to dinner one night. You may be surprised to see how pleased they will be if the father of the family shows them some attention. . . . The fathers left at home will be doing an invaluable service if they can find a way to be friends with those children whose fathers are away from home."[11]

The system of stratification had its bottom rungs, too. Men who were classified as IV-F (not qualified for military service) were almost always viewed with suspicion. If they appeared to be able-bodied but were not in uniform or ostensibly employed in a war-related job, they might be asked—

sometimes in public by complete strangers—to justify their actions and whereabouts.[12] Children whose fathers were not in the military also could be confronted or ostracized by their classmates. "The girls won't let me join their club because my daddy isn't fighting," said one young girl in tears.[13] Conscientious objectors were in a very precarious position and were routinely asked to defend themselves against the charge that they were draft dodgers or, worse, cowards. Being a conscientious objector, it is important to acknowledge, did not necessarily mean that one did nothing to help in the war effort. Some C.O.'s served as medics or filled other important roles. Still, they frequently were harassed.[14]

Fathers who were thought to be aiding and abetting the enemy—or believed to have the potential to do so—occupied the lowest rung. After Pearl Harbor, Japanese Americans were thrust into this category. (The absence of credible evidence of wrongdoing had little impact on how the suspicions played out.) An individual did not have to be classified as an "enemy alien" to be denounced. A father convicted of defrauding the government or of shipping defective parts, particularly if the parts had something to do with weaponry, was vermin in people's eyes. Such a father might be considered unworthy to be called a dad—or a man. A fictional example, reportedly based on actual events, is the three-act play, *All My Sons*, written during the war by Arthur Miller. In the play, a family discovers that its sixty-one-year-old patriarch, Joe Keller, has knowingly shipped faulty cylinder heads to the air corps. (Joe is a co-owner of a machine shop and admits that he was afraid of losing his contract with the government if he did not get the parts out on time.) The twenty-one planes in which the parts are used end up crashing, and all the pilots are killed. Joe's partner is convicted and goes to prison, but it is Joe who actually is to blame. When the truth finally comes out, Joe's son, Chris, cannot contain his rage: "God in heaven, what kind of a man are you? Kids were hanging in the air by those heads. You knew that! . . . Don't you have a country? Don't you live in the world? . . . Dad, you killed twenty-one men!"[15]

The different strata of wartime fatherhood were apparent both in people's words and in their actions. One war bond advertisement summarized the most basic rule of the ranking: "None of us in civilian life can match the sacrifices that fathers away from home and fireside—and many others in the armed services—are making for us on the fighting fronts."[16] Another advertisement conveyed the pride that children with a father in uniform could feel and the blanket of protection that a military warrior was assumed to provide. "I come from fighting stock," proclaimed an infant girl perched in a baby carriage. "You should see my father. Fighter's jaw, steady eyes, handsome uniform. . . . Nobody's going to push him around, him or his family."[17] The Savings Bank of Brooklyn ran an ad that pictured a young boy earnestly looking up at an adult and asking, "Won't you buy a bond, Mister, so's my Daddy can come home?" The child was one among thousands of "Victory Volunteers" who were "backing up our gallant Soldiers, Sailors, and Marines . . . fighting for America . . . for your future . . . and the future of your own children."[18] The Paul Revere Copper and Brass Company told the story of Sergeant Samuel Jones Jr., wounded in battle and now recuperating in a hospital. Sergeant Jones was "sent to do our fighting," stated the company, and had seen "the hell and evil of war." Yet he remained upbeat. "If he can smile, why should we cry? . . . The courage of such men."[19]

Given the nationalism throughout the United States and the symbolism of being in the military at that time, many fathers were eager to enlist. And enlist they did. It was estimated that between seven and eight hundred thousand fathers were on active duty in September 1943 (prior to the lifting of the draft exemption for certain categories of fathers).[20] The fact that racial and ethnic minorities, however, were denied the opportunity to join, at least in the beginning, meant that their access to the upper echelons of fatherhood was blocked.

In some cases, it was not the color of a man's body but its condition that kept him out of the service. Physical impairments could lead to one being classified as IV-F. Some men welcomed the dispatch to the sidelines; it meant that they would not be placed in harm's way. But others were saddened to learn that they were not "fit" to join. The actor James Stewart was turned down because he was underweight and was ridiculed in the press as a result ("Movie Hero Heavy Enough to Knock Out Villain but Too Light for Uncle Sam"). Stewart's dad threatened to come out to Hollywood and "punch a few noses among those reporters," but his son told him, "That wouldn't help things a bit." Stewart said that they "both knew what he had to do to retain [his] self respect." The actor went back to the induction center and "begged them to forget the fact [he] was underweight." The recruiters consented to do so, and Stewart "became a soldier—just as [his] father had been in two previous wars."[21]

There were also those who, craving to get into the war by whatever means they could, repeated their physical exams or lied about their health. This tactic often worked, for the military was eager to enlist as many as it could. If an individual was repeatedly rejected, he might agree to take on a lesser but still socially valued role (e.g., working in a shipyard). Alternative service, however, was not acceptable to everyone. For a few, not being in uniform was excruciating. One forty-one-year-old father of two, whose efforts to join were thwarted by a physical disability, shot and killed himself on the lawn of a church in the Flatbush section of Brooklyn. The shotgun he used was a birthday present he had purchased for his fifteen-year-old son.[22]

More than one hundred and eighty thousand children lost their fathers in World War II.[23] The grief that these sons and daughters experienced cannot be adequately expressed. We do know this: their painful mourning was sometimes anything but private. Granted, a child might be allowed periodically to steal away to suffer alone, and the funeral might be closed to anyone but family members and the dearest of friends, but a soldier's death was frequently interpreted as a community's loss, making the sorrow something of a civic event.

In wartime, it is not unusual for people with no apparent kinship or friendship relationship to the fallen to feel that it is their duty—indeed their right—to display their gratitude. For a downed combatant, one's respects must be paid. War memorials are but one example of the kind of public recognition that often is bestowed upon those who have given their lives for their country. Other acknowledgments exist as well.

Throughout the war, families would overtly communicate that one of their own was in the armed forces. A Blue Star Flag in a home's window signified that a family member was serving. A Gold Star Flag meant that a family member had been killed. People who passed by a family's home thus would be apprised of the anxiety and anguish inside.

Newspapers frequently offered personal stories of military deaths in addition to obituaries. Each tale of woe was more poignant than the next. Flight Officer George E. Larsen of San Angelo, Texas, died in a training plane crash "seventeen hours after he had first glimpsed his newly born son."[24] Private Joseph J. Short of Lake Ronkonkoma, New York, whose father was slain in World War I, wrote a letter to his wife, saying, "I hope my sons do not lose their father the way I lost mine." Three weeks later, he was killed while serving with a commando unit. His boys were six and three.[25] Captain Gerald Marnell of Parsons, Kansas, wrote his first letter to his two-year-old daughter just hours before he lost his life on a combat mission:

> I know that you can't read this letter now, but your mother will read it to you and she will save it for you until you are old enough to read it yourself. Your daddy held you in his arms when you were only a few minutes old. Your daddy saw you grow. He would beam with pride and joy when he

would watch your mother rock you to sleep in her arms. Daddy saw you start to crawl, and how you did get around! He remembered you standing alone and taking your first step and cutting your first tooth and saying your first word. Then came the day when your daddy had to say good-bye. You cried so hard when daddy was driving away and daddy shed a tear himself. Your daddy didn't want to leave you, but he had to go to help make your country a safe and free place to live in. Little baby, God has blessed you with the finest mother in the world and daddy loves your mother very much. Be good to your mother, Geraldine, there is no one else like her in the world. Daddy won't write much more to you. He will be back home some day and you and he will play together again. Daddy asks God every night to guide and watch over you and your mother.[26]

Medal ceremonies also were commonly covered in the news. These observances could be heartbreaking when the medals were given posthumously. Colonel George F. Marshall of Jacksonville, Florida, was awarded a Distinguished Service Cross. His three-year-old son, George Jr., accepted the award on his father's behalf. Private August Armocida of the Bronx, New York, was awarded a Bronze Star, and Private Tonny Hansen of Manhattan, New York, was given a Soldier's Medal. Their awards were pinned on their children, both no more than two years old.[27] A father-and-son ceremony was held for Lieutenant Colonel William H. Combs of New Rochelle, New York, and Lieutenant Richard M. Combs of Baltimore, Maryland. The father was awarded the Distinguished Service Cross, while the son was awarded the Silver Star. Their wives accepted their awards.[28]

The publicity attending a soldier's death could be intrusive. For some family members, death in war was not glorious, nor could military medals distract them from the pain. One widow, who asked to remain nameless and whose hometown was not revealed, refused to attend the ceremony where an Air Medal was posthumously awarded to her husband—a fighter pilot. She said that since he was not alive to accept it himself, the meaning of the medal was "gone for [her]."

I am used to the Government leaving things at my door, the telegram, the Purple Heart, and so I won't mind the Air Medal coming through the mail too. I would like to have it, you see, because of my son. He's never seen his father but still there's so much I want him to know of his dad. I guess the only way to start is to show off his dad's medals to him. I wish I could tell him his father died to save him from being drawn into a third World War. I'm afraid

I'll just have to tell him about his father as a civilian, a young man just out of college with his life ahead of him, dying before he had a chance to live for what he was fighting for.[29]

Soldiers killed in action were not only spouses and parents, but also sons and daughters. The social meaning of fatherhood during the war thus was also about the shock and suffering that thousands of men experienced when they learned that a child of theirs had been mortally wounded. Notable is the fact that, while fathers of the fallen were certainly revered, they generally were not accorded as much sympathy as the mothers. Gold Star status, intended to honor the parent of a child killed in action, was originally conceived to recognize mothers and mothers alone.

The practice of displaying a gold star following a battle death can be traced to at least as far back as World War I. In 1918, the Women's Committee of the Council of National Defense suggested to President Woodrow Wilson that instead of wearing black attire to mourn relatives who had died in a war, people should wear black arm bands with a "gilt star" to signify each member of a family who had been killed. (Gold Star flags already were being hung in windows to honor the dead.) The feeling of the committee was that wearing black attire, a practice that had existed for some time, negatively affected "the spirit and energy of soldiers, their families, and the public." Because so many had been killed in the war, the number of people wearing black had increased markedly—and in a very short period of time. (The United States had entered the war only the year before.) The gold star insignia, in the opinion of the committee, "[would] express better than mourning the feeling of the American people that such losses are a matter of glory rather than of prostrating grief and depression."[30]

The idea, however, was not that everyone in a family would wear the star; only women were expected to do so. This was probably connected to the fact that women more than men traditionally adorned themselves in black for months (and often years) after a loved one passed away. People apparently assumed that women would be the most devastated by the loss.[31] During World War I, however, the constant reminders of death were dispiriting, said the committee. And, in the end, President Wilson agreed: "I hope and believe that thoughtful people everywhere will approve of this action, and I hope that you will be kind enough to make the suggestion of the committee public, with the statement that it has my cordial indorsement."[32]

Some time later, in 1928, a group of twenty-five mothers in the District of Columbia came together to create a national organization called the American Gold Star Mothers (AGSM). The women were building on the efforts of another group of mothers who had formed a Washington-area organization some ten years before. The main objective of the AGSM was phrased as follows in its earliest constitution: "To unite with loyalty, sympathy and love for each other, mothers whose sons or daughters have made the supreme sacrifice while in the Service of the United States of America, or as a result of such service." In 1936, a bill was presented to the U.S. House of Representatives to incorporate the women's organization. Therein it was stated that "persons . . . may be chosen who are mothers who have lost a son or sons, a daughter or daughters," but "honorary members" could include "the fathers of such sons and daughters." Mothers, in other words, were the AGSM's principal figures. Fathers, if they were involved at all, were secondary.[33]

The extent to which parental suffering was presumed in World War II to be largely a maternal affair is also evident in the accounts surrounding the deaths of the five Sullivan brothers (Albert, George, Francis, Joseph, and Madison) who served on the USS *Juneau* and who perished together when it was sunk in the South Pacific on November 13, 1942. The saga of the brothers and of their parents, Alletta and Thomas Sullivan, was chronicled in newspapers throughout the country and made into a 1944 movie, *The Fighting Sulllivans* ("a deeply touching story," wrote one reviewer, "because of the personal sacrifice it represents").[34]

Soon after being told of the death of their five boys (after first being informed that they were missing in action), Mr. and Mrs. Sullivan embarked on a government-sponsored tour of industrial plants. It was believed that the couple's presence at the plants and, more important, their testimony to the workers would speed up war production. "What I feel is this," said Thomas Sullivan, during a stopover at a Philadelphia shipyard. "If we had more planes and more ships out there in the Solomons, the cruiser Juneau wouldn't have been sunk, and our boys wouldn't have been lost. Maybe if the men and women in war plants realize what it has meant to Mom and me, and to a lot of other mothers and fathers, that there weren't enough planes and ships, they will work their level best to make sure there will be enough from now on. And then the war will be over sooner."[35]

The meaning of the boys' deaths, however, apparently was not the same for Mr. Sullivan as it was for Mrs. Sullivan. At least this is the impression one gets from published reports. Alletta and Thomas Sullivan may have toured the country as a couple, but it was Mrs. Sullivan who mostly "[did] the speaking at the plants."[36] At the ceremony where a navy destroyer was named in honor of their sons, Alletta Sullivan was called upon to christen the ship, while Thomas Sullivan stood nearby.[37] When *The American Magazine* published an article about the tragedy, Alletta Sullivan was its sole author. "I Lost Five Sons," was its title.[38]

The article is especially revealing. "Here is one of the war's great human documents," declared the magazine. "Out of the depth of her experience, a mother whose boys went down with the cruiser *Juneau* in the Pacific brings comfort and courage to the women of American servicemen." Alletta Sullivan talked about how she and her husband were initially told about the *Juneau*'s sinking (by a neighbor) and what it was like to have three men in uniform show up at their home at seven o'clock in the morning.[39]

What was said to have happened when the men arrived is this: Mr. Sullivan answered the door; Mrs. Sullivan was upstairs, still in bed. (She was not feeling well that day.) When a navy officer informed Mr. Sullivan that he had "some news" about his "boys," Mr. Sullivan asked the man to delay the message so he could first get his wife. He then went up to wake Mrs. Sullivan and also called out to Genevieve, their daughter, and Katherine Mary, their daughter-in-law, both of whom were living with the Sullivans at the time. (Katherine Mary was the wife of Albert. The couple had an infant son.) The family members came down (the women in bathrobes). At that point, they were formally notified that the *Juneau* had sunk and that the boys were missing ("The Navy Department deeply regrets . . .").[40]

"Genevieve turned white and Katherine Mary looked as if she were going to collapse," reported Mrs. Sullivan. "I could hardly hold back the tears, but I wouldn't let myself cry in front of the three men." Although Mrs. Sullivan managed to remain composed at the announcement, she and her daughters went upstairs and "gave way to [their] grief" as soon as the visitors left. Mrs. Sullivan said, too, that she "cried a lot" in the following days and weeks and that she and her mother tried to keep busy to "soften" their sorrow.[41]

How did Thomas Sullivan react to loss of his boys? If the accounts are to be believed, he was indestructible. Mr. Sullivan pretty much knew why the navy personnel were there that morning, but he kept his emotions in check long enough to go upstairs to announce that the family had "visitors." Upon receiving the news, Alletta Sullivan controlled her tears (but only briefly); both the daughter and daughter-in-law bordered on shock. Thomas Sullivan, however, did not sob or turn pale or collapse. Rather, according to Mrs. Sullivan's memory of events, Mr. Sullivan's concern above all else was whether to head out to his job: "Dad turned to me," Mrs. Sullivan recounted. "He was due at work. He is a freight conductor for the Illinois Central. He had a record of 33 years without an absence, except for serious illness. His train was leaving in half an hour. He said, 'Shall I go?' "[42]

Yes, he should, insisted his wife: "I knew that his train was carrying war freight. If that freight didn't reach the battle fronts in time, it might mean more casualties. Dad holding up the train might mean other boys would die; that other mothers might have to face such grief needlessly, so I said, 'There isn't anything you can do at home. You might as well go.' So he did." A father's ultimate obligation—even at that moment of moments—thus was thought to be not to his own family but to his country and its war—and to its "other mothers."[43]

Each individual grieves in her or his own way, and Thomas Sullivan's way was not necessarily any less genuine than that of his wife or daughters. It was, however, unique within the family—and it was gender-bound. Stoicism in wartime was presented to the nation as Thomas Sullivan's patriotic duty as both a father and a man. When Mr. and Mrs. Sullivan eventually were told that their five sons had been killed, Alletta Sullivan succumbed to what she called "blind grief." ("It seemed as if almost everything I had lived for was gone.") Thomas Sullivan, in contrast, stood fast and left for work.[44]

A year later, at the launching of the USS *The Sullivans*, Rear Admiral Clark H. Woodward talked about the heroism behind the ship's name. When he did so, Alletta Sullivan, once again, began to cry. "It was really her tears which christened the ship," said the *New York Times*. As for Thomas Sullivan, "There was nothing . . . [he] could do about it except squeeze Mum's hand." Once more, Mr. Sullivan did not shed a single tear. If he did, he kept it to himself.[45]

Crying or, more precisely, *not crying* was central to the notion of the father as protector. Not crying shields others from your grief and makes it appear that you are available to absorb their grief, shielding them yet again. The taboo against crying that applied to soldiers (crying was not condoned in battle or anywhere else) also applied to fathers of soldiers who died. A "good" father was a "strong" man; a "good" father did not bend under duress.[46]

This does not mean that fathers did not mourn the loss of their children or feel, as Alletta Sullivan put it, that everything they had lived for was gone. There are cases of fathers who were so overcome with sorrow after learning of the death of a child that they keeled over. An eighteen-year-old sailor from Boston died while on furlough. His father, in "shock and grief," passed away the very next day. An aviator from Green Bay, Wisconsin, was killed in action in the Pacific. His father died, "presumably of shock," as soon as he heard.[47] Just the thought that a child might not be safe could be enough to demoralize or destroy some men. One Illinois father had difficulty sleeping during the time his boy was gone and would stare out a window in the middle of the night, uttering, "He's out there, that kid is out there."[48] A New

Jersey father was so troubled that his son was drafted that he had a heart attack within minutes of seeing him off. Five hours later he had another heart attack and died. The father reportedly had "tearfully told his family that induction of his second son into the Army would be the death of him."[49]

These examples, however, do not represent what was generally *expected*. The culture of fatherhood in wartime dictated that fathers be self-controlled and strong. To stare down death was the symbol of a "true" man. Twenty-four hours after learning that one of his boys had been killed "in performance of his duty," a Gloversville, New York, man marched his other boy, a younger child, to the induction station and ordered him to enlist. "When I left home this morning to come down here," the child said, "My father took me by the hand and told me, 'It is better that these sacrifices be made than to be ruled by the Axis. Good luck to you, son.'" A fifty-four-year-old farmer from Downing, Wisconsin, whose two sons had recently died in the fight on Bataan and Guadalcanal, "avenged" the deaths by enlisting in the Marine Corps. He did so, he said, so his remaining children, two daughters, "might continue to enjoy 'the advantages that were guaranteed [to him] under [America's] system of government.'" And then, of course, there were the thousands of fathers who, like Frank Sullivan, kept a stiff upper lip and simply *soldiered on*.[50]

The fact that Frank Sullivan left that fateful morning to go not just to any job but to a job transporting "war freight" shows the devotion that fathers in war industries were expected to have. These men, employed in factories and on farms, were thought to be combatants at home. Their status in the system of stratification, however, depended on how well they performed their assigned tasks. Alletta Sullivan mentioned that her husband "was a little shaky . . . about the idea of getting a leave of absence from his railroad" to participate in the tour that the navy had proposed. "After all," she said, "in his own way, he was doing war work, too." Only when his fellow trainmen agreed that it was okay for him to leave *his job* if it meant inspiring other defense workers to do *their jobs* did Mr. Sullivan feel it was appropriate to go.[51]

Given the need for war workers and the advantages to be gained if a company or farm were seen as contributing to the nation's defense, advertisements touted what the men in the war industries were doing. The General Electric Company's "Man of War" ad was emblematic of this genre. "Pete is a quiet, peace-loving man," began the ad. "Treats his family fine and pays his bills and gets along with his neighbors. Hasn't struck a blow in anger since he was a kid and caught another boy mistreating a dog." G. E. then talked about how Pete had changed, now that the country was at war:

But today Pete is mad clear through. You'd never guess it to see him at home; if anything he's quieter than ever. He isn't the kind to go around gritting his teeth and calling names. When you see him at work, though—then's when you realize the difference. For there's a deadly precision in the way he goes about his work. He's on the job a little before starting time; he pays more careful attention to what he's doing; he knows what he's building and for whom he's building it. And that's why he's probably the most dangerous, the "fightingest" enemy the Axis powers have. For it's men like Pete—who feel the way he does, who are doing what he is doing—who are manning the machines in America's factories today. And they're turning out the deadliest, most effective array of weapons the world has ever seen. There are lots of men like Pete among the 125,000 General Electric employees these days. In their off hours you'll find them acting as air-raid wardens in their communities. You'll find them among the more than 100,000 G-E men and women who, without fanfare or hurrah-boys, have signed up for the U.S. Defense Bonds to the tune of more than $20,000,000 a year. But most important of all, you'll find them on their job—doing what they know best, giving it the best they've got. Quiet, peaceable, determined men of war. They're the men who, a few months ago, took pride in building refrigerators, radios, washing machines, and all the other contributions of electricity to peace-time living. Today, they're putting their whole heart into the building of grimmer things—so that they and all of us may the sooner pick up the never-ending job of making better things for a better America.

Above the text was a photo of Pete, overall-clad and resolute-looking. The Petes of the nation—armed and dangerous home-front dads—were basically "peace loving" men (protectors of pets and other defenseless beings), who never shirked their responsibilities, but who now were "mad clear through" and willing to do what they had to do to win ("there's a deadly precision in the way he goes about his work"). Their fortitude was going to help make the difference in the war; indeed, they were the "fightingest enemy" Germany and Japan had to contend with. Pete and others like him were "Quiet, peaceable, determined men of war."[52]

PART TWO

FIVE

"Rights" of Passage

THE WAR IN EUROPE IS ENDED! SURRENDER IS UNCONDITIONAL; V-E WILL BE
PROCLAIMED TODAY; OUR TROOPS ON OKINAWA GAIN (May 8, 1945).[1]

JAPAN SURRENDERS, END OF WAR! EMPEROR ACCEPTS ALLIED RULE; M'ARTHUR
SUPREME COMMANDER; OUR MANPOWER CURBS VOIDED (August 15, 1945).[2]

First Germany capitulated; then Japan. The news was not unanticipated.
Rumors had been circulating for months that the end of the war was near.
Still, Americans waited for the official word. When it finally came, people
reacted swiftly, but not in the same way.[3]

With the announcement of Germany's defeat, thousands across the country poured into the streets. New York City residents "tooted horns, staged
impromptu parades and filled the canyons between the skyscrapers with
fluttering scraps of paper." More of them, however, "responded with quiet
thanksgiving that the war in Europe was won, tempered by the realization
that a grim and bitter struggle still was ahead in the Pacific." The nation was
still grieving from the loss of President Franklin D. Roosevelt, who had died
of a cerebral hemorrhage a few weeks before. Harry S. Truman, FDR's vice
president, was now in the White House.[4]

When Japan accepted defeat, the response from Americans was even
stronger—perhaps because their fears had been more intense. Again, rumors
that Japan was about to surrender circulated; and, again, only a formal announcement was able to put people at ease. The United States had dropped
the first atomic bomb on Hiroshima on August 6, and released another on
Nagasaki on August 9. The question was, would the complete destruction of
these two cities be enough to convince the Japanese Emperor Hirohito and
the Japanese Supreme Council to stop fighting? The answer, we know, was

yes. At seven o'clock on the evening of August 15, President Truman called reporters into the Oval Office to tell them that the Japanese government had accepted America's conditions.[5]

Informed of the surrender by radio and teletype, Americans could hardly contain their glee. "Restraint was thrown to the winds," reported the *New York Times*.

> Those in the crowds in the streets tossed hats, boxes and flags into the air. From those leaning perilously out of the windows of office buildings and hotels came a shower of paper, confetti, streamers. Men and women embraced—there were no strangers in New York yesterday. Some were hilarious, others cried softly. By 7:30 P.M., the crowd in the Square had risen to 750,000 persons; by 8:45 it had swelled to 800,000 and the number continued to rise. People were packed solidly between Forty-third Street and Forty-fifth street. Individual movement was virtually impossible; one moved not in the crowed but with it. . . . Everywhere noisemakers were in evidence. Automobiles, taxis, trucks ran through the streets with passengers not only inside but on running boards, shouting and blowing horns. Thousands of pedestrians carried small American flags and there was hardly a vehicle that did not display the Stars and Stripes.[6]

In the midst of all the revelry were the stories of pain and hope. The Roosevelts' third child, Elliott, happened to be near Forty-third Street in Manhattan. A sailor spotted him and said that he wished FDR were alive so he could see the celebration. "I do, too," the son softly replied. Elsewhere, an elderly couple surveyed the jubilation from the entrance of their home. In their window hung a gold star flag—a symbol that they had lost a child in the war. On another side of town, a man on the subway told a reporter that his kids had awakened him at 3 a.m. the day before, because they wanted to know for sure that that their older brother, who was overseas, would soon be coming back. Without that promise, the father said, the children refused to go back to sleep. Now he could tell them that their family would be together again.[7]

Victory prompted a range of feelings and actions. "My daddy was so excited," said one woman, "that he ran in the room and he got a pistol from World War One and he filled it and we went out of the front door. . . . He fired six rounds into the azalea bush, brought the pistol back in the house, and said to my brother and me, 'Come on, gang, we're going downtown.'"[8] Another remembered her parents waking her up to tell her that the war was over. The family went out to join the throngs already celebrating. "There in the dark of night, just before dawn of another day, the whole world suddenly became alive with excitement," the daughter said. "People outside were dancing in the streets with their nightgowns and pajamas on."[9]

Celebrating perhaps the most were the men in the Pacific who were poised to attack the Japanese mainland if the Japanese government had not surrendered. They knew only too well that the battles would have been hard and that the casualties—on both sides—would have been horrendous.[10]

And then there were the happy reunions that everyone looked forward to. But these did not occur immediately, or in one fell swoop. To deal with the logistics of bringing the soldiers home and to address the question of fairness, the War Department devised a point system which gave each G.I. credit for having achieved certain milestones or for holding a particular status. Formally called the "Adjusted Service Rating," the system was designed to create a scale by which soldiers could be not only classified but also stratified.[11]

Four types of credit were taken into account. All were arrived at after consultation with the troops themselves.[12] The first type was a "service credit." This was based on the number of months that a soldier had been on active duty since September 16, 1940. For each month in uniform, a soldier was given one point. The average time in the service was thirty-three months. The second type was an "overseas credit." Here, again, one month of service equaled one point; and September 16, 1940 was the start date. The average time overseas was approximately sixteen months.[13] Third was a "combat credit." In this instance, and with the same time period considered in the calculations, a soldier was awarded five points per battle participation star (i.e., being involved in a military campaign) and five points per combat decoration (e.g., Distinguished Service Cross, Silver Star, Purple Heart—the last for being wounded). Controversy surrounded the credit given in this category. Battle participation stars frequently were bestowed upon all members of a unit, regardless of whether they directly participated in battle. To some, this was grossly unjust. "The method of giving points for 'battle stars,' is an act of complete stupidity," said one lieutenant. "There is no distinction between front-line infantry and a service unit miles to the rear, or between those that fought campaigns from beginning to end, and those who ventured into a combat zone for one day."[14]

The fourth type of credit was a "parenthood credit." A soldier received twelve points for each child under eighteen years of age. No more than three children could be taken into account in the tabulation. Thus, a father who had three children and another who had five would both get thirty-six points. There was little to no controversy surrounding this category. The troops appeared to believe, from the start, that parental status should be recognized. In one survey, in fact, when asked what the rating scale should include, soldiers ranked having dependent children over both age and length of time in the military. (Age was not included in the point system that finally was decided upon.)[15] The value of parental status in determining when soldiers would get to go home was significant. All other things being equal, a *father of two children* who had been *stationed overseas for one year* and *not seen combat or received any medals* would receive a higher rating, and thus go home earlier, than someone who, though *not a father*, had been *stationed overseas for two years* and *been in combat and received two medals*.[16]

Because of the point system, soldiers did not return in one gigantic wave but dribbled home over a period months. Thus, there generally were no mammoth parades to honor the troops after World War II; rather, there were mostly smaller, albeit well attended, intimate reunions at seaports as well as train and bus stations. Men recalled coming down gangplanks and, once on American soil, dropping down and kissing the ground. Family members and friends, sometimes numbering in the thousands, cheered the arrival of returnees, especially if they were arriving by boat. (A single ship might have more than seven thousand soldiers on board.) "It was the greatest feeling in the world," said a former prisoner of war who returned to the United States on a navy transport.[17]

For some, their return seemed to fall flat. A bomber pilot in the Pacific said that when he walked in the door of his house and surprised his folks, their reaction was mundane: "When I came in, my mother said, 'Ah, I'll fix you a nice supper of Spam.' And that was my welcome home. I supposed my father might have given me a hug or shaken my hand. I don't remember."[18]

Winning the war made Americans fiercely patriotic and deeply appreciative of the men who, in subsequent years, would be dubbed the country's best. "Perhaps I am only thinking along the lines the nation's propagandists want me to think," a wife wrote to her husband on V-J Day. "But I know I am proud of the men of my generation. . . . I am proud to be an American, and married to one of its fighting men."[19]

Soldiers also took pride in what they felt they had accomplished, and they had their own ideas about what they had learned overseas and what they wanted when they got home. As one young corporal phrased it,

We know one thing absolutely. We don't want another war. And we know that with the invention of the atomic bomb, if there is another war not only our effort but every effort ever made by man will be in vain. We know also, although the feet of us infantryman will never admit it, that the world is now a very small place and that cooperation and understanding between all nations is the one thing which will keep it from flying apart. We have learned, too, what a priceless and easily lost thing freedom is, and what it means to be without it. The Army has taught us that in a way we will never forget, and as civilians we will jealously guard our freedom and watch carefully to see that it is not taken from others. We agree unanimously and are insistent that the draft be continued for a while, and that soldiers who have not left the States or been exposed to hazardous duty should make up the occupation forces. We have never felt that the point system made nearly enough distinction between combat men and other soldiers. . . . There is only one thing that every soldier agrees he is going to do for awhile when he gets home, and that is nothing; or rather nothing but satisfy all the desires for comfort, luxury and fun which have been building up every day he was in the Army. And mothers, fathers, sisters, brothers, wives, sweethearts, uncles, aunts and cousins: when we come home don't feel that we are strange, hurt creatures who need special handling. But do remember that deep down inside we'd like to be treated as heroes for just a little while.[20]

Many servicemen, no doubt, got the kind of reception they had long dreamed about; they were "treated as heroes." The honors accorded to some, however, were not accorded to all. Throughout the war, blacks faced one humiliation after another. Initially, they were prevented from joining the military; when they were given the chance to enlist, they were restricted to noncombat roles (e.g., serving as stewards). Life in the military also was segregated, with not only separate units but also separate dining and bathroom facilities. After the war was over, the racist policies continued. Although blacks had valiantly fought, the white establishment seemed unwilling to give an inch. The actions of some were surreal. When men were being out-processed at Camp Kilmer, New Jersey, and were standing in line to be fed, it was decreed that the white soldiers should be served by other white soldiers, but that the black soldiers should be served by Italian POWs.[21] (Months before, black officers were barred from the Fort Des Moines officers' club, while German POWs were invited in.)[22]

The bravery of blacks was repeatedly questioned, despite overwhelming evidence that, on the battlefield, they were just as capable as whites. Indeed, in the thick of combat, the color line could quickly become moot. One black veteran recalled, "When . . . Marines who may have thought Jim Crow was okay got pinned down under fire in places like Guam, boy—they just loved to see black Marines landing and bringing ammo. They were so relieved and delighted they hugged them."[23] Blacks who were not officially combat fighters also distinguished themselves, prompting at least some whites to view racial discrimination in a different way. A white veteran spoke highly of a black truck driver "who brought medical aid through the enemy passes to a group of trapped men, a ride to test the courage of any man." Witnessing such bravery made the veteran feel badly about all the times "he had not given colored boys a break" when he was a youngster. "War starts you thinking," he confessed.[24]

A significant number of black soldiers assumed that their willingness to stand up and fight would be rewarded, that they would have more rights and privileges after the war. As one black soldier put it in 1945, "I spent four years in the Army to free a bunch of Dutchmen and Frenchmen, and I'm hanged if I'm going to let the Alabama version of the Germans kick me around when I get home. No sirreee bob! I went into the Army a nigger; I'm comin' out a *man*."[25] Black leaders, indeed, had encouraged participation in the war and endorsed what they called the "Double V" campaign—victory for America abroad coupled with victory for blacks at home.[26]

Isolated cases may have given people reason for hope. At Fort Dix, New Jersey, a group of black and white soldiers were in their barracks waiting to be furloughed, when a white private marched in and bellowed, "I want all you niggers to fall out in the company area." Almost instantaneously, a white paratrooper stood up and pushed the private out the door. "The next time you come in here you'll know how to talk," the paratrooper commanded.[27] In another case, a black man recalled how, when he was nine or ten, he saw his father, a seaman, remove the "Colored" partition on a bus and proceed to sit down in the white section, with no apparent reaction from other riders.[28]

Scenes like these, however, were exceptional. More typical is what happened to Isaac Woodward who "survived fifteen months fighting the Japanese in the Pacific," but "[ran] afoul of two white men who saw fit to gouge out his eyes with the blunt end of a billy club," and to Wilson Head, another black veteran, who came close to being killed while in the custody of the police.[29]

In 1946 Isaac Woodward, a black veteran, was returning to his South Carolina home after completing three years of service in the army when he asked the white bus driver if it would be possible to stop so that he could use the bathroom. "Hell no!" the bus driver said. Still wearing the uniform that symbolized his service to his country, Woodward seethed: "Dammit, you've got to talk to me like a man." The bus driver then radioed ahead to the police, who pulled Woodward off the bus at the next stop and beat him until he was blind.[30]

Wilson Head, a courageous black World War II veteran . . . undertook his own personal freedom ride from Atlanta to Washington in July 1946. Traveling on the Greyhound line and insisting on his right to sit in the front of the bus, he braved angry drivers, enraged passengers, and menacing police officers—one of whom threatened to shoot him during a brief detention in Chapel Hill, North Carolina. Somehow Head managed to make it to Washington without injury or arrest.[31]

Two cartoons—one published in the *Chicago Defender* in 1946, the other the work of the renowned artist, Oliver W. Harrington—also portrayed the kind of world that awaited black veterans. The first showed a soldier staring up at the Statue of Liberty. In Liberty's raised right hand is a tree from which a man has been hung. The second depicted two young boys standing outside "Ye Olde Dixie Inn." Tacked to the wall is a poster: "Notice. Only white ladies and gentleman will be seated and served. Members of other races are considered undesirable." Seeing this, one youngster turns to the other and states: "My Daddy said they didn't seem to mind servin' him on the Anzio beach-head. But I guess they wasn't gettin' along so good with them Nazis then!"[32]

Another example of discrimination was the lack of access to programs that were specifically set up for veterans. The G.I. Bill of Rights, which grew out the Serviceman's Readjustment Act of 1944, provided veterans with funds to enroll in school and with low- to no-down-payment mortgages to buy homes.[33] In principle, the bill was supposed to provide benefits for all veterans, regardless of color. In practice, it existed mainly for whites. Said an author, whose father *and* mother had served in black military units,

Thousands of black veterans took advantage of the benefits immediately after they left the military. But many veterans were unable to access the education benefits. The few black colleges were flooded with applicants, and most other colleges accepted white students only. Job-training programs were segregated in the South and under local white supervision. Black veterans were one-third of the WWII vets in the South but got one-twelfth of the job-training slots.

Home buying was skewed against black veterans, too. Many black veterans bought new homes with the help of a Veterans Administration mortgage, but they were limited as to where they could buy homes.[34]

African Americans were frustrated at every turn. In a survey carried out under the auspices of the War Department, black veterans expressed their growing discontent. The unfairness of the system was obvious. Whites, however, tended to pretend that it was not. Said the white retired lieutenant colonel who oversaw the survey: "Traditionally the white population finds it more convenient to ignore his black fellow citizens, thus maintaining that there is no problem."[35]

Racial discrimination was not confined to the South. In 1946, Northwestern University in Evanston, Illinois, built new dormitories, to include 280 apartments for veterans and faculty members, but the administration announced that blacks would not be allowed to live there.[36] Reported the *Chicago Defender*,

Negro veterans, despite their years of service in the armed forces of this country, will never set foot in the dormitories of Northwestern University. So spoke the University's President Franklin Bliss Snyder this week in defiance of the National Housing Agency's ultimatum that "it would not approve issuance of priorities for the construction of housing from which Negro veterans are to be barred." Carrying out the Jim Crow policy of the board of trustees, but modifying his own flat statement, Dr. Snyder declared, "It is not in my power to commit the university on the question of housing Negro veterans; the university recommends that they stay with Negro families in Evanston and not on the campus. . . . I am merely carrying out the established practice of the university."[37]

Two years later, it was proclaimed that fifty-five commercial schools in Illinois had been approved to accept federal funds under the G.I. Bill. Of these, however, twenty-seven stated that they admitted only whites, while a scant eleven said that they had no racial restrictions. (The other schools did not specify one way or the other.)[38]

On the south side of Chicago, a mob of angry whites—including fathers with their children in tow—gathered and chanted "Niggers go home!" to protest the fact that black families were moving into veterans housing. The confrontation was punctuated by the actions of a black veteran who ripped open his shirt to reveal scars from wounds that he had suffered during the war. "This happened in Anzio!" he told the mob. He then proceeded to cry.

People "just stood there startled." Some of the older whites "felt guilty," inferred a *Chicago Defender* journalist who witnessed the event—and who also was among those attacked.[39]

The daring that this veteran exhibited in the face of discrimination was not unusual. The war had transformed the attitude of thousands upon thousands of blacks. Many returned from the war not simply seeking jobs and other rewards but ready to confront racial apartheid head on.[40] The National Association for the Advancement of Colored People (NAACP) "harnessed the organizing energy of returning veterans into a national campaign to overthrow Jim Crow."[41]

Militancy, however, could prove costly. If a black man stood up to the white establishment, he was putting his life at risk. Children could be targets, too. Even in circumstances when they were not physically harmed, young boys and girls, both black and white, could be brutalized, by being forced to witness the monstrous acts of white adults. (The children of the white fathers who instigated the violence were, in a sense, victims as well, in that they were being taught how to be racists.)[42] Consider the following account:

> On one occasion there was a black man—God bless his heart, I know not his name—but the rich white town boss approached with his two daughters up the sidewalk, and the black man didn't stop for him. All the rest of the folks were looking as to what he was going to do. The white boss got within 10 feet of this black man and addressed him: "Nigger, get off the sidewalk!" The black man stood there. The third time he addressed him, the rich white man said, "Do you know who I am?" And the black man said, yes, he knew who he was, but he didn't see getting off the sidewalk and into the street to let him pass. He said, "This sidewalk looks big enough for both of us." The town boss did not say a word. He turned around and took his daughters with him and went back to his house, got his gun and came back and shot the black man and kicked his body off the sidewalk into the gutter. He then dragged the body into the street and called the sheriff. And nothing was ever done about it. I didn't know how to forgive my dad for being one of the men who watched that and took no action. But he was wiser than I was. I said if I ever get the opportunity, I would do something.[43]

Anyone who actively demonstrated on behalf of civil rights or showed support for activists could be caught in racism's stranglehold. In the spring of 1947, sixteen men—eight blacks and eight whites—set out to challenge the South's Jim Crow laws and, in particular, its segregated policies dictating who, by virtue of their race, was permitted to sit where on a bus. The idea was to travel on buses that crossed state lines and thus bring into play a 1946 U.S. Supreme Court ruling (*Morgan v. Commonwealth of Virginia*) that segregated seating on interstate buses was unconstitutional. (The black demonstrators were to sit in the front of the bus; the white demonstrators in the back.) The sixteen men included students, ministers, journalists, a musician, a biologist, an attorney, a social worker, and a college instructor (among their other endeavors). Most were in their twenties. Seven had been conscientious objectors during the war.[44]

As the men traveled through the South, they were subjected to attack and arrest. When they stopped to stay overnight in the homes of sympathizers, neighbors and others in the town sometimes would threaten the hosts and their guests. During one weekend, in Chapel Hill, North Carolina, a white pastor, the Reverend Charles M. Jones, served as host. Following the men's departure the next day, Jones and his family were assaulted.

> As soon as the riders left, Jones took his wife and two children to a friend's house for protection, a precaution that seemed warranted by subsequent events. When Jones returned home Sunday evening accompanied by a friend, Hilton Seals, he found a crowd of angry white protesters in his front yard. The two men tried to ignore the crowd's taunts, but as they walked to the door Seals was struck by a rock. On Monday morning Jones received a second anonymous call threatening him with death.[45]

In Asheville, North Carolina, several of the demonstrators stayed at the home of the father and mother of one of the white riders. Their presence enraged at least one of the neighbors, who yelled, "How're your nigger friends this morning" to the son, as he and his fellow riders departed for the station.[46]

Although blacks ran into a significant amount of white backlash after World War II, the contribution of black soldiers to the war effort had one fairly immediate positive effect in terms of civil rights, and that was the *de jure* desegregation of the military. On July 26, 1948, President Truman issued Executive Order 9981 calling for "equality of treatment and opportunity for all persons in the armed forces without regard to race, color, religion or national origin."[47] In the wake of the order, optimism ran high. The editor and publisher of the *Chicago Defender* sent Truman a telegram and confidently predicted, "In the executive order dealing with the army we believe that you have set up the machinery for the abolition of segregation which will eventually destroy Jim Crowism in all aspects of our national life."[48]

The signs were indeed favorable. Fifty years later, and with the advantage of hindsight, one historian summed up what the order had accomplished:

In general, when presidents issue executive orders, they do so for political reasons. Certainly, Truman's reasons for issuing EO 9981 were political. The order was issued before an election—an election "surprise." Also, at the time Truman issued the order, the military was already beginning to integrate some of its troops. Perhaps most importantly, the government perceived a crisis in terms of segregation and military efficiency, and thus changed military policy to reflect a new integrationist thinking. Overall, the order was a presidential grand gesture aimed toward political and social equality. However, the gesture, political and expedient as it was, resulted in a change of culture within American society and started a movement toward equality in all social and political settings and institutions. EO 9981 was in many ways the political precursor to the civil rights movement. The executive order to integrate the armed forces had had long-term and long-reaching effects.[49]

In the 1950s, blacks would continue to push for "victory at home" and would set in motion changes that continue to be felt today. Black children, along with their parents, would be the main beneficiaries of these efforts, but only after they served as "foot soldiers" in the struggle for civil rights.

Members of the armed forces were not the only ones who were coming home. As the war drew to a close, thousands of Japanese American fathers and their families, many of whom had been locked up for years, were released from detention centers. Being physically free, however, did not mean being unencumbered. "'Camp' has never been 'all over,'" said one Japanese individual who had been incarcerated as a youth. "We children of the camps continue to measure our lives against where we came from." Another reported how "the scramble to reestablish lives and to become acceptable absorbed most [of the community's] time and energy."[50] Internment was, in the eyes of many third-generation Japanese Americans (*Sansei*) "an important factor contributing to the accelerated loss of Japanese language and culture." Also, second-generation (*Nisei*) parents often did not encourage their children's ethnic identification, which "added another source of sadness and anger" for first-generation (*Issei*) grandparents.[51]

Once the Japanese were released from the camps, getting a job was a top priority. From the beginning, however, the fathers faced major hurdles. "My dad . . . went back to this factory where he was a foreman for years and years," said one internee, "and now this little boy that he trained, the boss's son is grown and he was the one managing it. . . . When he came home, his face was just like a sheet, white as a sheet. . . . Things had changed during the war time and they have a different manager and a different way of operation and I guess the boss said 'Yama you stay home.'"[52] Even the educated and the highly skilled ran into roadblocks. A Japanese man who had graduated from the University of Oregon Law School but was unable to practice as an attorney because he was not a U.S. citizen earnestly looked for work, all to no avail. Recalled his daughter, "To me, the saddest thing that happened was when my father came out of internment, after being idle for four years. He had to resettle in Chicago, and he didn't have any money. No capital. No nothing, and even with his education. As you can imagine, a sixty-year-old man trying to get a white collar job—there was nothing available for him." She added, "My father kept looking for work, and he couldn't find anything. Finally, he decided that he would try opening some kind of an office and do bookkeeping services and try to sell real estate and things like that. He never was able to get back on his feet in the real sense of the word."[53]

Some Japanese fathers had volunteered for an all-*Nisei* unit and saw combat in Europe. In spite of their service, these men, too, had to contend with racism. One wife reported, "We started to look for a house and we did suffer discrimination, housing discrimination. . . . One real estate office told my husband that they're saving the homes for veterans returning from war, returning veterans. And so he got mad and he said, 'What do you think I am?'"[54] Another Japanese veteran, who had been wounded in action (his right arm was shattered in a one-man assault on a German machine-gun nest) and had been awarded the Bronze Star and Distinguished Service Cross, offered another story of abuse. After twenty months in the hospital, he set out for home and decided en route to, as he put it, get "all gussied up" for his parents ("so . . . Mama and Papa would see me in all my glory"). He walked into an Oakland, California barbershop, but promptly was told to leave:

> A barber comes up to me and wants to know if I'm Japanese. Keep in mind I'm in uniform with my medals and ribbons and a hook for an arm. I said, "Well, my father was born in Japan." The barber replied, "We don't cut Jap hair." I was tempted to slash him with my hook, but then I thought about all the work the 442nd had done and I just said, "I feel sorry for you," and walked out. I went home without a haircut.[55]

Not all Asians were treated in the same way. Whereas Japanese Americans continued to be demonized after the war, Chinese Americans were extended a hand of friendship (provided they were not mistaken for being Japanese). Because China was an ally of the United States, the status of Chinese Americans generally improved compared to what it was in the 1930s.

"To men of my generation, World War II was the most important historic event of our times," exclaimed one journalist. "For the first time, we felt we could make it in American society."[56]

After Pearl Harbor, Chinese Americans lined up with thousands of others to enlist. (One father, like many others, was told that he was too old, but he persisted and was finally accepted into officer candidate school.)[57] The men served in both integrated and all-Chinese units, and gained admittance to all branches of the military. They were in the infantry as well as in fighter and bomber squadrons, and could also be found in intelligence, engineering, and transportation specialties.

Being in the armed forces gave Chinese Americans a variety of skills they might not otherwise have had the chance to obtain. Some, seeing opportunity, stayed in the service, choosing to make it a career. While discrimination against Chinese Americans was certainly not eradicated by the war, the barriers that had been in place before were lowered (e.g., the Chinese Exclusion Acts, which placed severe limits on the number of Chinese who could enter the country, were rescinded). One veteran reported, "What wearing the uniform did was that it opened up things that gave you the confidence that you weren't going to get kicked around. So with the uniform on you felt that you had as much right as anybody else to go [wherever you wanted] or be whatever you wanted." As for finding work, he said he had little difficulty. "When I came back after the war I had no problem of going around and getting a job anywhere. I walked in as if I owned the place. Even without the uniform."[58]

There were other concrete benefits from having served. Before the war, Chinese Americans often made a living by owning and operating small stores, not because they necessarily wanted to be shopkeepers, but because other occupations were systematically closed to them. The G.I. Bill opened up new avenues of employment. The wife of one veteran explained,

> During WW II, after the kids went into the service, Uncle Sam gave them the opportunity to go back to college; he paid for the college education. So that's how a lot of us were able to get out of the grocery business. My husband was able to go to college, and to learn the air-conditioning/refrigeration business. So when he got to do that, his brothers took over the store. Most of the families who have stores, their children did not go back to the stores. Now you have doctors, technicians, engineers, draftsmen, architects. So you find that this younger generation has broken the gap between Mama and Papa stores. They go into professions and some of them have set up their own businesses and some are working in other organizations.[59]

Thousands of Chinese American immigrants, as well as émigrés from other countries (including Germany and Italy) applied for U.S. citizenship during the war. Among other motivations, becoming a citizen symbolized support for the war and the country where one yearned to stay. More immigrants became naturalized citizens between 1941 and 1945 than in any previous five-year period. Of these, more than one hundred thousand were armed forces personnel, and more than one-and-a-half million were civilians.[60]

SIX

Reentry

Long before Germany and Japan surrendered, Americans were anticipating what their lives would be like after the war. The anticipation was evident, to a certain degree, by the kinds of advertisements that began to appear in early 1945. Whereas before, many of the ads were about the war itself—and about a corporation's commitment to help win it—now the ads increasingly talked about the soldiers' return. Corporations, however, continued to associate their goods and services (and employees) with the war and, envisioning victory, its afterglow.

A Pennsylvania Railroad advertisement showed a veteran sporting conductor's attire, while his wife and daughter proudly gazed at him. "How do I look in *Blue?*" the father asked. "Just fine!" was the reply. "And we're glad to have him back! [the railroad interjected]. More than 4,000 of the over 53,000 Pennsylvania Railroad men who entered the armed forces have returned to their old posts—having honorably fulfilled one duty to resume another . . . *the pleasure of serving you.*"[1] A Worthington Air Conditioning Company ad depicted a family holding hands and scanning the sky. "You're going to be *babied* after these wars are over," said Worthington. "You're going to walk into stores and work in offices and eat in restaurants where the air makes you feel like a million dollars. . . . You're going to benefit from what companies like Worthington—an old hat at air conditioning—have done during the war."[2]

The Nash Motor Company tugged at people's hearts by portraying a father and son (in a new Nash, of course) as they left for a fishing trip: "You'll look down at the seat beside you, and there he'll be . . . your son. . . . Taller than you remember him . . . with freckles sprinkled across his nose and laughter in his eyes. You'll get acquainted all over again, you and that boy of yours. . . . And he'll beg for stories about the war . . . and you'll tell him some of the things you saw . . . because that will be far away, and you'll be home. Some bright day . . . You'll feel the thrill of a wheel again . . . You at the wheel of a Nash . . . and your son by your side."[3]

"Stories about the war" were central to Nash's marketing strategy. In another one of its ads, a uniformed air corps pilot is shown standing in front of an airliner. It is implied that he has just returned from overseas. The message from the company reads, "When victory comes, Nash will go on." How the company would go on, however, was what was central. "Nash will help contribute the jobs, the opportunities, the future which will insure [sic] the strong, vital and growing America all of us owe to those who have fought to preserve it." As for the soldiers, Nash said that they would remember the past, but also to look to the future.

> Back here . . .
>> Back home . . .
>> With our missions done and the roar of guns and the bombs fading and faint in my ears . . .
>> Back here, I remember, now, the power of America at war!
>> I don't want to kill any more . . .
>> I don't want to destroy . . .
>> I want to work and build and make things live and grow.
>> And now I know we've got the power and the
>> might to smash factories and cities and countries
>> into dust. . . . I know that here at home we've got
>> the power and the will to build new towns and
>> cities . . . to build an even finer, an even greater
>> country of our own.[4]

What is especially remarkable about the advertisements is how, by declaration or insinuation, they tended to profile battle-hardened veterans. A war bond ad, for example, published in 1944, long before V-J Day, showed a father returning home from the Pacific and being greeted by his son at the front gate. "Are you my daddy?" the son asks. "Yes, sonny boy, I'm your daddy—the daddy you don't remember because you were just a few months old when I left for war." Hanging from the father's valise is a Japanese sword—symbolic of combat and conquest.[5] A similar metaphorical device was used in a 1945 advertisement for Whitman's Chocolates. Now it is a young girl who not only greets but also embraces her dad, a naval officer. Unlike the war bond ad, this one has no words detailing the fathers' exploits; only the hint of such—a Japanese sword and helmet lashed to his briefcase.[6]

The advertisements thus tended to glorify the "fighting man," and, in doing so, they encapsulate what a number of soldiers went through. They also, however, invariably obscured what being *in* the fight actually meant. Advertisements alluding to World War II generally offered a sanitized picture of combat. The same was—and is—true of most movies and other cultural renderings, including newsreels and documentaries.

With a few exceptions, filmed scenes of a ground battle can lead one to believe that it is akin to a choreographed football scrimmage, where everyone charges ahead and hits the dirt with precision, and those who are "taken out" do not bleed, much less suffer (and almost always are shot in the chest or shoulder rather than the testicles). Likewise, aerial dogfight sequences frequently show aircraft spiraling out of control and crashing; rarely does a filmgoer witness, *for several minutes,* a pilot being roasted alive. Sailors on torpedoed ships are blown to smithereens and seemingly vanish, or jump, without consequence, into the sea; hardly ever are they shown gasping for air and, with terror in their eyes, drowning or succumbing to other gruesome deaths. Note, too, the reference in the Nash Motor Company advertisement to bombs that can smash cities "into dust." No mention is made of how the residents of those cities agonizingly died during and after attacks from the sky. Also virtually absent in nostalgic depictions of war is the pandemonium—and abject fright—that soldiers experience while under fire and duress.[7] It is, of course, a romanticized view of war that is instrumental to getting a country's citizens to enlist. The glory, more than the gore, seduces them.[8]

The soldiers themselves generally offered fictional accounts of what it meant to be in battle. Their letters seldom told the whole truth of what they were going through. Rather, for the most part, they accentuated the positive, so as to protect their families and friends and boost their loved ones' morale.[9] Thus, in the thick of the Battle of Bataan—when things looked pretty grim (America would suffer one of its worst defeats)—a sergeant wrote to his wife to say, "The boys here are in high spirit," and to inquire about his two-year-old daughter's Christmas, while a D-Day veteran spoke of the dead on the beaches as "the silent" and of his own maneuvering amidst a hail of bullets as "cover[ing] the ground at full speed."[10]

Unusual were letters offering graphic tales of destruction. One such letter was penned by an infantry private. "This is a horrible thing to write about," he said to his parents, "but people should understand what war means, then maybe they wouldn't start another, so soon." Reporting on fighting on Saipan and Okinawa, he described the following scenes:

> We were wading down the coast, and boys were being killed right and left. Mortar shells lit on their heads, and this really did something to all of us. Some boys were jumping into the sea, when their faces were blown away. Two of us, carried one boy back with us, and our aid man gave him plasma all night, but he died next morning. He had his jaw, tongue, and nose blown away. . . . All along the beach, men were dying of wounds. . . . Mortar shells dropping in on heads, and ripping bodies. Faces blown apart by flying lead and coral. It wasn't a pretty sight, and I will never forget the death and hell along that beach. . . . The artillery on Okinawa was terrific. Shells would hit, and bury you, or blow you out of your foxhole. The Catholic Chaplain was killed as he was blessing each foxhole. An artillery shell cut him in half at the waist.[11]

In World War II, as in other wars, men were killed not only by automatic weapons and artillery, but also by body parts and jewelry. A severed arm or head, even a wedding ring, could be a lethal projectile after a bombardment. Sheer terror also could immobilize soldiers or provoke them to run away from the action. Men in combat frequently wet their pants and lost control of their bowels. They convulsed and vomited. Sometimes they just cowered and cried (often calling out to their mothers). And they could feel deeply ashamed—even years later—for what they and their comrades did or failed to do.[12] Because the people at home were not fully apprised of what it meant to be in battle, an experiential gulf existed between soldiers overseas and those who got to stay home. It is in this context that we ask, what effect did the war have on the fathers who served and on their families? The answer is complex.

Among the combat veterans, there were many who came through the war with their bodies and minds basically intact. Yes, they had seen things that they wished they never had, and did things that they would just as soon forget, but for the most part they were able to put their service behind them and get on with their lives.

Other men, however, were not so fortunate. More than six hundred and seventy thousand American soldiers were wounded in the war, some very seriously.[13] Athletic men were reduced to vestiges of their former selves. Amputees had to confront the fact they might never know the joy of running with their children or the delight of playing ball with them in the backyard. Brain-injured fathers were faced with the prospect that they could be dependent on their families for life. Even mildly impaired men could expect uneasiness and pretense at home. The Child Study Association of America advised the wives of injured soldiers to warn the children of their fathers' injuries, but not tell them too much: "It is probably better not to give the children too detailed instructions about how to spare your husband's feelings. If they act natural it will probably be easier for all of you in the end."[14]

What also could be terrible but harder to identify was the plight of men who suffered psychologically—men who in World War II might be said to be suffering from "battle fatigue" but who today could be diagnosed as having "post-traumatic stress disorder."[15] Consider the case of Lieutenant Murray Greenberg, a crewmember on a B-17 "flying fortress" (immortalized in the film, *Memphis Belle*).[16] In 1944, Lieutenant Greenberg's aircraft was shot down over Leipzig while on a bombing run. He was able to parachute out, but was captured and sent to a German prisoner of war camp, where he was confined until the end of the war. Initially notified by telegram that her husband was missing in action, Shirley Greenberg eventually was told that he was being held by the enemy.

When Lieutenant Greenberg was released, he met his son, Steve, for the first time. He attempted to adjust to being a family man, but in the months after his return, something was not quite right. The former airman seemed unhappy and behaved oddly. Over time, his condition grew from bad to worse, and he became increasingly estranged from his wife and children. He eventually contracted amyotrophic lateral sclerosis (ALS or Lou Gehrig's disease) and died at the age of forty-nine. "Get a haircut" were the last words he said to his son. "Not 'I love you,'" the boy later remarked. "Not 'I love your mother.' Just 'Get a haircut.' It blew my circuits. At his funeral there were no tears." Looking back on it all, Shirley Greenberg theorized that the war had "killed" her husband. "He was never the same man."[17]

Another case is that of Lieutenant Thomas Richard Mathews, who was a veteran of the fabled 10th Mountain Division, a ski-combat unit that was engaged in heavy fighting in the Alps. Of the 19,780 men who served in the 10th in Italy, 25 percent were either wounded or killed.[18] When Lieutenant Mathews came back from the war, he was eager to be reunited with his son, Tom. On the day of his arrival, he found the boy, one day shy of his second birthday, sitting on top of the doghouse in the family's backyard. Expecting Tom to run and greet him, he was surprised when his son did not budge from his perch. Moving closer, Lieutenant Mathews held out his arms. "Jump." *No response.* "Jump." *Still no response.* "I said jump." There was a harshness to the father's voice, but it lasted only a second. "It's okay, Tommy. I'm your father." *The son remained frozen in place.* In a rage, Lieutenant

Mathews did an about face and stormed into the house. The son would later say, "For the rest of my life I will hear the screen door's sharp bang and the last thing [my father] said before he turned his back and walked away. 'No son of mine is a coward.'" Climbing down from the dog house and going into the kitchen, Tommy found his mother and asked, "What's a coward Mama?" Realizing what had happened, his mother rushed to the bedroom to confront her husband. Although the door was closed, Tommy could tell his parents were arguing. Suddenly, Tommy heard his father yell, "GODDAMMIT. YOU'VE SPOILED MY SON."[19]

Writing about "his father's war," Tom Mathews talked of the pain his father experienced and how it affected his relationship with his family. "He went into the war as an innocent, an idealist full of hope and energy; he came home an elusive shape-shifter. It was difficult for him [to] show the simplest expression of fatherly affection."[20] Some fifty years after the war, the father and son took a trip to the Alps, in the hope of repairing their relationship. In time, the father talked about the war, and shared something that he had never revealed before. "I killed a lot of people," he said, sobbing. "Jesus Christ . . . I killed so many people." The son put his arms around his father and held him close. "Wasn't your fault, Pop. Wasn't your fault."[21]

The killing certainly could take a psychological toll, but men were affected in other ways as well—ways that, ironically, were a counterpoint to killing. Almost always, when the subject of World War II and fatherhood comes up, attention is focused on the men who did the shooting. Understandably perhaps, their stories are the ones we want to hear about most; their stories also are the ones that have been meticulously preserved in books and in memorials. But combat constituted only a fraction of what happened during the war. The often-overlooked fact is that most of the soldiers in World War II were not directly involved in any fighting.

Of the 16.3 million U.S. personnel who served, 10 percent saw combat, while "fewer than 1 million, probably no more than 800,000, took part in any extended combat."[22] Many were close to battles but far from immediate danger; others served in an adjunct capacity (e.g., ferrying supplies) or in a subsidiary role (e.g., preparing food). Millions of men, in other words, never shot at someone or had someone shoot at them.

An experiential gulf thus existed not just between veterans and their families, but also among the veterans themselves. As one chronicler of the war put it, "If most civilians didn't know about [the horrors of war], most soldiers didn't either, since only a relatively small number did any fighting which brought them into mortal combat with the enemy. For the rest, engaged in supply, transportation, and administration functions, the war constituted a period of undesired and uncomfortable foreign travel under unaccustomed physical and social conditions, like enforced obedience, bad food, and absence of baths."[23]

The distinction between combat veterans and noncombat veterans was not lost on the soldiers. Those who fought railed against the point system used to determine who would get to go home first, because, in their minds, it did not draw as sharp a line between front-line and other troops as they thought it should.[24] Exclaimed one man who did more than his share of killing, "To me, there were two different wars. There was the war of the guy on the front lines. You don't come off until you are wounded or killed. Or, if lucky, relieved. Then there was the support personnel. In the Pacific, for every rifleman on the front lines there were nineteen people in the back. Their view of the war was different than mine."[25]

The multiple "realities" of war, even among the soldiers, introduces an element to the reentry process that cannot be ignored. It often is said that World War II veterans were reluctant to speak about the war because what they had gone through was too difficult to bear. Reliving it only brought back painful memories. Certainly, this was the case for many. "You could never get the father of my four children to talk about the war," said one woman, whose husband had been in combat. "It was like we put blinders on the past. . . . I don't think it was just [us]. It was everybody. You wouldn't fill your children full of these horror stories, would you?" Another combat veteran and father reported that while he told his children "some of the funnier stories" about the war, he never told them "all the things that happened." He did not want them to know.[26]

The "horror stories" could be a lot to absorb. A five-year-old boy, whose father was serving overseas, happened to ask his mother one day, "Mama, is my Daddy killing folks in the war?" The mother ignored her son's question because she did not know what to say. "I dislike to think what effect it may have on Perry if I answer his question truthfully. . . . Suppose I say, 'Yes, Perry, your Daddy is shooting real guns and killing people in the war.' Can I make the necessary follow-up explanations plausible to him without tearing down all that we have tried to teach him of kindness and consideration for others? Can I make the fact of war intelligible to his five-year-old mind?"[27]

Even adults could not fully grasp what combat veterans experienced. Sometimes only those who also had been in battle could relate to the enormity of it all. One man, who had served in World War I, reported that when he came home the only one interested in his stories was his Civil-War-veteran grandfather: "There was no one else I knew that understood my language."[28]

In certain circumstances, returning soldiers were ordered *not* to share their wartime experiences with their families or friends. A top-secret program that was kept under wraps for twenty-four years after the war was the military's use of Native-American code talkers to transmit messages in a language that the enemy could not translate. Although many of the code talkers "suffered from nightmares and depression" (as they sometimes were in the thick of battle), they "were denied much of the therapeutic advantage of talking about what they did." They also were long denied the recognition they deserved.[29]

An unwillingness (or inability) to talk about the war may not necessarily have its roots in battle, however. There can be other truths. When we think about why a veteran might not want to speak of his time in service, we should consider the possibility—indeed *probability*—that the veteran may not feel that he has much of a story to tell. Asked "What did *you* do in the war, Daddy?" some may find it difficult to offer an account that would satisfy their children's curiosity—and desire. Rather than admit that they were not the heroes their kids imagined them to be, they might even be tempted to fabricate a war record—or just "bend the facts" a little. Not wanting to lie or admit that they did not directly engage the enemy, when asked, "Did you kill anybody?" they might simply answer, "I'd rather not talk about it."[30]

Men who were discharged, because of psychological problems (e.g., classified as "neuro-psychiatric patients," or N.P.s), found themselves having to think about constructing narratives for why they were back home. "What will my parents think?" "How will I be able to face my brother who already has his medals?" Foreseeing the reaction they might receive from strangers could be particularly upsetting. "If I walk down the street in civvies, everyone will stare at me." "What can I say to people? How can I explain?"[31]

The multiple realities of war and the disappointment that could characterize a veteran's return were not totally unanticipated. Within weeks of the war's end, the philosopher and sociologist Alfred Schutz discerningly wrote that when the men came back, they would occupy a unique social world—a world where they would have to reconcile the discrepancy between what their friends and families assumed they did during the war and what they actually did, and the intrapsychic conflict between who they wished they were and who they thought they were in fact.

In times of war the members of the armed forces have a privileged status within the community as a whole. "The best for our boys in service" is more than a mere slogan. It is the expression of prestige deservedly accorded to those who might have to give their life for their country or at least to those who left family, studies, occupation, and the amenities of civil life for a highly valued interest of the community. The civilian looks at the man in uniform as an actual or future fighter; and so, indeed, the man in uniform looks at himself, even if he performs merely desk work in an army office somewhere in the United States. This humbler occupation does not matter; to him, too, the induction marked a turning point in his life. But the discharged home-comer is deprived of his uniform and with it of his privileged status within the community. This does not mean that he will lose, by necessity, the pres-tige acquired as an actual or potential defender of the homeland, although history does not show that exaggerated longevity is accorded to the memory of glory. This is partly because of the disappointment at home that the return-ing veteran does not correspond to the pseudo-type of the man whom they have been expecting.[32]

Being in battle or not being in battle was not the only personal experi-ence that complicated the relationship between soldiers and their families. Spending days and weeks in close proximity with other men, perhaps un-der grueling conditions, created an intimate bond between soldiers that, in different circumstances, would be perceived as odd, given the culture of masculinities at the time. In some cases, the bond was largely platonic; in other cases it became physical.

Homosexual encounters were more common during the war than be-fore, if only because the war created conditions for such encounters to take place. Wrote one scholar, "At no time before the Second World War had so many American men consciously felt deep affection for other males, and not since the previous century had romantic attachments between men been so widespread and little scorned."[33] Said two others, "For a generation of young Americans, the war created a setting in which to experience same-sex love, affection, and sexuality, and to participate in the group life of gay men and women."[34]

The degree to which a soldier's homosexual activities affected a man and his family was not predictable. If the activities came to the attention of military authorities, a soldier could receive an undesirable discharge and be denied G.I. Bill benefits. If the activities were not known to military au-thorities, the soldier had more control over whether and how to disclose his sexual behavior. What to do was not necessarily clear cut. One historian described the options as follows:

Veterans who had formed their first gay relationships or discovered gay so-cial life while in the military . . . had to make important life decisions about marriage and partners, education, where to live and work, how much to reveal about their sexuality to their families, and how deeply to become involved in a gay social life. They often had to choose between their families' expectations and their own needs. Some based their civilian decisions on their loyalty to their families and home communities, while others embarked on lives organized around their homosexuality. . . . As they tried to adjust to their new lives as civilians, some gay veterans realized that their identity as homosexuals was integral to the way in which they lived. . . . Having served their country well in a time of national emergency, gay veterans, especially those who had fought in combat, felt a heightened sense of legitimacy as citizens, entitlements as veterans, and betrayal when denied benefits.[35]

Sexual minorities who had fought in the war were ready once it was over to demand the rights they had been historically denied, much as racial and ethnic minorities were. They, too, believed that the time for America to change had come. "No one asked me if I was gay when they called out 'Medic!' and you went out under fire and did what you were expected and trained to do," declared a corpsman who was wounded in the Normandy invasion and in the Battle of the Bulge. "There were so many gays in the medics [and in other military occupational specialties] and so many of them gave their lives."[36]

Scholars did not wait until World War II was over or about to end to think about the war's impact. From the moment it began, they considered what it would do to individuals and especially how it might affect families. Given the theoretical inclinations at the time, most tended to talk in terms of social pathology, adjustment, and disequilibrium. In one of the earliest statements on the subject, sociologist Ernest W. Burgess predicted that the war would lead to a rise in "juvenile delinquency," because fathers would be conscripted into the service, and women would be pulled into the labor force.[37] H. J. Locke, also a sociologist, spoke of how the war would disturb "the settled habits of millions of persons, necessitating numerous readjustments," and couched his expectations for what lay ahead in social systems terminology: "War breaks up the normal equilibrium of institutional relationships, disrupts interrelations between institutions, and establishes more or less temporary new equilibriums."[38] Other authorities raised questions about marriage and divorce rates, husband-wife and parent-child decision making, and whether the war would make families more intimate— or less.[39]

Toward the end of the war, scholars often focused on returning soldiers. Family social scientist Reuben Hill zeroed in, for example, on how veterans might react to the changes in their wives.

> The well adjusted wife and mother faced with the necessity of mastering the combined job of father and mother has frequently grown as a result of the separation. The lore of masculine culture has been opened to her; she has been treated to a liberal and a technical education in the ways of a "man's world." Indeed, men have become dispensable as wives have mastered the traditional masculine duties of repairing light and plumbing fixtures, mowing lawns, filing tax statements, meeting mortgage installments and insurance payments, and meeting other responsibilities great and small for which men have claimed a special talent. Dr. Therese Benedek predicts woman's newfound self-sufficiency will prove a threat to the returning father, who will want to resume his role as head of the house, and will find a competitor in a working wife, a self-sufficient wife.

Hill, citing Benedek (who was a psychoanalyst), allowed that a "woman's newfound self-sufficiency" might prove to be a threat to a returning husband, but he also believed, as did others, that "many so called self-sufficient wives actually long to be dependent again, and will all too gladly resume the role of wife and mother."[40]

Not everyone was as convinced as Hill that women would be yearning to reoccupy a traditional place in the home. One group of scholars, who before the war had pushed for greater gender equality, offered an alternative perspective on how the war might shape people.[41] First, they insisted that the war would have a positive effect on women's lives. Second, they contended that the key factor in whether or not women remained in the labor force would be the nation's economy. If jobs were plentiful, women would continue to work. If jobs were scarce, women would be expected to step aside to make room for men.

> What will happen now that the bells have rung proclaiming that the war has ceased? Who can say at this writing? One *can* say "We will not go back to things as they were before the war." One does not *erase* the effects of war. Its impact on society goes too deep for that. Thousands of women have found certain satisfactions for themselves in work outside the home. Doubtless many of them will want to continue with such work. Others look with eagerness toward serving again in a home capacity and will gladly withdraw from the industrial world. Probably much will depend on our economic condition.

If work is available at good pay or is demanded of women they will work. If there is not enough work for all, the women to a great extent will give way to men.[42]

Regardless of what different scholars may have thought, women had their own ideas of what they wanted for themselves—and for their families. Although some were happy to embrace domesticity, others valued their hard-earned independence and had no intention of going back to how things were before. One wife told her soon-to-return soldier-husband, "Sweetie, I want to make sure I make myself clear about how I've changed. I want you to know *now* that you are not married to a girl that's interested solely in a home—I shall definitely work all my life—I get emotional satisfaction out of working; and I don't doubt that many a night you will cook the supper while I'm at a meeting. Also, dearest—I shall never wash and iron—there are laundries for that! Do you think you'll be able to bear living with me?"[43]

An issue that brought women's employment to a head was child care. During the war, publicly funded day care centers were opened to make it easier for mothers to work outside the home. When the war ended, many of these centers were either shut down or restricted to lower income groups. In New York City, mothers marched to protest the nursery cuts. In February 1948, the *New York Times* reported on one such demonstration: "A large group of women, many of them working mothers, picketed the Department of Welfare offices, 902 Broadway, yesterday morning in a protest over the curtailment of the day care nursery service in the city's child care centers." Accompanying the article was a photo of a mother and child, bundled against the cold. In the mother's hands was a placard that read, "Prices are going up, but the Dept. of Welfare says Income must come down. . . . OUR CHILDREN SUFFER." The previous year, the Child Welfare League of America published a study of six Connecticut centers, along with data from sites in other states. According to the study, "The war merely intensified a problem of long standing. Mothers still work for a living. Many homes do not offer space or companionship." Women were not the only ones affected. Men needed the centers, too: "It is estimated that approximately one million children under 16 are motherless. In such cases the father must find a female relative free to help him, be able to employ adequately paid help, or find a center that can care for the children in his absence."[44]

With the end of the war on the horizon or an already established fact, researchers accelerated their efforts to ponder and measure its impact. A study of thirty-two veterans found that being in the military could have a salutary influence. Asked how things were going after the war, only one of the veterans "said that being in service and away from his family made it harder to be a good father." The others spoke mainly in positive terms: "I realize more what the family means and what the children mean in my life." "I was father to so many young kids in service that I feel I was educated to help adolescents." "I saw things that I didn't want to have happen to my family; it stabilized what I want and made me more sensible." "I used to think I didn't want the responsibility of my family any more, but after seeing German kids wanting to eat scraps from my mess kit, I decided that I should accept the responsibility for my own family."[45]

Most researchers, however, warned families of the kind of trouble that they might encounter or, on the basis of studies carried out, pointed to difficulties that fathers, mothers, and children were already having. One scholar predicted that families probably would experience first a "reunion glow," but they "[are] not . . . likely to be aware of the hardships" to come.[46] Another said, "The first few months of a serviceman at home will try the nerves of the whole family."[47]

A study of nearly two hundred college men who had been in the service found that veterans sometimes "lack[ed] the motivation and habit necessary to accomplish day-to-day duties of the husband and father, even though they once were proficient in them." Fathers also could come to feel that they were on the outside looking in. "It's very ironical," said one wife of a serviceman. "I worried, read books, consulted experts in an effort to learn how to play both the mother role and the father role while my husband was in the service. Now he is back with us and I have realized that I have erred in that I have done the job too well. My husband feels that the children do not need him, that my personality is adequate to the situation. Intuitively I feel the same way. I am more worried about him than I am about the children. I think I can readjust them to need him much more easily than I can mend his damaged ego."[48]

The 1946 Academy Award–winning film, *The Best Years of Our Lives*, presented a fictionalized—but familiar—story about the difficulties that three veterans faced in adjusting to civilian life. When the father in the group is asked by his wife what he thought of his teenage daughter and son, whom had not seen in years, his response is that he didn't "recognize them," they had "grown so old" in his absence. "I tried to stop them, to keep them just as they were when you left," she says. "But they got away from me."[49]

A detailed investigation of the war's effect on families, comparing nineteen men who, because of the war, were absent during the first year of their first-born child's life with nineteen men who were not, also found that separated fathers could feel marginalized. "I think that something is wrong somewhere," one man exclaimed. "[My son] has not adjusted to me in general. . . . My wife is the main one in his life. I don't think that he's ever really accepted me. It is better now. I can do things for him my wife can't do and he's beginning to see a father's worth something. But mother is first. . . . Even now there are instances when he excludes me. If he says something at the table and I say, 'What did you say?' he will answer, 'I wasn't talking to you!' "[50]

One of the questions that the investigators wanted to answer was whether war-separated fathers would be closer to their second-born children than to their first-born children. Would the men's absence at a critical point in their children's lives make a significant difference? It was found that, in certain cases, it did. A war-separated father said, "Alice [the couple's second-born child] seems like a first baby—I feel like a first-time father. She's getting all the attention I would have lavished on Fran [the couple's first-born child] if I'd been around." Another separated father reported, "Albert [the couple's first-born child] is [my wife's] boy, Leslie [the couple's second-born child] is mine. . . . If Albert wants something fixed, he goes to his mother. When he is most worried it is about his mother's affection and the threat of its loss." A third offered, "I feel Pattie [the couple's firstborn child] and my wife are close, like my wife and her mother. I felt left out in the early days and I feel left out now."[51]

Soldiers lived for the day when they would be reunited with their families. For some, however, the moment proved to be bittersweet. One war-separated father, who had been "bubbling with enthusiasm and anticipation," was disappointed that his wife did not greet him at the station. She thought that he would enjoy seeing his daughter before he saw her. "I had expected to see my wife, of course. But my in-laws were there with Mary. I realize now it was planned as a grand surprise for me, to see my daughter first. But it was upsetting. She would have nothing to do with me. The grandparents were hanging around her. I felt sorta embarrassed. I was kind of let down not to see my wife. Sometimes I used to wonder afterwards if my wife really wanted to see me."[52] Another war-separated father remembered not having "any particular emotion" when he saw his newborn child. "I was just noncommittal about the whole thing. . . . It was a bitter disappointment."[53]

The early days and weeks of the reentry process could be especially trying as the men tried to come to terms with routines that had been established while they were away. Where children slept was a major bone of contention. "[My son] slept in the room with my wife while I was away and slept in the same room when I got back. . . . We'd put him to bed. He'd yell like mad. . . . The first night I got back I started working on him." Another father said, "My wife and the baby had always slept together. When I got home, of course, I think the baby grew a little jealous of me when she saw me sleeping with her mother, and she would beat me to bed and get in there with her. She had her own bed but she just didn't want to stay in it. . . . I spanked her. I felt the baby in our bed interfered with privacy with my wife."[54]

Discipline was an even bigger issue. Sixteen of the nineteen fathers thought their kids were always getting what they wanted, would not do what they were told, were stubborn and disrespectful, or believed the world revolved around them.[55]

I didn't take much responsibility for Joe when I first got back. For days and weeks I looked on while he was being brought up. He would take forever to eat his meals. My wife would beg him and promise him this and that and tell him to hurry up, but he just took his own sweet time and often he'd just refuse to eat altogether. She got upset and nervous. Then he would wet his pants. She never could catch him—looked like he was just perverse. He *knew* what to do, but would he do it? He sucked his thumb, too, not regularly but sometimes. It looked so silly to see a big boy like that sucking his thumb. That annoyed me. And he wouldn't obey my wife—no matter what, he just wouldn't obey.[56]

Fathers complained that their children treated their mothers like "servants," "monopolized mealtimes," and were "demanding." Several men decided it was their duty to "straighten out" their kids because their wives "wouldn't." As one father put it, it was time for him to "take over."[57]

War-separated fathers also were generally stricter than their wives, and they tended to punish their children more. Boot-camp tactics sometimes were incorporated into a fathers' child rearing regimen. Raising a child the military way did not always have the desired effect, however.

After I was discharged I can recall my training procedures; they were behavioristic—a slap was effective in training. I believe you spoiled babies by picking them up. I can recall feeding Ann when she was one year old and slapping her when she spewed food. . . . Once incident I remember which I have been ashamed of ever since—Ann was about 16 months old, she wanted to investigate a lot. We were on the train. Toward the end of the day I took her into the men's lounge. I was feeling rage. She was crying. I pushed her down roughly. . . . I decided to train Ann for the toilet in a week. I put her on the potty and kept her there until she'd defecate. She responded with rage. I would too. She would get off the potty and defecate in the corner.[58]

The men's approach to parenting put them at odds not only with their children but also with their wives. The question, for some mothers, came down to whether their husbands were expecting too much. "My wife and I had quarrels over the baby," said one man. "I thought she was stubborn. I tried to force her. My wife said, 'She's just a baby, you can't expect her to do things.' Probably I expected more of her than I should."[59] A wife reported, [My husband]

has always been hard on [our son]. When he was little his father used to lose control of himself and treat him much more roughly than he should. He didn't know what to expect of a child when he came back . . . for one thing, and he would do anything that came into his head. He'd shake him or dangle him by his heels and let him flop upon the bed from a distance and that would knock the breath out of him. . . . He frequently spanked him, but I don't think he ever took a stick to him, though he might have.[60]

Trouble in families also was evident in the stories that women told when they sought assistance from counselors, the police, and other specialists. In contrast to what might be revealed to an interviewer in a research situation, a plea for professional help often exposed a darker side to a family's life. "I have recently discussed my problem with a Social Worker and she was kind enough to suggest that I write to you as she feels that you'd be more capable of helping me in this particular case," said a mother in a 1949 letter to the psychologist and columnist, Rose Franzblau.

I've been married to my husband for seven years. During that that time he served 2 1/2 years in Service. We [had] gotten along fairly well until he came out of Service. Five months after his return, I became pregnant. When I was in my fourth month my husband struck me, and a good number of times after that too in my stomach. I was extremely nervous as I naturally feared for my child. She was unharmed. I knew then my husband wasn't quite himself but since he promised never to strike me again I was very tolerant with him. Well no sooner was my baby born than he started all over again, this time striking me with my child in my arms.

The husband eventually admitted that he had fallen in love with someone else, and he suggested to his wife that she leave him but also turn the baby over to his mistress because the woman could not have children.

> I said if he's in love with another woman its [sic] all right with me, but that I of all people would never give up my child. He was actually forcing me out so that it would look like I was deserting my baby God forbid. Since I had told him I never intend to do any such thing he again became very abusive and made many attempts of choking me. Well I finally took out a summons for him and had him put out of my house. . . . The Judge . . . explained to me that according to the [psychiatric] analyses of my husband he is a very sick man, mentally, and that I should use as much tact with him as possible when he comes to visit us on Sundays. . . . I'm actually left penniless and my husband had seen to it that I'd be in this predicament, and I owe two months' rent already. . . . I've been asking a nursery to please accept my child and they refused to do so as he's not quite three. . . . At this rate it may take years for a divorce. It isn't so much that as to feel that I'd like to have it come to some understanding that I don't have to be humiliated by this man any longer as my child and I have suffered too much already. I'm desperately in need of some good advice, and I do by all means want to get my child and me out of this rut.[61]

Although this woman could not easily extricate herself from her marriage, other women were able to find ways not only to separate, but also legally to uncouple from husbands who, as a result of being away (and maybe in battle), had markedly changed. Men, too, sometimes came home to find out that their wives had developed interests and goals that the men could not abide (e.g., wanting a career) or had fallen in love with someone else.

In 1940, the divorce/annulment rate in the United States was 2.0 (per 1,000 population). In 1945, it rose to 3.5; and in 1946, it jumped to 4.3. One year later, it dipped a bit, but it was still high, at 3.4. These breakups created thousands of single-parent families (more often than not single-mother families).[62] In numerous cases, the children in these homes were a lot better off in harmonious single-parent families than in conflict-ridden two-parent families. Still we may ask, what would these children's lives have been like if there had not been a war?

PART THREE

SEVEN

Father's Proper Place

From the turn of the century to the beginning of World War II, child-rearing experts were engaged in heated discussions over the proper place of fathers in American society. Often these discussions appeared in the press, especially in magazine and newspaper articles devoted to parenting and the home. During the early 1940s, the conversation continued, but was slightly different, in that the focus shifted to the question of the war's immediate effect. When the fighting stopped, it did not take long for the experts to pick up where they had left off. However, the conversation did not reach the fever pitch of the 1930s until the late 1940s and early 1950s. Only then do we begin to see some familiar themes.

The expectations for fathers that cropped up repeatedly in the first half of the twentieth century and that were resurrected, in full measure, at the beginning of the second half were the father as economic provider, father as pal, and father as male role model. These expectations complemented rather than competed with one another. Men were instructed to fashion their lives according to all three.[1]

The *father as economic provider* emphasized the importance of fathers as breadwinners. The experts did not go out of their way make this point; it was just assumed that men were the principal wage earners. To a certain extent, the experts were correct. Although the labor force participation rates of women in 1950s varied by race and ethnicity, on the whole women were far less likely than men to be employed for pay. For married women and married women with young children in particular, the differences between women and men were even sharper. Still, given that a sizeable percentage of women were employed—in 1950, for example, more than 10 percent of married women with children under six years of age were in the labor force—it is remarkable that the experts regularly ignored women who were working outside the home.[2]

An article in *Today's Health* in 1950 was devoted to reviewing the "new" responsibilities of being a father—which included being the family "playmate" and "funmaker"—but it said first that the "traditional role of Father was that of provider and disciplinarian." A *Parents Magazine* article the same year outlined the strategies that a father of four girls used to ease his transition from work to home. The inference throughout the piece was that the transition applied only to men.

> I resent problems and children heaped upon me as I enter the door. . . . I was a grouch, and a meany with a one-word vocabulary, "No." So we hit upon the idea of my greeting the family with a hearty "Hello," then marching straight up the stairs to our bedroom with the paper and a glass of milk. . . . I have found that all I need is fifteen minutes of quiet to organize my inner forces to pack away the grouch, the meany, and the "no."

Another article in *Parents Magazine*, again in 1950, titled "What Does Father Do?" advised mothers to "take the children to visit Daddy's place of work and let them see for themselves what he does while he's away from home all day." No mention was made of children possibly wanting to visit mothers at their jobs.[3]

The theme of the father as breadwinner was also evident when talk centered on how fathers should not be so preoccupied with their careers that they were unavailable to their families. A 1952 *New York Times Magazine* essay on "Father's Occupation" reported the results of a study in which children from seventeen to twenty-two "were asked to consider how their parents' work affected their development and to rate that influence in comparison with other factors in their early lives." The author found that the "complaint heard repeatedly from mothers that fathers are 'too busy' to function as parents is substantiated by many of the young people's comments—and 'the job' is frequently pointed at as the cause of it all."[4]

The second theme—that of the *father as pal*—included any and all references to the value of fathers being companions to their children and playing and kidding around with them. Often this theme was expressed in terms of how much fathers had changed in recent times—how they had become more involved at home. Typical was a 1954 article in *McCall's* that introduced, through a combination of text and photos, "a modern husband and father" named Ed.

Here's Ed Ritchtscheidt of Pines Lake, New Jersey, his wife Carol and their three children. They live in a gray shingle split-level house with three bedrooms, one bath and an unfinished basement room that will one day be the game room. On the north side of their lot, where they plan to build a barbecue, Ed has made a play yard for his children. We're introducing Ed and his family because, like millions of other married couples today, they're living the life of *McCall's*, a more casual but a richer life than that of even the fairly recent past. Ed's place in this new way of living is something he takes for granted. He doesn't stop to think about the great changes that have taken place since he was a boy. Had Ed been a father twenty-five years ago [in 1929] he would have had little time to play and work with his children. The running of the household would have been left entirely in the hands of his wife. Husbands and fathers were loved and respected then, but they weren't friends and companions to their families. Household chores were beneath them. Today the chores as well as the companionship make Ed part of his family. He and Carol have centered their lives almost completely around their children and their home. Every inch of their house and yard is lived in and enjoyed. And it's a very happy place.

Ed was said to like reading to the children, putting them to bed, and feeding and bathing them. He did not like picking up after the kids, buying their clothes, taking the babysitter home, and changing diapers.[5]

In a similar vein, an article in *Woman's Home Companion* the year before affirmed that "ideas about fathers have changed. The old-time picture portrayed a stern bewhiskered gentleman, seated in great dignity on a throne-like eminence, his children clustered in meek submissiveness at his feet. In today's picture the throne is empty, because its erstwhile occupant sprawls on the floor while boisterous youngsters clamber all over him!"[6]

What is interesting about these articles is not that they represent a new way of thinking about fatherhood—a new culture of fatherhood—but that they repeat statements made years before. Indeed, if we examine magazine articles published prior to World War II, we find the same kind of "dads-are-more-involved-today-than-they-were-yesterday" rhetoric. In 1934, for example, *Parents Magazine* published a piece that announced, "Father seems to be coming into his own these days so far as sharing the fun along with the responsibilities of bringing up children. Gone are the days when child training was considered entirely 'mother's job.'"[7] In 1933, it was likewise reported that "until the last ten years or so, a man married and had children and that was the end of it as far as he was concerned. The nursery wasn't his province, and he knew it. Without concern, he left the children to his wife, and more often than not was known to his offsprings merely as the man who stayed with them on week-ends." And what was it like "now"? "This now has *completely* changed. The old type of father is passing!" (Hyperbole was and is a commonly used rhetorical tool to characterize historical shifts in the expectations applied to fathers.)[8]

In both the prewar and postwar versions of the father-as-pal theme, men were encouraged to be less austere. A father did "not need to pretend that he . . . was perfect," a *New York Times Magazine* article suggested. "To hear about some of the mischief Daddy got into when he was a boy—some of the silly things he said, or did, or thought about—may be a real comfort to a child."[9] The realm of sports also was considered Dad's purview. Men were expected to be responsible for teaching daughters and especially sons the ins and outs of baseball, basketball, boxing, and other athletic pursuits. They also were accountable for educating their children in the art of tool use ("Dad's interest and help will make this scooter extra special").[10] And they were encouraged to share with their kids their favorite pastimes and hobbies—fishing, hunting, woodworking, stamp collecting, and so forth ("Through mutual enjoyments, Father and child discover how to be friends").[11]

The experts after the war—much like the experts before the war—directed their advice almost entirely to middle-class and upper-class parents. Owning a house with a fully equipped workshop seemed to be assumed. So was a certain amount of wealth. Several weeks before Christmas, a 1949 article proclaimed, "We know (and you know) that, no matter how much we stress the importance of 'basic toys'—blocks, cars, small 'people' scaled to fit into the block play, clay, paints, crayons, and so on—still, on some Christmas morning, Daddy's boy will have an electric train."[12] That a parent might not be able to afford an electric train set apparently was not imagined.

Fun with dad also could mean experiencing an adventure—one that might never happen, if it were left up to mom. "Sometimes mothers are afraid to climb high, or to go into dark caves, or to risk deep waters, or ride the roller coaster. Father can lead here, to the delight of the children."[13] The fun quotient, it was said, could rise as well when dad took over an activity that generally was in mom's domain. "When father's in the kitchen, that's where you're bound to find the children—watching, helping, tasting."[14] And merriment definitely was to be had when father and kids were left alone while mom was out of town. "Boy, oh boy, did they have keen fun with Daddy! . . . No one ever mentions that the children regard the whole affair as a very special sort of party."[15]

If reference was made to men spending time with their children or engaging in routine child care, they often were depicted as incompetent and in need of serious assistance. When a father volunteered to watch his son for a weekend ("I'll take care of Dennis"), his wife responded, "You!" ("I was incredulous"). When he agreed to do the same thing the next year, "he had to face a barrage of complaints from neighboring fathers" ("You want our wives to get ideas?"). The father did expect his wife to provide a list of what he was supposed to do. Also, "everything [was] made easy for his weekend duty: marketing done, meals prepared or ready for easy heating."[16]

Another father, a World War II veteran, who was pressed into taking care of his children while his wife went out to dinner with friends, was said to have "reluctantly agreed to try his hand at babysitting." Announced the wife: "Before I left, I gave him a written list of instructions, and the phone numbers where I could be reached. I never felt so guilty and uneasy in my life as I did that night as I started off, leaving the baby crying, our daughter tearfully waving good-by and my husband with a pathetic look of helplessness on his face."[17] Classifying a father's contribution to child care as *babysitting* is telling. By definition, to *babysit* is to "take charge of a child while the parents are temporarily away." A father who babysits for his own child is, connotatively, *not* the parent.[18]

An article entitled "Have Fathers Changed?" made the argument that "laughter at father . . . used to be behind his back," whereas now it had become "frank and open." The article also included a drawing of a father perched at the top of a castle, watching his wife and children hammering at the base. (They are attempting to bring the castle—and the father with it—down.) The author maintained that poking fun at dad was not necessarily bad. People were openly ridiculing the family patriarch, to be sure, but the father had also become, as he saw it, "much more a member of the family." In addition, the author argued that the father's "position in the group [was] much more real than it ha[d] ever been before."[19]

The condescension toward fathers in magazine and newspaper articles could be found in other aspects of the culture of fatherhood as well. Comic strip fathers were more likely than comic strip mothers in the early 1950s to be depicted as incompetent, whereas the reverse was true in the late 1940s. The more benign characterization of fathers immediately after World War II may have arisen out of respect for the sacrifices that men had made in the service. The dividend that fathers possibly gained by the war, however, seemed to dissipate by the early 1950s, even though the United States was engaged in yet another, albeit smaller, war in Korea.[20] One early 1950s comic strip, for example, depicted a father taking his child (Baby Snookums) into the family's yard to play baseball ("Now you just watch your daddy!!").

But when father bats the ball over the fence, it bounces off the head of his neighbor, who then throws it back and smashes a window ("Now—how in the world could that happen?").[21]

Fathers were also derided on the airwaves. The radio version of *Father Knows Best*, which showcased a married couple and their three children, routinely made fun of dad. Originally, in fact, the title of the show was a question (*Father Knows Best?*), "suggesting that father's role as family leader and arbiter was dubious." One radio script had the Child Welfare Society accusing the father of "beating and starving his children." Of course, it all turned out to be a huge misunderstanding—one that, predictably, grew out of father's "fumbling." (The television version of the series, which began its run in 1954, eliminated the question mark. It also offered a much wiser dad.)[22]

The earliest family TV sitcoms (some of which started as radio series) also lampooned dads. *The Life of Riley* (1949–50, 1953–58), *The Trouble with Father* (1950–55), *I Love Lucy* (1951–61), *The Adventures of Ozzie and Harriet* (1952–66), and *My Little Margie* (1952–55) all tended to portray fathers in an unflattering light. In the *I Love Lucy* episode that satirized Lucy and husband Ricky's transition to parenthood, Ricky acts as if Lucy is "going to blow up" when she announces that the baby is about to arrive and that it is time to leave for the hospital. Once they arrive, Ricky "[cannot] remember where he lives or even his own last name."[23]

Ironically, it was in this climate of making fun of dad, and perhaps in part because of it, that experts promoted a third theme—the *father as a male role model*. Central here was the notion that fathers had something unique to offer their children—something that mothers could not provide. Besides being the family's economic provider and fun guy, fathers were to be icons of masculinity—or at least of a certain kind of masculinity. By their actions, fathers would demonstrate, not just to their sons but also to their daughters, what it meant to be a "real" man. Ultimately, the men's task was to counteract the "softer" influence of women. Here also a certain kind of femininity was implied.[24] Those who embraced this theme essentially believed that no amount of mothering could substitute for fathering. They also believed that maligning fathers, even in jest, was not only misdirected but also destructive.

Two of the most ardent advocates of this view in the postwar era were psychiatrist O. Spurgeon English and his colleague Constance J. Foster. In their book, *Fathers Are Parents, Too*, they deplored how fathers were portrayed in comic strips and on radio and TV. "The patriarchal 'father' has been supplanted in our popular terminology by the effete 'papa,' the saccharine 'daddy,' the fraternal 'dad,' the ineffectual 'pop,' and the frankly scornful 'old man.' " As to who was at fault, English and Foster felt that fathers and mothers, as well as the media, should be held accountable.

> A share of the blame for [the father's] weakened position must be attributed to father himself. . . . He has failed to understand his psychological role, play it faithfully, and appreciate its full significance in the growth and development of his children. . . . Women are culpable, too. They have sometimes been unwilling or unable to accept their true femininity. They have often unconsciously resisted their biological destiny in life. Some have aggressively attempted to usurp man's place.[25]

In a series of related articles, English and Foster outlined how and why fathers were central. A father should get up in the middle of the night to soothe a colicky child *not* because he should do his fair share of baby care (why should the mother be the only one who is exhausted?) but because his "arms are strong and the child who experiences the security they give him grows up with the warm regard for some of the best qualities of masculinity—tenderness, protection, strength." A mother could "indulge" her children; fathers could not. "A father," they said, "while basically no less kind, should naturally be masculine and firm. As the more resolute of the two parents, he leaves Mother free to play her protective role properly." The job of raising children also was said to be "as thoroughly masculine an occupation as exploring darkest Africa, adjusting a delicate carburetor, or running a ball around your own end for a touchdown."[26] In a follow-up book, *A Guide to Successful Fatherhood*, English and Foster argued that the father was "the connecting link with the outside world," and that his job was to bring "the masculine viewpoint into the home to balance the prevailing feminine viewpoint presented by the mother and, in the early school years, by [female] teachers."[27]

The father as male role model was a theme that had been introduced before. It was popular between 1901 and 1909, and between 1930 and 1939. At both times, a "crisis" of masculinity was perceived to exist. In the early 1900s, the supposed calamity was rooted in the social transformation of the workplace and workforce (more desk jobs, higher numbers of women), and in the belief that, in the wake of economic change, American culture had lost its "cultural vitality" and "national virility."[28] In the 1930s, the Depression and high unemployment prompted a deeper conversation about the value of men in children's lives. Focusing on the "manliness" that fathers brought to parenthood steered attention away from the fact that many men had lost their jobs and were unable to fulfill the traditional role of breadwinner. Child-rearing experts rarely connected the father as male role model to the economic downturn. As a rule, they avoided talking about the Depression altogether.[29]

Did people come to think that there was a crisis of masculinity in the post–World War II era as well? If so, did that perception lead to a resurgence of the father-as-male-role-model theme? The answer to both questions, it appears, is yes. World War II prompted a nationwide discussion about whether America's sons and fathers were "tough enough" to fight. During the war, a particular kind of masculinity was glorified—a masculinity that emphasized strength, forbearance, instrumentality, and "nerves of steel." Assessing afterward how America's military had performed, some observers concluded that far too many U.S. soldiers were "soft" and "weak willed." As to how and why this could have occurred, a common explanation was that mothers were the root cause. Mothers, it was said, smothered their children with love—or, stated in the reverse, did not use enough discipline in raising them. Simply put, they were accused of pampering their kids.[30]

The antidote for what ailed America was a heavy dose of dad. Various authorities contended that men needed to step in and play a larger role in child socialization to counterbalance the debilitating influence of women. If men shirked their child-rearing responsibilities, the consequences for not only children but also the country, it was thought, would be dire. How could the United States hope to win a *third* world war—which some believed was imminent—if its fighters were not "hard"?[31]

An article in *Better Homes and Gardens* entitled, "Are We Staking Our Future on a Crop of Sissies?" defined a "sissy" as "a boy (or girl) who gets too much satisfaction from what his mother does for him and not enough from what he does for himself." Having a "sissy" for a child was a nightmare that only a father could dispel: "You have a *horror* of seeing your son a panty-waist, but he won't get red blood and self-reliance if you leave the whole job of making a he-man of him to his mother."[32] An article in *The Rotarian* asked a different, though related, question: "[Are you] confused about what it means to be good father?" It then immediately offered these words of encouragement: "Look at the three unique contributions you make to your children's development and you may feel better about the job you're doing: 1. *Father stands for 'Man.'* Your children learn about masculinity just from watching and listening to you. 2. *Father stands for the Outside World.* Aware of it or not, you are 'interpreting the codes of society' when you answer those endless questions about why teacher is a sourpuss. 3. *Father stands for Competence.* You may feel like Caspar Milquetoast, but to the children you represent all that is strong."[33]

Did men and women buy into the feminization/sissy rhetoric? Some did. One woman, seeking advice from psychologist and columnist Rose Franzblau, said that she was worried that her seven-year-old son spent a lot of time with his mother and older sister, but very little time with his father, and that the boy was at risk of developing into the wrong "type" of man.

> Since my son has two women around him so much of the time, I thought it would be good for him if my husband would take him to the playground. . . . My husband [however] complains of being tired. . . . I believe there is a tendency for these kind[s] of boys who are somewhat rejected by their fathers to incline to the scientific, studious type. In fact I [think] we have to be careful of feminine tendencies."[34]

Another mother, also writing for advice, expressed concern that her eleven-year-old son "[did] silly little things that girls do when he is in his room." ("[He] gets in my lipstick, etc.") Her husband, a factory worker and farmer, "[didn't] have time to take [the boy] fishing or play ball with him and to be a pal to him" because he was "tired at the end of the day and cross and irritiable [sic] . . . from overwork." The mother believed that her son was "a good boy" but felt that "he act[ed] like a little 'sissy' " because of how much he was around her.[35]

Concerns about a son being a "pantywaist" or about his exhibiting "feminine tendencies" often meant that a parent was afraid that a child might be homosexual. In postwar America, this was a fear that a number of parents shared. World War II created opportunities for soldiers to engage in homosexual behavior and to contemplate in earnest, maybe for the first time, what it meant to be gay. The war also helped to promulgate psychiatric concepts of homosexuality, as mental health professionals were called upon to screen inductees.[36] New research on the sexual habits and inclinations of American men—especially the landmark work *Sexual Behavior in the Human Male*, published in 1948—provided evidence that the number of homosexuals in the male population was much higher than previously thought, and that homosexuality cut across all socioeconomic and geographic groups.[37] This meant not only that most gay men kept their actions and impulses a secret but also that it was difficult, if not impossible, to identify individuals who were gay simply by observing how they behaved in public.[38]

The inability "to just know" who was gay intensified parents' scrutiny of their children's—especially their sons'—demeanor for telltale signs of homosexuality. The question of "who was and who was not" gay also extended to grown-ups. (After all, the Kinsey Report did focus on adults.) Thus, in the fifties, fathers tended to be scrutinized differently than they might have been before: people wanted to see men adopt a demeanor that supposedly established that they were heterosexual.[39] Here perhaps is another reason why the father as male role model was popular at the time. By emphasizing their purported "inner maleness," some men may have been trying to signal to observers that they were *not* gay.[40]

Among the many experts offering child-rearing advice in the postwar era, none was better known, or possibly more influential, than Dr. Benjamin Spock. What pushed Spock to the top of an already crowded field was the publication of *The Common Sense Book of Baby and Child Care* (hereafter *Baby and Child Care*), a five-hundred-page tome that he (and, we now know, his wife) began in 1943 and completed in 1946.[41] *Baby and Child Care* sold three-quarters of a million copies in its first year, and more than eight million copies by 1956. For many postwar parents, the book was a veritable child-rearing bible. Dr. Spock became a household name. (Parents frequently referred to *Baby and Child Care* as *Dr. Spock*—or simply *Spock*.)[42]

Historians of fatherhood often have examined the pages of *Baby and Child Care* to map the culture of fatherhood in the postwar era. Although it was the work of only one man (or one couple), the fact that the book was in so many homes prompts the question, what proper place did it prescribe for men? The fact that it was a book about baby and child *care* also allows us to ask, What were postwar fathers expected to do when it came to the "dirty work" of parenthood (e.g., diaper-changing and middle-of-the-night feeding)? A quick scan shows that only a few lines in the book alluded to fathers. This simple statistic, however, does not convey the book's nuances or its inconsistencies. A closer examination reveals more.[43]

Baby and Child Care opened with "A Letter to the Mother and Father," and followed with a section headed "The Right Start" and subsection headed "The Parents' Part." Given these headings, one might believe that Spock was writing for parents, regardless of their gender. Throughout, however, there were far more references to "mother" than to "father," strongly suggesting that Spock imagined he was speaking primarily to women.[44]

The subsection on "The Parents' Part" included a drawing of a father looking at his baby through the nursery window, with the caption, "The father is apt to get the mistaken idea that he's unimportant." Opposite the picture was a discussion headed "The Father's Part." (No similar discussion of the mother's part appears.) Spock's commentary on fatherhood was detailed but also contradictory.

Some fathers have been brought up to think that the care of babies and children is the mother's job entirely. This is the wrong idea. You can be a warm father and a real man at the same time. We know that the father's closeness and friendliness to his children will have a vital effect on their spirits and characters for the rest of their lives. So the time for him to begin being a real father is right from the start. That's the easiest time. The father and mother can learn together. In some cities, classes in baby care are given for fathers too. If a father leaves it all to his wife for the first two years, she gets to be the expert and the boss, as far as the children are concerned. He'll feel more bashful about pushing his way into the picture later. Of course, I don't mean that the father has to give just as many bottles or change just as many diapers as the mother. But it's fine for him to do these things occasionally. He might make the formula on Sunday. If the baby is on a 2 A.M. bottle in the early weeks, when the mother is still pretty tired, this is a good feeding for him to take over. It's nice for him, if he can, to go along to the doctor's office for the baby's regular visits. It gives him a chance to bring up those questions which are bothering him and of which he doesn't think his wife understands the importance. It pleases the doctor, too. Of course, there are some fathers who would get goose flesh at the very thought of helping to take care of a baby, and there's no good to be gained by trying to force them. Most of them come around to enjoying their children later "when they're more like real people." But many fathers are only a little bashful. They just need encouragement.[45]

Although Spock appeared to advocate that fathers should connect with their children from the very beginning, he blunted that advice when he said that fathers need only engage in routine child care "occasionally," and that men should *not* be "forced" to "help," if caring for the baby made them squeamish. Also, proposing that fathers "go along" to the pediatrician's office would seem to make fathers their wives' health-care partners, but then Spock quickly added that the main reason fathers would want to be in attendance was so they could ask, condescendingly, "those questions" that they thought their wives did not comprehend.

Other sections of the book prominently mentioned fathers. One talked about how important it was for children to have a "friendly, accepting father." Spock wrote, "Boys and girls need chances to be around with [*sic*] their father, to be enjoyed by him, and, if possible, to do things with him." (Note the caveat, "if possible.") He then warned, "Unfortunately, the father is apt to come home wanting most of all to slump down and read the paper. If he understands how valuable his companionship is, he will feel more like making a reasonable effort." As to what constituted a "reasonable effort,"

Spock was not asking much. "I say reasonable because I don't think the conscientious father (or mother either), should force himself beyond his endurance. Better to play for 15 minutes enjoyably, and then say, 'Now, I'm going to read my paper,' than to spend all day at the zoo, crossly." That a father might come home from work and relish spending more than a few minutes with his children seemed to be an odd concept—at least to Spock.[46]

Another section that prominently mentioned fathers was headed "The Fatherless Child." Here Spock spoke of the child whose father was gone for a long time, and the child whose father had died. For the first scenario, Spock echoed the view of other writers who expressed concern that, during the war and even after, many children were being raised without a father in the home. Spock said that letters back and forth helped to give the father "a feeling of taking part in the baby's care." Photos helped, too. "Take as many snapshots as you can," he advised. "Send along any that don't look like midnight. A proud mother feels like holding back on the pictures that make the baby or her look homely or silly or cross. But a father trying to imagine his family doesn't want all smiling faces any more than a hungry man wants all candy."[47]

When Spock talked about what to do if a father died, he emphasized that, without a father, children still could "grow up normal and well adjusted"— a comforting message, no doubt, given that so many fathers did not return from the war. It was important for the mother to recognize, however, that her children "need[ed] to be friendly with other men." Younger children gained a good deal if they could "just be reminded frequently that there *are* such creatures as agreeable men, with lower voices, different clothes, and different manners than women." Older children needed "chances to be with and feel close to other men and older boys." This companionship was invaluable not just to sons but also to daughters. "Grandfathers, uncles, cousins, scoutmasters, men teachers at school, the minister, old family friends, or a combination of these can serve as substitute fathers, if they enjoy the child's company and see him fairly regularly." (Others offered similar advice during the war and after.)[48]

Though Spock seemed to be careful to refer to both boys and girls, he ended the section on the fatherless child with a special piece of advice for the mothers of sons. Women were told that the sons of fathers who had been killed needed the "opportunity and encouragement to play with other boys, every day if possible." Moreover, said Spock, when a young man turned two years of age, he should "be mainly occupied with boyish pursuits." Why was this important? Said Spock, "The temptation of the mother who has no other equally strong ties is to make him her closest spiritual companion, getting him interested in clothes and interior decorations, in her opinions and feelings about people, in the books and other recreations she enjoys. If she succeeds in making her world appealing to him, easier to get along in, than the world of boys (where he has to make his own way), then he may grow up precocious and effeminate."[49] Spock's belief that sons who got close to their mothers were at risk of becoming "effeminate" mirrors what other experts were saying at the time about the importance of fathers as male role models. It was a standard argument among child-rearing experts, especially those who were drawn to psychiatry and psychoanalytic theory, which Spock was.[50]

Finally, Spock devoted a section in his book to separated parents. He counseled that, during and after a breakup, it was important that children be told two things: first, "Even though the parents separate, the children will still belong to both and will always be able to see both regularly"; second, "Neither parent is the good one or the bad one." Spock cautioned that the latter was "the hardest rule for parents to abide by." As to how to inform a child about a pending divorce, Spock offered the following as a possible narrative: "Your Daddy and I argue and fight too much, just the way you and Peter Jenkins do. So we've decided that we'll all have a better time if we don't try to live in the same house. But Daddy will still be your Daddy and I'll still be your Mummy."[51]

Far more mothers than fathers wrote to Spock. The letter-writing imbalance, however, does not directly reflect the degree to which fathers may have read and been influenced by Spock's ideas, or the degree to which fathers were involved in their children's lives. A survey of the letters indicates that the women who wrote to Spock often saw their husbands as partners in *"rearing,"* though not necessarily *"caring for"* their children. A number of them, in fact, "reported that their husbands were actively involved, at least as young parents, in making decisions about how to raise their children." Interestingly enough, it was not uncommon for the women to use the pronoun *we* to refer to themselves and their husbands when outlining their child-rearing concerns.[52]

Some women also would come right out and say that their husbands pored over Spock's book or column. When Spock wrote an article in favor of baby pacifiers, people wrote to express their support for his position, and a few mentioned who was paying attention to what. "Your discussion of pacifiers in the July *Ladies Home Journal* was of great interest to *my husband and me*," said one mother. Another wrote, "*My husband and I* feel that your book on the care of babies added a great deal to *our* courage and knowledge in the rearing of two boys, and I am looking forward to your following articles." A third wanted Spock to know that his book "has been a treasure" for *her and her husband*, while a fourth wrote of how much his book was a constant subject of conversation among their circle of friends: "As near as *my husband and I* can figure, your book, *Baby and Child Care*, has become the Modern Bible of American Parenthood. At least *everyone we know with a child, or children*, can reach quickly to some convenient place and pull down a copy of 'Spock' at the least provocation. At *many a social gathering* it has been the topic and center of no end of conversation and discussion."[53]

Fathers who wrote to Spock for advice might also mention *Baby and Child Care*. One father heaped such high praise on the book that Spock felt obliged to reply, "I certainly enjoyed your enthusiastic letter, in fact I swelled with pride when I read it. I appreciate your taking the trouble to write." Fathers outside the United States were also enamored with *Baby and Child Care*. A father in Australia wrote not so much to ask for advice as to pay Spock a compliment. "Just a short note telling you how wonderful your book has been to my wife and myself in regard to bringing up our child. . . . [We] have both learned a great deal from this edition which we would not have learned elsewhere. [O]ur baby (16 months) is quite a healthy and normal average baby thanks largely to your book. I have recommended this book to many friends and have given half a dozen away for presents."[54] Spock also had his detractors. One mother told Spock that her husband did not believe in raising children "by the book," and that he absolutely refused to read *Baby and Child Care*. As far as he was concerned, child-rearing manuals were "poppycock."[55]

Whether fathers and mothers actually followed Spock's advice—or the advice of any avowed experts—is difficult to determine. Reading a child-rearing book or parenting magazine article did not necessarily translate into compliance. In the 1940s and 1950s, as well as before, fathers and mothers selectively chose from a range of opinions (including the opinions of family members and friends), scrupulously adhering to some suggestions and just as scrupulously ignoring others. This "pick and choose" strategy did not make postwar parents unique. Fathers and mothers pretty much did the same thing before, and they pretty much do the same thing today.[56]

EIGHT

Baby Boom

Immediately after World War II, the birth rate in the United States increased sharply, and it continued at a high level throughout the 1950s and early 1960s. The twenty-some-odd-year "baby boom" was one of the most distinguishing features of the postwar era and is a phenomenon that has long intrigued scholars.[1] Why the boom occurred is open to various interpretations. Some point to a relatively healthy postwar economy as the reason. Others say the boom reflected couples' yearnings for stability and the glorification of family and home that seemed to grip the country. Still others contend that the boom was related to Americans' sense of security (helped by the war's end) and the increased confidence that many had about the future. In all likelihood, several factors were involved.

Looked at in concrete terms, the boom came down to the decisions made by two specific groups. One comprised older couples who had married either before or during the war and who had postponed having kids—or put off having more kids—until the war ended. This group was primarily responsible for the spike in birth rates in 1946 and 1947. A second group comprised younger couples who married in the late 1940s and early 1950s and became parents soon thereafter. This group was primarily responsible for the large number of births in the late 1950s and, to some degree, the early 1960s.[2]

Although the fertility rates in the fifties might make it seem that everyone in the United States was "kid crazy," some in America were not entirely comfortable with the idea of having children. One New York man, whose wife felt a "natural desire to become a mother," told her that he did not want children because, from his point of view, "the world [was] in a terrible state that could lead to war." A Virginia woman, the mother of an eighteen-month-old, confessed that she never liked children and was doing her best to resist her husband's request to have a second: "Where I cannot deny the advantages of another for the companionship and benefit, possibly, for the current baby, my stomach more than turns at even the thought."[3]

With all the babies being born at the beginning of the boom, it makes sense to ask, How much did men care for infants then? Did fathers in the late 1940s and early 1950s change diapers? Did they get up in middle of the night to calm cranky and colicky newborns? A judicious answer to these questions is that it is difficult to say. We cannot rely exclusively on what the child-rearing experts were recommending at the time; their axioms are a reflection more of the culture than of the conduct of fatherhood. In the 1946 edition of *Baby and Child Care*, for example, Benjamin Spock said that a father should consider making a baby's formula "on Sunday," but not necessarily on weekdays, and that he should volunteer for middle-of-the-night feedings "in the early weeks," but not necessarily after that. Do these pronouncements coincide with what fathers actually did? Were dads available only during the first few weeks of their children's lives and just on weekends? Spock's words are one thing; men's actions are another.[4]

Evidence suggests that some men in the postwar era at least *planned* to be active caregivers. Fathers-to-be attended "maternity" classes in order to learn how to feed, bathe, and dress a baby. They also were taught how to "bubble" (i.e., burp) a newborn and how to change a diaper. The formal lessons were not a new phenomenon but an extension of an educational program that had begun at least ten years before. Did fathers internalize the training they received and apply it? Did they *care for* babies?[5]

Detailed studies of father-infant interactions generally are the best way to answer questions like these. Studies of this nature, however, are few and far between. Researchers in the fifties, if they directed their attention to fatherhood at all, focused primarily on men's relationships with school-age children rather than with infants. One study (reported in chapter 6) found that fathers who were in the service during the war generally were more attached to children born after they got home than to children born while they were gone. This stronger attachment may have translated into a greater willingness on the part of the fathers to be involved with certain babies, but we can do no more than hypothesize since the researchers did not focus on infant care per se.[6]

Another study, completed in 1950, offered more information about the degree to which fathers cared for the very young, but it, too, is limited in some respects. In the 1940s, eighty-five New York City men, the majority of whom were between thirty and fifty years of age, were queried about their activities as fathers. The men were asked what they did with and for their children. More than 90 percent of the men said that they participated in routine daily care. When it came to specific duties, the fathers reported that they had fed children (62.4 percent), minded babies (43.5 percent), and cleaned children or groomed them (36.5 percent). They also indicated involvement in their children's sleeping (35.3 percent), toileting (31.8 percent), dressing (29.4 percent), and night-time routines (22.4 percent).[7]

These figures are nowhere near a totality (clearly some men did little or next to nothing); moreover, they could be construed to cover a lifetime of fatherhood (were the older men not talking about their care activities *before* the war?). Still, the study's results appear to paint a picture of greater father involvement in the immediate postwar period than the child-rearing experts would have us believe. The author's interpretations are especially striking on this count: "Fathers consider the role of child rearer in the sense of 'doing for' their children, not only an important function of motherhood but of fatherhood as well. Here . . . we find evidence that bespeaks a more equalitarian than patriarchal type of family pattern emerging." What was being said, in short, is that men as a group were taking on a larger share of child care. Perceiving a gap between the conventional wisdom at the time and the study's somewhat positive results, the author argued,

> Recent literature has characterized the role of the modern American father as "vestigial"; he is said to have "abdicated" the rearing of his children to the mother. The . . . conclusion of the present study, based as it is on the reports of the fathers themselves, indicates, rather, that the role of these fathers is an active one, and that not only do they participate in such duties as the routine daily care of the child, but the majority of them seem to consider child rearing as part of the requirements of the father role.[8]

The author did caution that the study, focused as it was on men living in New York City, was basically "an examination of the role of the *urban* American father" and that one "[could not] tell the extent to which [the] findings [were] applicable to other cultures."[9] Still, the author's findings are intriguing. Were men in the immediate postwar period more involved in infant care than the experts were suggesting?

Consider another project, which focused on, among other things, men's transition to parenthood and their involvement with infants and was one of the most comprehensive studies of child-rearing in the postwar era. In the project, 379 mothers living in middle-class or working-class suburbs surrounding a large New England city were queried in 1950–51 about their families' home life. Every mother had a kindergarten-age daughter or son, defined for the purpose of the project as the "focal child." The women were asked what their family life was like when the focal child was an infant (that is, what it was like in the late 1940s), and they were questioned specifically about their husbands' involvement at the time: "How much did your husband do in connection with taking care of [your son or daughter] when he or she was a baby?"[10]

The mothers offered a variety of answers, which were content-analyzed by coders working with the original team of researchers and ultimately placed into eight categories. The categories and results (percentage of fathers within each category) were as follows: did no infant care (15.8 percent); very little infant care (33.8 percent); between very little and some (8.3 percent); some (22.8 percent); between some and quite a bit (5.6 percent); quite a bit (11.0 percent); shared equally with mother (2.7 percent); did more than mother (one father). In general, then, half of the fathers did either no infant care or very little infant care; about a third did more than very little but less than quite a bit, and approximately one out of eight did quite a bit or shared equally with the mother or did more than the mother.[11] To place these findings in context, it is important to keep in mind that the vast majority of the fathers in the study were the sole or primary wage earners in their families.[12]

What explanations did the women offer for the division of infant care in their homes? Here, too, there was variation. Some of the wives said their husbands did little or no infant care because it was not their responsibility. As one mother put it, while it was true that, every now and then, her husband would "take over"—for instance, when she "wanted to go out for an evening" or if the baby "was sick"—for the most part, he did not do much. Change diapers? "Oh no, he never changed him." Wash the baby? "Oh, he'd wash his hands or face in a pinch, but not a bath. He would if he had to, but I mean—it isn't a man's job—just like washing the dishes."[13] A second mother acknowledged that her husband would "watch over [the baby] once in a while for [her]," but only rarely changed diapers or participated in feedings. How about giving the baby a bath? "No. (laughs)."[14]

A second group of mothers conveyed the sense that their husbands basically were unskilled when it came to infant care. One mother declared that her husband was "kind of afraid" to handle his daughter, while another reported that her husband was "always sort of nervous with youngsters and small children."[15] The husband of a third did not "bathe [the baby] himself" because "he wasn't too sure with him," though he did give the baby "certain feedings" and "tried to diaper him, which he didn't like to do."[16] Similar concerns were echoed by others.[17]

Such accounts are frequently offered to explain low levels of father involvement in the postwar era. Men, it often has been said, did not care for infants then because it was not among their duties (breadwinning, however, was); or they did not care for infants because they preferred not to. But do these accounts tell the whole story? Do they, by themselves, completely capture what the New England mothers ultimately revealed? It turns out that they do not.

One of the things that made the late 1940s somewhat unique is that World War II had ended only a short time before. Although the shadow of war would continue to influence family life throughout the fifties, the effects of the war were especially felt in the years that immediately followed its end. Some of the husbands in the New England study had served in World War II and remained on active duty after the war. Separation from their families left them with little opportunity to perform much infant care. "Nothing," said one mother, when asked how much her husband did. "Because he wasn't here.[. . .] He was overseas when [our son] was eight months old." What about when the father returned? "He cared for him for 3 weeks when I was in the hospital. So he had to take over, but otherwise nothing." Did he ever change diapers? "No, not outside that three weeks." Feed him? "No, he wouldn't feed [him]. He [the baby] wouldn't eat for him [the father]." Give him a bath? "No."[18]

Another woman talked of how her husband had been "injured quite badly in the war," and how he "sometimes los[t] his patience because of that." She also felt that the fact he was older when he became a father was instrumental: "If there hadn't been the war we would have had our children sooner. I think that makes a difference—your age and patience with children. He's 40. If he had had his children when he was 30 he would have been better." Asked how much her husband cared for their son after he was born, the mother said that he did "very little." He did change diapers "occasionally" and fed the baby "once in a while," but never gave the baby a bath.[19]

Some men could not contribute as much as others, the mothers said, because of their heavy schedules. After the war, the G.I. Bill of Rights, which grew out the Serviceman's Readjustment Act of 1944, provided veterans with funds to enroll in school and with low- to no-down-payment mortgages to buy homes.[20] The G.I. Bill afforded returning soldiers the chance to attend school and acquire diplomas and degrees, but veterans with children were not always in a position to quit their jobs to get an education. Frequently, fathers went to work *and* class on the same day. Asked how much her husband took care of their baby daughter, a mother replied: "He had little time to spend with her. He was going to school nights, and working."[21]

Even without trying to combine work and school, some fathers spent long hours at their places of employment and were not able to pitch in on a regular basis. Still, some tried. Granted there were fathers who stood idly by, even when they were available to take a turn at changing a diaper or feeding the baby, as some of the women's responses indicate, but there were others who endeavored to lend a hand. One man was described as doing "a little bit of everything when he had a chance, when he was at home." Said the mother: "[He would] do anything that I asked, that I happened to need at the moment. He would give her her bottle certain times, and change her diapers. He never gave her a bath when she was an infant. He did later on when she got older and got into the bathtub."[22] Another father was reported to have taken care of the baby "a great deal" and was characterized as an outstanding dad: "I could depend upon my husband to take care of him. I could go off any Saturday I felt like it as my husband is very capable and willing. [. . .] He is an ideal father as far as loving and caring for his children [are] concerned."[23] Still another man was said to be "very good." The mother noted that when the baby was "tiny" her husband "would wash him, change him, and treat him like a King."[24] A third dad "help[ed] very much," by giving the baby a bottle when he cried and getting up "all the time for him at night."[25]

In another family, a mother had to return to the hospital for several weeks after the baby was born. "Except for the time that my husband was at work or at the hospital visiting me he had full care of him. We had a nurse come in the morning and prepare him and my mother stayed with him in the daytime but at night [my husband] had complete care of him." Did he change the baby's diapers and feed the baby or do anything? "Complete care at night. . . . He would [give the baby a bath] for me and as well as I [could]. In fact I think he really enjoyed it." The focal child also had arrived early, which added to the amount of attention that was required. "Being a premature child [also meant that the baby] was quite a care. It was 24 hour care and being so small [he] had to be fed practically an ounce at a time and whenever he would awaken a bottle was stuck in his mouth."[26]

One father did a sizeable amount of feeding and diapering, but also specialized in caring for the baby on weekends. How much did your husband do? "Oh, he used to do quite a bit—give her the bottle, make the formula; he still does." Change her? "Oh, yes." Give her a bath? "Yes." How did you work that out? "Well, on Saturdays when he'd be home, or Sunday when he'd be home, he'd just take care of them." Did he seem to like it? "Oh, he'd love to—he always made the formula for the baby. He's even done diapers."[27]

One especially interesting case involved a father who taught his wife how to diaper the baby and prepare a bottle. "The first time I came home from the hospital, I had to change [the baby], and I was ascared to, so I called my husband, and he said, 'Don't be so frightened,' and I said, 'He's so tiny, I can't handle him,' so he changed his diaper and put powder on him, as though it was nothing to it. He really enjoyed doing it." Did he ever feed him or give him his bath?

> Well, the first night he had to give him his two o'clock feeding, so I had my nipples all sterilized and ready to give him a feeding if he woke up, and so the milk wasn't coming out of the nipples, and he was sucking on the bottle, and I said, "These nipples, the holes aren't big enough," so I was getting nervous, and I started to cry, you know the first time you're so nervous, and I hadn't felt very well anyhow, so [my husband] took the nipples, and he sterilized the needle, and he made the holes bigger, and then he put them in a pan of water, and he boiled the nipples up again, and he had the baby fed in about twenty-twenty-five minutes. [. . .] He is wonderful with a baby, and he loves them.[28]

Another mother reported that her husband "helped a lot," particularly when the baby was very sick. "He washed diapers, and he did bottles. She cried all day long with the colic and everything, and I just couldn't do everything at once. I was so tired out that he had to help." Did he feed her? "Yes, he fed her, and bathed her for me." Change diapers? "Yes, and washed them too." He did that regularly while she was sick? "Yes; oh she got me scared one day, I had to call from work. He used to work [for a company in another town], and I called up there, and he came running home. She was in such pain and everything; I didn't know what to do, so he gave her an enema to relieve her [and] went down to get the doctor. We had quite a session with her that day."[29]

One woman talked about having a "hard child" who "didn't need sleep very much." The doctor said that the baby "required little" in the way of rest. "She would wake with the slightest noise, telephone, door bell. Every time she awoke, he would go in, and he'd hold her and comfort her until finally she fell asleep again in his arms. [. . .] This would go on practically every night." Did he do things like changing diapers, feeding her, bathing her? "He did everything." He did that regularly when she was a baby? "Yes."[30]

A father's flexible schedule and freedom to be home from work in the afternoon also could facilitate a greater connection with the baby. One case entailed a father who was a teacher and was able to be home soon after school let out. How much did your husband do? "He did a lot. He really does a great deal. He takes over a lot, and if at night he hears anyone cry, why he will get up, rather than call me. He is a school teacher, and has the extra time off—you know in the afternoons, and has a chance to play with the children." Did he feed [the baby], change him? "Oh yes, yes. He did a great deal, and those two o'clock bottles, you know, and before we went to bed at night around ten or eleven, and he helped out on that a great deal."[31]

One couple tried to "share" child care—at least to some extent. Who took care of the baby mostly? "Well, I'd say we shared, really and truly, my husband and myself." How much did your husband do? "Bathe him, put him to bed, give him his bottle, get up in the middle of the night. He'd do anything that had to be done." Did he work all day and just see him in the evening, or did he see him in the day too? "Well, he's home at noon time, and he's home early, four o'clock in the afternoon, and for breakfast, so he sees a lot of him."[32]

Finally, in some families, the father's participation in infant care seemed to be viewed as "natural," and not requiring much of an explanation. How much did your husband do? "Oh, he'd feed him at night, when he came home—possibly the six, and quite often the ten, and he was very helpful with all of them—he has done a lot of that." And a few seconds later: Did your husband ever change the baby's diapers? "Oh yes." Give him a bath? "Yes, surely." [33] Another mother offered: "[My husband] would help give [the baby] her bottle and sometimes he would rock her before she went to bed. He would do just about everything. I mean there wasn't anything he wouldn't do or that I could do that he couldn't do."[34] Still another said that she felt her husband "[could] take as complete care" of the children as she could. "[My daughter] is just as much at home with him as if he were her mother.[35]

The New England mother study, in short, indicates that the division of infant care in the immediate postwar period was basically traditional, with many mothers doing the lion's share and many fathers either contributing little or nothing, or "helping" whenever they could. However, the study also indicates that the contribution of some men, albeit a minority, was not insignificant. In certain instances, a particular "problem" (e.g., a mother's hospitalization, a premature baby) set things in motion. In other instances, men seemed to embrace the role of caregiver either because they felt they should, or because they simply enjoyed being directly involved.

―――――――――――――――――

Although World War II came to an end in 1945, it was not too long before Americans were fighting again. The Korean War—a battle between North Korea and South Korea, with China weighing in on the side of the North and the United States weighing in on the side of the South—began on June 25, 1950, and reached a decisive (though not an end) point when a cease fire was declared on July 27, 1953. (Technically, the Korean War is still going on. The "cease fire" was not a "truce.")[36] More than 5.7 million U.S. soldiers served in the conflict—about one-third of the number that had served in World War II. Close to thirty-four thousand Americans died in battle, and more than one hundred and three thousand were wounded.[37]

The Korean War was, in part, a by-product of World War II. The line drawn at the thirty-eighth parallel, separating the two Koreas, was a compromise reached between the United States and Russia after the defeat of Germany and Japan.[38] The Korean War also was the first military conflict of the Cold War and the first limited war in the atomic age.[39] The significance of the Korean War reached far beyond the borders of East Asia. After World War II, the United States reduced its armaments, as it had done after other wars, but doing so made the country, in the words of one historian, "woefully unprepared to fight even a limited war." With the beginning of hostilities in Korea, the United States expanded its defense budget and stayed on high alert throughout the fifties and beyond.[40] In World War II, Americans were afraid of being firebombed and overrun by invading armies. In the fifties, they lived in fear of seeing a mushroom-shaped cloud erupt over their hometown.[41]

The Korean War was an unpopular war, with many in the United States wondering whether it should have been fought at all. Although soldiers who died in battle were honored for their sacrifice, the war itself and the president who chose to wage it were not held in the highest regard (at least at the time). One father, whose two sons had been killed in action, refused to accept the Medal of Honor awarded to one and the Silver Star bestowed upon another, because he felt that President Truman was "unworthy to confer them on [his] boys or any other boys."[42]

Despite its long-term impact, the Korean War has sometimes been called America's "forgotten war."[43] It was anything but forgotten, however, by the men who served and the loved ones they left behind. To them, the three years of conflict were "unsettled times" with "unfortunate effects."[44] Men who served in Korea, similar to those who served in World War II, often were away from home when a daughter or son was born; indeed, numerous men were in the armed forces in the fifties and absent from the home, even if they were not stationed in a war zone. A father in the military might earnestly believe that he was "making the world better for his child," but he also might understandably wonder whether, as far as his kids were concerned, he was simply "a thing that goes away to war."[45]

How much did men care for infants during the Korean War era, when America's birth rate was rising sharply? Again, it is hard to say. Child-rearing prescriptions cannot be taken as a direct reflection of men's conduct, and researchers at the time, like researchers before, often paid scant attention to father-infant interactions. Still, there are data that can be brought to bear. An in-depth study of eight New Haven families' transition to parenthood in the early 1950s found a wide range of caregiving levels among the men. Some fathers engaged in no care, others engaged in some, while at least one did a fair amount.[46] A man who worked as an architect had only a "small part in child-care routines but shared experiences with the child in play and in the interchange of teaching and learning." When his wife was ill, he "took over [the] care adequately."[47] Another man, a disabled veteran who was unemployed for long stretches of time, "participated to a considerable extent in child-care routines" from the time his son was three months old to when he was a year and a half. Assuming "many aspects of the mothering role," he "diapered and fed [the baby], rocked him to sleep when he was ill, and played with him."[48] Overall, the researchers found that "even the most demanding and adult-oriented fathers did take some active part in the rearing of the child," and that "seven of the eight fathers were involved to a considerable degree" by the time the children were two years old.[49]

In another project—supervised by the same researcher who directed the New England mother study—forty California married couples were interviewed and asked how they organized the care of a kindergarten-age child (the "focal child") when that child was an infant (that is, in the early 1950s). A limitation of the California couple study is that it relied on a much smaller sample than did the New England mother study. A strength is that it gathered information from both women and men. In individual interviews, fathers were asked: "How much did you help to care for [the focal child] during his [or her] first year of life? Feeding? Toileting and cleanliness?" Mothers were asked (separately): "How much did your husband help to care for [the focal child]?" (Note the use of the word *help.*) The interviews with the mothers were conducted by a woman. The interviews with the fathers were conducted by three different men.[50]

The fact that men's reports were included in the study probably increased the level of infant care that was found, since men and women in the United States tend to display an egocentric or credit-taking bias when they describe their division of child care. (An egocentric or credit-taking bias also may have affected the study of the eighty-five New York City men, discussed earlier.)[51]

One thing that is unfortunate about the data in the California couple study is that questions about the father's level of infant care were often handled in a perfunctory manner and occasionally with a lack of seriousness. The interviewers, for example, might laugh along with a father when it was suggested that infant care was something to be avoided. Also, although the interviewers sometimes probed for additional details, they did so haphazardly; and when they did probe, they sometimes disparaged the replies they received. One father was asked whether he enjoyed spending time with the baby. "Oh, very much so." You did? "Oh, sure." You like babies? "Oh, absolutely."[52] (Similar kinds of problems beset the New England mother study, though not as much.)

As with the New England mother study, the answers provided during the interviews were content-analyzed by coders working with the original team of researchers. When it came to evaluating the men's level of infant care in the forty families, the division of labor was broken down, once again, into eight categories. The categories and results (percentage of fathers within each category) were as follows: did no infant care (10.0 percent); very little infant care (7.5 percent); some infant care (27.5 percent); quite a lot (17.5 percent); between quite a lot and equal with mother (15.0 percent); equal with mother (12.5 percent); between equal with mother and more than mother (5.0 percent); more than mother (5.0 percent). Thus, about one-fifth of the fathers did either no infant care or very little infant care; about a fourth did some; a third did quite a lot or somewhat more than that; and just under a quarter shared equally with the mother or did more than the mother.[53]

These figures suggest a higher level of father involvement with infants than was found in the New England mother study, which, when it came to infant care, focused on the late 1940s. One possible explanation for the difference is that fathers were included in the California study but not in the New England study. Another is that the California families were middle to upper middle class, whereas the New England families were both middle class and working class. Finally, a high number (30 percent) of the California fathers were students; some were enrolled full-time.

Among the fathers who contributed the least amount of infant care were fourteen men who (according to the transcripts) were in the armed services around the time that the focal child was born. The proportion of fathers in uniform is noteworthy. If one estimates the number of men on active duty in the fifties and considers the impact of their absence from the home, one would have to conclude that understanding American fatherhood in the postwar era requires an appreciation of the military demands being placed on men at the time.

Asked what he was doing at the time his wife was pregnant, one father said that he was in the navy when his daughter was born and that she was sixteen-and-a-half months old by the time he got back. How much did you help care for the baby during that first year? "Not much," the father replied with a laugh. "I sent her dolls." What about when you came home, did you help with diaper changing and feeding? "I avoided the diapers as much as possible." With respect to feeding, the father said that his daughter did not seem to want to "have much to do with [him]" early on. "We just sort of had to get used to each other for a while."[54]

Another man also mentioned being in the navy when his daughter arrived. The mother said that her husband did not return from active duty until the child was nine-and-a-half months old. How much did you help care for the baby? "Oh, not very much. By the time I got home, . . . [she] would sleep through the night. Oh, I'm sure I fed her, I can't remember changing her—I guess consciously I would try to avoid that." (The father's sarcasm prompted the father and interviewer to laugh.) What about when the baby cried? "My wife handled it."[55]

Men who were in the military and stationed far away were unable to help with infant care, even if they were inclined to. A few, however, did what they could when they could. One father, who was on leave for the first two-and-a-half weeks after his son was born, tried to pitch in during the brief time that he was around. He had to "get over being afraid to touch [the baby]," according to the mother, but, once he became accustomed to picking his son up, he did his share. "[When our son] was about a week old, [my husband] took over during the day time. I was up most of the night with him, so during the day time I think he probably changed him as much as I did." The mother went on to say that her husband was "just wonderful with all three of the babies when they were little."[56] A second father was in an aviation cadet program for about the first seven months of his son's life and "was completely separated" from his family during that time. His wife said that she was "surprised" at how much he "helped" after he returned: "He'd never been around children, there weren't younger ones than him in his own family, and he seemed to take over naturally—playing with him and caring for him, etc."[57] Yet another father, who served in Korea and was often away during the summer (possibly in the reserves), made it a point to participate in child care when the opportunity arose. "I think I have always taken a lot of care of [my son]. For example, I have always made breakfast for [my wife] so that she can take it easy. I've always helped with changing him. I've always read to [him] even before he could. I sang to him and patted him . . ." The mother concurred: "Oh, [my husband] did everything. Changed his diapers, and . . . I had . . . some trouble nursing him, . . . I had infected breasts, and he helped make formula. Oh, [he] just did everything."[58]

Also among those unable to provide much infant care were twelve men who, because of their jobs or schooling, had limited time to be around the house. Interestingly, it was often the mother rather than the father who mentioned the men's competing responsibilities. One father proudly announced to the interviewer that he "did as little as possible." Because his daughter was breastfed, he said he had "nothing" to do with feeding her— or, as he put it, "with *that*"—and he added he would only on "rare" occasions change her diapers. "I think it was more the wife's duty than mine," he exclaimed, with a laugh. When his wife, however, was asked how much her husband did with their daughter during the first year, she agreed that her husband only "took [the baby] occasionally," but, rather than declare that it was her duty as a mother to care for the baby, she said her husband's lack of involvement was because he "wasn't around most of the time." She explained that he was "gone at school or work all day and [their daughter] wasn't up very long in the evening when he was home."[59] A second father reported that he did "very little," changing only "a few diapers" and pitching in with only "a few feedings." The wife concurred that her husband did not do very much ("he didn't help at all"), and mentioned, too, that she thought "he was kind of afraid of the idea of a baby." But she also said that he was a student whose family time was confined largely to the weekends.[60]

Because the fathers and mothers were interviewed separately, a couple might offer conflicting perceptions on who did what. One mother, for example, said that her husband was "very cooperative in everything" and "would do anything [she] asked him to do." Queried about the kinds of things that she wanted his help with, she alluded to "changing the baby," "washing the floor," and "doing the wash." But she also said that she would not ask her husband to help with the nighttime feedings: "I didn't ask him to get up at night, because I felt I could take a nap during the day, and I—I felt that [requesting his help] was an imposition." During his interview, however, the father claimed that he "took [his] crack at the two o'clock deal," meaning that he *did* get up for nighttime feedings. Interesting, too, is that while the mother said that she did not want to impose on her husband in the middle of the night, because he had to get up for work the next day, the father attributed his involvement to the fact that his work hours were flexible: "Most of the men have to get up a little earlier than I do and get home a little later, and they never get home at noontime, [. . .] so [. . .] I spend more time than the average father."[61]

A couple's division of child care could be a source of tension. One man, who confessed he did next to nothing, suggested that taking care of the baby was more his wife's "job." It was not, he insisted, that the couple explicitly defined the division "as such," but that "it just worked out that way." He said that he would step in during "emergencies" ("where of course she's busy or she's occupied"), but those occasions were "more the exception you know, certainly than the rule." The mother offered a different account and expressed disappointment in the level of care her husband provided. Interestingly enough, she did not directly condemn her husband, but straddled the fence between severely criticizing him and not leaving too negative an impression with the interviewer about the kind of father she believed he was. There was, however, no mistaking that she was peeved: "I don't mind work, but sometimes it just seems I can't manage, and if I don't get any help then, I get kind of angry! (laughs)."[62]

A father who was in the service when his wife gave birth to a baby girl but discharged when his daughter was about seven months old, admitted that he did not care for the baby "as much as [his] wife thought [he] should've." He noted that the daughter was born with a congenital heart defect and was, in his words, "hyperactive" and difficult to "quiet down." He agreed he may not have pitched in as much as his wife would have liked, but he also tried to convey that he did not disregard his daughter's needs, pointing out, for example, that he sometimes drove her around in the car to calm her down. The mother, in her interview, said that the daughter was "a very active child" and that caring for her restricted how much time the mother had to do things: "I'd always been used to going, coming and going as I wanted to, not having to stay home, and she cried so much I was so worn out all the time that sometimes (mother laughs) I felt like giving her away." The mother made no reference to what the father might have contributed, but said, with anger implied: "I felt tied down 'cause he never helped. [. . .] He never offered to help, one bit. So I felt like I was a prisoner."[63]

What about the fathers who were more involved; how much did they contribute and why? Among the more active fathers was a man who, in the course of the interview, referred to Benjamin Spock's advice in *Baby and Child Care* on how to respond to a crying baby. The implication was that he was at least aware of the pediatrician's prescriptions. When the father was questioned about how much he "helped" care for his daughter during the first year, he said that he was not sure that he could compare himself with other fathers, but that some of his parental activities included changing her diaper, feeding her, and preparing her meals. Did you do this regularly, or did you do it when your wife was busy with something else? "Well . . . [it] might have gone to twice a week—and I'd feed her, say, twice a week. The diaper chang[ing] would be [determined] more or less [by] whoever was there or handy, and I used to do it quite often. More like a team approach to the children." The wife, in turn, said that the father "helped a great deal." What kinds of things would he do? "Oh, I guess just whatever needed to be done. He'd change the baby if I needed it or feed the baby—just about anything that I didn't feel like doing at the time. [W]hy if I asked him to do it, he'd do it."[64]

Another father, whose wife suffered from postpartum depression, also seemed to do a fair amount of care. "[My wife's depression] meant extra number of hours of daddy looking after the boy." How much did you help care for the baby in the first year?

> Well, I wanted to do my share. In fact, I feel very strongly that a child who has only one parent in attendance on him is only getting half of what he deserves in the world. This doesn't mean his daddy has to cater to him all the time either, but I think—like any other activity in a home situation whether you're out camping or whatever, you get together and get the jobs done that are the dirty nasty things so you all have time for a little more relaxation.

When the mother was asked how much her husband had helped care for the baby, she responded: "A great deal. I don't know how he survived that strain, he was just wonderful about it."[65]

One couple with twin boys talked about the challenges of caring for two babies simultaneously. "We were quite tired because we really didn't [know] much about raising children," reported the father, "and . . . with twins it sort of doubled the effort [. . .]" Asked about how much help he provided, the father replied,

> I naturally had to do quite a bit more, even though we did have a maid. [. . .]
> They were *quite* difficult at first. We had . . . a very serious feeding problem. [. . .]

Both of us had to get up to feed the babies . . . and so I put in quite a bit of time . . . and I obviously feel that it's a very good thing. I'd advocate this for many fathers because . . . my own feelings are that you get to know your child much better. I feel I'm much closer—know the twins better than [I do my younger son] because when [he] came along, it was easier from me to take the twins . . . take care of them, let my wife take care of the baby . . . and as a result I did very little of the, you know, diaper changing and feeding and everything else with [my younger son] but with the twins it was almost constant and I did . . . a lot with them.

When the mother was asked as well whether her husband helped with the twins, she answered, "Yes, yes." (She also explained that she did not want the maid they hired to do too much, especially during the night.)[66]

Another father, also asked about how much care he provided, replied,

Uh—well my wife has never been too strong, so I—I just sort of started help-ing out at the beginning, it sort of worked out to 'bout where she would take the two o'clock feedings during the week when I had to go to work, and I would take them on weekends, when I could rest a little bit. And, in the mat-ter of toilet training, later on, when he got out of diapers, uh—the pediatri-cian told us the way to get him started is to watch me [go to the bathroom] . . . so we used to spend our time in the bathroom together [. . .] (laughs).

The interviewer then inquired about whether the father's care was limited to weekends and helping out and changing him "now and then," to which the father replied: "Um-hum. Yes. I changed him now and then [. . .] Here again it's awfully difficult to separate it from what has happened after we had more children: it's gotten to be routine; she's handling one, and I'm handling the other." When the mother was asked how much her husband helped with the baby, she said,

A great deal. [. . .] Of course I don't have any experience with how interested other men are, but I do remember that my husband was interested in every little detail, as far as that baby was concerned. Almost to the point (laughs) where he probably looked a little silly at times. I mean, I really think that his taking the pictures that they take within the first twenty-four hours, taking that to the office with him—I'm sure that everybody he came in contact with heard exactly how much that baby weighed, and when that baby opened its eyes. [. . .] The nurse that we happened to have was . . . interested in having him change—in teaching him how to change the baby, and he sure acted like he was interested—in fact, he was very much interested in making formula, and—not as interested in getting up at two a.m. That's about the only thing is—although he did it, but he wasn't enthusiastic about that part, but the rest of it, he [was] very interested in.[67]

Again, it appears that the division of infant care at the beginning of the baby boom was more varied than might be assumed, if one were to rely simply on what child-rearing experts were saying. Although it is true that mothers generally spent more time with newborns and almost always shouldered the major responsibility for a baby's day-to-day well-being, more than a few men in the postwar era participated in infant care.

NINE

"Adventure . . . Begins at Home"

In the late 1940s and early 1950s, the United States faced a housing shortage, particularly in urban areas. During World War II, millions of Americans
had left rural towns and villages to seek work in plants and factories, which
tended to be located in or near cities. When the war ended, the country
entered a period of high inflation, and jobs continued to be more available
in the nation's metropolises than elsewhere, prompting another period of
migration. Making a living became increasingly difficult.[1] So did finding a
place to live. With limited options, veterans and their families doubled up
with relatives and friends, creating a tight if not uncomfortable situation
all around. Responding to the shortage, the U.S. government built wooden
structures that resembled military barracks. In some neighborhoods, rows
of prefabricated metal buildings—semi-circular-roofed Quonset huts—were
erected.[2]

The gap between demand and supply soon caught the attention of the
private sector. Among the entrepreneurs who quickly saw an opportunity,
the most astute perhaps was William J. Levitt, who became the leading manufacturer of houses in the United States. Levitt had gone into the building
trade with his father and brother in the late 1920s and had experimented
with mass-assembly building techniques. During the war, he was a navy
Seabee (assigned to a construction battalion, or C.B.) and discovered just
how efficient these techniques could be. Levitt figured that streamlining the
process—boosting the use of precut materials and systematizing on-site fabrication—could mean huge profits. He was right.[3]

Two years after he was discharged from the service in 1945, Levitt began
construction on 17,447 homes approximately thirty miles east of Manhattan, converting land that once was a potato farm into residential terrain. By

1951, his first suburban development, eventually named Levittown, was complete. Levitt would go on to build similar communities in New Jersey and Pennsylvania, increasingly relying on—and refining—the principles of mass production, as the automobile industry had done in the early 1900s. He soon became the "Henry Ford of housing."[4]

Time magazine did a cover story on Levitt, and reported that builders throughout the country were duplicating his techniques. "The biggest housing boom in U.S. history," in the magazine's estimation, was "changing the way of life of millions of U.S. citizens." As to what was changing, the news report said, "[Families] are realizing for the first time the great American dream of owning their own home. No longer must young married couples plan to start living in an apartment, saving for the distant day when they can buy a house. Now they can do it more easily than they can buy a $2,000 car on the installment plan." One veteran, who had been living with his family in a one-room dwelling, told *Time*, "Getting into [a Levittown] house was like being emancipated."[5]

Buying a suburban home may have been the fulfillment of the "American dream" for some and "emancipation" for others, but not everyone was given a chance to share in the vision. Black families generally were excluded from postwar temporary housing and, in keeping with real estate practices in place at the time, were denied the option to live in Levittown and most other suburban neighborhoods. Levitt justified his policy of discrimination as a matter of economics, saying that opening Levittown to minorities would amount to financial suicide. "As a company," he said, "our position is simply this: we can solve a housing problem, or we can try to solve a racial problem, but we cannot combine the two."[6] Other builders and realtors pushed the same logic. So did the Long Island newspaper, *Newsday*, which tagged the activists who opposed discrimination "local troublemakers" and the organizations that supported their cause as "communist dominated" and "communist inspired." *Newsday* was especially miffed that the individuals and organizations fighting for racial justice linked their goals to the war: "Their sneaky tactics are demonstrated by mimeographed hand bills which they slip under doors at night in Levittown. Addressed to Levittown veterans, one of these rants, 'Remember how we were told that we were fighting for the four freedoms which were supposed to be for ALL. We believed in it then and we believe in it now. BUT IT'S TIME WE SAW IT IN REAL LIFE!'"[7]

The phrase "four freedoms" alluded to beliefs that President Franklin D. Roosevelt had spoken about in his State of the Union address on January 6, 1941. "We look forward to a world founded upon four essential freedoms," FDR declared. "The first is freedom of speech and expression. . . . The second is freedom of every person to worship God in his own way. . . . The third is freedom from want. . . . The fourth is freedom from fear."[8] The protesting veterans were appropriating the rationale used by the U.S. government to support fighting in World War II to justify what they saw as their inalienable right to live wherever they desired.

Regardless of what the editors at *Newsday* thought about the activists' tactics, the war did make it possible for hundreds of thousands of veterans to purchase the houses that Levitt and his fellow contractors had built. The G.I. Bill not only provided former soldiers with funds to enroll in school, but it also enabled them to buy property with little or no down payment. Blacks who served in World War II had been denied access to colleges when they tried to gain entry. Now they were being denied access to affordable housing. How were the liberties they had fought for being guaranteed?

Opposition to integration often went well beyond newspaper editorials. Blacks who ventured into white neighborhoods routinely were terrorized, vandalized, or beaten. One well-known case is that of Harvey Clarke, a bus driver, who in 1951 tried to move into an apartment in Cicero, Illinois, a suburb of Chicago:

> First, the police stopped him by force [telling him he had to have a "permit"]. . . . With help from the NAACP, Clark got an injunction barring the Cicero police from interfering with his moving in and ordering them "to afford him full protection from any attempt to so restrain him." As he moved in, a month after his first attempt, whites stood across the street and shouted racial epithets. That evening, a large crowd gathered, shouting and throwing stones to break windows in the apartment Clark had just rented. Prudently, the Clark family did not occupy the apartment. The next night, the mob attacked the building, looted the Clarks' apartment as well as some adjoining flats, threw the Clarks' furniture and other belongings out the window and set them afire in the courtyard below. Local police stood by and watched. The following night, a mob of 3,500 gathered and rioted. [The Governor called out the National Guard, and] . . . 72 persons were arrested, 60 were charged, 17 people were hospitalized.[9]

Although the racist policies of Levittown and other white-dominated suburban communities continued throughout the postwar era—in 1960 not one of the Long Island's Levittown's residents was black—other suburban neighborhoods were more open. For the most part, however, these were spaces that white families had either fled or never tried to occupy in the first place.[10]

Nonetheless, in the late 1940s and early and late 1950s, the number of black suburbanites grew significantly, with gains being greatest in the Northeast and Midwest. Central to the expansion was the increase in incomes. "Rising earning power laid the foundation for a greater black middle class and expanded the number of families who could afford well-built housing in the suburbs," reported one historian. "Unlike earlier status-based black elites, this new group was larger in size—representing 20 percent of the black population—and economically situated in the same income and occupational categories as members of the white middle class."[11]

In the cover story on Levittown, *Time* called the new suburban neighborhoods "fountains of youth"— not because living in Levittown made the old feel young again, but because older people were nowhere to be found. "Few of [the] more than 40,000 residents are past 35," *Time* reported. "Of some 8,000 children, scarcely 900 are more than seven years old. In front of almost every house along Levittown's 100 miles of winding streets sits a tricycle or baby carriage. In Levittown, all activity stops from 12 to 2 in the afternoon; that is nap time. Said one Levittowner last week, 'Everyone is so young that sometimes it's hard to remember how to get along with older people.'"[12] In short, the families of baby boomers and their not-much-older siblings pretty much dominated the place.[13]

The "place" included a number of special features. Levittown homeowners had the benefits of parks and "countless" playgrounds, baseball diamonds, handball courts, six "huge" swimming pools plus a "kiddy" pool, shopping centers, and "60 odd fraternal clubs and veterans' organizations."[14] All the houses had yards, where children could romp and where barbecues and gardens could be enjoyed. Interestingly, the floor plans for the first houses that Levitt built—the 1947 Cape Cod models—encouraged families to orient their activities not toward the back but toward the front. The kitchen, for example, was to your immediate right or left as you walked in the door, allowing the homeowner (while cooking or washing dishes) to keep an eye on children's activities on the sidewalk and beyond. Underlying this design "was the assumption that the street was the center, the playground, the focus." Interaction within and between families thus was vigorously promoted, making Levittown an ensemble in both word and deed. At least that was the idea. (Later-built homes—ranch models, for example—situated the kitchen toward the backyard.)[15]

The prominent writer and philosopher Lewis Mumford conveyed something of this idea in an article he wrote for *House Beautiful* in 1952. Although a harsh critic of suburbanization (he felt it reduced rather than enhanced primary group ties), he was an ardent advocate of the benefits of open space. "In the days to come," he proclaimed,

> the family will be a reality of incomparably higher importance than it has been for the last century. And why should it not? For as our modern age reorients itself toward life, it will bring to the culture of the family a wealth of scientific and imaginative interests that our ancestors did not possess. Many of us will find that *adventure*, even more than charity, *begins at home*. Our homes and communities will, even as physical structures, express the central importance of family. . . . They will be designed to make love possible.[16]

Much has been made of how suburbanization altered postwar family life. But studies of suburbia in the 1950s show that, although people's everyday living changed somewhat, "their basic ways [remained] the same," and that "many of the changes that [did] take place were desired before the move." In other words, "Rather than forcing the new suburbanites to behave in certain ways, . . . the new environment *permitted* them to behave exactly the way they wanted."[17]

What was true for suburbanites overall was also true for fathers in particular. That is, although suburban living changed men's relationship with their children to a certain degree, their basic ways of relating to their kids essentially were the same. It has sometimes been suggested, for example, that the morning and evening commutes of postwar suburban fathers left them with little time to interact with their families during the week. Although this may have been true for some fathers, it was not true for all, or even most. Evidence indicates that the move to the suburbs "did not cut into the time available for family activities." Indeed, it appears that suburban living "provided *more* opportunity for parents and children to do things together."[18]

First, men who were employed in the 1950s generally were away from home between 8:00 a.m. and 6:00 p.m. on weekdays, which allowed them to spend time with their families in the morning and evening. In addition, the overall length of their average work week was significantly lower than it had been in generations before (e.g., forty hours per week in 1950 compared to just under fifty hours per week in 1920 and close to sixty-two hours in 1890), which meant more free time on weekends.[19] Second, the journey between home and work "did not change significantly" among those who moved to the suburbs.[20] Third, not every suburban father commuted to the city; some worked in their suburb's surrounding area. Thus, while 80 percent of Long Island Levittown fathers may have traveled back and forth between their homes and Manhattan, as *Time* reported, this was not the general pattern, even in New York.[21] A study that looked at not just at one suburb in the metropolitan area, but several, found that only 40 percent of the commuters worked in the central city; the rest worked in the suburbs.[22]

"These data," concluded one sociologist, "sorely strain the classic image of the suburbanite as the dutiful commuter bound forever to the 7:02 [morning train] and a desk in the big city."[23] The findings also challenge the stereotype that, in the fifties, suburban fathers' commutes invariably precluded their having much contact with their children at the end of the workday. It is true that suburban men did not spend *as much time* with their children as did their wives, especially if their wives were full-time homemakers, as was often the case. And it is true that fathers' time with children could be fleeting, especially on commute-to-work days. But it is inaccurate to suggest that fathers living in postwar suburbia spent hardly any time with their kids. Like men and women who today work outside the home for large chunks of the day and for most days of the week, suburban fathers in the fifties had to make an effort to be with their children and invest in their development, but they were not, uniformly and without exception, the absentee parents they often have been made out to be.[24]

The suburban mothers (introduced in chapter 8), who were interviewed in the early 1950s, support and illustrate the basic point. When these women were queried about their husbands' relationship with their children—and specifically about their relationship with their kindergarten-age daughters or sons (the "focal" children for the project)—they were expressly asked about the warmth between their husbands and children (e.g., the quality of their affectional bond); the family's activities at the end of a workday (e.g., "What happens when your husband comes home?"); and the activities the fathers and kids shared (e.g., "What kinds of things do they do together?").[25]

Some mothers spoke of men who had only minimal attachment to their children, while others talked of fathers who were significant figures in their children's lives. For example, close to 14 percent of father-child relationships were said to exhibit "not much warmth" or to be "ambivalent," while almost 50 percent were said to show high levels of warmth (rated one, two, or three on a nine-point scale). Approximately 22 percent of the relationships were "extremely warm" or were one notch below that level. When it came to the father-child emotional connection, the results again were by and large positive. Hardly any fathers were characterized as "cold," while approximately 60 percent were reported to display high levels of affection. Exactly 29 percent showed "lots of affection" or were one notch below that level.

When asked about what happened at the end of the day, the mothers indicated that there were indeed fathers who got home late several nights a week and did not interact much with their children before they went to bed. This was especially true for men who worked two jobs or attended school in the evening. In a few cases, the children were already asleep when the father walked in the door. If the kids were in bed but still awake, they might come out to say goodnight, or the father might go in to give them a hug. Several mothers also said that, because of their husbands' late or erratic hours on weekdays, the children's time with their dads was often reserved for Saturdays and Sundays. Here, too, there was variation, with some fathers interacting little and others interacting a fair amount.[26]

One father—an unusual case—"never ha[d] time at night" because of the work he often did at his desk after dinner, and he regularly traveled on weekends, which further removed him from the household. "I have had the raising of [the children] most of the time," the mother said. "There are occasions maybe once a month or once every two months that he will get down on the floor and wrestle with all of them." The mother reported that her husband did put the children to bed now and again, but only "very, very seldom."[27] Although distant and aloof fathers were represented in the study, the majority of them got home from work early enough to devote time to their children—yet how much time was available depended on when the focal child went to sleep and the presence and age of siblings. Granted, the men's family time during the week may have been restricted, particularly when compared to that of their wives, but the majority of fathers made an effort to be actively engaged with their daughters and sons. In fact, 32 percent of the fathers were said to provide a level of child care that ranged from "moderate" to "quite-a-bit."[28]

The patterns observed in the New England study appear in other studies as well. In 1953, more than one thousand Florida high school sophomores living in and around the Tampa area were queried about their married parents' participation in child-rearing activities. About half of the families were working-class, with the median education of the parents being about nine years. In two out of five families, the wife worked outside the home.[29]

The students were asked, in addition to other things, who cared for the children when they were sick and who saw to it that they got dressed. Responses were broken down by whether the father, mother, teenage son, or teenage daughter carried out the activity. It was found that, in general, "fathers participated less in activities concerned with the early training of the children than those concerned with their later socialization." The most striking disparity, in terms of the father's vs. the mother's care, centered on children's clothing. Fewer than 6 percent of the fathers individually (i.e., not conjointly with other family members) saw to it that their children wore the right clothing, or were involved in getting their daughters and sons dressed. In contrast, more than 60 percent of the mothers individually carried out these activities.[30]

As rigid as the division of labor may seem to be, however, there were also patterns that suggested greater flexibility. Little to no difference was found in the proportion of fathers and mothers who individually taught their children facts and skills (75.5 percent vs. 76.9 percent) or who individually punished their kids for doing wrong (76.0 percent vs. 77.4 percent). Significant numbers of fathers, as well as mothers, individually helped their children with their school work (42.9 percent vs. 56.6 percent), and individually made sure they got to bed on time (45.7 percent vs. 71.9 percent). Almost all the mothers individually cared for their children when they were sick, which is not surprising. Interestingly enough, however, more than one-third of the fathers individually cared for sick children, too.[31]

In the New England families, a father's return from work typically was a dramatic moment in the day. Virtually every household had a welcome-home ritual, which could be very imaginative, usually followed a customary blueprint, and frequently set the tone for the evening. Rare was a home where a father's entrance was not marked.[32] One mother described her husband's arrival as "bedlam" for the couple's three girls. "You'd think they hadn't seen him for six years. Course, usually they're all out front. At nighttime I try to get them around the house, say that daddy will be home in a few minutes, watch for him and sometimes if he's not going out that evening, he puts the car in the yard and they jump in at the foot of the driveway with him. And, oh, lord, I always know the minute that he arrives. 'Here comes Daddy' then they all run, you know."[33]

After dinner, the father usually went out to chase the children around the yard, or they might plant some flowers in the garden. The mother acknowledged that her husband recently had "been rather tied up with work and of course his lodge affairs," but that he "always manage[d]" to find "five or ten minutes to romp around with them or something at night after supper." When she was asked whether her husband helped with the evening meal, she offered, "As far as his dinner time at night, he serves them, gets their meals ready for them, couple of servings and hands them out. [. . .] [Also] there are nights when I've gone out, sometimes if we're late with dinner at night, he does the dishes and puts the children to bed and things like that. So he has time to play with them before they go to bed."[34] (The suburban New England mothers also were asked at one point whether their husbands ever stayed with the children when they, the mothers, were out. About 46 percent said their husbands stayed alone with the children either "[more than] occasionally," "fairly often," or "frequently." About 21 percent said their husbands "practically never," if ever, did. In this latter group, about 2 percent said that staying alone with the children simply was "not his job" or that he "didn't want to do it.")[35]

Another mother, asked how her five-year-old son greeted her husband upon his arrival, replied: "It's dangerous to be in the path between the boy and the door. He races to the door. He opens the door and my husband hops out and calls—'Hi son,' and [the boy] climbs all over him and that's the general procedure night after night." During dinner, the father "more or less converse[d]" with the children (besides a son, the couple had a daughter) and played with them afterward, but not for as long as the father would have liked: "It is one of his great regrets that he doesn't have sufficient time with the children." Still, she said, he generally "put the children to bed at night [. . .] and he roughhouses with them and tells them a little story."[36]

A third mother talked about how roughhousing was central to her husband's evening interactions with their daughter and son: "Oh they just fall all over each other, and after supper we often have what you call 'rough time.' I can't play rough. The living room is just shambles. They play bicycling and all the rest of it. Handstands. That is what we call rough time. So it has quite a connotation [commotion?] when [my husband] comes home, that I just couldn't give them, and it is wonderful that [my husband] loves them that much. There is a wonderful comradery between the two of them and their father."[37]

For one father and his three daughters, the conversations at the end of the day were especially important. "He speaks to [the focal child] and kisses her and if she has been bad she tells him right away—as a matter of fact, he speaks to the children before he speaks to me. I don't know, we have come to the conclusion that they may be jealous if he pays too much attention to me." After dinner, the father "play[s] with [the children] a lot." Moreover, said the mother, "He always puts them to bed, he tucks them in and gives them their baths, especially in the summer when they stay up a little later." The mother indicated that recently the father had been working "day and night" and "[didn't] have time to go through that bathing business now." Nonetheless, she said, "He does show them a lot of attention. He brushes their hair at least every other night and they seem to get a lot of enjoyment out of that. They brush his hair [too], at least [the focal child] does, she loves to do that."[38]

A television set often figured prominently in the New England families' early evening activities. One mother reported, "Well the minute he sees him, of course, he'll run to him and kiss and come right up and he'll read the funnies to him and he'll sit on his lap and watch television until supper is ready. [. . .]"[39] Another remarked, "He always greets his father. He'll either put his arms up to be hugged or he'll kiss him or he'll say—here's my Daddy." Before bed, the father and son sometimes "just sit and talk and watch TV together."[40] A mother of two girls and a boy declared, "They all run to meet him. They all throw their arms around him and oh, it's always a wonderful reunion." After supper, "Well, they always go and watch television together."[41] Another mother talked of how her five-year-old daughter would "hide under the table or buffet" when her husband came home, while he pretended not to know where she was, and that after dinner he would watch television with his two children, holding one or both in his arms while the other sat on a footstool beside him.[42]

In 1950, only 9 percent of American households had a television set. By 1951, when the women were first interviewed, the number had skyrocketed to 24 percent. One year later, when the study was concluding, the figure shot up again to 34 percent. The ascent would continue. By 1960, televisions could be found in nearly 90 percent of American households.[43] On this count, the families in the study were unique. Approximately 90 percent of the mothers said that they had a television set in their home. And in almost 77 percent of the cases, the set had been purchased at least a year before.[44] They were not that different among *suburban* homeowners, however. In Levittown in the early 1950s, a television—installed in the living room—came with the purchase of the house. In postwar suburbia, watching television rapidly became a central feature of family and community life.[45]

Much the same as fathers and mothers at the turn of the twenty-first century have had to deal with the Internet and the impact it might have on their children, fathers and mothers in the early 1950s were confronted with the advent of television and its effects. A Cambridge, Massachusetts, study, carried out in 1950–51, found that children spent, on average, two-and-one-half hours watching TV on weekdays and three-and-one-half hours on Sundays. (For some reason, Saturdays were not asked about.) Mostly, they watched "with family members," which could include a parent or a brother or sister. Seldom did youngsters watch TV by themselves. (Part of the reason may have been that in 84 percent of the homes the TV was in the living room. Levitt's sense of where a TV should be placed was widely shared.) When asked, "Has TV made it easier or harder to take care of the children at home?" 54 percent of the mothers said that TV made it easier, while

33 percent said that it made no difference at all. Although 20 percent reported conflict with children over turning the TV off when it was suppertime, and 36 percent acknowledged conflict at bedtime, for the most part the mothers felt that a TV was a worthwhile addition to the household. Beyond citing the entertainment and educational value of the broadcasts, the women said that they liked having a TV because it kept their children "quiet" and "off the streets" and also prevented them from "harassing their parents." One commented that having a child in front of a TV was "just like putting them to sleep." According the study's author, "Parents very commonly use[d] TV as a 'pacifier.'"[46]

Lower-income families were less likely to own a television set. Those who did appreciated the fact that watching TV was a relatively inexpensive form of entertainment. For black families in the south, owning a TV could be a godsend. As one black mother explained, she lived in a town where blacks were barred from going to the movies, and so "for enjoyment" she stayed home and watched her "second-hand television."[47]

Middle- and upper-income families generally were the first to own a TV, but some made conscious choices *not* to buy one because they were "concerned about the effects of TV on family life and school work" or they "in general disapprove[d] of TV."[48] In the suburban New England study, a mother of a boy and a girl exclaimed, "I am bitterly against TV. We won't have one if I have my way. We very, very seldom have the radio on—Sunday afternoons for a musical program—or we turn on the record player for 'Peter and the Wolf' records, like that, 'Winnie the Pooh,' but we aren't a radio family. There are weeks that the radio is never turned on. And I bitterly oppose the business of sitting in front of a TV. He [the focal child] has never seen a TV in his life." Although she was able to restrict her younger child's access to TV, she was less successful when it came to her older child. "Our daughter," the mother confessed,

has [watched television] because a little girl across the street has TV and last year she had an urge to go there, quite a bit and we limited her to three times a week—one hour—and the newness soon wore off and she hasn't asked. And now we hear her airing our views as her views on television. But perhaps the day will come when they have programs that I consider good enough to be of value to a child. But just now I think there are other things that are more important to them.[49]

Some parents, though they owned a TV, had regulations on how often it could be turned on. In one family, the rule was that the children were not allowed to watch any shows after dinner during the week (but Friday nights were okay), and they were limited to one hour of TV in the afternoon. "I've heard of boys and girls having trouble with their eyes, and I think an hour is enough," said the mother. "My husband agrees with me there, he told me he wants it limited to that."[50] In another family, the prohibitions were more severe.

> Television is strictly taboo. We have a television set but she doesn't watch it at all. [. . .] I disapprove of a child seeing some of the stuff that's on the air, and on a day like this I think it is practically a sin to come in and look at television instead of being outdoors. There has been no battle, no battle at all—every other kid runs home like a bat out of hell to watch *Howdy Doody*, but she has never asked to see it. When we first got it there was a problem, but she is an active child, and she just can't sit still long enough for one thing, and for another thing we made fun of it—we said we thought it was a poor way of getting your entertainment, that you should be able to entertain yourself. [. . .][51]

Significant is the mother's reference to watching *Howdy Doody*, by which she meant *The Howdy Doody Show*, an afternoon television program that targeted preschool and elementary-school children. Notable for its opening ("Say kids, what time is it?" "It's *Howdy Doody* time!"), *The Howdy Doody Show* was one of the most popular TV programs of the postwar era, beginning its run in December, 1947 and ending in September, 1960. The suburban New England mothers mentioned *The Howdy Doody Show* when they spoke about their husbands' coming home, because the men's return at the end of the day sometimes coincided with when the show was being broadcast. Other shows might overlap as well with a father's arrival, depending on when he walked in the door.

Given the choice between saying hi to dad and continuing to watch television, some kids opted for the TV.[52] "Oh nothing [happens when he comes home]," said one mother. "Usually they're very interested in television and they pay no attention to anybody."[53] In other families, children briefly greeted their fathers and then turned their attention back to the television: "My husband comes home about quarter to six, and [the focal child] has time to say hello to him, and then run back to *Howdy Doody*."[54] On occasion, dinner time might be scheduled around particular TV shows: "We eat at five, and then [the focal child] goes in to watch *Howdy Doody*."[55] Or watching TV might supplant other father-child activities: "After we eat [his father] takes [the focal child] up to bed and talks with him, or he might get him to read him a story. But since the television, especially there hasn't been too much story telling."[56]

Although mothers in the New England study did not bring up the point, in some American homes it was not the children's attachment to television that stood between them and their father, but a father's love of TV that made for an absentee dad. A New York mother complained to psychologist and columnist Rose Franzblau that her husband "never plays" with the children—or even eats with them—preferring instead to pick up his plate and sit "in the living room with the TV set."[57] A Massachusetts mother indicated that her spouse, a World War II veteran and former prisoner of war, would come home only after "stop[ping] with the boys to have a cocktail" and then, upon arriving, "immediately" eat his dinner and "retire to the TV and to sleep."[58] (An interesting counterpoint is the New York father who forbade his wife and child to watch television. He referred to it as "a jukebox in the living room.")[59]

Needless to say, the children in the study were not simply inanimate objects to be noticed or ignored. Rather, they were social actors who regularly demanded—and often successfully got—their dad's attention. Fathers also were not unemotional beings. Men enjoyed it when they were raucously welcomed and bristled when they were placed second after the TV. As one mother mentioned, "The only time she doesn't [run to the door] is when there is a particularly good television program, . . . and he will feel very insulted."[60]

It is noteworthy that, in the open-ended interviews, the New England mothers typically did not talk about their husbands contributing to routine child care at the end of the day. Though some referred to husbands who did the dishes after dinner or other household or child custodial work, for the most part, they highlighted their husbands' play activities with the children. This may reflect an assumption on the family's part that because the men had just gotten home from their jobs, they should not be expected to perform additional jobs when they got home. But we should not forget that the mothers also were at their jobs throughout the day, too—doing housework and taking care of the kids—and they were still at their jobs in the late afternoon or evening (e.g., preparing dinner) when their husbands arrived. The fact that the mothers typically did not talk about routine child care also could have been a function of how the questions to them were posed. The women were expressly asked what happened when their husbands came home, not what happened throughout the evening. (Yet in the standardized survey, one-third of the mothers did report that their husbands provided a level of child care *overall* that ranged from "moderate" to "quite-a-bit.")

What about weekends? When the suburban mothers were asked about the kinds of things their husbands did in general with the children, they often launched into a discussion of the fathers' activities on Saturdays and Sundays. Men fortunate enough to have these days off from work, when their kids were not in school, had the opportunity to strengthen their ties with their daughters and sons—and many took advantage of it. For the most part, the weekends, like the weeknights, were devoted to joint leisure activities. Woodworking, repairing, and gardening appeared to be especially favorite father-child pastimes.[61]

"[My husband] loves to make things and so does [the focal child]," said one mother. "They both go in the barn, and he will fix his bike, or make a car, or something, and [the focal child] will be thrilled to death, or he will put a plane together, that is what they generally do."[62] Exclaimed another, "He does as many things with her as he possibl[y] can. When he is home, she is always around him. Working down in the basement, he is just as pleased to have her have a hammer and nails, as if she were a little boy. He has always had her work in the yard with him and help him all she can although at times she is not much help."[63] Said a third, "Oh they do a lot of yard work together, and hammering nails, and raking up the lawn, and they do the shopping. [. . .] He loves to get the car checked at the gas station. [My husband's] uncle has a jeep there and he rides around in that and he has a grand time."[64] And a fourth said, "[My husband] has a woodworking shop downstairs and he has taught the kids how to hammer and that. [. . .] [My husband] is never too busy to stop and explain what he is doing to the children. He is the most patient man with them." (The mother said also, "There is a very tender relationship there that I think is very, very beautiful. She would turn to him as quick as to me.")[65]

Coincidental with suburbanization was the growth of Little League baseball. Founded in 1939 in Williamsport, Pennsylvania, Little League baseball expanded during the war and became especially popular soon thereafter. Baseball for kids was not a new idea. Organized youth baseball leagues had existed as far back as the nineteenth century and were common in the 1920s and 1930s, when they were viewed as antidotes to juvenile delinquency. But none of these earlier leagues came close to matching Little League's enrollments.[66]

During the war, Little League baseball grew by only a few teams, because men who might volunteer as managers and coaches were in short supply and equipment and cloth for players' uniforms were harder to obtain. After the war, though, the program picked up. In 1946, the number of leagues, each with several teams, increased to 12, all in Pennsylvania. By 1948, the figure jumped to 94 in several states. By 1949, it had increased again, to 307. One explanation for the growth was veterans' interest in the program. As one observer put it, "Fathers returned from the battlefields of Europe and the Pacific to families whom they may not have seen for several years. Having played the game as boys, many American men knew enough about baseball to teach it to their sons. So Little League provided a way for families to become reacquainted."[67]

It was in the 1950s, however, that Little League baseball really flourished. From 1951 to 1956, the number of leagues rose from 776 to more than 4,000—a fivefold increase in as many years. By the end of the decade, the program had more than 5,000 leagues. Many of the teams sprouted in suburban developments, which were being built at a record pace.[68]

Not everyone was enamored with Little League baseball. Some believed that playing baseball on a regular basis was unhealthy for youngsters and forced them to "specialize too intensively in one activity." One father of a ten-year-old thought the arguments against Little League baseball amounted to "pure spinach." Said the dad, "I look forward to my Brian playing his eighteen games with the Exchange Club next year." A number of other parents appeared to disregard the critics as well, given the Little League's rate of growth.[69]

Fathers were pressed into helping in a variety of ways. Not only were they recruited as managers and coaches, but they also were called upon to construct and maintain the fields. Mothers got involved, too, and not just at the concession stands. In 1951, a "minor league farm system," where younger kids prepared to move up to the Little League level, had 870 women (as "supervisors") in addition to some 11,000 men. (The Little League program itself was open only to boys from eight to twelve years of age. Girls were excluded from the teams in the 1950s, though one girl masqueraded as a boy to join.)[70]

As often happens when kids engage in competitive games supervised by adults, the action in the stands could be more dramatic than what was happening on the field. Watching their children play and hoping they did well made for a lot of anxious parents. One father at a Little League World Series announced, "My wife's a nervous wreck." A mother exclaimed, "My husband only shouldn't have a stroke."[71] The games, which lasted six innings as opposed to the nine innings that professionals played, were frequently scheduled at twilight, giving fathers who worked the 9:00 a.m. to 5:00 p.m. shift (or something close to it) an opportunity to see their sons perform. Fathers who were at work or commuting in the early evening, however, might miss a child's baseball heroics. The dad who "wasn't in the stands when I hit a home run" or who "didn't see me pitch a no hitter" became a problem for kids in fact—and in lore. The stories that baby boomers often tell about their parents frequently include references to dads who were "not there" for "the big game." The fact that their fathers may have been at most of their games could be eclipsed by their not being at the one game (or games) that, *to the child,* was particularly special. Organized youth sports increased the rate at which these special moments—and disappointments—occurred.[72]

The growth of Little League baseball also contributed to the symbolism associated with the game of playing of catch.[73] Often portrayed today as a father-and-son drama on a suburban-backyard stage, playing catch actually has had three different meanings over the years.[74] In the early twentieth century, a common justification for playing catch was that playing with a child would help a father to get to know that child. Playing catch thus was placed in the same category as playing marbles or playing hide-and-seek.[75]

With the burgeoning of the Little Leagues, however, playing catch became an instructional activity. Learning how to throw and catch "correctly"—which generally meant "not like a girl"—ascended in importance.[76] Recalling what it was like to grow up in the 1950s, one former Little-Leaguer asserted, "I was lucky to have a dad who cared enough to teach me the basics."[77] Said another, remembering the same,

> I'm 8 years old and I'm playing Little League Baseball for the first time and my dad's the coach! It's my first tryout/practice and it's an exciting, confusing, scary affair, with what seems like hundreds of boys. . . . Later at home, my father informs me that there are two boys on the team who throw like girls, and that I, unfortunately, am one of them! By the next practice, he tells me, we will have corrected that problem. That evening, with glove and cap securely in place, I anxiously face my father on the front lawn. And we play catch. For quite a while, I am concentrating, working hard to throw correctly ("like a *man*"), pulling my arm back as far as I can and snapping the ball overhand, just past my ear. When I do this, it feels very strange—I really have very little control over the flight of the ball, and it hurts my shoulder a bit—but I am rewarded with the knowledge that *this is how men throw the ball.* If I learn this, I won't embarrass either myself or my father.[78]

In the late twentieth century, in the wake of a new fatherhood movement that emerged in the 1970s (mirroring somewhat a movement that emerged in the 1920s), playing catch appeared to take on yet another meaning. The game was still about play and instruction, but it had been transformed, at least for some, into a celebration of fatherhood: "There's something about a father playing catch with his son that is just so pure, so iconic, so American."[79] Baseball also came to be defined by its association with the symbolism of the game: "Baseball is fathers and sons playing catch, lazy and murderous, wild and controlled, the profound archaic song of birth, growth, age, and death."[80]

Little League baseball was not the only parent-organized/child-centered activity in the fifties. Many children also participated in other kinds of sports leagues (e.g., swim meets), enrolled in after-school classes (e.g., piano lessons), and joined youth groups (e.g., Girl Scouts). For some fathers and mothers, their children's extracurricular commitments got to be all-consuming. Reminiscent of the concerns that parents today have about "overscheduled" children, fathers and mothers in the fifties sometimes wondered whether the orchestration of childhood perhaps had gone too far. One set of parents, whose daughter took synchronized swimming classes three days a week and was a Girl Scout, feared that the organized activities were beginning to detract from family life. "I'm all for Scouts," said the mother. "But too much of it is for the birds." A neighbor of the couple recalled how one little girl who wanted to play with another little girl discovered, after checking *her* personal calendar, that the only time she had free was between 2:00 p.m. and 4:00 p.m. on Thursday.[81]

Organized youth activities could provide more opportunities for a father and child to relate to one another (e.g., with the father serving as a coach or as an authority on how to throw a ball). For a father whose time at home might be limited to begin with, however, a child's busy schedule could create barriers that stood in the way of his being more involved.

PART FOUR

TEN

Picture Imperfect

On April 9, 1959, the ABC network televised an episode of *Leave It to Beaver*—a situation comedy about June and Ward Cleaver and their two sons, Wally and Theodore (a.k.a. "The Beaver")—that centered on Ward's military service during World War II. The episode, titled "Beaver's Hero," begins with Wally, age thirteen, and Beaver, age eight, in their bedroom getting ready for school.[1]

Beaver tells his brother that he is learning about the World War in class. "Which World War?" Wally asks. "You mean there was a lot of 'em?" Beaver replies. "Well, there was two of 'em that I heard about," says Wally. "I think it was the one with President Eisenhower in it," Beaver suggests. "Yeh," Wally answers. "That's the one that Dad was in, too."

June comes by to tell the boys that they should hurry up or they will be late. "Was Dad and Mr. Eisenhower both in the same war?" Beaver asks his Mom. "Why, yes, Beaver, why?" "I don't know. But it's something having your father in the same war with the President."

In the next scene, Beaver is in a classroom where his teacher, Mr. Willet, is concluding the day's history lesson and asks whether anyone has something to add. Beaver raises his hand and says that his father was in World War II. This prompts another student to announce that his uncle was "almost a General." "Is that so?" says the teacher. "Yes, sir, he was a Sergeant," the boy responds, seemingly unaware of the span between the two ranks. The girl seated next to Beaver chimes in to declare that her father was a hero and that he had an airplane with his name on it—one that "he didn't even have to give back, unless he wanted to," she proclaims.

The school bell rings, signaling the end of the class, but the students continue to talk about the war as they get up and go out into the hallway. Beaver is asked whether his father was a general. "Uh, I don't think so,"

Beaver answers. "Then what was he?" "Well, he was a *hero*." "Aw, you're just sayin' that, Beaver. I'll bet he wasn't a *real* hero." This from the girl whose father was said to be a fighter pilot. "He was, too," Beaver replies. "He's got a great big trunk out in the garage and it's full of guns and hand grenades and all kinds of stuff he took off enemy guys."

Unconvinced, the daughter of the war-time airman accuses Beaver of being a liar. "I am not!" shouts Beaver. "You better take that back!" Hearing the ruckus, Mr. Willet approaches the group, is apprised of what Beaver has told his classmates, and expresses his confidence in Beaver's integrity. "Well, I'm sure if he said that, we can count on it being the truth. Can't we Theodore?" "Um, yes sir," Beaver replies. The scene ends with Mr. Willet telling Beaver that, if his father does not mind, "it might be very interesting to bring some of those souvenirs around for the class to see." That evening, he phones Beaver to ask him to bring in the souvenirs the very next day, and cautions him not to include anything dangerous. "You'd better check with your father," he advises.

The television audience soon discovers—or already has figured out—that Beaver does not actually know what his dad did in the war. Beaver simply has assumed that when he looked in his father's footlocker he would find evidence that Ward was, indeed, in combat.

Beaver and his brother are next shown opening Dad's "old war trunk" and pulling out a T-square and a surveyor's telescope or transit. Not understanding what the instruments are, Beaver speculates (hopes) that they were used to track enemy planes. Their dad, seeing the boys in the garage, goes out and asks if he can "join the fun." At this moment Beaver asks what, for him—and for many other baby boomer children—was the crucial question, at least when it came to their fathers and World War II. *"How many guys did you kill in the war, Dad?"*[2]

Ward hesitates for a moment, then slowly replies, "Well, Beaver, I didn't kill anyone. I was in the Seabees." (He was, in other words, assigned to a Navy construction battalion, as was William J. Levitt, of Levittown fame.) When Wally asks what the "telescope" was for, Ward tells him it was used to survey whether the ground was level. "Gee, Dad," says Beaver, "was all you did in the war was to see if the ground was level?" It is beginning to dawn on Beaver that his father is not the fighter he had made him out to be.

Back in their bedroom, Wally admonishes his brother for getting himself in such a colossal jam. "Heh, Beaver, what did you have to go and tell all the guys that stuff about dad bein' a war hero?" "Well I didn't mean to tell 'em so much, but I just started talkin' and it all slipped out," Beaver confesses.

"How was I supposed to know that all dad ever did in the war was measure dirt?" "Yeah, well, it must have done some good," Wally answers, "or dad wouldn't have done it."

Without "guns and hand grenades and all kinds of stuff" to bring to class, Beaver concocts a "goofy idea" to forge a wartime letter from his dad—a letter that would falsely substantiate Beaver's assertion that his father was a combat veteran. ("Dear June, I'm sitting here with my submachine gun waiting for the enemy to attack. . . . Me and all the other brave men have been on Wake Island for two weeks. This morning I volunteered for a dangerous patrol and captured sixty-five prisoners single-handed, and the General said, 'Good going, Ward.' He said he wished he had more men like me. I have to finish now as I hear the enemy approaching. . . . P.S. I got your last letter and I'm very sorry that you lost all those medals that I sent you.")

After giving it some thought, Beaver decides to abandon the letter idea. ("Wally, I don't think this is going to work.") Soon thereafter, however, Ward happens to come across the letter, which had been left in the boys' room. He puts two and two together, and quickly calls Beaver's teacher to ask that he *not* put Beaver on the spot in class. When the subject of war comes up in the history lesson the next day, the topic of the discussion "miraculously" has shifted to the War of 1812. Beaver is spared the embarrassment of explaining why he cannot produce his father's World War II souvenirs.

Being the wise and all-knowing father he has been scripted to be, Ward leaves work early so he can to talk to Beaver about the letter as soon as he gets home from school. "Beave," he asks, "why would you write a thing like that? . . . Why would you make up stuff about me and the war?"

"Well, I knew you were in the war, and I figured if you were in the war you just had to be a hero."

"Well, I'm glad you think of me that way, Beaver, but, you know, there were thousands of us in the service who weren't heroes."

"Yeah. But a guy likes to think his father was."

"Well, I can understand that, but I guess you're just gonna have to take your old dad the way he is."

"Yeah, but when I looked in your trunk, I thought there'd be guns and hand grenades, instead of just tools and stuff."

"Well, you see, Beaver, they put a man where they thought he could do the best job. Now I was an engineer, so I could do a better job with tools than I could with guns. There were lots of fellows in the Seabees who were heroes, but I just didn't happen to be one of them."

"You know, Dad, I'll bet you were the best dirt leveler in the whole Seabees."[3]

The creators of *Leave It to Beaver* guessed that "Beaver's Hero" would touch a chord, and they were probably right. A decade and a half after World War II had ended, what fathers had done in the war remained a salient issue. Recollecting his own youth experiences in the fifties, a man talked about going on a twelve-hundred-mile family road trip in 1958, when he was six years old, and how, while on the journey, his dad talked about the war and his involvement with the Red Ball Express, a convoy that trucked fuel and supplies across Europe in the fall of 1944. The father's wartime exploits made the son proud. He noted, too, how the war was a central theme in the games that postwar children played.

> As a kid in the 1950s, our favorite sport was baseball, but our favorite game was war. We called it playing war. . . . Our war games were stocked with weapons. Toy pistols, rifles, and machine guns were plentiful. . . . We used real helmets, but only if they were battered and not a prized possession of our fathers. . . . Most of the authentic stuff we kept in a clubhouse museum. We had great respect for these items, especially the battered helmets, a rusty Japanese sword, about one dozen empty shell casings, and a grenade (defused). High-ranking captured enemies were required to wear a German helmet, which my older brother found buried in a cousin's backyard. No one wanted to wear the dread[ed] helmet because an actual German soldier had worn it. Worse, he probably died wearing it.[4]

What effect "Beaver's Hero" may have had on viewers is impossible to assess. (We may wonder what the Red Baller's son thought of the episode, since he admitted to being an avid fan of the show.)[5] We do know that, in 1959, close to forty-four million homes (86 percent of all households in the United States) had TV sets.[6] Numerous families watched "Beaver's Hero" on the night that it aired.

The influence of the series itself is even more profound—and also more intricate.[7] *Leave It to Beaver* occupies a special place in America's collective imagination. It is a show that some believe veritably defined television in the fifties. It is not alone in this regard. When people talk about the fifties—and particularly when they talk about fatherhood in the fifties—they often mention *Leave It to Beaver*, along with three other family-oriented sitcoms: *The Adventures of Ozzie and Harriet*, *Father Knows Best*, and *The Donna Reed*

Show. Over the years, these shows—which caricatured *and* celebrated white, middle-class, suburban domesticity—"have become synonymous with our ideas about family life during that period."[8] They are said to reflect "the postwar emphasis on men's family roles."[9]

Why would these shows be identified with fatherhood in the fifties more than others? Some might hypothesize that it is because they dominated the television schedule back then. But did they? *The Adventures of Ozzie and Harriet*—the fictional account of a real-life family, Ozzie and Harriet Nelson (musicians by trade), and their sons, David and Ricky—started as a radio series in 1944, was first telecast in October 1952, and ended in September, 1966. *Father Knows Best*—a program about Jim and Margaret Anderson and their children, Betty, Bud, and Kathy—also started as a radio series (in 1949), but did not become a television sitcom until October 1954, ending its run in April 1963. (The 1959–60 season was the last to use original episodes. Thereafter the network broadcast repeats.) *The Donna Reed Show*—in which Oscar-winner Reed played Donna Stone, wife of Dr. Alex Stone and mother of Mary, Jeff, and later Trisha—began in September 1958 and ceased production in September 1966. *Leave It to Beaver* first aired in October 1957 and continued to September 1963. Thus, two of the shows that have come to symbolize fatherhood *throughout* the fifties did not go on the air until the *late* fifties, while one did not begin until the *mid*-fifties.[10]

Then there is the question of ratings. How popular were these shows when they were broadcast? During its entire run, *The Adventures of Ozzie and Harriet* never made it into the top twenty-five in the Nielsen ratings. *Father Knows Best* was canceled at the end of its first season, but was picked up by a rival network when viewers complained. Still, it did not rank in the top ten until its last new-show season (1959–60). In every other year, it was ranked either thirteenth (1958–59), twenty-third (1957–58), or did not make it into the top twenty-five. Neither *The Donna Reed* Show nor *Leave It to Beaver*, which also was dropped by one network and picked up by another, ever ranked among the top twenty-five.[11]

This is not to suggest that the shows were unpopular or that no one watched them. Given that the three major television networks (ABC, CBS, and NBC) had a virtual monopoly on what people could see during prime time (compared to the number of stations and choices available today), a show that ranked as low as twenty-third, as *Father Knows Best* did in the 1957–58 season, could receive a fairly hefty rating of 27.7, which meant that, over the course of that season, 27.7 percent of TV households tuned in.[12] Significant, too, is the fact that on four different occasions—in 1956, 1958, 1959, and 1960—one or more of the cast was featured in *TV Guide.*

The U.S. Treasury Department also commissioned a special episode of *Father Knows Best*, which was distributed in schools throughout the country to promote the purchase of government savings bonds. No doubt this contributed to the show's notoriety and demonstrated also that people did not have to watch the show to know about it. Finally, *Father Knows Best* was one of those rare TV series to end at its peak. (Actor Robert Young tired of the role, having also played Jim Anderson on the radio.) But however popular *Father Knows Best* may have been, on the Monday evenings (at 8:30 p.m.) that it was broadcast in 1959–60, the show's highest-rated season, it enticed fewer viewers than the family sitcom that immediately followed it, *The Danny Thomas Show* (originally titled, and hereafter referred to as, *Make Room for Daddy*), about which I will have more to say in a moment.

If *The Adventures of Ozzie and Harriet, Father Knows Best, Leave It to Beaver,* and *The Donna Reed Show* were not necessarily the most popular shows of their time, why are they accorded so much attention today? One answer, simply, is reruns. Their resurrection, every now and then on afternoon or late night TV, accounts in part for why these programs are collectively remembered.[13] The fact that these shows are routinely mentioned in both popular and scholarly articles, as well as in textbooks and on Web sites, also helps to explain why they stand out. They have their "historians," so to speak—people willing to tell their tale.[14] Because of their repeated mention, our memories of these shows are very sharp, perhaps even sharper and "fresher than memories of real life."[15] In other words, people may have come to think that *The Adventures of Ozzie and Harriet, Father Knows Best, Leave It to Beaver,* and *The Donna Reed Show* are representative of what TV viewers mostly watched in the fifties. Some may go so far as to believe that the fictional households in the shows were what families in the fifties were "really" like.[16] So, what were people watching, besides these four shows? To put the shows of the late fifties in the proper historical context, we need to go back and see what was being broadcast in the early fifties.

The most popular evening shows at the dawn of the television age were dramatic anthologies and comedy variety shows: for example, *Texaco Star Theater, Fireside Theatre, Philco TV Playhouse, Kraft Television Theatre, Your Show of Shows, The Colgate Comedy Hour,* and *The Toast of the Town* (later called *The Ed Sullivan Show*). The earliest shows to center on families, fathers or mothers, grandfathers or grandmothers (as well as parental figures), children, and domestic life in general were the following, in chronological order by their debut dates: *The Goldbergs* (1949), *I Remember Mama* (1949), *The Life of Riley* (1949), *The Aldrich Family* (1949), *Beulah* (1950), *The Trouble with Father* (a.k.a *The Stu Erwin Show*) (1950), *I Love Lucy* (1951), *Life* with *Luigi* (1952), *My Little Margie* (1952), *Bonino* (1953), *Life with Father* (1953), *Make Room for Daddy* (1953), *My Favorite Husband* (1953), *My Son Jeep* (1953), *Sky King* (1953), *The Wonderful John Acton* (1953), and *Lassie* (1954). Between 1955 and 1960, another set of shows, often focusing on fatherhood, premiered. These were: *The Adventures of Champion* (1955), *Brave Eagle* (1955), *Circus Boy* (1956), *Fury* (1955), *Professional Father* (1955), *My Friend Flicka* (1956), *Bachelor Father* (1957), *The Real McCoys* (1957), *The Rifleman* (1958), *Bonanza* (1959), *Dennis the Menace* (1959), *The Dennis O'Keefe Show* (1959), *Dudley Do-Right* (1959, a cartoon series), *The Many Loves of Dobie Gillis* (1959), *The Andy Griffith Show* (1960), *Guestward Ho!* (1960), *Harrigan and Son* (1960), *My Three Sons* (1960), and *Peter Loves Mary* (1960).[17]

Historians of fatherhood often have limited their analysis to domestic comedies or dramas. Seldom are westerns, action shows, or animated series looked at. But if these shows depict fathers or father figures, there is no reason that they should be excluded. Why should we assume that a child who watched television in the 1958–59 season would not draw conclusions about "what it meant to be a father" from the story lines presented in *The Rifleman*, as opposed to *Father Knows Best*? *The Rifleman* was pitched as "the saga of Lucas McCain, a homesteader in the Old West struggling to make a living off his ranch and make a man out of his motherless son, Mark."[18] The fact that *The Rifleman* was set in the "Old West" and not in the fictional "Midwestern community of Springfield" (circa late 1950s), where the Andersons reportedly lived, does not make the fatherhood messages in *The Rifleman* irrelevant. TV shows that are set in the past almost always are anachronistic, relying more on strained contemporary relevancy than on historical accuracy to connect with their audience. Producers and advertisers would not have it any other way. Incidentally, more people watched *The Rifleman* than *Father Knows Best* in 1958–59, when the two shows were ranked fourth and thirteenth, respectively.[19]

Significant, too, were the number of shows depicting single fathers or father figures. In addition to *The Rifleman*, the count included *My Little Margie, Bonino, My Son Jeep, Sky King, The Wonderful John Acton, The Adventures of Champion, Brave Eagle, Fury, Circus Boy, My Friend Flicka, Bachelor Father, The Ed Wynn Show, Jefferson Drum, Bonanza, The Dennis O'Keefe Show, Dudley Do-Right, The Andy Griffith Show,* and *My Three Sons*.[20] The most popular shows, besides *The Rifleman*, were *Bonanza, The Andy Griffith Show,* and *My Three Sons*. Bonanza was "set in the vicinity of Virginia City, Nevada, during the years of the Civil War." In the series, "Widower Ben Cartwright was the patriarch of the all-male clan and owner of the thousand-square-mile

Ponderosa Ranch. Each of his three sons had been borne by a different wife, none whom was still alive."[21] *The Andy Griffith Show* and *My Three Sons* told the story of two widowers, one a small-town sheriff and the other an aviation engineer. Single TV fathers in the fifties almost always were widowers, as opposed to divorcees.

Some of the shows that debuted in the fifties did not last very long, while others grew to become legendary. *Bonino*, starring opera star Ezio Pinza as a widowed father raising seven kids, was on the air for only three months. *I Love Lucy* was—and is—one of the most renowned shows of all time. *Make Room for Daddy* ran from 1953 to 1965. The show got off to a slow start but caught on in its fourth season. In 1957–58, 1958–59, and 1959–60 (when *Father Knows Best*, *Leave It to Beaver*, and *The Donna Reed Show* were also vying for attention), *Make Room for Daddy* ranked second, fifth, and fourth, respectively. The title of the show was based on nightclub-entertainer Thomas's real-life experiences as a father. Thomas said that when he came home after being on the road, his children had to move to different bedrooms to "make room for Daddy."[22] Curiously, *Make Room for Daddy*, set in the city rather than suburbs, is rarely cited today as an example of how fathers were portrayed in the fifties. Although it was a very popular show at the time, without recurring reruns it has been largely forgotten.

Looking beyond *The Adventures of Ozzie and Harriet*, *Father Knows Best*, *Leave It to Beaver*, and *The Donna Reed Show* reveals that several shows in the fifties portrayed men in caregiving roles. The presence of shows depicting single fathers/grandfathers, or father/grandfather figures, indicates as well that, while the breadwinner father married to the homemaker mother was a powerful symbol at the time, it was not the only family scenario found on the small screen. Fatherhood images in the fifties also were not limited to suburban dads. *The Goldbergs* was set in an apartment in the Bronx. *I Remember Mama* was about a family living in San Francisco at the turn of the century. *Brave Eagle* focused on a Native American chief and his foster son in the southwest during the mid-1800s. *Lassie*, in its first three seasons, often pictured Gramps Miller dispensing sage advice to his grandson, Jeff, on their small farm. In *Circus Boy*, Joey, a professional clown, guided twelve-year-old-orphan, Corky, as they picked up stakes and moved from town to town. These are but a few of the shows that deviated from the white-picket-fence ideal. There also was, at the beginning of the fifties at least, more racial and ethnic diversity. The Goldbergs were Jewish. The Hansens (*I Remember Mama*) were Norwegian. Bonino was Italian, as was Luigi, whose best friend was a father. Beulah was a black woman working as a maid for a white family. (Ethnic and racial stereotypes, needless to say, were the norm.) Then, "as the decade wore on, TV families became almost exclusively white as well as middle class." Schedulers appeared to "assume" that "*everyone* would want a family like the Nelsons or Cleavers."[23] The homogenization of family life on TV thus was more characteristic of the *late* fifties.

How were fathers in particular portrayed? Some have suggested that fathers were uniformly depicted as incompetent.[24] Others have contended that the portrayals varied.[25] The weight of the evidence supports the second view. First, there was a class effect. In general, working-class TV fathers were presented as less competent than middle-class TV fathers,[26] although the correlation was not perfect. The father in *The Trouble with Father*, for one, was middle-class and inept. But overall, working-class fathers were more likely to be the brunt of the joke.

Second, there was a vintage effect. *I Remember Mama, The Life of Riley, The Aldrich Family, The Trouble with Father, Life with Father,* and *Make Room for Daddy* all tended to depict fathers as inept. All of these series also debuted in the early part of the fifties (between 1949 and 1953). By contrast, comparable family sitcoms, which began later, tended to depict fathers as competent. This latter group included *Father Knows Best, Leave It to Beaver,* and *The Donna Reed Show.*[27] Although some scholars have classified Jim Anderson of *Father Knows Best* as a bumbler, the argument has been made that he was just the opposite—"superdad incarnate,"[28] "the symbol of the ideal American father."[29]

Critics in the fifties complained about how fathers were being portrayed, much as they do today. Highlighted for their negative portrayals were *I Remember Mama, The Life of Riley,* and *Make Room for Daddy.*[30] *Father Knows Best* also was targeted, but it was the radio version, not the TV version, that bothered a few. In its transformation from audio in the early fifties to video in the late fifties, Jim Anderson became the mid-twentieth-century poster guy for "New Fatherhood." "Robert Young proves a TV dad doesn't have to be stupid," reported *TV Guide* in 1956.[31] Perhaps therein lies the reason that *Father Knows Best* and, to a lesser degree, *Leave It to Beaver* and *The Donna Reed Show* continue to reside in our imagination of fatherhood past. The men on these shows were designed to be liked. They were manufactured "heroes."[32]

It has often been assumed that the images of families in the fifties shown on TV mirror not only how parents and children behaved then, but also what occupied their thoughts. The nostalgia frequently associated with the fifties can be traced to these images as well. For some, especially those who never directly experienced the era, TV-based recollections constitute the most striking memories that they have of the time. However vivid these images are, and however genuine they seem to be, *Leave It to Beaver* and the other TV shows that have come to be synonymous with the fifties did not represent all families.[33]

Most glaring is the fact that the casts of the shows were almost always white. This was not an accident; minorities were deliberately and systematically excluded. Exceptions proved the rule. In the 1958–59 season, one writer for *The Donna Reed Show* said he "felt like Abraham Lincoln" because he insisted that "a black face" appear in a segment. If you look very closely at one of the episodes in that cycle, you will see a black woman and child in the *background* of a scene in a department store. In 1965, the same year that President Lyndon B. Johnson signed the Voting Rights Act, the show's writers thought of creating a part for a black neighbor boy, but the idea was jettisoned because the network and sponsor feared the show would be "blacked out in the South"—an ironic choice of words. The part eventually was offered to a white actor.[34]

Millions in the fifties thus may have watched TV shows en masse, but how they *perceived* the shows could be very different. A white child might identify with Beaver or Wally (or with Betty, Bud, Kathy, Mary, or Jeff, etc.). He or she might imagine being a sibling or the kid next door. A black child, on the other hand, might contemplate something else entirely. The man who recalled what it was like as a kid to play war ("our favorite game") was the son of parents who had served in black units in World War II. (His father was in the 3,438th Quartermaster Corps; his mother was assigned to a postal battalion.) Sharing his fascination with TV as a youth, he remarked,

> Like many American kids, I watched television nearly every day of my life. I knew then that there were two Americas, but I didn't really care. All of the characters in my favorite shows were white. Lassie and Timmy didn't need colored friends to make me watch. The only colored kids on television were Buckwheat and Stymie, and they were nothing to me. Such a personal embarrassment were they that it never crossed my mind to ask for more colored characters on the *Little Rascals* or any other show. And as much as I wished to be Beaver's pal, he did have a friend whom he called Whitey. I dreaded to think what Beaver and his buddies might have called me.[35]

The moral lessons of a TV show thus were in the eye of the beholder. Some children might very well have felt a certain kinship with the Cleavers, Andersons, and Stones. But other children, though they enjoyed the shows, might understandably have been troubled by the stereotypes on the screen ("I dreaded to think. . . .").

Largely absent as well in the TV shows of the fifties were tales of domestic abuse. If one were to think of the shows' plotlines as perfectly accurate portraits of everyday life, one might conclude that all postwar fathers were honest gents who, every now and then, were stymied by unfamiliar situations (e.g., not knowing what to do when their pregnant wives went into labor) or puzzled by their kids' antics ("Beave, why would you write a thing like that?"). It is certain, however, that thousands of men in the fifties—men who, to neighbors and friends, might appear to be above reproach—bullied and maltreated family members, creating an atmosphere that was more suffocating than serene.

Accurate statistics are difficult to come by because researchers in the postwar era for the most part turned a blind eye to domestic violence. It was not until the 1960s and 1970s that child abuse, spousal battering, intimate partner rape, and child sexual victimization were empirically examined. The earliest U.S. studies revealed that domestic violence was a social problem of immense proportions. The first nationwide survey, carried out in 1975, found that more than 2 million Americans had been beaten up by a spouse, and as many as 2.3 million American children had been beaten up by a parent. (The study focused only on married couples and children growing up in two-parent households, and it did not measure the number of family members who were psychologically abused or sexually terrorized.)[36]

There is little reason to believe that the figures would be lower in the 1950s. Indeed, if anything, they probably were *higher*. The 1940s and 1950s, said one historian, "represented the low point in public awareness of family-violence problems and in the status of child-protection work within the social work profession."[37] In other words, victims of abuse were less visible to the helping professions during the 1940s and 1950s than they were in the decades that came immediately before or after. High marriage and low divorce rates in the 1950s also suggested trouble for victims. Men and women in the postwar era were more likely than men and women today to marry individuals who were abusive (thinking "they will change once the knot is tied") and less likely to leave spouses who battered them or their children (in part because of the greater economic dependence of wives on husbands then). These mate-selection and retention dynamics worked to entangle victims in a web of abuse and keep them trapped for years.[38]

Although violence in the home was something that researchers in the postwar era generally ignored, the plight of at least some abuse victims was known to social workers and other therapeutic professionals. Among the letters written to the psychologist and columnist Rose Franzblau were a number of pleas for help. The letters, of course, do not capture the full range of the kind of abuse that family members experienced, but they do provide an inkling of what was going on behind some of America's picture-perfect front doors.[39]

A mother of two—a boy, eleven, and a girl, seven—wrote to say that her husband had "severely beaten [her] in front of the children" and "made [them] all into a very unhappy family." She said she called the police several times, but was offered only the idea that she take the father to court. She did so, but was told then that as long as he financially supported the family there was "very little they [could] do" to assist her. "I am in no position to obtain a lawyer," she said, "and I need help desperately."[40]

A twenty-four-year-old woman, who had been married for four years and was the mother of two children, spoke of the cycle of violence that she had been repeatedly subjected to.[41] "We had many arguments where my husband punch & slap me about. Whenever we ma[k]e up, [h]e becomes a different person. Always kissing me i[n] front of anyone & calling [me] pet names. I can't understand him. If I express my opinion & he disagrees, [i]t becomes a nightmare. Hateful words are said." When the woman complained to her father- and mother-in-law, they refused to believe her but simply said that their son had "always been a good boy."[42]

A woman talked of being married to a man who was a "good provider," but who, as of late, had taken to "beating [their twelve-year-old] daughter again." (Note the *again*.) "The other day she was fooling around with her cousin, having a grand time but getting under her father's skin. He leapt up from his chair and beat her without her knowing he was coming at her." The wife said she tried to get her husband to read books on the "psychology of raising children." His response to her suggestion was that she was a "crackpot." When she insisted that he "consult a family guidance service," or else she would leave him, he "refused." Later, he said that he would "commit suicide," if he had to "live without his family."[43]

A teenager disclosed two family situations, both frightful. In her letter, she spoke of a father who brutally spanked her—and seemed to relish doing so. "My father was born and raised in England and he strongly believes in the English tradition of strict discipline and corporal punishment." She said that she had always been spanked when she was "naughty," and had accepted her father's discipline as "normal and logical when [she] was small." What surprised and disappointed her, however, was that the spankings continued after she got older. If anything, in fact, her father's use of corporal punishment had "become much worse." When she came home from a date that her father had "not approved beforehand" or performed a household task less precisely than he would have liked, he got especially agitated. "He waits in his study until I am ready for bed," she said. "Then he takes me across his knees, pulls up the back of my nightgown above my waist and paddles me long and severely with a hairbrush. . . . He often leaves me so badly blist[er]ed it hurts to sit down for as long as three or four days. . . . I sometimes have a horrible suspicion that he spanks me because he enjoys it, especially since he thrashed the daylights out of me for what he called my 'inexcusable carelessness' in burning his morning toast." She went on to say that "most of the time" her father was "kind and considerate," yet she acknowledged that he did seem to expect "more kissing and physical affection than a father should want from his grown-up daughter." She interjected that she did not want to give the impression that her father would do anything "improper or immoral to [her]—except to denude [her] bottom for punishment." She also pleaded, "Now please do not misunderstand me. I certainly do not intend to accuse him of evil or incestuous ideas."[44]

In the next paragraph of the letter, the focus shifted from her father to the father of a girl she knew. "A friend of mine is very much worse off than I am," she said. "Her father not only makes her strip completely naked to be whipped, he actually forces her to have sex relations with him. The poor girl is nearly crazy. As far as she can make out, her mother knows about it but for some reason does not dare to protest. I don't understand how so-called human beings can treat their own child that way. I think she should go to the police."[45]

Despite this and other evidence of physical and sexual violence in families in the postwar era, there was little organizational or emotional support for women and children who were abused. Franzblau, as far as we know, did not write back to the teenager to offer any advice. Also nothing in the file indicates that anyone in her office contacted the authorities. The only thing we know about how the letter was interpreted was that Franzblau or someone on her staff scribbled "Oedipus in reverse" on the envelope, an allusion to the Freudian principle that children will be attracted to their opposite-sex parents. It is this theoretical principle that, for years, contributed to America's failure to take child sexual victimization seriously. Parents and others were told that a child's report of sexual abuse was fanciful and not to be believed.[46]

Even when there was a sense of alarm in response to abuse, it did not necessarily translate into the kind of action that would help the victims.

Secrecy within a family and the desire to avoid making waves were the rule. A woman who wrote to Franzblau revealed that a male boarder in her mother's house "on occasion" was "handling" her eight-year-old daughter's vagina. "He has given her trinkets and I guess fondled her when she was near him," she said. The eight-year-old had told her five-year-old sister about what was happening to her, and the younger girl had "casually mentioned" the news to her mother. "Now, what can I say to my child?" the mother asked. "I don't feel that confronting her with this incident would be wise. She is merely a victim of a crafty fool." Her reason for keeping things quiet was partly financial: "I don't want my mother to lose her income." She also thought it would not be smart to tell the child's father: "I hate to think what my husband would do should this be told [to] him." She did ask whether she should "confront the man & warn him." Was she thinking about "warning" the man to stop, but still letting him remain a boarder in her mother's house? It is hard to know. That possibility was hinted at: "Our visits to grandma's house are very infrequent." In the main, however, what the mother seemed to want to know most was, "What [was] the right thing to say to the little girl from a psychological point of view?"[47]

Franzblau did not reply to the mother. Nor did she answer another mother who reported coming home from work "exceptionally early" one day and finding her fifteen-year-old daughter in bed with her husband.

> I ran out the room crying hysterically. I soon gained control of myself. My daughter said that this is the first time she has ever had sexual relations with a male. However, I don't believe this is true. Since that incident, I have not talked to my husband. I am under great emotional strain and am on the verge of a nervous breakdown. I long to have relations with him just as before the incident occurred. My daughter never talks to her father now. She refuses dates with boys now and keeps to herself all the time. How can I reunite my once-happy family?[48]

Three months before the *Leave It to Beaver* episode on heroism aired, a twelve-year-old girl—only a few years older than Beaver and close in age to Wally—wrote to Franzblau about an issue that often arose in family sitcoms with characters who had reached or were about to reach driving age. In the TV world of the 1950s, the question of whether Ricky, Betty, Wally, or Mary should be given the keys to the family car or be allowed to have his or her own car was designed to generate laughter and usually was resolved in the space of a half-hour episode. In the non-TV world of the 1950s, however, things did not necessarily go as smoothly.

I think I have a very serious problem. My father and my brother who is 20 years of age are constantly bickering. My brother wants my father's car, but my father refuses to give it to him. He doesn't think my brother deserves it, because he doesn't like the way he is behaving. My father tells him he is not mature. My brother wants my mother to persuade my father to give him the car. If my mother says something in favor of my brother, my father gets mad at her. If my mother says something in favor of my father, my brother accuses her of being against him and he gets so angry, that he starts hitting me. When my mother doesn't voice any opinion they both get angry at her. I can't see them treating my mother like that. They are having so many fights that it's rather unbearable. This fighting goes on day in and day out. I wonder how long this will continue. Many nights I can't sleep, as they continue their argument into the early hours of the morning. I am ashamed to meet any of the neighbors, and I imagine my mother is too, as I can hear them opening their windows to listen. I can't stand this much longer. My father has threatened to leave home many times. My father gets histerical [*sic*] and throws things and my brother does the same. Our home is no home any more. Please help me try to bring peace in our home.[49]

Again, many children might have felt a certain kinship with various TV characters. But other children might understandably be disappointed by the lack of correspondence between the stories played out on their TV screens and the stories that were their lives: How come my father is not like Beaver's dad, waiting for me when I get home from school? How come my father screams and hits? Beaver's dad never does that. Beaver's dad treasures his wife and kids. My dad. . . .

ELEVEN

"What a Man!"

A combat veteran of the Vietnam War once remarked that most of the soldiers he served with "were the first generation of American fighting men to have television," and that all of them "were brought up on *Leave It to Beaver* and *Father Knows Best*." He also made the point that the shows on TV were not always comforting. For at the same time that he and his friends were watching Beaver and Wally and an assortment of other television characters lead their cheery lives, they also were seeing black adults and children in the South "murdered because they demanded their right to vote or attend a school."[1] America in the fifties routinely has been characterized as a *Leave-It-to-Beaver*-like world, but for many individuals, it was anything but. Struggle, rebellion, and agony also were part of the era, with the black civil rights movement making significant strides and encountering vicious opposition in the process.

Three events—all in and around 1955 (a "watershed year")—occupied center stage. One was the torture and murder of a black youth, Emmett Till, by two white men (fathers and veterans both) in the small town of Money, Mississippi. The public display of Till's mutilated body inspired thousands of blacks and whites, in the North as well as the South, to rise up in protest. The second was the Montgomery, Alabama, bus boycott, which lasted for more than a year, and helped to launch the career of a young black leader, Martin Luther King Jr. The third centered on two U.S. Supreme Court rulings in *Brown v. Board of Education*, a school-integration case that ultimately transformed the social terrain of the entire country. These three events, and the events that followed in their wake, had a significant impact on fathers and their families.[2]

In May of 1955, the body of Emmett Till was dragged from the Tallahatchie River in Money, Mississippi. The fourteen-year-old black child, a citizen of Chicago, "had been shot through the head, one eye had been gouged out, and a seventy-five pound cotton gin fan was wired around his neck."[3] At the time of incident, Till was visiting his great aunt and uncle, Elizabeth (Lizzy) and Moses (Papa Mose) Wright, and spending time with his cousins.[4]

The slaying was thought by townspeople to have been sparked by something Till said or did several days earlier while buying treats at a country store. What happened is not exactly known. Some claimed that Till had made "indecent advances" and wolf-whistled at a white woman, Carolyn Bryant, whose family owned the store.[5] Emmett Till's mother, Mamie Till-Mobley, however, rejected this assertion, saying that her son sometimes whistled when he got stuck pronouncing a word (she gave, as an example, *bugglegum*). It was possible, too, that Till whistled in response to a checker move being made on the store's porch.[6]

Whatever occurred was perceived to be insulting, as far as Carolyn Bryant and her husband, Roy Bryant, were concerned. Roy Bryant later would confess to murdering Emmett Till out of revenge. His admission, revealed in an article in *Look* magazine, came four months after an all-white and all-male jury *acquitted* the husband and his half-brother, J. W. (Big) Milam, for the crime.[7] The jury's publicly proclaimed rationale for delivering a not guilty verdict was that "the state failed to prove the identity of the body."[8]

Emmett Till's face and head had, in fact, been significantly disfigured. Still, there was little doubt among blacks as to whose body it was. The day before Emmett Till left for Mississippi, his mother gave him a signet ring that once belonged to his father, who had died just months before the end of World War II. When Till's uncle was asked if he could identify the corpse, he said yes, pointing to the ring. The item of jewelry that Emmett Till had inherited from his father was, for the prosecution, a crucial piece of evidence at the trial (though in the end the jury ignored it). But it was not the only thing that made people contemplate a son's connection to his dad. The social meaning of fatherhood would prove to be a prominent theme in the case. So would the social meaning of war.

Emmett Till's father, Louis Till, had served in World War II, but was dead before the war was over. In July of 1945, Mamie Till-Mobley received a telegram, notifying her that Private Till had passed away. She also was informed that he had been found guilty of "willful misconduct." His offense was not made clear. Over the years, she tried to learn more about what occurred, but apparently was never given a full explanation. Part of the problem was that she and Louis Till had separated before he went overseas, and he had listed his uncle rather than her as his next of kin.

After Roy Bryant and J. W. Milam were acquitted of murder, prosecutors attempted to charge the two with kidnapping. When the grand jury was deciding whether to indict them on this count, a newspaper story was published, claiming that Louis Till had been court-martialed in Italy and been found guilty in 1944 of raping two women and murdering another. He was condemned to death and hanged. From the defense's perspective, the account, which has been disputed, could not have been better timed. "The uproar was deafening," said Mamie Till-Mobley. "That story was used in Mississippi just the way it was intended by the people who leaked it. For people who didn't know any better, it would provide the justification for everything that happened to Emmett. The suggestion was clear: 'Like father, like son.'"[9]

Press reports about the service records of the defendants infused the proceedings as well. J. W. Milam was said to be "a much decorated veteran of World War II who won a battlefield commission while fighting in Europe." He also was said to have been awarded a Silver Star and a Purple Heart in the war.[10] Milam had achieved a reputation for being a tough interrogator of German prisoners. The .45 Colt automatic pistol used to kill Emmett Till purportedly was one of his war mementos.[11] Roy Bryant was described as a Korean War veteran and former paratrooper who, according to one neighbor, had served once under a black noncommissioned officer. ("He didn't seem to mind him," the neighbor offered. "They understood each other.") The two men's "war biographies" and other said-to-be admirable qualities (e.g., their "athletic" and "handsome" looks and "unusually attractive" wives) were paraded out for the express purpose of making them seem like honorable men, "heroic defenders of the country generally and Southern white womanhood particularly."[12]

The most insidious element, however, in the defendants' carefully fashioned personas was the theatrical use of their children as props. During the trial, the men's sons, all between the ages of two and four, were allowed to "frolic about and roam freely while court was in session."[13] Photographs of the proceedings show the children positioned on Bryant's and Milam's laps. The father-son tableaus were crucial to the men's presentation of themselves as men of repute. How could the jury possibly believe that these two ostensibly "caring" fathers tortured and murdered anyone, much less someone else's son? Certainly, it could not find these *dads* guilty?[14]

Upon receiving her son's mutilated remains, Mamie Till-Mobley opted for an open casket, saying, "people needed to know what happened to Emmett Till." Some fifty thousand mourners came to the Chicago funeral, "with many people leaving in tears or fainting at the sight and smell of the body."[15] Others throughout the nation saw newspaper photos of Emmett Till in his casket. The senseless execution of a fourteen-year-old child and the display of his beaten body prompted thousands of blacks and whites to become involved in the fifties' struggle for civil rights.[16]

As the Emmett Till case illustrates, black adults in the fifties were put in the impossible position of teaching their children to stand up for themselves while, at the same time, telling them not to appear so independent as to draw a white person's ire. What made the difference, *at least in the murderers' minds*, between whether to whip Emmett Till to "scare some sense into him" or to kill him outright was Emmett Till's insistence that he was their equal. "You still as good as I am?" J. W. Milam supposedly asked. "Yeah," Till supposedly countered.[17]

U.S. Representative John Lewis, who was a young activist in the fifties, remembered reading about Emmet Till in the newspapers and talking about the homicide with his father and mother. One thing that made an impression was the daring that Moses Wright showed when he pointed to Bryant and Milam at the trial and identified them as the kidnappers. This may have been the first time a black man "stood in open court in the South and accused a white man of a crime—and lived."[18] Said Lewis, "We read about Moses Wright's testimony, my family and I, and we marveled at his bravery, to do what he did in that time, in that place." Lewis also could not help relating personally to Emmett Till: "As for me, I was shaken to the core by the killing. I was fifteen, black, at the edge of my own manhood, just like him. He could have been me. That could have been me, beaten, tortured, dead at the bottom of a river."[19]

Ten weeks after the verdict in the Emmett Till murder trial, on December 5, 1955, a forty-two-year-old black seamstress refused to give up her seat to a white passenger on a city bus in Montgomery, Alabama, and was arrested and detained for violating Alabama's bus segregation laws. The woman's name was Rosa Parks. When her mother got the call that Parks had been arrested, her first question was, "Did they beat you?" Parks could have pleaded guilty and agreed to a fine, and the status quo in Alabama would have been preserved. Drawing on her own anger and daring, and with encouragement from others, she chose instead to fight. (Parks had long been active in the civil rights movement, and black leaders were looking for a fitting case to challenge the law.) Parks understood and was apprised by family and friends what the consequences of her decision might be. "The white folks will kill you, Rosa," her husband warned. But she knew also that standing up to segregation at that moment could make a difference. To those who vowed to back her if she pressed on, Parks said, "If you think it will mean something to Montgomery and do some good, I'll be happy to go along with it." [20]

In a show of support, the Women's Political Council encouraged blacks to boycott the city's buses on the day the case would be coming to court. Among those who were asked to endorse the boycott was the twenty-six-year-old pastor of the Dexter Avenue Baptist Church, Martin Luther King Jr. King at first said that he wanted to think about whether to get involved. He hesitated in part because he had just become a father; his first child had been born only a few weeks before. He eventually agreed to join the protest and, at a meeting on the evening of the court case, King was elected president of the nascent Montgomery Improvement Association. [21]

What began as a one-day demonstration continued for more than twelve months, ending effectively on December 20, 1956, when the Supreme Court ordered Montgomery to integrate its buses. "This morning the long awaited mandate from the United States Supreme Court concerning bus segregation came to Montgomery," King announced. "In light of this mandate and the unanimous vote rendered by the Montgomery Improvement Association about a month ago, the year old protest against city buses is officially called off, and the Negro citizens of Montgomery are urged to return to the buses tomorrow morning on a non-segregated basis." [22] The Montgomery bus boycott "created a model for challenging segregation in the South with nonviolent protests," and helped to establish King as the foremost figure in the postwar black civil rights movement. [23]

From the very beginning, the Montgomery bus boycott was a logistical challenge. Without public transportation, how were parents supposed to get themselves to work and their daughters and sons to school? Most demonstrators simply walked to wherever they needed to go, which made them heroes in the eyes of many. At one meeting, a minister talked about seeing a group of women who were on their way to work. "They were walking in pride and dignity," he declared, "with a gait that would 'do justice to any queen.'" The minister also praised "an elderly woman who had told him that if her feet gave out she would crawl on her knees before riding the buses." [24]

Initially, organizers thought that they could call on the eighteen black taxicab companies in Montgomery to form a "taxicab army" that would offer reduced fares, but they had to abandon the plan when the city police commissioner announced that any cabbie who charged less than the minimum forty-five-cent fare would be arrested. Seeking advice, Martin Luther King Jr. contacted a college friend, T. J. Jemison, who had organized a bus boycott in Baton Rouge in 1953, and learned how the leaders of the boycott had effectively employed carpools. Figuring that carpooling could work in Montgomery, too, King called for owners to offer their automobiles and for volunteer drivers. In this arrangement, "no money could change hands directly, but passengers would make contributions to the MIA, and the MIA could in turn subsidize the costs of the car pool." Between 275 and 350 vehicles were commissioned for the cause.[25]

Throughout the year of the boycott, Montgomery's black citizens repeatedly were harassed. Carpool drivers were pulled over "for minute and imaginary violations of the law." In January, King himself was arrested and jailed, supposedly "for speeding thirty miles an hour in a twenty-five mile zone." When he finally was released, the organizers of the boycott decided that it was too dangerous for King to drive a car and that he should have bodyguards always by his side.[26] Death threats also were commonplace. "Listen, nigger," said one middle-of-the-night caller to King's home, "we've taken all we want from you. Before next week you'll be sorry you ever came to Montgomery."[27] On January 30, a bomb was thrown onto King's front porch, while his wife, Coretta Scott King, and daughter, Yolanda Denise, were inside. (Neither was physically injured.)[28]

Black leaders were not the only ones under attack, nor did the end of the boycott mean that hostilities ceased. On Christmas Eve in 1956, four days after the boycott was officially over, five white men beat a fifteen-year-old black girl as she stood at a bus stop.[29] Having some understanding of the oppressive conditions in the fifties requires imagining the horror that this young woman experienced before and during the beating, the panic of other black youngsters in anticipating that they might be next, and the anxiety that black fathers and mothers felt as they tried to sort out how best to shield their children from harm.

The Montgomery bus boycott sparked other boycotts throughout the South; one of the most notable occurred in Tallahassee, Florida. What made the boycott in Tallahassee different is that it was initiated by students. Wilhelmina Jakes and Carrie Patterson, undergraduates at Florida Agricultural and Mechanical University (FAMU), were arrested for sitting in the white section of a city bus. Unlike Parks, who was jailed, Jakes and Patterson were handed over to the university, and the charges against them were dropped. Soon thereafter, however, a cross was burned in front of the house where one of the students lived. Angered over the threat, FAMU students met and decided to boycott the city's buses. Others in the black community quickly joined the demonstration, which lasted for eighteen months.[30]

Throughout the fifties, college students increasingly participated in the civil rights movement, which sometimes put them at odds with their parents. John Lewis, who helped organize the Student Nonviolent Coordinating Committee (SNCC), was inspired by the events in Montgomery and the charismatic leadership of Martin Luther King Jr. He traveled to Montgomery to meet with King and eventually became one of his most trusted aides. Lewis said his parents "would talk about 'that young preacher' who was leading [the boycott]" but sensed "a mixture of both awe and disapproval in their voices." Lewis's father and mother were not alone in their doubts. A number of older blacks worried that the actions of the twenty-something demonstrators, however well intentioned, could lead to increased levels of violence.[31]

Another concerned father was Martin Luther King Sr., affectionately known as Daddy King. He was uncomfortable with developments in Montgomery and was especially troubled by the large number of arrests. The elder King feared that his son would be sent to prison for a lengthy period on a trumped-up charge. When the younger King came home to Atlanta to visit his family in February of 1956, Daddy King called together a select group of friends to urge his son not to return to Montgomery—at least for a while, "until things cooled down." Martin Luther King Jr. told his father that he had to go back, that he refused to "hide." Stunned, the father "burst into tears." Only after Daddy King was assured that the National Association for the Advancement of Colored People (NAACP) would throw its legal support behind his son did he relent. Martin Luther King Sr. also promptly announced that he would be returning to Montgomery, too. "He was going to *stick by his son*. He would accompany him to the jailhouse."[32]

The thought of their children being arrested was of great concern to black fathers and mothers—as it would be for any parent. Lewis said that, after he was jailed in the spring of 1960 for demonstrating against segregated lunch counters in Nashville, he "lost" his family. "When my parents got word that I had been arrested—I wrote them a letter from the Nashville jail explaining what had happened and that I was acting in accordance with my Christian faith—they were shocked. Shocked and ashamed. My mother made no distinction between being jailed for drunkenness and being jailed for demonstrating for civil rights. 'You went to school to get an education,' she wrote me back. 'You should get out of this movement, just get out of that mess.'" Lewis said that, while he deeply loved his father and mother, he was unwilling to accept things as they were. "I could not live the way they did, taking the world as it was presented to them and doing the best they could with it."[33]

The early 1960s saw a variety of student demonstrations against segregated lunch counters in cities throughout the South, including Greensboro, North Carolina; Tallahassee, Florida; and Atlanta, Georgia. In Tallahassee, students at Florida Agricultural and Mechanical University again took the lead.

On February 20, a group of mostly FAMU students walked in the door of the Woolworth store on Tallahassee's Monroe Street and sat at the "whites-only" counter. There they were met with the usual jeers. "I thought I smelled niggers," said one diner. Another yelled, "You niggers sit in back!" After an hour and a half, the police, with explicit orders from the mayor, arrested the protesters "for disturbing the peace by 'engaging in riotous conduct.'"[34]

A letter that two participants in the sit-in, Patricia and Priscilla Stephens, received from their father after they were arrested and put in jail further illustrates the ambivalence that black parents could feel about what their daughters and sons were doing. The sisters were first asked whether they had "counted the cost" of their behavior. The father then went on to say that, in his estimation, only 10 to 15 percent of the black community was "ready for what [they were] trying to accomplish." Next, he talked about how their protest activities could mar their lives and hurt the family.

> Yes, I know it looks big and you feel like you are doing something, but stop and take stock and put the matter in balance. Right now you stand chances of being expelled from school, as FAMU is a State School, run with State Funds, and dictated to from the State's governing powers. This might lead to your not being able to get employment anywhere in the State, unless you have money enough to open your own business, but right now all of us are living day to day with no preparation for tomorrow—financially nor for business. This thing could even come to the point of me losing my job—I do work for the County and State, you know—and I am too old to look for any type of job now, nor would anyone employ me at my age. You may come out all right, but on the other hand you stand a great deal to lose and nothing to gain but short-lived satisfaction. . . . I know both of you are going to do what you want to do. I think I know you that well. All I can say is weigh the matter, consider all that might be affected, and then do what you are going to do. I know neither of you think Daddy Marion has any sense, but he has lived in this world a long time and what you are now doing is nothing new to him.[35]

While still in jail, one of the daughters replied to her father's pleas. Her motivation to become involved in the movement was similar to that of John Lewis and other young activists. "We cannot be contented with the condition here in the South any longer," she exclaimed. "Our very souls are taken from us by discrimination. How can we be content, saying we'll put it off until we're independent? How many independent people are willing to make the necessary sacrifices for freedom. You know, and I know, that there are only a few. I hope my parents are included in that few. . . . We cannot sit back any longer. I'd rather not have an education if it is going to make me afraid for my rights."[36]

When the mother came to visit once, she asked her daughters, "Girls, are you sure you want to do this?" The response that they gave exposed the complexity of the parent-child differences on the matter. "We reminded them that she and Daddy Marion were the ones who taught us that all citizens must stand up for their rights. Further, we pointed out what we considered a painful truth: 'Mother, if *your* generation had done this, we wouldn't have to do it now. It's time for all of us to be free.'"[37]

Years later, one of the daughters reflected on her father's letter, sent to her and her sister in jail. "Daddy Marion's conservatism was a bit of surprise to us," she said, "considering how much he had influenced our thinking in terms of the rights and responsibilities of citizens." In retrospect, however, she also acknowledged that her father was caught between his general belief in racial equality and his immediate desire to protect his daughters. "He was a parent first," she conceded. "No one wants his children to be on the front lines. No one wants his own family to suffer."[38]

While it is true that, in some black families, parents and children did not see eye to eye on certain issues, the younger generation had much to thank their parents (and grandparents) for. Were it not for the pioneering efforts of older civil rights workers (including scores of black veterans) who, for years, had struggled against the white establishment, the younger civil rights workers would not have had the personal and organizational resources to accomplish what they did. In a number of instances, too, we should not forget, the young and old demonstrated together.

Joining the FAMU students at the Tallahassee sit-in, for example, was forty-three-year-old Mary Ola Gaines. "I was not afraid," Gaines told an interviewer years afterward. "I was doing something I thought would help." In 1960 in Atlanta, seventy-eight-year-old John Wesley Dobbs also marched in support of students who were protesting the segregationist policies of Rich's department store. Some time later, Maynard Jackson, Dobbs's grandson and

Atlanta's first black mayor, was shown a photograph of his grandfather picketing the store. Dobbs was attired in "a fine three-piece suit and gray trench coat" and carried a placard that read "Wear Old Clothes With New Dignity. Don't Buy Here." Seeing his grandfather in the photo brought tears to Jackson's eyes. "Look at that jaw set," the grandson declared. "He would've walked through hell—*bare feet, if he had to!* What a man!"[39]

In May of 1954, another Supreme Court ruling played a significant part in the black civil rights movement. The Court ruled in *Brown v. Board of Education* that the "separate but equal" clause used to justify public school segregation was unconstitutional. On the surface, it appeared that the Court was declaring that schools must be immediately integrated. In actuality, it "did not order the states to enforce the rights [it had] just announced, but instructed the *Brown* lawyers to return a few months later to address specific questions concerning the scope of their ruling." While the *Brown* lawyers argued that segregation should be dismantled posthaste, the lawyers representing the states countered that the Court's ruling could do "irreparable harm" and predicted that "there would be sustained hostility by whites, withdrawal of white children from integrated schools, racial tensions, violence, and loss of jobs for black teachers."[40]

In August of 1955, the Court issued a second ruling, *Brown II*, one that was intended to appease southern segregationists and also had the effect of diluting *Brown I*—or at best delaying its implementation. The Supreme Court instructed the District Courts to "enter such orders and decrees consistent with this opinion as are necessary and proper to admit to public schools on a racially nondiscriminatory basis with all deliberate speed the parties to these cases." *With all deliberate speed* was the key. Those four words effectively gave the states the license to drag their feet. Be that as it may, *Brown* ushered in a new dawn.[41]

Of all the acts of courage that took place in the late fifties on behalf of civil rights, the most significant—and most far reaching—were those that grew out of the Supreme Court's ruling to integrate the nation's public schools. The advantages that blacks would gain as a result of the ruling were tremendous. In effect, *Brown* had "destroyed the legal basis for segregation." The risks to blacks were also real, for many whites throughout the South, some extremely powerful, were intent on doing whatever they felt was necessary to avoid school desegregation. Besides the public officials who campaigned against integration—among them state governors—there were the newly formed White Citizens' Councils (WCC), which, at their peak, had chapters throughout the South and two hundred and fifty thousand members rabidly devoted to "stop[ping] the emerging Civil Rights Movement in its tracks." The WCC "flooded the South with racist propaganda, subjected civil rights activists to threats and economic pressure, erected new barriers to black voting, tried to suppress the NAACP, condemned white liberals as traitors, and made segregation, and how to defend it, the central issue of Southern politics." The members of the Councils claimed that they had no connection with the Ku Klux Klan and "presented themselves as God-fearing, hardworking, and peaceable middle-class folk." In actuality, however, they were not much different from the Klan.[42] Dressed in coats and ties, rather than robes and hoods, and allying themselves with Rotary and Kiwanis clubs, they were dubbed the "Uptown Klan" by one observer.[43]

In the line of fire stood the children and their parents, some of whom had been fighting in the courts to integrate the public schools long before the Supreme Court issued its *Brown II* ruling in 1955. The beginnings of the Brown case, itself, date back to 1951, when thirteen black parents in Topeka, Kansas, tried to enroll their children in the neighborhood school. When they were rebuffed, they collectively sued the Topeka Board of Education, drawing on the legal assistance of the NAACP. (Technically, it is not *Brown v. Board of Education* but *Brown et al. v. Board of Education of Topeka, Kansas*. The case before the Supreme Court, however, joined several separate cases stemming from suits in Delaware, South Carolina, and Virginia.) The "Brown" in the case refers to thirty-two-year-old Oliver L. Brown, one of the parents/plaintiffs. He was listed first not because his name alphabetically came first, but because the NAACP lawyers thought he would present a better public face to the Court. He was a father, whereas all the other plaintiffs were mothers; and he also was a World War II veteran.[44]

Brown's daughter, who was a third-grader at the time, recalled what happened when her father tried to enroll her in school.

We lived in an integrated neighborhood and I had all of these playmates of different nationalities. And so when I found out that day that I might be able to go to their school, I was just thrilled, you know. And I remember walking over to Sumner School with my dad that day and going up the steps of the school and the school looked so big to a smaller child. And I remember going inside and my dad spoke with someone and then he went into the inner office with the principal and they left me out . . . to sit outside with the secretary. And while he was in the inner office, I could hear voices and hear his voice raised, you know, as the conversation went on. And then he immediately came out of the office, took me by the hand and we walked home from school. I just couldn't understand what was happening because I was so sure that I was going to go to school with Mona and Guinevere, Wanda, and all of my playmates.[45]

The Court's ruling on *Brown I* was enthusiastically received by many in the black community. "I was so excited about the *Brown* decision, it's almost too difficult to describe in words," recalled Patricia Stephens, who had participated in the Tallahassee sit-in. "I was in the ninth grade at the time, and I immediately had a grand vision of Negroes and whites sitting side by side, building a future *together*."[46] John Lewis expressed a similar kind of optimism. "I remember the feeling of jubilation I had reading the newspaper story—*all* the newspaper stories—that day. Everything was going to change now. No longer would I have to ride a broken-down bus almost forty miles each day to attend classes at a 'training' school with hand-me-down books and supplies. Come fall I'd be riding a state-of-the-art bus to a state-of-the-art school, an *integrated* school."[47] Maynard Jackson was seated in a school assembly at Morehouse College when the announcement came down. "It was like the second Emancipation. We didn't know the first one, but we imagined what it was like for a slave to hear that you are free. This was unbelievable. *Unbelievable!* And unanimous? It was too good to be true."[48]

Others in the black community, however, were unhappy with the ruling and what it might portend. Indeed, in the beginning, the full consequences of *Brown* were largely unknown.

Integration was uncharted territory: how would it work, what would it mean? If it entailed black children applying to attend white schools, then the pressures, dangers, and uncertainties would be immense; few parents would be happy volunteering their children as guinea pigs. And what would happen to the small number of children who might gain admission to white schools? Evidence from the North suggested they lagged behind white children, becoming frustrated and demoralized, often dropping out. NAACP officials had a hard time convincing their members that integration would be more effective than equalization in obtaining a better education for their children. For black teachers, integration posed an obvious threat to their jobs. If Southern states really did merge the inefficient and wasteful dual school systems, there would be fewer schools, fewer principals, and fewer teachers. Some feared that up to 75,000 jobs might be jeopardized.[49]

Those who opposed *Brown* also felt uncertainty and trepidation—but of a different kind. Before the decision was handed down, Robert Patterson, a white World War II paratrooper and father of two, lay awake at night distraught at the prospect that his daughter would have to sit in a first-grade classroom with black girls and boys. He started a letter-writing campaign in which he characterized school integration as "mongrelization," and was one of the founders of the Citizens' Councils. Robertson had little difficulty finding sympathizers. Many white parents throughout the South were hysterical over *Brown*. They could not get their minds around the concept that their children would have to go to school with blacks.

The WCC's segregationist newspaper stoked people's fears with headlines like "Rape [and] Assault in [Integrated] New York Schools" and "Sex Atrocities in Massachusetts: Blacks Rape White Girl Repeatedly." The WCC's leaders cast themselves as chivalrous fathers who were protecting their children from "animalistic" blacks. In an open letter to President Dwight D. Eisenhower, a WCC member and former air force officer explained, "Do you think any American father with any red blood in his veins is going to allow his dear, little girl to be insulted, possibly sexually molested and exposed to disease?" Though he eventually would send troops to enforce integration, Eisenhower, himself a father, expressed a view that could be construed as accommodating but was, in fact, both racist and sexist. "These [segregationists] are not bad people," he told Supreme Court Chief Justice Earl Warren. "All they are concerned about is to see that their sweet little girls are not required to sit in school alongside some big overgrown Negroes."[50]

To be sure, not every white Southerner was willing to use violence to oppose integration. A Gallup Poll conducted in 1956 found that the majority of southern whites felt that school integration was pretty much inevitable, though they were not necessarily in favor of it or happy about it.[51] Still, regardless of how many were either for or against the *Brown* decision, it did not take a lot of people to stop, if only temporarily, the process that *Brown* had set in motion; cadres of ruthless people would be enough.

The most effective (at least initially) strategies of the WCC and their allies were legislative and economic. In 1956, nineteen southern senators and eighty-two southern representatives signed a "Southern Manifesto" condemning *Brown*. "The unwarranted decision of the Supreme Court," the declaration began, "is now bearing the fruit always produced when men substitute naked power for established law." Then, after claiming that the ruling had no foundation in the Constitution, the legislators offered their own understanding of prior law. "This interpretation . . . is founded on elemental humanity and commonsense, for parents should not be deprived by Government of the right to direct the lives and education of their own children." The decision by the Court, they further argued, "is creating chaos and confusion in the States principally affected. It is destroying the amicable relations between the white and Negro races that have been created through 90 years of patient effort by the good people of both races. It has planted hatred and suspicion where there has been heretofore friendship and understanding." As strong as the declaration's language was, it apparently was not strong enough for some. According to one spokesperson, as reported in a *Chicago Defender* editorial, "the manifesto was re-worded several times so as not to reflect the bitterness of most of its signers."[52]

At the state level, lawmakers passed bills that denied public funds to integrate schools and gave governors the power to close schools that were intent on implementing *Brown*. Several cities shut down their classrooms for a time. Prince Edward County in Virginia boarded up its public schools for several years. Closing schools did not sit well with most white voters. The tactic also failed to daunt the Supreme Court, which in 1959 ruled that a state could not lock *just* its integrated schools. Either all or none had to be closed.[53] Some white parents pulled their children out of public schools and sent them to private institutions—or at least they tried to. In 1958, more than eighteen hundred students were denied admission to Westminster, a private academy in Atlanta. There simply was not enough room to accommodate the flood of applicants.[54]

The economic strategy of the WCC was to strike at any family breadwinner who expressed support for *Brown*. "They would use all kinds of sanctions," said a white Catholic priest who set up a store-front church for poor blacks in Mississippi in 1953. "If they found out you were involved in civil rights, the next day you would be out of a job."[55] A reporter in Mississippi recalled what transpired in Yazoo City in 1955 when people took a stand against segregation:

> A group of middle class blacks signed a petition asking to integrate the local schools. Almost immediately all of them lost their jobs. Banks suddenly called in their mortgages. The young head of the state NAACP, Medgar Evers [a father who in 1963 would be shot dead in his driveway because he fought for civil rights] . . . arranged for me to be smuggled into Yazoo City to meet the victims of the economic backlash. All were quite properly terrified and in no way anxious to continue any further challenges to the power structure. It was clear to me that night how difficult a struggle it was going to be.[56]

Blacks had every reason to be terrified—and not just of losing their jobs. Some southern whites believed that the only way to keep their schools from being integrated was to resort to force. Although the signers of the "Southern Manifesto" had pledged "to use all lawful means to bring about a reversal of" *Brown* and discouraged "disorder and lawless acts," it also charged that "outside agitators" (by which it meant not only northerners but also, as other documents indicate, individuals they perceived to be Communists) had "invaded" the Southern states and were "destroy[ing] the system of public education" for what they termed "our people."[57] Some whites in the South thought they were at war. And to a certain few, this meant doing anything, no matter how cruel, to destroy those who were thought to be the enemy.

In 1957, when Reverend Fred Lee Shuttlesworth and his wife Ruby tried to enroll their two daughters in the all-white Phillips High School in Birmingham, a white mob, brandishing chains and knives, attacked them. Ruby Shuttlesworth was stabbed. (A policeman and television crew stood by and watched.) On Christmas Eve, the Shuttleworths' home was destroyed by a bomb.[58] That same year, in one of the most famous struggles for school integration, nine black students tried to enroll at Central High School in Little Rock, Arkansas, and were soon met by hostile students and parents. On the first day, the nine were prevented from entering. ("Chaos reigned supreme and was replete with racial epithets, threats of lynchings, and physical assaults.")[59] President Eisenhower deployed federal paratroopers to escort the students to class. Arkansas Governor Orval Faubus, opposed to integration, responded, "We are now an occupied nation."[60]

The night before the scheduled day, the father of one of the students could not hide his fear: "Dad was walking back and forth, from room to room, with a sad expression. He was chewing on his pipe and he had a cigar in hand, but he didn't light either one. It would've been funny, only he was so nervous." During the ordeal, parents, concerned about their children's safety, sometimes chose *not* to send their children to school. When the publisher of a local newspaper, friendly to the cause, showed up at the home of a student in the middle of the night to inform the parents that she had gotten word that there would be heightened protection the next day, the father answered the door with his shotgun in hand. Upon being told that the superintendent of schools had instructed her to encourage the students to come to school, the father testily replied, "I don't care if the President of the United States gave you those instructions. I won't let Gloria go. She's faced two mobs and that's enough." He eventually changed his mind and permitted his daughter to join the other students. (In some cases, the children first approached their parents about attending Central High.)[61]

Other black families at other times were able to escape attack, but not intimidation. In June 1960, the local newspaper reported that, come fall,

Carol Swann and Gloria Mead would be integrating the eighth grade at Chandler Junior High School in Richmond, Virginia. The paper also published the parents' names and addresses. "Almost immediately, we began to get threatening phone calls. My parents didn't curse. But in a week I think I heard every word there was, just by virtue of those calls. All summer. The callers hoped we would not go to school, and they could say to the courts, 'Well, you know, we offered a spot to them and they declined—it's not our fault.'"[62]

On November 15, 1958, the headline on page one of the *Chicago Defender* read "U.S. Maps War on Terrorism." The *Defender* was referring not to foreign but to home-grown terrorists—American citizens who were intent on dynamiting (frequently occupied) homes, churches, schools, and other locations to preserve racial segregation.[63] In the previous year alone, there had been more than forty-five bombings in the South, many of which were in response to the *Brown* decision.[64]

It is important to acknowledge that the movement included not just blacks. There were white men and women throughout the country who favored integration. A number of the supporters were willing to put their lives and the lives of their families at risk to fight for racial equality. Atlanta Rabbi Jacob M. Rothschild, a World War II veteran (in the chaplain corps) and married father of two young children, had long been a strong advocate for integration and an ally to black civil rights leaders. In the early morning hours of October 12, 1958, a Sunday, the synagogue he headed was dynamited. (No one was inside.) Rothschild was the terrorists' "chief target," as was the movement, itself. A "General Gordon of the Confederate Underground," taking credit for the attack, said in a phone call to the United Press: "We bombed a temple in Atlanta. This is the last empty building in Atlanta that we will bomb. All nightclubs refusing to fire their Negro employees will also be blown up. We are going to blow up all Communist organizations. Negroes and Jews are hereby declared aliens." Rothschild was undeterred and continued to speak out. (Later in his life, he said that his commitment to black civil rights was "his greatest cause" and that "without it his pulpit would not have been worth as much.")[65]

"The Temple Bombing," as it has come to be known, was not an isolated instance. Between 1954 and 1959, 10 percent of the bombings in the United States involved Jewish targets. Sometimes, it was rabid anti-Semitism that pushed the fanatics' psychological buttons. At other times, it was the allegiance that Jews were perceived to have (and did, in fact, have) to the black civil rights movement that provoked the thugs. Racism coupled with anti-Semitism was a deadly mix.[66]

Other examples of white supporters of the movement include the editor-in-chief of the *Virginia-Pilot*, Lenoir Chambers, who angered legislators, neighbors, and fellow journalists when he took a public stand in favor of school integration. His editorials on the issue earned him a Pulitzer Prize and are credited with encouraging calm and significantly influencing the debate. Because of the progressive position he took on racial equality, the sixty-year-old World War I veteran and married father was repeatedly harassed and physically threatened. At one point, he met with the FBI "to determine the best strategy to protect himself and his family."[67] Not as famous, perhaps, but still courageous were the countless numbers of white students who helped to organize rallies and demonstrated with black protestors to show their allegiance. Noteworthy, too were the white families who welcomed out-of-town activists into their homes—a gesture that often resulted in their being targeted for attack.

Finally, there were the whites who in small but still significant ways communicated their approval of what civil rights workers were striving to accomplish. A poignant example was a jailer who, days before the Tallahassee demonstrators were about to be released, brought his young son to a cell where three of them were imprisoned. Other jailers had been verbally abusive toward the women, but this jailer was different. "Say hello to them," the father instructed his son. "Hi," the boy complied, smiling. The father then turned to his son and said something he hoped would make an indelible impression on the child.

> I know Daddy has told you only bad people go to jail. Well, you may be too young to understand, but these three ladies aren't in jail because they're crooks, or because they're bad people. They're in jail because they're trying to change the laws that say Negroes and whites can't eat together. They want to be treated just like anybody else. And they believe in what they're doing so much, they were willing to go to jail to make it right. So you try to remember that, okay? One day, you'll look back and realize how important it was for them to do this.[68]

Black children in the fifties understandably looked to their parents for role models. But under the tyranny of racism, black fathers and mothers often were forced to choose discretion over valor, simply for the sake of their own and their children's survival. Youngsters might not understand why black adults were treated the way they were, and why their response to how they were treated could seem meek. A cartoon published in the *Chicago Defender* in 1956 depicted a black man sitting on the ground and a preschool-age child standing in front of him. "If you're a man, Granpa," the child inquires, "how come they call you 'boy'?" Drops of sweat fall from the grandfather's face, conveying his disquiet.[69]

Black parents had to make excruciatingly tough decisions about how much to tell their children and whether it might be best, in some circumstances, to keep them unaware. One father, stationed in Europe during World War II, lost his eye in a baseball game when a white pitcher deliberately threw at his head. The man apparently had never told his kids how he was injured. Later, a nephew would say that his uncle did what many black parents chose to do. As the nephew saw it, his uncle as well as others "would not pass racial fear on to his children." He went on to explain, "At a time when vicious racial hatred was featured on the front pages of newspapers and on television, they felt the need to create a safe haven of equality for their children, even if it was not entirely real."[70]

White parents also could be confronted by daughters and sons who had yet to fully grasp the range and depth of America's racial divide. In another *Chicago Defender* cartoon, also published in 1956, a white youngster is shown looking out a bus window at two buildings—one that is small, dilapidated, and marked "For Colored" and another that is two stories high, well-kept, and marked "For White." Turning to his mother the youngster asks, "What country are we in now, Mom?"[71]

TWELVE

"Daddy, That's Not Your Job"

Among the many advertisements that appeared in magazines like *Time* and *Life* during World War II, there were virtually none that depicted a father caring for a baby. If and when a father was pictured (or alluded to at all), the message often centered on the role of men in wartime. Eight months after the war ended, however, the John Hancock Life Insurance Company ran an advertisement unlike those it had run only a few years before. It showed a dad, sleeves rolled up and in an apron, bathing a baby, while another child, about seven years old, watches nearby. "How good a father are you?" the insurance company asked. "A man doesn't have to hand his children the world with a white picket fence around it to be a good father." True to its intentions, John Hancock pitched the value of life insurance. But it did so only after answering the question it initially posed. To be a good father, the company said, one had to be "a good man and an understanding man" *and* be involved in "home training" (e.g., diapering and, by implication, other aspects of routine child care).[1]

One might surmise from the John Hancock ad that, with the end of World War II, the arbiters of culture expected fathers to do more day-in-and-day-out parental work. It turns out, however, that the norms for being a dad were a bit more ambiguous than that. First, the expectation that fathers should know how to change a diaper was not new to the postwar period, but had been applied to fathers decades before.[2] Second, the norms applied to fathers in the fifties did not remain constant, nor did they change in a more progressive way. Rather, from the beginning to the end of the postwar period, they became more traditional.

In the roughly ten years since *The Common Sense Book of Baby and Child Care* was first published, sales of the book had soared. So had Benjamin Spock's reputation and fame. "This past Sunday I saw your television program for the first time," wrote a mother to Spock in 1956, "and it confirmed the opinion that I had formed from reading your articles in the [*Ladies Home*] *Journal* and *Baby and Child Care*; namely, that you are the most intelligently perceptive and human authority in the pediatrics field today. How I wish there were more like you out practicing!"[3] The mother then went on to suggest how Spock could be more perceptive still: *pay more attention to fathers*. The mother's husband, it was said, "took over complete care of the baby" once when she was ill and "became as efficient and relaxed in baby feeding and care as any mother." The change that came over him as a result of this experience led the mother to conclude that fathers should be encouraged to become more involved with their newborns. "Much is made of the feeling of warmth and security between a nursing baby and its mother, but there is something to be said for letting father know the closeness of feeding his offspring, too."[4]

When Spock revised his manual, he appeared to heed the request of this mother (and others, too).[5] The second edition of the manual, published in 1957, devoted more space to men than did the 1946 edition. Judged on this alone, it would have to be categorized as a more father-inclusive text. A detailed examination of the revision, however, reveals that, despite the extra pages, it tended to draw sharper boundaries between fatherhood and motherhood. Contrary to what might be presumed, the new manual was a more gender-polarizing text.[6]

Consider the following. The 1946 edition opened with "A Letter to the Mother and Father," whereas the 1957 edition began with "A Letter to the Reader of This New Edition." The change in wording eliminated the open invitation to fathers. The 1946 edition had a drawing of a father gazing at his baby in the nursery. The 1957 edition reproduced the drawing, but the discussion surrounding the drawing, though lengthier, was phrased in such a way as to suggest that men were being disregarded. In the 1946 edition Spock remarked, "Some fathers have been brought up to think that the care of babies and children is the mother's job entirely. This is the wrong idea. You can be a warm father and a real man at the same time." In contrast, he declared in the 1957 edition, "Some fathers have been brought up to think that the care of babies and children is the mother's job entirely. But a man can be a warm father and a real man at the same time."[7] This modification not only removed the direct statement about how it was "wrong" to think that caring for babies and children was the mother's job alone, but it also grammatically shifted the text from the second to the third person. Thus, in the 1946 edition Spock appeared to talk to fathers as well as mothers ("You can be a warm father and a real man at the same time"), whereas in the 1957 edition he appeared to talk to mothers *about* fathers.

Subsections in the 1947 edition that dealt with the need of boys and girls for a "friendly, accepting father" were subsumed in the 1957 edition under a more general heading, "The Father as Companion." Also included under the heading were two new subsections: "A Little Rough-Housing Goes a Long Way" and "A Father Should Go Light on the Kidding." Both cautioned fathers to be sensitive to their sons' and daughters' perceived frailties, implying that men's and women's approaches to child rearing were not socially but intrinsically unalike: "On the average, men seem to have more fierceness in them than women do," the new edition proclaimed. "In civilized life, they have to keep this under control."[8] A section headed "Discipline" also was expanded, with fathers being mentioned more, and a subsection, "A Father Should Share in Discipline," was added. This change may have been an effort on Spock's part to encourage fathers to be equally involved in child rearing, but the language he employed shows that the nature of men's involvement was sharply delineated. Spock, for example, gave greater attention in the 1957 edition than he did in the 1946 edition to the notion that fathers and mothers should serve as masculine and feminine role models, with the emphasis being on how men and women were fundamentally dissimilar. Enlarging a section on three-to-six-year-olds' "devotion" to parents, Spock ventured into a discussion of how "a boy wants to be like his father" and "a girl wants to be like her mother." He also talked about the supposed "romantic attachments" that boys developed toward their mothers and girls developed toward their fathers. The insinuation was that these desires and attachments were not a matter of convention but a consequence of biological differences between males and females.[9] Noteworthy, too, were Spock's admonitions to fathers to be stern with sons whose connections to their mothers had gone "so far" as to possibly last beyond childhood.[10]

The new edition of *Baby and Child Care* thus may have expanded the amount of space it devoted to men, but the content of the book tended not only to inscribe but also to *reify* a distinction between fatherhood and motherhood. Ultimately, and paradoxically (assuming Spock's aim was to come across as more father-inclusive), the new edition promoted a more conservative view than that of the first one. If Spock's book can be considered an indicator of the times, one would have to conclude that the culture of fatherhood in the fifties had traditionalized.[11]

Other signs point to the same conclusion. Indeed, evidence of tradition-alization in the fifties appears in a variety of works. Consider, for example, the turnaround in the U.S. Children's Bureau manual, *Infant Care*. Beginning in the late 1920s and continuing through the early 1950s, the bureau gradually modified its manual and called for closer contact between fathers and young children. In other words, initially its position shifted toward a more "modern" approach to the division of child care. Later, however, its position seemed to shift back toward a more "traditional" approach.

When the manual first came out in 1914, it was addressed mainly to mothers. The same was true for the 1921 (second) edition. The 1929 (third) edition, on the other hand, under the influence of the psychology of behaviorism, emphasized the idea that "parents must work together from the baby's birth to teach him [or her] good habits." The 1935 printing of the 1931 (fourth) edition changed the title of the bibliography from "Selected Books of Interest to Mothers" to "Selected Books of Interest to Parents," while the 1942 (seventh) edition, put together before the war, and the 1945 (eighth) edition, which was essentially the same as the 1942 edition, stated that the purpose of the manual was "to help mothers and fathers in taking care of babies." The same thing was said in the 1951 edition.[12] In the late 1950s, however, the Children's Bureau took a different tack; it *reversed course*. Without explanation, in the 1955 edition of *Infant Care*, the bureau chose to delete the father-inclusive opening, which gave the impression that the manual was now addressed exclusively to women.[13]

Additional examples are not hard to find. Television programs featured more conservative portrayals of family life in the late fifties than the early fifties (see chapter 10). Sunday comic strips published between 1955 and 1959 were less likely than Sunday comic strips published between 1950 and 1954 to portray fathers as parentally nurturant and supportive.[14] Hollywood films "offered an ambivalent image of the father": some stressed men's roles as breadwinners (e.g., *The Man in the Gray Flannel Suit*); others stressed their domestication (e.g., *Rebel Without a Cause*); and a third group depicted "strong, autocratic, even despotic" patriarchs (e.g., *Giant*). The films in the third group were the most prevalent. They also were generally produced in the late fifties.[15] Fewer magazine articles on fatherhood were published in the mid-1950s than were published in the mid-1940s. The mid-1950s articles tended to place more emphasis on men's roles as economic providers (vs. their roles as parental nurturers), compared to the mid-1940s articles.[16]

The theme of the father as male role model was touted more in the late fifties than in the early fifties. In the wake of the Korean War and in anticipation of future wars, it was a theme that resonated among some individuals. The theme had not disappeared and now reappeared. It had always been around in one form or another, if only at certain times and in certain circumstances. But in the late fifties, the father as male role model appeared to be embraced, in part because of heightened concerns about men's "place" in the family—concerns that were related to questions about whether encouraging men to be involved with their children had sidetracked them from what they "should" be doing (i.e., breadwinning) and stripped them of their "masculinity."[17] "Father's role has undergone a revolutionary change, raising the disturbing question of whether it is possible to be both a family man and a man," said the anthropologist Margaret Mead in 1959. "There seems to be a real danger that the care of young children will prove both so time-consuming and so fascinating that many men will skimp their careers in order to get more time with their families."[18]

The psychologist Bruno Bettelheim in 1956 disparaged the fact that, in the writings of some child-rearing experts, fathers were being "advised to participate in infant care as much as mother does so that he, too, will be as emotionally enriched as she." Bettelheim believed that this was an "empty" recommendation "because the male physiology and that part of his psychology based on it are not geared to infant care." He maintained, too, that men were better suited to be a family's "protector" and "breadwinner" and model of "deep concern for matters beyond the day-to-day struggle." The male of the species, as he saw him, was the family member "whose role is clearly to protect against the outside world and to teach how to meet this world successfully" and "[whose] greater objectivity can be trusted in all emergencies just because he is not so immediately involved in the picayune squabbles."[19]

Writings on fatherhood and motherhood in the late fifties (and before) were not totally uniform or consistent. In truth, they could be anything but. Sometimes Margaret Mead waxed nostalgic about the traditions of the past. Sometimes she encouraged people to think about gender and parenthood in seemingly novel ways. Sometimes she tried to occupy a middle ground between the two positions: "If taking care of children is seen as playing a woman's part, being a sucker, being dominated by women, it will be looked at one way. If it is seen as an extension of manhood, as an exercise of strength, imagination and tenderness it will be looked at the other way."[20]

Contradictions could be found in other writings, too. The historian Arthur Schlesinger argued in 1958 that "the key to the recovery of masculinity" was that men needed to locate their true "identity." (He apparently believed it had been lost.) "For men to become men again, . . . their first task is to recover a sense of individual spontaneity," Schlesinger advised. Men also needed to recover their sense of humor and appreciation for art. And they should recognize that one "means of liberation" was politics. "Not the politics of rhetoric and self congratulation," Schlesinger offered, "which aims at burying real issues under a mass of piety and platitude; but the politics of responsibility, which tries to define the real issues and present them to people for decision."[21]

Given that Schlesinger did not mention caring for children as a way for men to "recover" their masculinity, one might think that he was separating "manhood" from "fatherhood." But he may also have been endeavoring to join the two. Earlier in the piece, he wrote, "The American man is found as never before as a substitute for wife and mother—changing diapers, washing dishes, cooking meals, and performing a whole series of what once were considered female duties," and he said that, to some, this indicated an absence of masculinity. (He cited Bettelheim as someone who believed this.) In Schlesinger's mind, however, "The willingness of a man to help his wife around the house may as well be evidence of confidence in masculinity as the opposite; such a man obviously does not have to cling to masculine symbols in order to keep demonstrating his maleness to himself."[22]

On the whole, then, there was considerable angst in the late fifties over whether men could be involved fathers *and* simultaneously "true" to their "nature" as "males." The question occupied the attention of both academics and the general public. After the anthropologist Ashley Montagu—known to take a progressive stance on matters of gender (in the context of the era)—appeared as a guest on a 1957 television show devoted to the topic of American husbands, viewers wrote in to ask Montagu what he thought fathers and mothers should do.[23] The letters, which were mostly from women, included questions such as the following:

- Do American husbands change more baby diapers than other countries?[24]
- Should husband[s] take turns with wives in getting up and feeding [a] new baby during those first 5–6 weeks?[25]
- How often and how long should I expect my husband to "baby-sit" for me?[26]
- Why [do] some husband[s] have children and never play at home with their wife and children. Do you call that a husband[?][27]
- Is there real co-operation between father and mother today in bringing up a family? Or has the American father left nearly the entire business to his wife, without much objection? What, eventually, will the father's position in a family be?[28]
- Should the husband regain his position as head of the home and family?[29]

Not as many men as women may have watched the show (which was broadcast during the day), and few men chose to write. One who did said that he hoped Montagu would weigh in on whether it was okay for a father—and particularly for him—to be observed steering a baby carriage. To the father, such a sight was embarrassing.

> Everything was fine in our home until [the] baby came, and though I adore the mite, a problem has arisen which perhaps you and your listening audience can help us settle. When we go out with the baby my wife thinks that I should wheel him, as she does this daily. However, I feel it is not a man's job (though many men do it) and I feel not only sheepish, but downright silly. One afternoon I met my boss, while engaged in this un-pleasant-to-me chore, and got red to the ears. Now mind you, I do love my wife and baby, and I would work my fingers to the bone for them, but I don't like the idea of my hands pushing a baby carriage. I'm twenty-seven, my wife twenty-one. Man to man, please advise me.[30]

The cultural boundary between fatherhood and motherhood hence may have been fortified in the late fifties. Comments made by the California fathers and mothers, interviewed in 1958, seem to suggest this possibility. These were the couples (discussed in chapter 8) who had a four-to-five-year-old child—the focal child for the project—enrolled in a nursery school. Besides being asked about their infant care arrangements five years earlier, they also were questioned about their current division of child care. The families were middle-class, with the men holding professional positions or going to college or graduate school, and the women working primarily as homemakers.[31]

One father had a job that kept him pretty busy (he worked in a physics lab) and gave him less time at home than some other men seemed to have. But his not taking a larger share in child care appeared to have little to do with his demanding profession and everything do with his patriarchal principles. He simply wanted the division of labor in his home to be rigidly partitioned—by gender.

> Well it's just my feeling that there ought to be a clear-cut division of responsibility. I feel that the husband's main responsibility is to make a living for the family and in essence the one time—possibly more the old-time pattern for a father and a wife, with the father making shall we say the intellectual decisions and supposedly being a symbol of reasonableness and logic and high standards and so on, and the wife being a symbol of motherly love and affection

and day to day physical care of the house, the washing the dishes and the clothes and such things, so we try—at least I feel [we] have tried—and both of us agree on the fact that there should be a fairly clear-cut division of labor between the husband and wife, except of course when [the mother] is sick. I certainly have no objection to doing the dishes, or washing or taking care of the kids under those circumstances, but in general I don't change diapers or feed the children or do the dishes or do the washing.

The wife confirmed the husband's account. "Things are divided up," she said. "I do the dishes, barring some unusual thing—like if I go out and baby-sit for the pool, he'll sometimes do the dishes. Or, y'know, if I'm sick or something. Otherwise I do all the undressing and dressing of the children, and washing of the children, and dishes; and he takes care of the car, and the lawn."[32]

Other couples conveyed, too, a sense that they had consciously chosen traditional child care arrangements. A father who was questioned specifically about "the division of labor within the household" said that, in his view, there was "a pretty complete" separation on who did what. "She's expected to handle most of the household chores concerned with cooking, washing, and raising the children and—I—handle little repairs—to the kids' toys and—round the house—and—most of the yard work, although she does flower gardening—quite a bit. [. . .] Ah—I'll occasionally help with the children and—about every two months, wash the dishes—but (chuckle) not more often than that, I guess. Don't want her to get in the habit."[33]

Another father stated that he "hate[d] to get [the division of labor] mixed up." As to why, he explained, "You read so many articles there are about the poor children in families nowadays, in certain families where they don't know [who's] the mother and [who's] the father because of the division of duties. I mean, there is no division as such of duties and they say the men now are helping too much and, they're, they're you know getting away from mother and father separation entirely. I hope that's not happening in our family." The mother, who also was asked about how duties in the home were divided, corroborated her husband's insistence on gender boundaries. "My husband considers it that his main job is being the provider of the family, that's his main idea. He thinks everything else is mostly my job."[34]

Yet another father—a physician with a "very time-demanding" medical practice—was away from home so often that his kindergarten-age son already had announced to the family that he had no interest in becoming a doctor when he grew up because "he [didn't] want to work that hard." The youngster also apparently had embraced the idea that a sharp division of labor between husbands and wives was best. When he saw his mother, along with his father, laying pipe in the yard, he demanded that she return to the house and start cooking. When he observed his father doing what he considered women's work, he chastised him: "Daddy, that's not your job."[35]

The culture of fatherhood, we thus may conclude, was in a state of flux in the late fifties and was more traditional than it was in the early fifties. What about the conduct of fatherhood? Did it traditionalize, too? This is a harder question to answer. Determining whether the culture of fatherhood changes generally entails a close examination of a society's child-rearing books, television shows, comic strips, magazines, and the like—from one year to the next, or from one decade or half-decade to the next. A similar kind of analysis for plotting changes (or continuities) in the conduct of fatherhood in the postwar era cannot be carried out, because the information necessary to test the hypothesis simply is unavailable.

There were no postwar surveys in which researchers asked one cohort of men in the early fifties how much they interacted with their kids, and then, in the late fifties, asked a second cohort of men, equivalent to the first (i.e., similar in age, education, income, etc.) how much they interacted with their kids. Nor were there studies in which successive waves of women were asked to report on the child-rearing patterns of their husbands. Without such reports, we are forced to rely on fragments of evidence that are, at best, incomplete. In the same way that paleontologists must be satisfied with fragments of bone to visualize the actions of prehistoric creatures, "parentologists" often must work with fragments of one kind or another to formulate hypotheses about the conduct of fatherhood in the past.[36]

Consider, for example, a research project carried out in 1956 in which 391 wives residing in Omaha, Nebraska, were asked who "usually performed each of one-hundred household duties." The choices presented to the respondents were: "wife always or almost always"; "wife sometimes and husband sometimes, or both spouses jointly"; and "husband always or almost always." Included among the duties were (1) bathe and feed preschool children; (2) put preschool children to bed; (3) discipline school children; (4) supervise children's school work; and (5) teach school children manners. For each of these, the proportion of responses in the "wife always or almost always" category was, respectively, 89 percent, 66 percent, 55 percent, 59 percent, and 55 percent. Thus, nine times out of ten the wives were the ones who usually bathed and fed children; and six times out of ten they

were the ones who usually taught school children their manners. These results suggest a sharper division of child care than had been reported in studies carried out in the early fifties.[37]

Or do they? The Nebraska study may seem to provide concrete results
about men's conduct, but there is a measurement issue, related to the struc-
ture of the interviews, which cannot be ignored. The women were not asked
who did what and when (as they might have been in a time-diary study);
rather, they were asked who "usually performed" certain tasks.[38]

To ask "who *usually* did what" places limitations on the study's results—
limitations that the researchers openly discussed. "Because of [the] wording
of the questions," they warned, "the results show only primary responsibility for any one task" and "do not reflect cases in which a second family
member might occasionally help with the task." The Nebraska mothers, in
other words, may have had primary responsibility for the bathing and feeding of children, but that did not necessarily mean that the fathers did not
also perform these duties. The men could have pitched in periodically, but
not have been deemed (by their wives) to be customary caregivers.[39]

Even if we concede that the Nebraska project is a reasonably accurate
measure of the child care activities of men in the late fifties, the project cannot, by itself, answer the question of whether the conduct of fatherhood
changed (or stayed the same) in the postwar era, because all the interviews
for the study were carried out at a single point in time. Also, the women
were not asked how their current division of household duties compared
with what it was five or ten years before.

The same inability to tap change and continuity in the fifties applies to
two other projects, both based in California, which have been used to make
claims about father involvement in the postwar years. The Berkeley Guidance Study and the Oakland Growth Study, as the projects are called, were
longitudinal in design, with data collection commencing in the late 1920s
(Berkeley) or early 1930s (Oakland) and occurring also in later decades.
The follow-up interviews in the fifties, however, were scheduled just once,
in 1958 or 1959, which means that systematic comparisons *across* the fifties
cannot be made.[40]

The Berkeley Guidance Study and the Oakland Growth Study nonetheless are revealing. Similar to what we see with the Nebraska project, the
picture of fatherhood that emerges from the California projects is fairly traditional. A post-hoc analysis of the interview transcripts of one hundred
couples (half of the subsample drawn from each project) indicated that
only eight of the men were significantly involved "in their children's devel-

opment" (*involvement* being defined as "companionship, affection, and effort"). Fourteen of the men "acknowledged that they were supposed to invest time and effort in their relationships with their children," but admitted that they "had not succeeded in doing so." The researcher who pored over the transcripts concluded that the men in the two studies "seemed removed from most of the actual childrearing in their homes."[41]

In some of the late-fifties' studies, interviewers did not even bother to ask about men's child care work, but focused almost exclusively on men's play time with their kids. For example, when the California fathers of kindergartners—not the Berkeley or Oakland fathers, but the fathers talked about earlier—were queried about their *current* level of parental involvement, they were asked, "How much time does [the focal child] spend with you?" The mothers, in turn, were asked, "How much time does [the focal child] spend with his [or her] father?" Follow-up probes included, "How much of this is alone with [you/him]?" "What do [you/they] do together?" When the researchers, however, wanted to know about the men's *past* level of involvement with the same children (i.e., their level of involvement when the children were infants), they asked the fathers, "How much did [you] help to care for [the focal child] during his [or her] first year of life? Feeding? Toileting and cleanliness?" The mothers were asked, "How much did your husband help to care for [the focal child when he or she was a baby]?" (No follow-up probes.)

The answers that the fathers and mothers offered, when talking about their late-fifties' level of involvement probably reflected, to some degree, what the men actually did with their children. But the answers also probably reflected how the interview questions were phrased. The researchers appeared to believe that, when it came to older children, it was more important to ask about the fathers' interaction than about their possible participation in feeding, carting, and consoling their kids.[42] Given this, it is not surprising that the men came across as primarily engaged, if they were engaged at all, in child care *play*. When the focus of the interview was on infant care in the early fifties, on the other hand, more attention was devoted to child-care *work*.[43]

How questions in a study are worded ultimately says more about the culture than the conduct of fatherhood. Implicit but unexamined assumptions about what fathers do represent researcher-held biases rather than paternal actions. Thus, although the interview studies cannot directly answer the question of whether men were less involved in child care in the late fifties compared to how involved they were in the early fifties, they do offer additional evidence (albeit only fragments) that the culture of fatherhood in the late fifties was more "traditional" than it was just a few years before.

Altogether, books, films, television shows, comic strips, popular magazines, and interview transcripts from the fifties indicate a process of traditionalization from the early to the late fifties. Though it may seem improbable that such a transformation could take place in so short a period of time, we have other information about the postwar era that also suggests that the late fifties were an especially traditional moment in America's history. The late fifties were marked by a high number of births (the postwar baby boom peaked in 1957) and a thriving economy (though there was a recession in 1958)—societal-level patterns that may very well have reinforced an ideology of "separate spheres," with parenthood and breadwinning being seen as women's and men's domains, respectively.[44] The labor force participation rate for women did increase from 1950 to 1960, but the earning power of women declined.[45] The earning-power differential could have further accentuated men's status as economic providers and more readily cast them as mothers' "helpers" when it came to child care work. Finally, new parents in the late fifties tended to be more politically conservative than new parents in the early fifties. One reason is that the young men and women who had become parents in the early fifties mostly were children of the Great Depression and World War II. Those who became parents in the late fifties, on the other hand, generally were born at the end of the Depression and were infants or toddlers just as the war was ending. The first group grew up under the most trying conditions. The second group grew up in a time of prosperity. The intersection of historical circumstance, chronological age, and family biography produced divergent sets of attitudes.[46]

If there is a methodological lesson to be taken from this, it is that historians of fatherhood must be careful not to presuppose that the late fifties represent the entire post–World War II era. Materials from the late fifties sometimes have been used as the primary (or sole) data to support the claim that fatherhood was sharply traditional. Although I certainly would agree that fifties' fatherhood as a whole was traditional, I also would challenge the notion that it was *as traditional* as some have made it out to be. Relying primarily or exclusively on materials from the late fifties (e.g., examining the second edition of *Baby and Child Care* but not the first; focusing on interview studies carried out in 1958 or 1959 but not before) ignores the changes that occurred *during* the fifties and often results in hyper-traditional portrayals of postwar dads. Broader investigations—those that look at an assortment of evidence gathered at different points in time—demonstrate that fatherhood in the fifties was significantly more variable than the standard accounts would have us believe.

There is an important theoretical point here, too. The modernization of the culture of fatherhood in the prewar era, coupled with the traditionalization of the culture of fatherhood in the postwar era, makes for a fluctuating pattern and supports the proposition that the institution of fatherhood in America has not inexorably "evolved," but has shifted "up" and "down" in the wake of large-scale social forces (e.g., ideological and political movements, economic booms and busts, wars and revolutions). The history of fatherhood, in short, is a product of circumstance, and it does not always travel in a straight line.

THIRTEEN

"Tempered by War, Disciplined by . . . Peace"

The 1960 presidential campaign was a contest between two World War II veterans. It also was a contest between two dads. Richard Milhous Nixon, the Republican candidate, was forty-seven years old and the vice president of the United States under Dwight David Eisenhower, who was completing his second term as president. Nixon had served as a naval officer in the war, but had not been in combat. He was the father of two daughters, ages twelve and fourteen. John Fitzgerald Kennedy, the Democratic candidate, was forty-three years old and the junior senator from Massachusetts. Kennedy, too, had served as a naval officer in the war, but he also had been awarded the Naval and Marine Corps Medal and Purple Heart for his heroics as the skipper of a patrol torpedo (P.T.) boat. He was the father of a two-year-old girl; another child was expected in the fall.

Kennedy won the election, but only by the slimmest of margins. Fewer than 113,000 ballots separated the two opponents. Had 4,500 voters in Illinois and 28,000 voters in Texas switched sides, the electoral-college count would have flipped in Nixon's favor.[1]

A variety of reasons have been offered for why the election turned out the way it did. Skill, money, religion, virility, even the candidates' facial appearance are frequently are cited. One factor, not talked about much, was the social meaning of fatherhood. The 1960 election may very well have been decided by the attention that one candidate gave to his daughter, and by a *non*-candidate's love for his son and his family.

America in 1960 was very different from America in 1952 when Eisenhower ran against Governor Adlai Stevenson of Illinois. A cease fire in the Korean

War had been declared seven years earlier; America was at peace. Or at least it was in a formal sense. Although the United States was not engaged in battle, the country was on a high state of alert. Its new foe was Communism, the personification of which, for most Americans, was the Soviet Union, a former ally. The Cold War had begun almost immediately after Germany and Japan surrendered in 1945, but it had escalated since, fueled by the proliferation of nuclear weaponry and the dogged efforts of the U.S. government to identify Communist sympathizers.

A "missile gap" between the United States and the Soviet Union, with the United States generally thought to be at a disadvantage, was of great concern. Although it was later learned that the Soviet Union had far fewer missiles than did the United States, at the time the balance of power between the two countries was thought to be in doubt.[2] To be able to win the election, a candidate had to show resolve against the country's enemies. Accusing one's opponent of being weak on national security was a standard campaign tactic.[3]

The Cold War was such a key feature of late fifties' American culture that it influenced not only affairs of state but also how individuals, and in particular men, viewed themselves. Brute strength was prized, much as it had been in earlier times (e.g., in the late nineteenth century).[4] Magazine articles on fitness and health, published in the years leading up to the election, talked about the dangers of "fragile males" and "flabby Americans," more so than did the same kind of articles published several years earlier. Thus, in addition to talk of a "missile gap," there was thought to be a "muscle gap." Both gaps, it generally was believed, had to be eliminated; otherwise the country would not survive. (Popular remedies at the time: personal exercise programs and backyard bomb shelters.)[5]

Important as well to understanding the social landscape in 1960 was the black civil rights movement. The highly publicized murder of fourteen-year-old Emmett Till and the intractability of Jim Crow laws, available for the world to see during the Montgomery bus boycott (and other demonstrations), in conjunction with the South's vicious resistance, particularly in Little Rock, to federally mandated school integration after the *Brown v. Board of Education* ruling, compelled the nation to acknowledge racist policies and practices that had long been ignored—at least by whites (see chapter 11). Racial stratification was not destroyed by any means in the wake of these events. But the political realities of race in America definitely had changed in the span of eight years. How all of this figured into the 1960 election is an interesting story. So is the part that fatherhood played in determining who won.

The Democratic Convention was held in mid-July; the Republican convention, about a week later. Four months before Americans entered the polling booths on November 8, Nixon, by most accounts, had the edge. The Republican nominee could claim more experience on the international stage, and his was the incumbent party. He was helped, too, by the fact that Eisenhower's approval ratings in the late fifties were high.[6] Kennedy, besides being perceived as both inexperienced and young (though Nixon was only four years older), had to deal with voter concern about his religion. Specifically, he had to convince people that he would not allow his Catholicism to interfere with his presidential judgment. Anti-Catholic sentiment in national politics was strong. Kennedy did what he could to put the religious issue to rest by affirming his belief in the separation of church and state. For the most part, he was able to minimize the Catholic factor, though there were some who refused to vote for him simply because of his faith.[7] As for the youth factor, it ended up being an asset.

A turning point in the campaign was the first televised debate, which was held on September 26 and was watched by more than twenty-eight million households.[8] Appearing next to Nixon on a national stage boosted Kennedy's standing in the eyes of many. (As a rule, debates generally increase the exposure of anti-incumbents.) Kennedy also benefitted from the fact that Nixon had been ill during the two weeks prior to the event. Nixon's gaunt appearance, coupled with his refusal to wear theatrical makeup to counteract the harsh studio lights, made him "haggard-looking to the point of sickness."[9] Kennedy also refused the cosmetics offered by the TV crew, but one of his aides "did a slight touch-up with commercial makeup bought at a drugstore two blocks away."[10] A Republican aide applied a pancake powder to conceal the vice president's heavy beard. The powder, however, made Nixon appear worse on TV than he might have without it.

Besides having the good fortune to stumble upon the right facial, Kennedy also had relaxed in the days before the debate, acquired a radiant suntan, and exhibited calm from the beginning of the debate to the end. Kennedy's hale-and-hearty persona and energetic performance would have worked to his advantage no matter when the debate took place. But in the health-conscious America of the late fifties, "the total look" served him particularly well. Because of how he appeared and acted in the debate, Kennedy was said to acquire "a 'star quality' reserved only for television and movie idols." An immediate "quantum jump in the size [of his] crowds" was reported.[11]

During the campaign, Kennedy and Nixon repeatedly tried to "out-muscle" each other. A "cult of toughness" made aggressiveness an admirable trait. Not surprisingly, both wanted to be viewed as "hard" on Communism.[12] There were risks, however, with being perceived as too aggressive. Americans had come to enjoy the rewards of prosperity and peace.[13] A certain amount of "softness" thus had to be shown as well. At one point, in an attempt "to take the 'peace' issue away from the Republicans," Kennedy accused Nixon of being trigger happy. "He wants us committed to the defense of every rock and island around the world," Kennedy exclaimed, "but he is unwilling to admit that this may involve American boys in an unnecessary and futile war."[14] Being concerned about "American boys" allowed JFK to be perceived as an empathetic father who deeply cared about the nation's children.

On the issue of who knew more about what it meant to "involve" troops, Kennedy had the advantage, because he could depict himself as a war hero.[15] How he performed in the war, in fact, did make a difference to people. A Wisconsin man who generally voted Republican said he had decided to vote for Kennedy because he felt that JFK was "a young guy and kind of all-around fellow *with his war record* and everything."[16] The media also touted Kennedy's military exploits. Two days before election day, the *New York Times* ran a photo essay, titled "Evolution of a President," which offered a comparison of the nominees. Nixon, pictured in his World War II uniform, was said to have "joined the Navy in 1943," while Kennedy was shown in uniform "attend[ing] a reception in his honor" and was declared a "WAR HERO," in bold type, for having "saved ten of his crew" after "the P.T. Boat he commanded was sunk."[17]

On October 19, 1960, less than a month before the election, Martin Luther King Jr. was arrested for leading a sit-in at a prominent Atlanta restaurant and sentenced to serve time in a maximum-security state prison (rather than a county or city lockup). His detention was widely covered by the press, putting Kennedy and Nixon in the position of having to choose how to respond publicly. Nixon decided to employ a laissez-faire approach and issued a "no comment," stating that he did not think it appropriate for a lawyer (Nixon) to give the appearance of trying to influence a judge.[18] The Kennedy camp opted for a more direct approach. JFK personally phoned MLK's wife, Coretta Scott King, who was pregnant at the time, to offer his sympathies. Meanwhile, JFK's thirty-four-year-old brother, Robert F. Kennedy, worked behind the scenes to help secure Martin Luther King Jr.'s release.

Although Martin Luther King Jr. never formally endorsed Kennedy, Martin Luther King Sr. did. "Because this man was willing to wipe the tears from my daughter's [i.e., daughter-in-law's] eyes," said the father of the young civil rights leader. "I've got a suitcase of votes, and I'm going to take them to Mr. Kennedy and dump them in his lap." Millions of blacks, also impressed by the Kennedy camp's gesture, joined Martin Luther King Sr. and vowed to cast their votes for JFK.[19] Some friends and confidantes of Daddy King were disappointed in his decision to support a Democrat. Though criticized for "confusing politics with personal emotion," the elder King stood his ground. "You don't understand," he explained. "You can't have a man do what Kennedy did and not pay your debt." Polls after the election showed that nearly seven in ten blacks voted Democratic. Martin Luther King Sr.'s proclamation of paternal love was instrumental to Kennedy's victory.[20]

Another factor that appeared be instrumental to Kennedy's becoming president was his presentation of self when he was around a young child—and especially when he was around one particular child. "Kissing infants is a traditional prerequisite for American political success," declared the *New York Times* in October 1960. Included with the article was a photograph of Kennedy "juggling" a six-month-old child while at an airport in Maine. "Mr. Nixon, too, observes the rules of classic campaigning," added the *Times*, showing Nixon cooing at a baby who was being held in his mother's arms. "Here, [Nixon] essays the kitchy-koo approach with a youngster from Illinois." Being seen with a youngster was such an important element in the 1960 presidential campaign that the *Times* saw fit to impart, *as news*, the exact date and location that Kennedy "kissed his first baby of the campaign." (For the record, it was Saturday, October 16, in Beaver Falls, Pennsylvania.)[21]

What does a politician gain by holding or kissing a baby? One answer is that voters tend to attribute positive personality traits to people who appear to like kids. If this is indeed the case, an even greater advantage is to be gained if a candidate can regularly be seen not just with any baby but with *his or her own baby*. Kennedy often was photographed on the campaign trail with his baby daughter, Caroline, and his wife, Jacqueline Bouvier Kennedy. The week after the Democratic convention, while in the middle of a "part-time vacation," he was shot grasping Caroline's hand as she sat on her mother's knee.[22] Returning from a Cape Cod weekend at the end of August, he was photographed again, this time carrying Caroline as he was about to get on a plane. (Jacqueline Kennedy walked alongside.)[23] In October, he was pictured once more with Caroline as he was about to leave a plane. Caroline was held in his right arm and a large Raggedy Ann doll was held in his left. The caption under the photo read: "CAREFUL OF HER, SHE'S MINE: Caroline

Kennedy, 2 years old, with her father Senator John F. Kennedy, and the doll he gave her yesterday before he left Hyannis, Mass., in his plane on presidential campaign."[24]

Caroline was mentioned in newspaper articles, even in the absence of a photo of her with her dad. A piece that reported on how much Jacqueline Kennedy was "charming" voters also said that she "did not discuss issues but hit a sympathetic chord with parents, talking about their children and her daughter Caroline, 2, home in Washington." When Jacqueline Kennedy was escorted to a school gymnasium, she "pointed to kindergartners and said they made her feel lonesome."[25] She also was asked at one point "about the kind of disciplinarian the Senator [was]," and answered, "He is strict—but very affectionate, like I try to be." Mentioned, too, was that "Their 2-year-old daughter, Caroline, . . . is 'excited but doesn't know why,'" and that she is "'too little to know what it is all about.'"[26]

One press report described Caroline as "blonde and blue-eyed," and characterized her as "one of the best vote-getters in her age group."[27] The Kennedy camp produced a television documentary stressing that JFK was "the father of a beautiful two-year-old daughter."[28] And, for further effect, Kennedy's chartered plane was named *Caroline*.[29]

Did Kennedy's fatherhood displays help him win? There is a good chance that they did. Although the culture of fatherhood was more traditional in the late fifties than in the early fifties, men still were expected to play with children and occasionally "assist" mothers with diaper changing, infant feeding, and the like (see chapters 7 and 12). Some women bragged about their husbands' contribution to child care. Others, dissatisfied with the aid they received, hoped their husbands would do more. Mothers of small children were especially likely to monitor how much a politician-father did or did not do. Given that it generally takes a lot more energy to mind babies and toddlers, these women would be especially appreciative of a father who appeared to be willing to pitch in.

If Kennedy's fatherhood displays did contribute to the outcome of the election, the impact would be most discernable in women's voting patterns—and especially in mothers' voting patterns. The Kennedy camp anticipated this. When Benjamin Spock endorsed Kennedy, taped television interviews with Spock and the Kennedys were quickly arranged. "We felt," said a member of Kennedy's team, "that a lot of ladies in the United States, seeing Ben Spock and Jack together, might be persuaded to vote for Jack."[30]

As the campaign progressed, Kennedy could see the strength that he had among mothers. "Young mothers with children in their arms formed a substantial part of the crowds that turned out to greet [JFK]," reported the *New*

York Times.[31] Young mothers, post-election analyses showed, also formed a substantial voting bloc. A Gallup poll conducted in December 1960 indicated that Kennedy and Nixon broke even with middle-age women, but that Kennedy beat Nixon by 10 percent among young women.[32] Of course, not all young-women voters are mothers. But given the high marriage and childbearing rates in the late fifties, most probably were.

Other factors, to be sure, also may have accounted for the gender split (e.g., Jacqueline Kennedy's popularity among the young women; Spock's endorsement), but it is reasonable to hypothesize that the physical and psychological presence of Caroline was a significant advantage in a very close race.[33]

Jacqueline Kennedy gave birth to a boy. John Fitzgerald Kennedy Jr. was born on November 25, 1960, seventeen days after the election. Nicknamed John-John, he was the first child to be born to a president-elect.[34] The press announced that JFK had told Caroline that she had a baby brother while he walked alongside her as she pushed a toy stroller near their Georgetown home: "He talked to her in a quiet voice, and from time to time helped her steer the doll carriage over the rough brick sidewalk and around tree trunks." A photo of father and daughter, taken from a distance, was published with the account.[35]

JFK was relieved that the birth had gone relatively smoothly and that his wife was doing well (John-John, like Caroline, was delivered by Caesarean section), and he was absolutely ecstatic over the fact that he had a son.[36] Unlike a number of other fathers in the fifties, JFK did not change many, if any, diapers, nor was he apparently comfortable, at least at first, in holding his children when they were small. Three weeks after Caroline was born, he tried to give her a bottle, but asked the family's nanny, Maud Shaw, to stand nearby because he feared his daughter would slip out of his hands. In a matter of a few seconds, he apparently decided he was not up to the job. "Miss Shaw," he said, "how have you got the patience to feed the child all this bottle? You take the bottle and finish her." As far as we know, Jacqueline Kennedy did not do much diapering either—or infant feeding. She also did not routinely get up in the middle of the night to respond to a baby's cries. The child care work in the household was largely left to nannies, cooks, maids, and laundresses. This was a common pattern in very wealthy families, and was the pattern that John and Jacqueline Kennedy had experienced and witnessed in the homes in which they grew up.[37]

Voters who identified with the Kennedy family, seeing in them a reflection of themselves, may not have fully appreciated just how far removed the lives of the Kennedys, and the lives of most upper-class Washington politicians, were from theirs. The first couple may have been perceived, or been portrayed, as the embodiment of "American Fatherhood and Mother-hood"—as if either existed in the singular—but, in truth, they occupied a rarified world.

Still, how voters thought about the Kennedys, and especially how they thought about the Kennedys, *as parents*, was very much connected to the culture and conduct of fatherhood and motherhood at the time. To a certain extent, people saw what they had been trained to see and, depending on their political inclinations, perhaps also what they wanted to see. A father carrying his two-year-old in his arms when he steps off a plane, or telling his daughter about the arrival of a baby brother as he gently (and publicly) helps her navigate an uneven sidewalk, is interpretable only within identifiable sociocultural contexts.

John F. Kennedy was inaugurated as the thirty-fifth president of the United States on January 20, 1961. The day was sunny, and the temperature in Washington was below freezing. More than seven inches of snow had fallen on the capital the day before.[38]

The Kennedy clan, including not only Jacqueline but also JFK's father, mother, brothers, and sisters, occupied an honored place behind and to the right of the new president as he took the oath of office and delivered his inaugural address. Caroline, who had turned three since the election, was not on the dais, but she did watch the festivities on TV in the White House. Two-month-old John-John was reported to have "spent most of the day sleeping peacefully in his crib."[39]

When JFK finished his address, he turned to look at Jacqueline who, in response, gave her husband what the *New York Times* described as an approving smile. During the swearing-in ceremony, JFK's father, Joseph P. Kennedy, had tears in eyes. Later in the afternoon, when JFK approached the reviewing stand where he would watch the inaugural parade, his father, who was already there along with the rest of the family, solemnly stood up and took his hat off "in a gesture of deference to his son." The new president, in turn, tipped his hat to his Dad.[40]

In his address, JFK said that the United States was prepared to defend itself against any who posed a threat, even if it meant going to war. "Let every nation know, whether it wishes us well or ill, that we shall pay any price, bear any burden, meet any hardship, support any friend, oppose any foe to assure the survival and the success of liberty." Acknowledging the sacrifices that had been made during World War II, he praised the millions of Americans, soldiers and nonsoldiers alike, who had banded together in a time of dire need. "In the long history of the world, only a few generations have been granted the role of defending freedom in its hour of maximum danger." At the end of the speech, JFK proclaimed that the "fire" that could "truly light the world" was devotion not to self but to others, and then uttered what has since become the inaugural's most memorable line. "And so, my fellow Americans: ask not what your country can do for you—ask what you can do for your country." [41]

What JFK said at the beginning of his address, however, best captured the significance of the moment and also managed to convey eloquently how World War II and its aftermath had altered the lives of the men, women, and children in whose hands the future now lay. "Let the word go forth from this time and place, to friend and foe alike, that the torch has been passed to a new generation of Americans—born in this century, tempered by war, disciplined by a hard and bitter peace." [42]

The key to appreciating the effects of World War II on the history of fatherhood, as stated in the introduction, is not to presuppose what fatherhood was like in the 1950s, and retrospectively wonder how it was affected by the war, but to begin with the war itself and prospectively examine how it affected society in general, of which fatherhood is a part. This alternative perspective—made concrete in the lives of the ordinary and extraordinary people who are the heart of this book—underscores the importance of context and brings into view a host of war-related effects that are often excluded from scholarly and popular accounts of fatherhood, but routinely included in basic historical works.

One thus cannot truly understand the culture and conduct of fatherhood in America if one does not examine the plight of the Japanese on U.S. soil in the immediate wake of the attack on Pearl Harbor; the effects of the conflict on all nationalities, especially those who were thought to be on the wrong side of the war; the brutality of combat and what it signified both to the men who lived through it and to those who never came anywhere near it; the abject fear that families on the home front felt and how their dread of being vanquished changed how they thought and behaved; the anger of black soldiers who were asked to fight in a battle for freedom but were denied freedom themselves, and how the incongruence between the country's ideals and its practices motivated thousands of fathers and mothers and sons and daughters to rise up and strike a blow at racial apartheid.

Likewise, one cannot truly understand the culture and conduct of fatherhood in America if one does not examine how the war further reified lore and law, and led to the creation of more sharply delineated gender and sexual boundaries; how it accelerated the pace of suburbanization, but did not necessarily alter the connections that fathers had with their kids; how the advent of television and the proliferation of other technologies, some potentially lethal, transformed the collective mentalities of the nation; how political affairs, both stylized and raw, not only directly and indirectly influenced fathers and their families, but also, in a manner both predictable and not, was influenced by them.

———————

Some writers have implied that the effects of the war were virtually erased in the fifties, as other historical forces came into play. Scholarly and popular works often emphasize how a thriving postwar economy increased consumerism and accentuated breadwinning, and how a postwar baby boom gave additional impetus to an ideology of domesticity.

These are, without a doubt, important shifts, and I have made a point of discussing them here. But I have underscored, too, that World War II continued to have a major influence throughout the fifties, and that the story of fatherhood from 1945 to 1960 cannot be divorced from the war itself. It is not just that major events in the fifties were set in motion by the war, but that the war cast a shadow on people's lives long after it was over.[1] A writer remarked in 1959 that America's children were almost constantly told about war, despite parents' efforts to shield them from it. "Even in homes where television is carefully controlled, war scenes may intrude in the act of switching the dial," she exclaimed. "Talk of war on news reports is incessant. . . . Signs, portents, reminders of war are everywhere."[2]

Benjamin Spock also appeared to believe that World War II and its aftermath would affect youngsters for a long time and that its simulation provided a valuable object lesson. In the 1957 edition of *Baby and Child Care*, he preserved the point on war gaming that he first made in the 1946 edition, and said, "A crowd that wants to play war divides itself into teams." He then added, "When your child at 2 bangs another over the head, or at 4 plays at shooting, or at 9 enjoys blood-and-thunder comic books, he is just passing through the necessary stages in the taming of his aggressive instincts that will make him a worth-while citizen."[3]

Given the staying power of war, it is not startling that a nursery school girl would say, "Fathers are to go to the army," when asked in 1957 "What are fathers for?"[4] Nor is it mysterious that a 1959 episode of *Leave It to Beaver* would be devoted entirely to men's combat records.

Placed in the social context of the fifties, the fact that shoot-'em-up TV westerns were more popular than situation comedies is understandable.[5] So is the fact that a seven-year-old boy, born after the war, would write in 1960 to the Fort Dix Post Exchange to request, in his size, "an army uniform" just like his dad's. The child's father was among the soldiers who had landed on the beaches of Normandy and survived the D-Day assault, but had passed away twelve years later. "My Dad is dead," the youngster reported. "He was a Regular Army man, and I want to be like he was."[6]

In 1985, a representative sample of 1,410 Americans, eighteen years and older, was asked in a telephone survey "to think about 'national or world events or changes' that have occurred over the past 50 years and to name 'one or two . . . that seem to have been especially important.'" The most common event or change that the respondents named was World War II. After it came the Vietnam War.[7] When the survey was replicated in 2000 and 2001, but prior to the September 11 attacks, World War II again was mentioned the most. Unlike before, however, the Vietnam War was no longer second; it had slipped to fourth place behind the "end of Communism" and (the invention of) computers and the Internet.[8]

Between November 2001 and January 2002, the survey was repeated again to determine whether the September 11 attacks had had an appreciable effect on what Americans identified as historically important. Not surprisingly, given the recency of the attacks, September 11 was at the very top. World War II, however, was a strong second, mentioned by 28.2 percent and ranked first by 19.5 percent. A comparison with the second survey showed World War II rising in importance in the immediate wake of September 11. To a lesser but still significant degree, the Vietnam War rose in importance, too.[9]

Evident in all three surveys, and helping to clarify why certain events or changes were chosen, was a generational effect. People in their teens or twenties at the time of the event or change were more likely to mention that event or change. The researchers discovered, moreover, that the imprint of an event or change on the mind, if it were made at that "critical age," remained throughout a person's life. In the post September 11 survey, the men and women in their teens or twenties during World War II were, on average, more likely to mention World War II than they were to mention September 11. For those who came of age in the 1940s, the September 11 attacks did not eclipse but in fact magnified the memories they had of the war.[10]

The thoughts that people have about the past include not only the salience of events or changes (e.g., how often they are recalled), but also the value that is attached to them (e.g., how much events or changes are conceptualized in positive or negative terms). In the 1985 survey, the researchers asked the respondents which events or changes were important *and why*. It was found that people who lived through World War II were more likely to say the war was significant because of how it affected them personally. One man, for example, said, "A lot of lives were lost. I came home but a lot didn't." A woman reported, "Because my husband was away from me for three and a half years and it changed my life a lot. I had a child when he was gone, and I had to go through that alone."[11]

People born after the war, on the other hand, took a larger and, in some respects, impersonal view. They were more likely to talk about how the war "changed world relations" or how it "affected more people than any other war." Especially striking was their emphasis on the idea of "winning the good war." One woman, who was born in 1949, remarked, "That was a victorious war so it was exhilarating to bond together in the country." Another, who was born in 1954, observed, "If we didn't win the war, this would be a different kind of world—not much freedom." Thus, those who did not live through World War II were more likely than those who did to look back at what happened in wistful terms.[12]

It is noteworthy that the children of the fifties—the baby boomers—tended, more so than others, to frame World War II as the "good war." As to why they did so, the researchers hypothesized that the children of the fifties viewed World War II through the prism of the Vietnam War, which was a war that members of their generation had fought in, and one that, in comparison to World War II, was widely protested and did not result in a victory for the United States.[13] The children of the fifties, having come of age in the Vietnam War era, were "vicariously nostalgic," said the researchers, "for a world they [had] never known directly, in contrast to the world of their own youth during the divisive late 1960s and early 1970s."[14]

Examining the effects of World War II thus must take into account not only the political, economic, and technological developments that the war brought about, but also the changes in people's social mindsets. Indeed, it appears that, as an event or change recedes in time, the cognitive realm pertaining to that event or change becomes increasingly more important. The power of World War II today rests, to a large extent, on what people choose to remember about the war—and also what they choose to forget. The legacy of the war lies partially in its retelling.[15]

Regardless of whether a war is thought to be "good" or "bad," its most visceral effect is represented in the lives that it claims. The cemeteries speak of the legions that died, but they do not reveal all. What about the tens of thousands who never came back? According to U.S. government records, 74,213 American G.I.'s from World War II—mostly fathers, grandfathers, sons, brothers, and uncles—have not been officially recovered and identified.[16] To this day, Defense Department teams continue to search for them.[17] For the family members of the World War II soldiers missing in action, lost at sea, or interred as unknowns, the war has not ended.[18]

INTRODUCTION

1. Richard Guy Wilson, "America and the Machine Age," in *The Machine Age in America, 1918–1941*, ed. Richard Guy Wilson, Dianne H. Pilgrim, and Dickran Tashjian (New York: Harry N. Abrams, in association with the Brooklyn Museum, 1986), 23–42.

2. To a certain degree, men remain mothers' "helpers" or "stand-ins." Although their involvement in child care has significantly increased in recent years, men still do not do as much child care as women do. Moreover, women continue to be the ones who "orchestrate" the care (by lining up babysitters, keeping track of the kids' progress in school, etc.). See Suzanne M. Bianchi, John P. Robinson, and Melissa A. Milkie, *Changing Rhythms of American Family Life* (New York: Russell Sage Foundation, 2006); Kathleen Gerson, *The Unfinished Revolution: How a New Generation Is Reshaping Family, Work, and Gender in America* (New York: Oxford University Press, 2010).

3. On fatherhood in nineteenth-century America, see Stephen M. Frank, *Life with Father: Parenthood and Masculinity in the Nineteenth-Century American North* (Baltimore, MD: Johns Hopkins University Press, 1998); Shawn Johansen, *Family Men: Middle-Class Fatherhood in Early Industrializing America* (New York: Routledge, 2001).

4. The main findings from the fatherhood-in-the-machine-age project were detailed in Ralph LaRossa, *The Modernization of Fatherhood: A Social and Political History* (Chicago: University of Chicago Press, 1997).

5. General works on the history of American fatherhood have acknowledged the impact of World War II but (as a matter of focus and probably also for lack of space) have not fully explored its wide-ranging effects. See, for example, John Demos, "The Changing Faces of Fatherhood: A New Exploration in Family History," in *Father and Child: Developmental and Clinical Perspectives*, ed. Stanley H. Cath, Alan Gurwitt, and John M. Ross (Boston: Little, Brown, 1982), 425–45; Steven Mintz, "From Patriarchy to Androgyny and Other Myths: Placing Men's Roles in Historical Perspective," in *Men in Families: When Do They Get Involved? What Difference Does It Make?* ed. Alan Booth and Ann C. Crouter (Mahwah, NJ: Lawrence Erlbaum, 1998), 3–30; E. Anthony Rotundo, "American Fatherhood: A Historical Perspective," *American Behavioral Scientist* 29 (September/October 1985): 7–25; Joseph H. Pleck, "American Fathering in Historical Perspective," in *Changing Men: New Directions in Research on Men and Masculinity*, ed. Michael S. Kimmel (Newbury Park, CA: Sage, 1987), 83–97; as well as Elizabeth H. Pleck and Joseph H. Pleck, "Fatherhood Ideals in the United States:

Historical Dimensions," in *The Role of the Father in Child Development*, ed. Michael E. Lamb (New York: John Wiley and Sons, 1997), 33–48; and Peter N. Stearns, "Fatherhood in Historical Perspective: The Role of Social Change," in *Fatherhood and Families in Cultural Context*, ed. Frederick W. Bozett and Shirley M. H. Hanson (New York: Springer, 1991), 28–52; John R. Gillis, "Marginalization of Fatherhood in Western Countries," *Childhood* 7 (May 2000): 225–38. The first book-length treatment of the history of American fatherhood, which chronicled continuities and changes from 1800 to 1993, devoted an entire chapter to World War II and another chapter to the postwar era; see Robert L. Griswold, *Fatherhood in America: A History* (New York: Basic Books, 1993). Though detailed in many important respects, there are significant experiences and events in the 1940s and 1950s that were not fully examined. Griswold said that he "tried to capture changes in the history of American fathers in [the twentieth] century, fully aware that [he] . . . often painted with a broad brush," but that he "hope[d] and expecte[d] that finer strokes [would] be added by later historians" (x). My goal in this book is to add some of these "finer strokes." Informative accounts of the history of fatherhood in the 1940s and 1950s also include works that are histories of World War II or the postwar era, of family life or childhood, of masculinities or femininities, or of popular culture. See, for example, Lizabeth Cohen, *A Consumers' Republic: The Politics of Mass Consumption in Postwar America* (New York: Knopf, 2003); Rachel Devlin, *Relative Intimacy: Fathers, Adolescent Daughters, and Postwar American Culture* (Chapel Hill: University of North Carolina Press, 2005); Stephen Mintz and Susan Kellogg, *Domestic Revolutions: A Social History of American Family Life* (New York: Free Press, 1988); Elaine Tyler May, *Homeward Bound: American Families in the Cold War Era* (New York: Basic Books,1988); Stephanie Coontz, *The Way We Never Were: American Families and the Nostalgia Trap* (New York: Basic Books, 1992); Jessica Weiss, *To Have and to Hold: Marriage, the Baby Boom, and Social Change* (Chicago: University of Chicago Press, 2000); William M. Tuttle Jr., *"Daddy's Gone to War": The Second World War in the Lives of America's Children* (New York: Oxford University Press, 1993); Steven Mintz, *Huck's Raft: A History of American Childhood* (Cambridge, MA: Harvard University Press, 2004); Susan Faludi, *Stiffed: The Betrayal of the American Man* (William Morrow, 1999); James Gilbert, *Men in the Middle: Searching for Masculinity in the 1950s* (Chicago: University of Chicago Press, 2005); and Michael Kimmel, *Manhood in America: A Cultural History* (Free Press, 1996). Studies of the incarceration of Japanese Americans after World War II and accounts of the postwar black civil rights movement, to name just two areas, also are valuable sources for understanding the history of fatherhood. See, for example, Stephen S. Fugita and Marilyn Fernandez, *Altered Lives, Enduring Community: Japanese Americans Remember Their World War II Incarceration* (Seattle, WA: University of Washington Press, 2004); Taylor Branch, *Parting the Waters: America in the King Years, 1954–63* (New York: Simon and Schuster, 1988).

6.   In *The War Complex: World War II in Our Time* (Chicago: University of Chicago Press, 2005), Marianna Torgovnick noted that when she thought back over the materials she had examined and the memories she had received about World War II, she was "struck by how almost all led back to families." The war complex, Torgovnick argued, "lives where we live, in families" and "begins by imagining historical disaster in the home" (143). In *This Republic of Suffering: Death and the American Civil War* (New York: Random House, 2008), Drew Gilpin Faust talked about the connection that families had with the Civil War. "Perhaps the most distressing aspect of death for

many Civil War Americans," Faust said, "was that thousands of young men were dying away from home" (9).

7. Frank Pittman, "Bringing Up Father," *Family Therapy Networker* 12 (May/June 1988): 22.

8. The phrase "strides toward freedom" is derived from Martin Luther King, Jr., *Stride Toward Freedom: The Montgomery Story* (New York: Harper and Row, 1958).

9. The "fifties" (vs. "1950s") generally is understood to encompass more than the years 1950 to 1959. For some, the period began at the end of World War II and ended in 1963 with the assassination of John F. Kennedy and the publication of Betty Friedan's *The Feminine Mystique* (New York: W. W. Norton, 1963). See Jessamyn Neuhaus, "The Way to a Man's Heart: Gender Roles, Domestic Ideology, and Cookbooks in the 1950s," *Journal of Social History* 32 (Spring 1999), 529–55. Others define the fifties as the time between the end of World War II and the election of John F. Kennedy (i.e., 1945 to 1960). I use the second definition here. See Steven Cohan, *Masked Men: Masculinity and the Movies in the Fifties* (Bloomington, IN: Indiana University Press, 1997); David Halberstam, *The Fifties* (New York: Villard Books, 1993); Joanne Meyerowitz, ed., *Not June Cleaver: Women and Gender in Postwar America, 1945–1960* (Philadelphia, PA: Temple University Press, 1994).

10. Jonathan W. Gould and Robert E. Gunther, *Reinventing Fatherhood* (Blue Ridge Summit, PA: TAB Books, 1993), vii, 4.

11. Quoted in Travis Grant, "Fatherhood," online at *About.com*, http:fatherhood.about .com (accessed January 23, 2000; my italics).

12. It is not that no research was being conducted on fatherhood, but that the amount of research was both sparse and limited in its scope. One set of authors reported searching the literature between 1929 and 1956 and finding "160 publications" dealing with mothers and children but only "10 articles, one convention address, and one book" providing information on fathers and children. See Donald R. Peterson, Wesley C. Becker, Leo H. Helmer, Donald J. Shoemaker, and Herbert C. Quay, "Parental Attitudes and Child Adjustment," *Child Development* 30 (March 1959): 119–30.

13. B. W. (man) to Rose Franzblau, no date (in all likelihood, 1949), box 27, Rose Franzblau Papers, Columbia University (hereafter cited as RFP). The writer said that his wife had an operation five months earlier, which resulted in her going through menopause and losing the ability to have children. "What is to be done? Where do we go from here?" he asked. Rose Franzblau was a prominent New York psychologist who wrote a syndicated column for the *New York Post* ("Human Relations") and, in that capacity, received thousands of letters from individuals asking for personal and family advice. The letters to Franzblau, a number of which I introduce in the chapters to follow, offer a side to family life that sometimes has been overlooked in historical accounts of fatherhood in the fifties.

14. M. N. (man) to Rose Franzblau, 21 August 1949, box 27, RFP. The writer was a thirty-five-year-old black man who was formerly married to a white woman hospitalized for mental illness. The father said that he hoped to remarry: "I'd like to find a nice woman who is looking for a good companion & also wouldn't mind helping me with my son." The father had written to Franzblau to ask for the name of a "good mental doctor" for himself and "a good little private school" for his son. At the top of the letter, there is a scribbled message that reads, "Answered Aug. 30 '49, M. L. M," suggesting that someone in Franzblau's office replied. A copy of the reply is not in the file.

15. Father 38, pp. 44–45, in Robert R. Sears, Lucy Rau, and Richard Alpert, "Identification and Child Rearing" (ICR) interview, Murray Research Center (MRC), Harvard-
MIT Data Center. This interview was part of a study carried out by Robert R. Sears,
Lucy Rau, and Richard Alpert, entitled "Identification and Child Rearing, 1958." For
a detailed description of the study, see Robert R. Sears, Lucy Rau, and Richard Alpert,
Identification and Child Rearing (Stanford, CA: Stanford University Press, 1965). Additional information about the study is provided in subsequent chapters. Ellipses
without brackets denote ellipses in the original transcript, while those in brackets
denote instances where I have omitted or skipped over sentences that were in the
original transcript. When the mother was asked in a separate interview about how
much time the focal child in the study (the four-year-old) spent with his father, she
said, "Oh, a great deal. I mean, at least, well his father generally gets home around
six or six-thirty; sometimes he's a little earlier, sometimes a little later, and from then
on, until he goes to bed, he is with his father, and weekends, he is with his father."
She added, "[H]is father has long put him to bed, and they talk about things—they
have one game of 'What did you do today? You tell me everything you did today,
and I'll tell you everything I did today.' And my husband lies down on the bed with
him, and that sometimes goes on for a half-hour, and—ah, they read—they draw . . .
[the focal child] loves to draw [. . .] with a pencil or with crayons, and my husband
has—is pretty good, and he draws pictures for [the focal child]" (Mother 38, second
interview, p. 30, in Sears, Rau, and Alpert, ICR Interview, MRC, Harvard-MIT Data
Center.

16. LaRossa, *Modernization of Fatherhood*; Ralph LaRossa, "Mythologizing Fatherhood,"
NCFR Report: Newsletter of the National Council on Family Relations 54 (Spring 2009):
F3, F4, F6.

17. M. Robert Gomberg, "Father as a Family Man," *New York Times Magazine*, 6 September 1953.

18. Miriam Selchen, "What Are Fathers For?" *Parents Magazine*, June 1957.

19. Examples of this compensatory process appear in Scott Coltrane, *Family Man: Fa-
therhood, Housework, and Gender Equity* (New York: Oxford University Press, 1996);
Kerry Daly, "Reshaping Fatherhood: Finding the Models," *Journal of Family Issues*
(December 1993): 510–30; John Snarey, *How Fathers Care for the Next Generation: A
Four-Decade Study* (Cambridge, MA: Harvard University Press, 1993).

20. Michael Chabon, *Manhood for Amateurs: The Pleasures and Regrets of a Husband, Father
and Son* (New York: Harper, 2009), 11.

21. A notable exception in the popular press to the tendency to assume that yesterday's
fathers did not care for children and were lacking in paternal emotion is Susan Jacoby's essay, "A Good Dad in Any Age," *New York Times Magazine*, 17 June 17 1990.
Jacoby noted that invidious comparison with fathers in the past "assuages the guilt of
men who aren't nearly as involved with their children on a day-to-day-basis as they
ought to be. Denigrating Dour Old Dad becomes a way of asserting superior sensitiv-
ity while avoiding the fundamental issue of what men's responsibilities ought to be
in a radically altered, two-earner domestic economy" (20).

22. The *culture of fatherhood* and *conduct of fatherhood* are terms first employed in Ralph
LaRossa, "Fatherhood and Social Change," *Family Relations* 37 (October 1988): 451–
57. See also LaRossa, *Modernization of Fatherhood*.

23. For an interpretive view of culture, see Clifford Geertz, *The Interpretation of Cultures*
(New York: Basic Books, 1973); and Peter L. Berger and Thomas Luckmann, *The
Social Construction of Reality: A Treatise in the Sociology Knowledge* (Garden City, NY:

Doubleday/Anchor, 1966). For a discussion of how culture is a complex of cultural objects, cultural creators, cultural receivers, and social worlds, see Wendy Griswold, *Cultures and Societies in a Changing World* (Thousand Oaks, CA: Pine Forge Press, 1994). For a discussion of the multifaceted and fragmented quality of culture, see Paul DiMaggio, "Culture and Cognition," *Annual Review of Sociology* 23 (August 1997): 263–87. For a discussion of this topic in the context of the postwar era, see Joanne Meyerowitz, "Beyond the Feminine Mystique: A Reassessment of Postwar Mass Culture, 1946–1958, in Meyerowitz, *Not June Cleaver*, 229–62.

24. See R. W. Connell, *Masculinities* (Berkeley and Los Angeles, CA: University of California Press, 1995; 2nd ed., 2005), 34–37, 77, 82; Harry Brod, ed., *The Making of Masculinities* (Boston: Allen and Unwin, 1987); Charlotte Hooper, *Manly States: Masculinities, International Relations, and Gender Politics* (New York: Columbia University Press, 2001). I have borrowed Connell's references to "alliance, dominance, and subordination" and "patterns of hegemony" from his discussion of masculinities and adapted them to the culture of fatherhood. Connell's "multiple masculinities" concept has been questioned, and a response and reformulation has been offered. See R. W. Connell and James W. Messershmidt, "Hegemonic Masculinity: Rethinking the Concept," *Gender and Society* 19 (December 2005): 829–59; as well as the introduction to the second edition of *Masculinities*. The "basic idea," however, has stood up to the test of time. "The fundamental feature of the concept," according to Connell and Messerschmidt, "remains the combination of the plurality of masculinities and the hierarchy of masculinities." The proposition that the culture of fatherhood and culture of masculinity are constructed and disseminated within a political context is axiomatic among fatherhood and gender scholars. See, for example, Mark C. Carnes and Clyde Griffen, eds., *Meanings for Manhood: Constructions of Masculinity in Victorian America* [the full collection of essays] (Chicago: University of Chicago Press), 1990; Richard Collier and Sally Sheldon, *Fragmenting Fatherhood: A Socio-Legal Study* (Portland, OR: Hart, 2008); Coltrane, *Family Man*; Jeff Hearn, *The Gender of Oppression: Men, Masculinity, and the Critique of Marxism* (New York: St. Martin's Press, 1987); Hooper, *Manly States*; Kimmel, *Manhood in America*; Michael S. Kimmel and Michael A. Messner, eds., *Men's Lives*, 2nd ed. [the full collection of essays] (New York: Macmillan, 1992); LaRossa, *Modernization of Fatherhood*; Deborah Lupton and Lesley Barclay, *Constructing Fatherhood: Discourses and Experiences* (London: Sage, 1997); William Marsiglio, *Procreative Man* (New York: New York University Press, 1998); and E. Anthony Rotundo, *American Manhood: Transformations in Masculinity from the Revolution to the Modern Era* (New York: Basic Books, 1993). Some have observed that the attention given to cataloguing diverse masculinities has sometimes steered scholars away from studying men's practices—particularly men's practices that create gender inequality. See Douglas Schrock and Michael Schwalbe, "Men, Masculinity, and Manhood Acts," *Annual Review of Sociology* 35 (August 2009): 277–95.

25. For a discussion of how "hard" masculinity became a standard during and after World War II, see Cohan, *Masked Men*; Faludi, *Stiffed*; Christina S. Jarvis, *The Male Body at War: American Masculinity During World War II* (Dekalb, IL: Northern Illinois University Press, 2004). For a discussion of "hard" masculinity during and after the Vietnam War, see Susan Jeffords, *The Remasculinization of America: Gender and the Vietnam War* (Bloomington, IN: Indiana University Press, 1989). For a discussion of "hard" masculinity and war in general, see Joshua S. Goldstein, *War and Gender: How Gender Shapes the War System and Vice Versa* (Cambridge: Cambridge University Press, 2001).

26. Other researchers studying the history of fatherhood also believe it is important to distinguish culture and conduct. In *Fatherhood in America*, Robert Griswold talked of "a sharp disjunction between what fathers think they should do at home and what they actually do" (227). See also Johansen, *Family Men*; LaRossa, *Modernization of Fatherhood*; Pleck and Pleck, "Fatherhood Ideals in the United States." On a more general level, in *A World of Their Own Making: Myth, Ritual, and the Quest for Family Values* (New York: Basic Books, 1996), John R. Gillis drew a distinction between culture and conduct when he referred to the family we live *by* and the family we live *with*.

27. Coontz, *The Way We Never Were*, 29.

28. On how letters, notes, and the like are inscriptions, where "active processes of interpretation and sense-making are involved," see Robert M. Emerson, Rachel I. Fretz, and Linda L. Shaw, *Writing Ethnographic Fieldnotes* (Chicago: University of Chicago Press, 1995), 8, drawing on Geertz, *Interpretation of Cultures*.

29. Philip Abrams, *Historical Sociology* (Ithaca, NY: Cornell University Press, 1982); Berger and Luckmann, *Social Construction of Reality*; C. Wright Mills, *The Sociological Imagination* (New York: Oxford University Press, 1959).

30. On the importance of age in the study of history, and particularly in understanding how people experienced World War II, see Glen H. Elder Jr. and Avshalom Caspi, "Studying Lives in a Changing Society: Sociological and Personological Explorations," in *Studying Persons and Lives*, ed., Albert I. Rabin, Robert A. Zucker, Robert A. Emmons, and Susan Frank (New York: Springer, 1990), 201–47; Tuttle, *"Daddy's Gone to War."*

31. On the importance of contingency in the historical process (and in understanding the process of war), see David Hackett Fischer, *Paul Revere's Ride* (New York: Oxford University Press, 1994); James McPherson, *Battle Cry of Freedom: The Civil War Era* (New York: Oxford University Press, 1988).

CHAPTER ONE

1. Department of Defense, Fiftieth Anniversary of World War II Commemorative Committee. *Pearl Harbor: Fiftieth Anniversary Commemorative Chronicle, "A Grateful Nation Remembers," 1941–1991* (Washington, DC: World War II Commemorative Committee, 1991), online at http://www.history.navy.mil/faqs/faq66-1.htm (accessed 28 March 2006). Gordon W. Prange, *At Dawn We Slept: The Untold Story of Pearl Harbor* (New York: McGraw Hill, 1981), 539–40, 777; Jean Edward Smith, *FDR* (New York: Random House, 2007), 536.

2. Robert Sullivan, "Pearl Harbor Timeline," *Time*, online at http://www.time.com/time/sampler/article/0,8599,127924,00.html (accessed 24 March 2006).

3. Steven Mintz, *Huck's Raft: A History of American Childhood* (Cambridge, MA: Harvard University Press, 2004), 254, citing a story told in Dorinda Makanaonalani Nicholson's book, *Pearl Harbor Child* (Honolulu: Arizona Memorial Museum Association, 1993).

4. William M. Tuttle Jr., *"Daddy's Gone to War": The Second World War in the Lives of America's Children* (New York: Oxford University Press, 1993), 4, 5. The personal accounts in this book were taken from letters that the author solicited through newspapers.

5. "Following the outbreak of war in Europe in 1939, the Coast Guard carried out neutrality patrols. . . . Port security began on 22 June 1940 when President Roosevelt invoked the Espionage Act of 1917 which governed the anchorage and movement

of all ships in U.S. waters and protected American ships, harbors and waters. Shortly afterwards, the Dangerous Cargo Act gave the Coast Guard jurisdiction over ships carrying high explosives and dangerous cargoes. In March 1941, the Coast Guard seized 28 Italian, two German and 35 Danish merchant ships." See United States Coast Guard, "U.S. Coast Guard: A Historical Overview," online at http://www.uscg.mil/hq/g-cp/history/h_USCGhistory.html (accessed 24 March 2006).

6. Kevin Coyne, *Marching Home: To War and Back with the Men of One American Town* (New York: Viking, 2003), 19.

7. Bell Aircraft Corporation ad, *Time*, 22 July 1940.

8. Lehigh Portland Cement Company ad, *Time*, 21 October 1940.

9. New England Mutual Life Insurance Company ad, *Time*, 17 March 1941.

10. White Motor Company ad, *Time*, 14 July 1941. Companies seemed eager to capitalize on the war, connecting their products in whatever way they could to the defense of democracy. In October 1941, the American Seating Company promoted its line of classroom desks by asking, "How well will your children take care tomorrow of the democracy you are defending today?" Its reply: "The answer lies with how well you equip them for the future. Good education creates good citizens. And good school equipment helps make education good . . . especially does this apply to school seating." American Seating Company ad, *Time*, 6 October 1941. For other examples of businesses couching their products in terms of the war, see Kenneth D. Rose, *Myth and the Greatest Generation: A Social History of Americans in World War II* (New York: Routledge, 2008), 72–77.

11. David M. Kennedy, *Freedom From Fear: The American People in Depression and War, 1929–1945* (New York: Oxford University Press, 1999), 565–72; Smith, *FDR*, 542. During the early months of the war, German submarine captains were so confident that the U.S. Navy could not protect ships going in or coming out of New York harbor that they attacked in broad daylight. Bodies along with debris from the torpedoed vessels would wash up on shore. Lorraine B. Diehl, *Over Here! New York City during World War II* (New York: HarperCollins, 2010), 91.

12. Warner and Swasey Turret Lathes ad, *Time*, 2 March 1942.

13. Warner and Swasey Turret Lathes ad, *Time*, 11 May 1942.

14. Warner and Swasey Turret Lathes ad, *Time*, 13 April 1942. A number of companies conveyed the message that America was in a fight for its life. Warner and Swasey, however, appeared to have developed an entire advertising campaign around this theme. Another of its ads warned, "America has lost too many battles in this war—always because that extra piece of equipment was still on somebody's machine here . . . your machine. Fighting men know the whole war can be lost that same way." And in still another, "If this war is lost (and it is dangerously close to it) don't blame your soldiers and sailors—blame yourself. Not the man or woman in the next block or at the next machine or desk, but *yourself*. All wars are lost by the people back home who want somebody else to do the fighting, the dying, the sacrificing for them." Warner and Swasey Turret Lathes ads, *Time*, 25 May 1942, and 7 September 1942.

15. Magazine Publishers of America ad, *Life*, 5 April 1943.

16. United Gas Pipe Line Company ad, *Time*, 12 July 1943.

17. See, for example, Deborah Dash Moore, *G.I. Jews: How World War II Changed a Generation* (Cambridge, MA: Harvard University Press, 2004).

18. Japanese American Internment Curriculum, "Posters from World War II," online at http://bss.sfsu.edu/internment/posters.html (accessed 23 March 2006).

19. Tuttle, *"Daddy's Gone to War,"* 172.

20. Bill Hosokawa, *Nisei: The Quiet Americans* (New York: William Morrow, 1969), 42. Hosokawa reported the total population of Japanese in the mainland United States (excluding Hawaii), by year, as follows: 55 in 1870; 148 in 1880; 2,039 in 1890; 24,327 in 1900; 72,157 in 1919; 110,010 in 1920; 138,834 in 1930; and 126,947 in 1940. See also Roger Daniels, *Prisoners without Trial: Japanese Americans in World War II* (New York: Hill and Wang, 1993; rev. ed., 2004), 8; Darrel Montero, *Japanese Americans: Changing Patterns of Ethnic Affiliation Over Three Generations* (Boulder, CO: Westview Press, 1980), 7.

21. Patricia Wakida, "Preface," in *Only What We Could Carry: The Japanese American Internment Experience*, ed. Lawson Fusao Inada, xi–xiv (Berkeley, CA: Heyday Books, 2000). The Japanese who entered the mainland United States between 1901 and 1940 numbered 108,163 between 1901 and 1907; 74,478 between 1908 and 1914; 85,197 between 1915 and 1924; and 6,156 between 1925 and 1940. See William Petersen, *Japanese Americans: Oppression and Success* (New York: Random House, 1971), 15.

22. Stephen S. Fugita and Marilyn Fernandez, *Altered Lives, Enduring Community: Japanese Americans Remember Their World War II Incarceration* (Seattle: University of Washington Press, 2004), 49 (Frank Fujii). The personal accounts in this book are taken from video-recorded interviews.

23. John Tateishi, *And Justice for All: An Oral History of the Japanese American Detention Camps* (New York: Random House, 1984), 16 (Eddie Sakamoto). The personal accounts in this book were taken from audio-recorded interviews.

24. Studs Terkel, *"The Good War": An Oral History of World War Two* (New York: Pantheon Books, 1984), 27 (Peter Ota). The personal accounts in this book were taken from audio-recorded interviews.

25. Tateishi, *And Justice for All*, 239–40 (Chiye Tomihoro).

26. Lorraine Glennon, ed., *Our Times: The Illustrated History of the Twentieth Century* (Atlanta: Turner Publishing, 1995), 264.

27. Tateishi, *And Justice for All*, 27, 28 (Haruko Niwa). The man went to say, "I didn't want to cause any hardship for two boys. So we took a picture and sent [it] to father along with the letter saying we're not going back to Japan with the last boat."

28. Ibid., 101 (Miyo Senzaki). A father who had come to the United States in 1906 burned the awards he had gotten in Japan, as well as letters and photos from Japan. Other mementos were hidden (ibid., 228 [Frank Chuman]).

29. "In 1942, we were dismissed from working for the state of California because we were of Japanese ancestry. We were given a piece of paper saying we were suspended. . . . We were accused of something, but I can't even remember any of the allegations" (ibid., 60 [Mitsuye Endo]). "In January, following Pearl Harbor, the Western Pacific kicked my father out—took his job away, claiming he was a security risk. . . . He and Mom were ordered to leave their house and get off railroad property" (Roy Nishiguchi, "'We Nisei Were Americans,'" in *War Stories: Veterans Remember WW II*, ed. R. T. King, 111–15 [Reno: University of Nevada Oral History Program, 1995], 113).

30. Hosokawa, *Nisei*, 255.

31. Tuttle, *"Daddy's Gone to War,"* 171–73.

32. Ibid., 172.

33. Tateishi, *And Justice for All*, 68 (Minoru Yasui).

34. Thomas James, *Exile Within: The Schooling of Japanese Americans, 1942–1945* (Cambridge, MA: Harvard University Press, 1987), 3; Roger Daniels, "Incarcerating Japanese Americans," *Organization of American Historian's Magazine of History* 16 (Spring

2002): 19–23; Fugita and Fernandez, *Altered Lives*, 50; Alison M. Wrynn, "The Recreation and Leisure Pursuits of Japanese Americans in World War II Internment Camps," in *Ethnicity and Sport in North American History and Culture*, ed. George Eisen and David K. Wiggins, 117–31 (Westport, CT: Praeger, 1995), 119–20. If we include not only those Japanese Americans who were interned in the War Relocation Authority's camps, but also those who were "held in Justice Department internment and isolation camps, Hawaiian ethnic Japanese brought to the mainland for detention, and births during the period of internment," the total number of Japanese Americans incarcerated is closer to 120,000. See Erica Harth, "Introduction," in *Last Witnesses: Reflection on the Wartime Internment of Japanese Americans*, ed. Erica Harth, 1–18 (New York: Palgrave/Macmillan, 2001), 16.

35. Masao Takahashi, quoted in Fred Barbash, "'Evacuation' of the Japanese Americans," *Washington Post*, 5 December 1982, cited in Tuttle, *"Daddy's Gone to War,"* 167–68.

36. Sonoko U. Iwata to Shigezo Iwata, 18 April 1942, and 5 October 1942, in Judy Barrett Litoff and David C. Smith, eds., *Since You Went Away: World War II Letters from American Women on the Homefront* (Lawrence: University Press of Kansas, 1991), 216.

37. Ibid., 221–22. In another letter, dated 18 June 1942, Sonoka U. Iwata wrote: "This coming Sunday is Father's Day and our thoughts will be with you especially. We certainly hope and pray that you will be able to join us soon" (219). The fact that a husband and wife might go together to a camp did not eliminate the pain of leaving home. "There were tears everywhere; Grandma couldn't leave her flowers, and Grandpa looked at his grape vineyard. We urged him to get into the car and leave" (Tateishi, *And Justice for All*, 11 [Mary Tsukamoto]).

38. John Y. Tateishi, "Memories from Behind Barbed Wire," in Harth, *Last Witnesses*, 134, 135.

39. Tateishi, *And Justice for All*, 34 (Donald Nakahata).

40. Daniels, "Incarcerating Japanese Americans."

41. Timothy J. Holian, *The German-Americans and World War II: An Ethnic Experience* (New York: Peter Lang, 1996), 132.

42. Ibid., 134.

43. Some 2,800 ethnic Germans also were transported to the United States from twelve Latin American countries and imprisoned (ibid., 143).

44. Edith Anson Howard to Alfred Ryland Howard, 3 July 1944, in Litoff and Smith, *Since You Went Away*, 243.

45. Tuttle, *"Daddy's Gone to War,"* 180, 181.

46. "On December 10, 1941, FBI Director Hoover announced that 1,291 Japanese, 857 Germans, and 147 Italians had been taken into custody. By June 30, 1942, the FBI had arrested a total of 9,405 suspect enemy aliens, including 4,764 Japanese, 3,120 Germans, and 1,521 Italians. After one year of war, internment figures reflected an even more glaring gap. At this juncture, only 210 Italians were interned"; Gary R. Mormino and George E. Pozzetta, "Ethnics at War: Italian Americans in California during World War II," in *The Way We Really Were: The Golden State in the Second World War*, ed. Roger W. Lotchin, 143–63 (Urbana: University of Illinois Press, 2000), 146–47. According to some, the number of Italians interned was closer to 1,500. See Nancy C. Carnevale, "'No Italian Spoken for the Duration of the War': Language, Italian-American Identity, and Cultural Pluralism in the World War II Years," *Journal of American Ethnic History* 22 (Spring 2003): 3–33.

47. Stephen Fox , *The Unknown Experiment: An Oral History of the Relocation of Italian Americans during World War II* (Boston: Twayne, 1990), 59 (Benito Vanni), and 65,

64 (Nida Vanni). A photographer in San Francisco was put in the position of having to take the photos that would be affixed to alien registration papers. His son recalled the noncitizens who came to the studio: "I never forgot their sadness, their tears. It was a very emotional experience for me. . . . Many had no relatives here, just themselves. . . . I'll never forget Mr. Maniscalco. He was a fisherman, the most respected at the wharf. . . . Italian aliens were compelled to remain fourteen blocks away from the waterfront. He couldn't comprehend. With tears in his eyes, he told me, 'I'm gonna breaka the law. My boat is my life.' He would sneak out to see his boat and the waterfront" (ibid., 710.

48. Carnevale, " 'No Italian Spoken for the Duration of the War,' " 7.

49. Ibid., 10.

50. Ibid., 8.

51. Mormino and Pozzetta, "Ethnics at War," 147.

52. Tuttle, *Daddy's Gone to War,* 183, 184.

53. David S. Wyman, *The Abandonment of the Jews: America and the Holocaust, 1941–1945* (New York: Pantheon Books, 1984).

54. Edward J. Escobar, "Zoot-Suiters and Cops: Chicano Youth and the Los Angeles Police Department during World War II," in *The War in American Culture: Society and Consciousness during World War II,* ed., Lewis A. Erenberg and Susan E. Hirsch, 284–309 (Chicago: University of Chicago Press, 1996), 295. See also Carey McWilliams, *North from Mexico: The Spanish-Speaking People of the United States* (Philadelphia, PA: J. B. Lippincott, 1948).

55. Ibid., 166–67.

56. See, for example, Angelo Falcon, "A History of Puerto Rican Politics in New York City: 1860 to 1945," in *Puerto Rican Politics in Urban America,* ed. James Jennings and Monte Rivera, 15–42 (Westport, CT: Greenwood Press, 1984).

57. Benson Tong, *The Chinese Americans,* rev. ed. (Boulder, CO: University Press of Colorado, 2003), 100.

58. Ibid. Iris Chang, *The Chinese in America* (New York: Viking, 2003), 224, 225. See also Nellie Wong, "Can't Tell," in Inada, *Only What We Could Carry,* 51–52. Wong, whose "father owned a grocery store in Berkeley next to a Japanese American butcher shop," wrote, "Shortly [after war was declared] our Japanese neighbors vanished and my parents continued to whisper: We are Chinese, we are Chinese. We wore black arm bands, put up a sign in bold letters."

59. George H. Roeder Jr., "Censoring Disorder: American Visual Imagery of World War II," in *The War in American Culture: Society and Consciousness during World War II,* ed. Lewis A. Erenberg and Susan E. Hirsch, 46–70 (Chicago: University of Chicago Press, 1996), 52; "How to Tell Japs from the Chinese: Angry Citizens Victimize Allies with Emotional Outburst at Enemy, *Life,* 22 December 1941; "How to Tell Your Friends from the Japs," *Time,* 22 December 1941.

60. "How to Tell Japs from the Chinese," 81.

61. "How to Tell Your Friends from the Japs," 33.

62. "How to Tell Japs from the Chinese," 81.

63. Mary Paik Lee, *Quiet Odyssey: A Pioneer Korean Woman in America* (Seattle: University of Washington Press, 1990), 95, 96.

64. Ibid., 95. Hoping not to be mistaken for Japanese, some Korean Americans also wore buttons proclaiming their ethnic identity. In 1942 Sammy Lee was on his way to a national swim meet and was wearing a button that said, "I'm a Korean, not a Jap." While on the train, he ran into two Japanese Americans who were members of the

Hawaiian swim team—people he knew them from previous meets. Lee admitted that he was embarrassed about wearing the button in front of them. "We understand. Don't worry about it," they said. He removed the button and never put it on again. (Lee won a gold medal in diving for the United States at the 1948 Olympics.) See also Juan Williams, *My Soul Looks Back in Wonder: Voices of the Civil Rights Experience* (New York: AARP/Sterling, 2004), 47.

CHAPTER TWO

1. "Storm Moving Up Atlantic Coast," *New York Times*, 15 September 1943.
2. "Manpower for Victory," *New York Times*, 15 September 1943.
3. "Nine Day Nightmare," *Time*, 9 November 1962, reporting on the U.S. publication of Hugh Pond's book, *Salerno* (Boston: Little, Brown, 1962). Pond noted that "Salerno was operationally coded Avalanche, and some people have described it as an 'Avalanche of Errors'" (vii). Eric Morris, in *Salerno: A Military Fiasco* (New York: Stein and Day, 1983), observed, "For the Allies at Salerno only the weather was favorable." On the German counterattack, which occurred between September 12 and 14, see Historical Division, War Department, *Salerno* (1944; repr., Washington, DC: Center of Military History, U.S. Government Printing Office, 1990); see also "Germans Claim 'Dunkerque' on Beachheads at Salerno," *New York Times*, 15 September 1943.
4. Drew Middleton, "London Is Anxious," *New York Times*, 15 September 1943.
5. "Manpower for Victory." Not everyone thought Germany had the strength to continue the war. Several days later, California Senator Sheridan Downey "predicted . . . the collapse of Germany within four months" ("Nazi Fall Is Near, Downey Predicts," *New York Times*, 26 September 1943).
6. "Kurile Battle Described," *New York Times*, 15 September 1943. The casualty figures made it the Eleventh Air Force's "most disastrous day." See "USAAF Chronology: Combat Chronology of the U.S. Army Air Forces, September 1943," online at http://paul.rutgers.edu/~mcgrew/wwii/usaf/html/Sep.43.html (accessed 8 May 2008).
7. Other news that day: German paratroopers were reported to have taken over the "policing" of St. Peter's Square in Vatican City. The German commander in chief in southern Italy said the action was done "in the normal course of their duty of suppressing 'unrest'" ("German Troops Enter Vatican City After Battles in Streets of Rome," *New York Times*, 15 September 1943). The Department of the Navy announced that another submarine had been lost and that, since the war began, the combined navy, Marine Corps, and Coast Guard casualties "divided into 10,143 dead, 5,169 wounded, 9,908 missing and 4,161 prisoners" ("Loss of Submarine Announced by Navy," *New York Times*, 15 September 1943; "Navy Casualties 29,381," *New York Times*, 15 September 1943).
8. Senate Committee on Military Affairs, *Married Men Exemption (Drafting of Fathers): Hearings on S. 763*, 78th Cong., 1st sess. (revised consolidated print), 15 September 1943; hereafter Senate Committee, *Drafting of Fathers*. Seven days of hearings were held on 5 May (when only a subcommittee met) and on 15, 16, 17, 20, 22, and 23 September (when the full committee met).
9. "Local Board Memorandum No. 3, Subject: Married Men in Class I-A" effective 1 July 1941 (changed from 12 July 1941), in *Local Board Memoranda, Nos. 1 to 195* (Washington, DC: United States Government Printing Office).
10. "Local Board Release No. 123, Subject: Dependency," effective 21 April 1942; and "Local Board Memorandum No. 123, Subject: Class III Deferments," amended 31 July 1943 (both directed by Lewis B. Hershey), in *Local Board Memoranda, Nos. 1 to*

195. Having a child who was conceived on or before the day of the attack on Pearl Harbor (December 7, 1941) qualified a man for the exemption. Thus, as written, "A child born on or before September 14, 1942, [was] considered as having been conceived prior to December 8, 1941, unless there [was] affirmative evidence of a medical character which clearly establishe[d] that birth was delayed" ("Local Board Memorandum No. 123").

11. Some critics said, too, that because "draft boards have varied widely in their rulings, . . . many men with pre–Pearl Harbor families have long been in uniform" (" 'Father Draft' Mis-Called," *New York Times*, 29 September 1943). Estimates at the time were that more than 800,000 fathers were already on active duty in the army and navy (Senate Committee, *Drafting of Fathers*, 15 September 1943, 53). Father and son enlistments were especially noteworthy. See, for example, "Father-Son Draft Begins in Suburbs; City Starts Today," *New York Times*, 15 February 1942; "Father and Son Report for Draft," *New York Times*, 21 August 1942. Among the fathers and sons who enlisted together were men in their forties who had served in World War I.

12. Statement of Lt. Col. Francis V. Keesling Jr., Chief Liaison and Legislative Officer, Selective Service System, at the Downey Subcommittee of the Senate Committee on Military Affairs, 9 September 1943, "Size of Armed Forces as of July 31, 1943, and Contemplated Increases." Reprinted in Senate Committee, *Drafting of Fathers*, appendix, 450.

13. Senate Committee, *Drafting of Fathers*, 15 September 1943, 32–33, 52.

14. Robert L. Griswold, *Fatherhood in America: A History* (New York: Basic Books, 1993), 169. Griswold, who wrote about the 1943 hearings, noted that some religious leaders and draft board members were also opposed to drafting fathers.

15. Ibid., 171. See also "Draft of Fathers Opposed by Public," *New York Times*, 15 September 1943. Wheeler claimed that he had gotten thousands of letters from people "opposed to taking these fathers and breaking up the American home until all the other available people are taken into the Army and Navy" (Senate Committee, *Drafting of Fathers*, 16 September, 1943, 190). As to exactly how many letters Wheeler had received, at one point the senator said that he had gotten two thousand letters just "in the last few days" (Senate Committee, *Drafting of Fathers*, 23 September 1943, 392). I had hoped to review the letters, but they were not to be found among the Hearing's files at the National Archives and Records Administration, or with the senator's papers at the Montana Historical Society. A 1942 advertisement for the New England Mutual Life Insurance Company captured the sentiment of Wheeler and perhaps of the many others who did not want fathers to be drafted. The ad included a photo of a small girl. "Her daddy's been drafted—for service at *home!* He's in Class 3-A . . . deferred from army service for family service. *Pigtails and pinafores are still just as important as Panzer divisions!* While fighting power is essential, the loving care and education of American children are also vital to the nation's future. . . . How can he best protect his home and family through the uncertain years ahead? . . . One safe, sure ally is the New England Mutual . . ." (*Time*, 9 March 1942).

16. Ralph LaRossa, *The Modernization of Fatherhood: A Social and Political History* (Chicago: University of Chicago Press, 1997).

17. Senate Committee, *Drafting of Fathers*, 15 September 1943, 22. Later in the morning, Senator William Chapman Revercomb asked Undersecretary of War Robert P. Patterson, "Is it your feeling, Judge Patterson, that right now is a very crucial point in the whole war effort, that up until now, so to speak, we have been fighting in the minor league and now we are up against the major league?" Patterson replied, "There is a

certainty that the military operations will be continued on a vaster, larger scale in the future than they have been in the past" (55). A few minutes earlier he had reported, "With the surrender of Italy, we have entered a new phase of World War No. 2. The Mediterranean is open from end to end. The prospects of victory are brighter. But it is the considered judgment of our military leaders that we still have a long, hard fight ahead" (51).

18. Ibid., 31; my italics. McNarney was speaking not just on behalf of the War Department but also on behalf of the president. According to the *New York Times*, Roosevelt "intimated . . . that he would oppose legislative attempts to prevent the drafting of pre–Pearl Harbor fathers." At his press-radio conference the day before, he "indicated his belief that those fathers of military age who were not in essential war service should be inducted," but he apparently "declined to answer directly questions on the father-draft issue" ("Roosevelt Backs Draft of Fathers; May Fight Bills," *New York Times*, 15 September 1943). At a news conference several months before, Eleanor Roosevelt was asked what she thought of drafting fathers. She said that local draft boards should make case-by-case determinations. "Because, while nothing can make up in a personal sense for the loss of a parent, still I think there are families that suffer less by the drafting of a husband and father than by that of an 18-year-old," she elaborated. "In the case of my own sons, all are fathers of young children and all are in the service and I think they should be, because whatever happens, their families are taken care of, the care and education of their children assured" ("First Lady Opposes Fourth Term Talk," *New York Times*, 9 March 1943). The arithmetic of war was something that presidents and generals were forced to confront. Abraham Lincoln's White House secretary said that both Lincoln and General Ulysses S. Grant were well aware of how winning a war could come down to "simple arithmetic." See William O. Stoddard, *Abraham Lincoln: The True Story of a Great Life* (New York: Fords, Howard, and Hulbert, 1885), 387. See also Doris Kearns Goodwin, *A Team of Rivals: The Political Genius of Abraham Lincoln* (New York: Simon and Schuster, 2005), 486. On the arithmetic of war prior to U.S. involvement in World War I and the risks associated with predicting "the rate at which human material is consumed," see "Arithmetic of War," *New York Times*, 4 February 1916.

19. Senate Committee, Drafting of Fathers, 15 September 1943, 45. On another day, Colonel Lewis Sander, an adviser to the Committee on Manpower, offered an assessment: "The question came up yesterday as to whether men with children make as good soldiers as single men. I have commanded a body of troops in the last war made up of single men and of married men, of fathers and of men who became fathers while we were overseas, which is probably the most trying condition a man could be in. I checked up with one of my battery commanders yesterday to see whether his impression of them was the same as mine. Those men were every bit as good soldiers as the single men. Whatever private worries they may have had, *like men* they kept to themselves, and they did not affect their military value in the slightest degree" (my italics). Wheeler vehemently disagreed: "I have six children. I think I know something more about the rearing of the family than many people who have never had families. I have found a lot of old women who have never had families and who do not know anything about families giving their advice. There are also those people who have had children but who think nothing of paying no attention to their children. But I say this: That the right kind of father and the right kind of mother, who are the heads of the right kind of American home, cannot help but worry if they know that their little children may be running around the streets. All

you have to do is read the statistics of any community in the country today" (Senate Committee, *Drafting of Fathers*, 17 September 1943, 224).

20. Senate Committee, *Drafting of Fathers*, 15 September 1943, 53 (my italics).

21. Ibid., 52–53.

22. Ibid., 57.

23. Ibid., 20 September 1943, 294. LaGuardia went on to report, "Now our police department has given 695 men to the armed forces. We have married men between the ages of 21 and 38 who would be subject to this [new] call in the number of 5,194, out of a present strength of 17,000, and we are about 1,200 short of the authorized strength. It is becoming increasingly difficult for me to properly police the city."

24. Ibid., 296, 295. When the subcommittee had met in May, Wheeler said, too, "[People] see the young men out there guarding these places, doing the various things, and they say, 'Why in the name of God should you take married men when you could use older men?'" (Senate Committee, *Drafting of Fathers*, 5 May 1943, 8).

25. Senate Committee, *Drafting of Fathers*, 22 September 1943, 343, 344.

26. Senator Wheeler: "If . . . standards were lowered and a full check was made of the available single men in the country, and if the Army and Navy standards were lowered to take in some of the classifications you have named today, you would not have to take married men at least for a long time, would you?" (Senate Committee, *Drafting of Fathers*, 16 September 1943, 190).

27. Ibid., 191.

28. Ibid., 23 September 1943, 400–401. The letter writer was Lt. James A. Love, who, according to the signature block, was a member of the 370th Infantry Regiment, 93rd Division in World War I.

29. Christopher Paul Moore, *Fighting for America: Black Soldiers—The Unsung Heroes of World War II* (New York: Ballantine Books, 2005), 29, 261. See also Neil A. Wynn, *The Afro-American and the Second World War* (New York: Holmes and Meier, 1976). Moore recounts a story that demonstrated Eleanor Roosevelt's commitment to the Tuskegee Airmen and to civil rights. While visiting the Tuskegee pilot project in March 1941, the first lady "asked to be taken on a ride in an airplane with a black pilot at the controls" and "insisted that her flight . . . be photographed and the film developed right away." She then presented the photograph to the president "to urge him to reject the opinion of his very capable but bigoted military advisors who staunchly opposed the presence of black pilots in the U.S. military" (28).

30. Andrew E. Kersten, "African Americans and World War II," *Organization of American Historians Magazine of History* 16 (Spring 2002), 13–17.

31. Roger Daniels, "Incarcerating Japanese Americans," *Organization of American Historian's Magazine of History* 16 (Spring 2002): 19–23.

32. Pre–Pearl Harbor fathers, though now eligible for the draft, were still given preferential treatment, by, for instance, being placed "at the bottom of eligible lists" ("President Signs Bill to Postpone Draft of Fathers," *New York Times*, 11 December 1943). Draft boards also continued to take fatherhood into account, even in the final year of the war. When it was announced in February 1945 that more men between the ages of thirty and thirty-four might be needed to meet the "demands for the armed forces," a memorandum from Selective Service headquarters stated that "if all other factors are equal, a father should be given greater consideration for occupational deferment than a non-father in this age group." Occupational deferment would mean that a man was "'necessary to and regularly engaged in' an activity in war production or in support of the national health, safety or interest" ("More Men, 30 to 34, to be

Drafted Unless Necessary to Industry," *New York Times*, 25 February 1945). Noteworthy, too, is the fact that Senator Burton K. Wheeler refused to give up. As late as April 1944, he was still trying to have fathers deferred. See "Wheeler Moves to Defer Fathers Over 30 in Cases Where Their Children are Minors," *New York Times*, April 19, 1944. Immediately after World War II, the father draft was suspended ("Induction of All Fathers Discontinued; Those with Two Children May Volunteer," *New York Times*, 20 December 1945). The issue, however, would come up again during and after the Korean War (1950–1953).

CHAPTER THREE

1. William M. Tuttle Jr., *"Daddy's Gone to War": The Second World War in the Lives of America's Children* (New York: Oxford University Press, 1993), 30.
2. "Floyd H. Bidleman, 27-Year-Old Army Inductee and Father of Seven Children, Left Home Today with Lockport Contingent" (opening sentence of article), *New York Times*, 30 June 1945.
3. Tuttle, *"Daddy's Gone to War,"* 30.
4. Isabel Alden Kidder to Maurice A. Kidder, 16 August 1943, in Judy Barrett Litoff and David C. Smith, eds., *Since You Went Away: World War II Letters from American Women on the Homefront* (Lawrence: University Press of Kansas, 1991), 96.
5. "Fathers Shun Draft Stay to Avoid More Farewells," *New York Times*, 4 April 1944.
6. Edward and Louise McDonagh, "War Anxieties of Soldiers and Their Wives," *Social Forces* 24 (December 1945): 196; see also Juliet Danziger, "Daddy Comes Home on Leave," *Parents Magazine*, October 1944.
7. Alex Kershaw, *The Bedford Boys: One American Town's Ultimate D-Day Sacrifice* (New York: Da Capo Press, 2003), 17.
8. Catherine Mackenzie, "Father Goes to War," *New York Times*, 17 October 1943.
9. "FBI Seizes 80 During Week in Draft Evader Round-Up," *New York Times*, 28 September 1943; "Indicted for Listing Mare as Dependent, Alleged Draft Evader Cites the Cost of Oats," *New York Times*, 4 February 1944. The "father" of the horse said that he answered the Selective Service form honestly and blamed the government for not knowing what questions to ask. "Why, I am not even married. If there had been any blanks on that questionnaire about being married, I would have [honestly] filled them in, too."
10. "Fears Draft, Ends Life," *New York Times*, 6 August 1943.
11. "Draft of Pre-War Fathers Begins Here; First to Be Called Says 'I Don't Mind,'" *New York Times*, 2 October 1943.
12. "Westchester Board Drafts Father of 7," *New York Times*, 30 December 1943; see also "Chooses Draft to Job," *New York Times*, 26 August 1943. Needless to say, not everyone believed that their jobs would be waiting for them when they returned. A police officer and father of six children who was facing induction asked, "What am I going to do? If I quit here I lose my seniority and everything I've been working for for twelve years. If I stay and wait to be drafted, who is going to support my family?" ("Policeman-Father is Called in Draft," *New York Times*, 22 August 1943).
13. "Westchester Board Drafts Father of 7"; "Father of 14 Seeks to Join Navy," *New York Times*, 28 March 1944; Father of 13 Joins Son in Navy," *New York Times*, 6 May 1944.
14. Anna Rush to Franklin D. Roosevelt, November 18, 1943, in Dwight Young, ed., *Dear Mr. President: Letters to the Oval Office from the Files of the National Archives* (Washington, DC: National Geographic, 2005), 76.

15. Carolyn Weatherhogg to Franklin D. Roosevelt, 14 October 1943, in Young, *Dear Mr. President*, 77.

16. Geoffrey C. Ward and Ken Burns, *The War: An Intimate History, 1941–1945* (New York: Knopf, 2007), 72; see also 5, 13, 22, 122, 369, 403. Recalled one woman, "You kept track of the war either by newspaper or by the *Movietown News*. . . . When we saw those newsreels you were always looking for a familiar face, looking to see if there was somebody that you knew" (334). Parents periodically would read the war news to their children, making the war, for some youngsters, "a source of constant excitement" (243).

17. "Japanese Pounded in Luzon, Warships Chased"; "Russians Rout Nazi Armies on Moscow Front"; "House Gets Bill to Register All Men 18 to 64," *New York Times*, 13 December 1941. Depending on the day and the amount of action in the previous twenty-four hours, more than 90 percent of the *New York Times* front page might be devoted to news of the war. Prior to U.S. involvement in the war, the *Times* published a daily column called "The International Situation." Soon after the country entered the war, the column was renamed "War News Summarized." Newspapers throughout the country also reported war news. In the early 1940s, there were more than eleven thousand local papers in the United States (Ward and Burns, *The War*, 72; see also 403–4).

18. "Tobruk Falls, Axis Claims 25,000 Prisoners"; "Germans Drive Wedge into Sevastopol Lines"; "Japanese Ashore on Kiska in the Aleutians," *New York Times*, 22 June 1942.

19. "U.S. Force Wins Beaches on Marshalls Atoll"; "Battles Rage on First Japanese Soil Invaded"; "Allies Attack Below Rome"; "Russians Advance," *New York Times*, 2 February 1944.

20. "Allied Armies Land in France in the Havre-Cherbourg Area"; "Great Invasion Is Underway," *New York Times*, 6 June 1944. The *Times* also reported that the Allies had captured Rome. In a radio address the night before, Roosevelt warned the country of the battles to come: "Germany has not yet been driven to surrender. Victory lies some distance ahead. . . . It will be tough and it will be costly" ("War News Summarized," *New York Times*, 6 June 1944.

21. "U.S. Marines Storm Ashore on Iwo Island"; "509 Planes, 36 Ships Smashed in Tokyo Blow"; "British at Edge of Goch"; "Patton Strikes Again," *New York Times*, 19 February 1945. The front page of the *Times* also carried an Associated Press photograph entitled "American tank running a gauntlet of steel in Manila," with the caption, "An amphibious vehicle crossing the Pasig River under Japanese machine gun fire while shells from a protecting barrage laid down by artillery burst on the far shore."

22. "Okinawa Is Ours After 82 Days"; "45,029 U.S. Casualties, Foe's 94,401"; "Gen. Stillwell Heads 10th Army," *New York Times*, 22 June 1945.

23. James Bradley, with Ron Powers, *Flags of Our Fathers* (New York: Bantam, 2000), 218.

24. Bill Madden to his father, in *War Letters: Extraordinary Correspondence from American Wars*, ed. Andrew Carroll (New York: Scribner, 2001), 297–300. Private First Class Madden ended his letter, "Well, I haven't said all I wanted to, but it's all I can think of now. My arm is doing o.k., so don't worry about it. Oh yes—Happy Birthday Pop!" The fight to control Iwo Jima remains the costliest battle in Marine Corps history.

25. For accounts of the fighting on D-Day, see Stephen E. Ambrose, *D-Day, June 6, 1944: The Climactic Battle of World War II* (New York: Simon and Schuster, 1994); Cornelius Ryan, *The Longest Day: The Classic Epic of D-Day* (New York: Simon and Schuster,

1959). The term *D-Day* has come to be associated with the Allied invasion of Normandy on June 6, 1944, but D-Day, in military parlance, generally refers to the day of a planned attack.

26. Bradley, *Flags of Our Fathers*, 218.

27. "President Orders 48-Hour Week in War Effort"; "Great 'Invasion of Europe' in 1943 the Goal"; "Guadalcanal Is Ours"; "Russia Takes Belgorod," *New York Times*, 10 February 1943. On the element of surprise on D-Day, see Ambrose, *D-Day*, 71–89.

28. "Country in Prayer, President on Radio Leads in Petition He Framed for Allied Cause, Liberty Bell Rings, Lexington and Boston's Old North Church Hold Services," *New York Times*, 7 June 1944.

29. Virginia Moore, "When Father Comes Marching Home," *Parents Magazine*, January 1945, 112.

30. "'Let Our Hearts Be Stout': A Prayer by the President of the United States," *New York Times*, 7 June 1944. This is less than one-third of the entire prayer.

31. Ambrose, *D-Day*, 183, 199, 219–20, 325–26; Ryan, *Longest Day*, 113–14, 133–35, 194–200.

32. See Ambrose, *D-Day*; Ryan, *Longest Day*. One World War II veteran, on the sixty-fifth anniversary of D-Day, recalled what it was like to be in the first waves of the assault. "[The Germans] had you pinpointed," said Lenny Lisoovicz, who was an infantry lieutenant in 1944. "It was just like shootin' ducks on a pond. Your comrades would get artillery busted. A hand flying here, a leg there, guts laying out on the ground, asking for help and you couldn't help them. You had to move. You just had to push them aside." CNN.com, "After 65 Years, Hero Talks about D-Day Assault," 5 June 2009, online at http://www.cnn.com/2009/US/06/05/dday.lisovicz/index.html (accessed 6 June 2009). George A. Davison, who was a sergeant in a black anti-aircraft barrage-balloon battalion, remembered seeing a soldier "blown apart." He talked "of ducking bullets and anything that would kill a man" (Brian Knowlton, "Last Soldier of a Forgotten Battalion Returns to the Beachhead," *New York Times*, 6 June 2009.
The phrase, *fog of war*, is generally attributed to Carl von Clausewitz, *On War*, trans. Michael Howard and Peter Paret (1832; repr., New York: Oxford University Press, 2007), xxxi.

33. Kershaw, *Bedford Boys*, 165, 223–25; David Fortuna, "World War II: The Town of Bedford, Virginia Loses Many Men on D-Day," World War II, June 2004, reprinted in 2008 on HistoryNet, online at http://www.historynet.com/world-war-ii-the-town-of-beford-virginia-loses-many-men-on-d-day.htm (accessed 29 May 2008).

34. Kershaw, *Bedford Boys*, 215.

35. Flora Gaitree Southwick to Erman D. Southwick, 6 June 1944, in Litoff and Smith, *Since You Went Away*, 115.

36. Catherine "Renee" Young Pike to George Pike, 6 June 1944, in Litoff and Smith, *Since You Went Away*, 87–88, 91. This soldier did come back from the war and was discharged soon after it ended. The husband and wife went on to have two more children.

37. The veteran who talked about "mutual survival" was in combat on Okinawa. Glen H. Elder Jr. and Avshalom Caspi, "Studying Lives in a Changing Society: Sociological and Personological Explorations," in *Studying Persons and Lives*, ed., Albert I. Rabin, Robert A. Zucker, Robert A. Emmons, and Susan Frank, 201–47 (New York: Springer, 1990), 238. Gerald F. Linderman contended that "within the world of war" family roles "became remote and at least temporarily irrelevant," but he made this point in a chapter on the value of comradeship in combat. Later, he explicitly acknowledged

the importance of mail to soldiers, thus reinforcing the difference between what men might view as important in the thick of battle as opposed to other moments in the war. He noted, for example, that soldiers often wanted reports from home about "the little things." The men "solicited a ritual of reassurance that family and friends were doing what the soldier wished them to do, what he missed doing, [and] what he would surely do again." See Gerald F. Linderman, *The World within War: America's Combat Experience in World War II* (Cambridge, MA: Harvard University Press, 1997), 273, 304.

38. Linderman, *World within War*, 303. One thing that helped to increase the volume of mail was the use of V-Mail. As Geoffrey C. Ward and Ken Burns explained, "V-Mail [was] a simple but ingenious space-saving system devised by the British—who called their version the airgraph. Letters were addressed and written on a special one-sided form, sent to Washington where they were opened and read by army censors who blacked out anything that might give useful information to the enemy, then photographed onto a reel of 16-millimeter microfilm. The reels—each containing some 18,000 letters—were then flown overseas to receiving stations. There, each letter was printed onto a sheet of 4¼- by 5-inch photographic paper, slipped into an envelope, and bagged for delivery to the front. A single mail sack could hold 150,000 one-page letters that otherwise would have required thirty-seven sacks and weighed 2,575 pounds. Between June 15, 1942 (when the first V-mail station began operation in North Africa), and the end of the war, anxious families sent more than 556 million pieces of V-mail to their sons overseas—and received some 510 million in return" (Ward and Burns, *The War*, 121).

39. Tuttle, *"Daddy's Gone to War,"* 36. Some men in the military were illiterate and unable to write letters on their own or personally read any that they might receive. "My father could not read or write," a daughter recalled, "[so my mother] never received a letter from him in the four years he was gone" (43).

40. Ruth Erling to Bertil A. Erling, [no date], 1943, in Litoff and Smith, *Since You Went Away*, 16; Farrell Faubus to Orval Faubus, cited in Linderman in *World within War*, 311. Orval Faubus was an army lieutenant who would go on to become the governor of Arkansas (1955–67) and famously defy a federal order to integrate the public schools in Little Rock in 1957.

41. Isabel Alden Kidder to Maurice A. Kidder, 29 April 1943, in Litoff and Smith, *Since You Went Away*, 95. Sonny was the fiancé of a woman who lived for a while with Isabel. He was killed only days before the wedding.

42. Marjorie Kenney Haselton to Richard S. Haselton, 6 September 1944, in Litoff and Smith, *Since You Went Away*, 105–7.

43. Shirley Greenberg to Murray Greenberg, June 1944, in Tom Mathews, *Our Father's War: Growing Up in the Shadow of the Greatest Generation* (New York: Broadway Books, 2005), 55. When Lieutenant Murray Greenberg received this letter, he was a prisoner of war in Germany. The plane in which he was the navigator had been shot down over Leipzig.

44. Walter Schuette to Anna Mary Schuette, 21 December 1943, in Carroll, *War Letters*, 227 (my italics). Lieutenant Schuette wanted his wife to read the letter to his daughter if he did not survive the war. He did return and was able to read the letter to her on her tenth birthday (229).

45. George Rarey to Betty Lou (June) Rarey, 22 March 1944, in Carroll, *War Letters*, 229. Three months later, Captain Rarey was killed in action, a victim of German antiaircraft fire (230).

46. Arthur Miller, *Situation Normal* (New York: Reynal and Hitchock, 1944), 145, cited in Linderman, *World within War*, 277. Sadly enough, not all labor and delivery announcements brought good news. While lying in a hospital bed recovering from wounds received in France, George Fisher received a message from his mother informing him that both his wife and baby daughter had died in childbirth (Mrs. George Fisher to George Fisher Jr., 1 September 1944, in Litoff and Smith, *Since You Went Away*, 239–40. George Fisher was paralyzed from the neck down and died on July 25, 1945.

47. Audie Murphy, *To Hell and Back* (New York: Henry Holt, 1949), 147; cited in Linderman, *World within War*, 277.

48. Sidney Diamond to Estelle Spero, 2 January 1944, in Carroll, *War Letters*, 289.

49. John Waldman, "Attention: New Fathers! Don't Let Your Wife Have All the Fun of Caring for Baby," *Parents Magazine*, May 1946.

50. Whitman M. Reynolds, "When Father Comes Home Again," *Parents Magazine*, October 1945.

51. Katherine I. Miller, "My Father and His Father: An Analysis of World War II Correspondence," *Journal of Family Communication* 8 (April 2008): 148–65.

52. Dwight Fee to William Fee, no date, in Carroll, *War Letters*, 188. Mr. Fee concluded his letter to his son with the encouragements: "Have at em!" "Keep busy." "Keep bucking." William Fee was wounded in battle, but eventually came home from the war.

53. George S. Patton Jr. to his son, George S. Patton, 6 June 1944, in Carroll, *War Letters*, 239, 240. Patton also said to his son, "I have no immediate idea of being killed but one can never tell and none of us can live forever so if I should go dont [sic] worry but set your self to do better than I have." Patton survived the war but died soon thereafter from medical complications after an auto accident in December, 1945 (Kathleen McLaughlin, "Patton Seriously Injured as Auto Hits Army Truck," *New York Times*, 10 December 1945, and "Gen. Patton Dies Quietly in Sleep; Burial in Europe," *New York Times*, 22 December 1945.

54. Fred Sheehan, *Anzio: Epic of Bravery* (Norman: University of Oklahoma Press, 1964), 179–80. The "old Army friend" was General George S. Patton Jr.

CHAPTER FOUR

1. Robert L. Griswold, *Fatherhood in America: A History* (New York: Basic Books, 1993); Ralph LaRossa, *The Modernization of Fatherhood: A Social and Political History* (Chicago: University of Chicago Press, 1997).

2. James Bradley, with Ron Powers, *Flags of Our Fathers* (New York: Bantam, 2000), 4; see also 258.

3. A Gallup Poll conducted in early 1943 showed that just under one-third of all husbands unequivocally supported the idea of women being employed in war-production jobs (Susan M. Hartmann, *The Home Front and Beyond: American Women in the 1940s* [Boston: Twayne, 1982], 82, cited in Emily Yellin, *Our Mothers' War: American Women at Home and at the Front During World War II* [New York: Free Press, 2004], 45).

4. American Mutual Insurance Company ad, "She's in the Army Now!" *Time*, 20 April 1942. Advertisements rarely showed men in kitchen aprons; if they did, the purpose often was to ridicule the men. The Aetna Fire Group Insurance Company ran an ad with a man in a kitchen apron, but he was made to appear sheepish and under his wife's control ("Who Wears the Pants in This Family?" *Time*, 3 August 1942). In a study of 495 comic strips published on Father's Day and Mother's Day between 1945 and 1999, only 1.9 percent of the fathers, compared to 8.7 percent of the mothers, were pictured in kitchen aprons. If we focus, however, on the period between 1945

and 1959, the difference is much sharper. By half-decade (1945–1949, 1950–1954, 1950–1959), the percentages for fathers were 5.9, 0.0, and 0.0. The percentages for mothers were: 37.5, 27.3, and 20.0 (Ralph LaRossa, Charles Jaret, Malati Gadgil, and G. Robert Wynn, "Gender Disparities in Mother's Day and Father's Day Comic Strips: A 55 Year History," *Sex Roles* 44 [June 2001]: 693–718).

5. Dixie-Vortex Company ad, "A Furnace Won't Make Guns . . . By Itself!" *Time*, 30 March 1942. In another ad, the company said, "We are at war. The health of our manpower is of vital consequence. Men must quench their thirst . . . but not at the work-interruption of leaving their jobs. . . . Used but once and thrown away, [Dixie Cups] break the chain of contagion" ("Water Bo-o-oy!" *Time*, 25 May 1942).

6. American Thermos Bottle Company ad, "High Time for 'Thermos,'" *Time*, 15 June 1942. Other examples abound. The Scott Paper Company said that its paper products "help[ed] reduce the heavy toll of communicable illness and [built] morale through personal cleanliness." The Texaco Company talked about how its scientists were contributing to the war effort. General Electric said that by manufacturing better light bulbs it was helping in the fight because "while battles are still fought out of doors, *wars are won indoors*." Campbell Soup contended that its soups offered "nourishing food for a two-job man" (i.e., one who works in an office during the day and in civil defense at night). The Mimeograph Duplicator Company said, "Wherever you finally fight—from a destroyer, a marine-held island, or an office in some war-vital plant, and regardless of your regular duties—a working knowledge of the Mimeograph duplicator may come in very handy at a very important time" (Scott Paper ad, "America Owes a Lot to Tremendous Trifles," *Time*, 19 January 1942; Texaco ad, "Helping Make America Strong," *Time*, 9 February 1942; General Electric ad, "The Army That Travels on Its Eyes," *Time*, 26 January 1942; Campbell Soup ad, "Nourishing Food for a Two-Job Man," *Time*, 19 April 1943; Mimeograph Duplicator ad, "Wherever You Land This Extra Skill May Be a Help to Victory," *Time*, 19 April 1943). For other examples of businesses couching their products in terms of the war, see Kenneth D. Rose, *Myth and the Greatest Generation: A Social History of Americans in World War II* (New York: Routledge, 2008), 72–77.

7. Exide Batteries ad, "Grandpa Enlisted Today," *Time*, 23 March 1942; Oldsmobile ad, "Oldsmobile: Offering Hydra-Matic—The Drive that Saves 10 to 15% on Gas!" *Time*, 12 January 1942; General Tire Company ad, "Everything's Changed Now," *Time*, 18 January 1943. President Franklin Roosevelt certainly reinforced the idea of sacrifice. "Not all of us can have the privilege of working in a munitions factory or shipyard, or on the farms or in oil fields or mines, producing the weapons or the raw materials that are needed by our armed forces," he said in an April 1942 speech. But people could still contribute. "All of us are used to spending money for things . . . which are not absolutely essential. We will all have to forgo that kind of spending. . . . [and] put every dime and every dollar we can possibly spare out of our earnings into war bonds and stamps." He added that "the demands of the war effort require the rationing of goods of which there is not enough to go around" (excerpts from, "A Call for Sacrifice," Franklin D. Roosevelt, 28 April 1942, *Organization of American Historians Magazine of History* 16 (Spring 2002): 51.

8. Mutual Life Insurance Company ad, "Dad . . . The Man the Army Left Behind," *Time*, 17 August 1942. It was striking to see how often insurance companies ran advertisements during the war.

9. "War Job 'Orphans' a Major Problem," *New York Times*, 10 August 1942. A 1944 journal article noted, "The nomenclature of social work literature has been enriched

during the war by such terms as 'latchkey' or 'doorkey' children and 'eight-hour' orphans. Unfortunately, these newly coined phrases describe the unhappy social condition of many young children left to shift for themselves while their mothers work." Also reported: "It is estimated that on April 18, 1944 there were 16,850,000 gainfully employed women in a total labor force of 51,290,000, as compared with a prewar total (March 30, 1940) of 11,240,000 in a total force of 45,060,000. In other words, the wartime gain in employment of women up to the spring of this year was over five and one-half million, and women now comprise about one-third of our total labor force as against one-fourth in prewar days" (Henry L. Zucker, "Working Parents and Latchkey Children," *Annals of the American Academy of Political and Social Science* 236 [November 1944], 43, 44).

10. Tuttle, *"Daddy's Gone to War,"* 40. Tuttle also pointed out that "not all grandparents were warm and loving" (41).

11. Laura C. Reynolds, "Calling All Fathers," *Parents Magazine,"* March 1945, 33, 102. On uncles, cousins, and others see Hope Ranslow Bennett, "Living Without Father," *Parents Magazine*, July 1943: "Yes, your children need a masculine influence and they know it instinctively. So call in stray uncles or cousins, enlist the services, occasionally, of a high school boy, who will come and play 'catch' or go in for a little carpentry or just roughhouse in a good wholesome boy way, and so provide a needed male influence" (57).

12. An essay on war anxieties noted, "Some service men's wives report that they feel like flinging some uncomplimentary epithet at men of military age, such as 'Why aren't you in uniform?' or 'Look at 4F!'" (Edward and Louise McDonagh, "War Anxieties of Soldiers and Their Wives," *Social Forces* 24 (December 1945): 200).

13. Ruth Heller Freund, "When Father Stays Home from War," *Parents Magazine*, April 1945, 152. Freund offered this advice to families: "If a father is a war worker, one who is directly connected with a factory making guns, airships, tanks, or other products directly connected with war, it is a little easier to explain that father is doing his share, since it is evident that the men who are doing such work at home are as much needed in the war effort as those who shoulder guns. But what about those fathers who are not called because they are over age or physically unfit, or too important in an industry or profession which in the children's mind is not connected with the war? The situation should be made clear to them before any problem arises. It is no easy matter to explain to a child that his father is too old to shoulder a gun, for to a child 'old' means decrepit, and father does not care to be thought of in that way. 'Physically unfit for active service' may also build up an unpleasant picture in the child's mind, [thus] it must be explained that physically unfit does not necessarily mean that father is sick. It may be that his eyes are not up to par, or that he has flat feet, or his back is not strong enough to carry the necessary loads, so that the Army and Navy feel that he can be of more help to the war effort in civilian life" (152).

14. Desmond T. Doss, a conscientious objector and "medical aide man" during the war, was awarded the Congressional Medal of Honor for heroism in the Battle for Okinawa (W. H. Lawrence, "Medical 'Objector' an Okinawa Hero," *New York Times*, 12 May 1945; "Medal of Honor Won by Objector," *New York Times*, 9 October 1945). During his training, he was harassed by fellow soldiers. One officer tried to have him discharged "on the ground of mental illness" (Richard Goldstein, "Desmond T. Doss, 87, Heroic War Objector, Dies," *New York Times*, 26 March 2006.)

15. Arthur Miller, *All My Sons: A Drama in Three Acts* (1947; repr., New York: Penguin, 2000), 70. Joe Keller, in denial, refuses to admit that he killed the airmen. "I didn't

kill anybody!" he says. "Then explain it to me," his son responds. "What did you do? Explain it to me or I'll tear you to pieces!" At the end of the play, Joe kills himself.

16. War bond ad, "Are You My Daddy?" *New York Times*, 19 June 1944. This and other war bond ads cited herein are drawn from the Ad* Access Project at Duke University, online at http://library.duke.edu/digitalcollections/adaccess/.

17. Beech-Nut Packing Company, war bond ad, "The Girl He Left Behind," 1944 (see n. 16 above).

18. Savings Bank of Brooklyn, war bond ad, "Won't You Buy a Bond, Mister, So's My Daddy Can Come Home?" 1944 (see n. 16 above).

19. Paul Revere Copper and Brass, Inc., war bond ad, "If He Can Smile, Why Should We Cry?" 1944 (see n. 16 above).

20. Senate Committee on Military Affairs, *Married Men Exemption (Drafting of Fathers): Hearings on S. 763*, 78th Cong., 1 sess. (Revised Consolidated Print), 15 September 1943, 53, 82.

21. James Stewart, "This Was My Father," as told to Floyd Miller, *McCall's Magazine*, May 1964, 210. This, at least, is the story that Stewart told to the press twenty years after the fact. In the article, Stewart also reported that when he and his father said goodbye to each other before he was to go overseas (to serve as a bomber pilot), they embraced but hardly said a word. His father handed him a letter, which Stewart did not read until he was alone. In the letter, the father told his son that he was "on [his] way to the worst sort of danger," and enclosed a copy of the 91st Psalm. He ended the letter with "I love you more than I can tell you." Stewart said that before that time his father had never said he loved him, though he "always knew he did." Stewart confessed that he wept after reading the letter.

22. "Unfit for War, Takes Life," *New York Times*, 9 April 1943.

23. Tuttle, *"Daddy's Gone to War,"* 44.

24. "Flier, Just a Father, Is Killed," *New York Times*, 2 September 1943.

25. "Soldier Dies, Losing Wish Sons Might Avoid His Fate," *New York Times*, 1 July 1944.

26. "Last Day in War, Dad Writes Baby," *New York Times*, 3 December 1944.

27. "War Hero's Child Receives His Decoration," *New York Times*, 16 March 1943; "Children Get Medals Awarded Posthumously to Veterans," *New York Times*, 8 September 1945. Other awards were given as well. For example, the Bronze Star was posthumously awarded to Sergeant E. T. Connolly of Long Island, New York. It's not clear whether Sergeant Connolly was a father. His brother, Gerard Connolly, a toddler, accepted the award on his behalf at a multiple-medal ceremony held five days after the Japanese surrendered to end the war.

28. "Father and Son Honored," *New York Times*, 28 October 1944.

29. "Hero's Widow Refuses to Attend Ceremony to Receive Posthumously Awarded Medal," *New York Times*, 14 March 1945.

30. "President Approves War Mourning Bands," *New York Times*, 26 May 1918; "Insignia, Not Black Gowns, as War Mourning," *New York Times*, 7 July 1918; American Gold Star Mothers, Inc., "History of the Gold Star Insignia," 1940 (box 6, American Gold Star Mothers Papers, Library of Congress).

31. Referring to the norms of mourning in mid-nineteenth-century America, specifically during the Civil War, Drew Gilpin Faust noted, "The work of mourning was largely allocated to women" (*This Republic of Suffering: Death and the American Civil War* (New York: Random House, 2008), 148).

32. "President Approves War Mourning Bands."

33. American Gold Star Mothers Constitution, undated, box 6, American Gold Star Mothers Papers, Library of Congress; *A Bill to Incorporate the American Gold Star Mothers*, HR 9, 72nd Cong., 1st sess. (8 December 1931), box 6, American Gold Star Mothers Papers, Library of Congress. There is some confusion on the dating of the constitution. Although it is said to be "undated," it is referred to as being written "c. 1917 or 1918." According to the official Web site of the organization, the American Gold Star Mothers was established as a group in 1928, but it says, too, that this came "after years of planning." Mention is made of a group being formed in 1918 under the leadership of Grace Darling Siebold. The Siebolds' son, George Vaughn Siebold enlisted (at the age of twenty-three) in World War I, and was commissioned and assigned to the British Royal Flying Corps. The family received notice on August 26, 1918, that First Lieutenant Siebold was killed in action in France. The Web site also reports that Grace Darling Siebold, "realizing that self-contained grief is self-destructive, devoted her time and efforts to not only working in the hospital but extending the hand of friendship to other mothers whose sons had lost their lives in military service. She organized a group consisting solely of these special mothers, with the purpose of not only comforting each other, but giving loving care to hospitalized veterans confined in government hospitals far from home. The organization was named after the Gold Star that families hung in their windows in honor of the deceased veteran" (American Gold Star Mothers, Inc., "History," online at http://www.goldstarmoms.com/WhoWeAre/History/History.htm [accessed 23 May 2008]).

34. Bosley Crowther, "*The Sullivans*, an Appealing Film about the Five Brothers Who Died on the Cruiser Juneau, Presented at Roxy Theatre" (film review), *New York Times*, 10 February 1944.

35. "Sullivans Urge Need of More Planes, Ships," *New York Times*, 6 February 1943.

36. "Sullivans Typify War Spirit of U.S.," *New York Times*, 8 February 1943.

37. "Mother's Tears for Her Five Heroic Sons Christen New Destroyer *The Sullivans*," *New York Times*, 5 April 1943.

38. Mrs. Thomas F. Sullivan, "I Lost Five Sons," *American Magazine*, March 1944. The article also included two photos, one of Mrs. Sullivan and another of the five Sullivan brothers. Mr. Sullivan was not pictured. Here and elsewhere, Mr. Sullivan was effaced (Rebecca Jo Plant, *Mom: The Transformation of Motherhood in Modern America* [Chicago: University of Chicago Press, 2010], 79–80). Another example of effacement is a poster that was sponsored by the National Industrial Information Committee and intended to serve as a "message to Americans in war work." Mr. and Mrs. Sullivan are pictured together on the poster, while their sons are shown in the background. Mrs. Sullivan has a handkerchief in hand and looks to be crying. Mr. Sullivan, turned toward his wife, strikes a sympathetic pose. "There are other sons of *Mothers* who are Fighting Our Cause," reads the message. "Give them everything you have! They need it!" (my italics).

39. Sullivan, "I Lost Five Sons," 17. The story told in Alletta Sullivan's magazine article is different from the story told in the Hollywood movie. Though both probably employ some poetic license, I assume that the movie relied more on dramatization and thus base my account of events on the article and on newspaper reports.

40. Ibid., 92.

41. Ibid., 92, 94.

42. Ibid., 92.

43. Ibid. Alletta Sullivan's account was deeply personal. In the opening paragraph of

the article, she said, "It is inevitable that during the course of this war, many mothers, wives, and sweethearts of men fighting for the United Nations will receive the news that the men they loved have died. I know how they will feel, for it happened to me" (17). And in the closing paragraph, she stated that she gave her consent to the making of the film. "I hope that *The Sullivans* will make other people more conscious of the importance of working, giving, living, and, if need be, dying to make our country live. In that way, my five boys will still be fighting" (95). Mrs. Sullivan also revealed that the testimonials given at the plants were not entirely of their own making. "Admiral Clark H. Woodward, head of the newly created Industrial Incentive Division of the Navy . . . suggested that my husband and Genevieve and I go on a tour of the country and address defense workers who were carrying out navy contracts. 'What could we say?' we asked. He said we could truthfully say something like this: 'We lost our boys. They died in the naval battle at Guadalcanal. We can't help feeling that if there'd been more planes over Guadalcanal, our boys might have come back. Nothing will bring them back now. But there are other American boys on battle fronts in many places. Maybe some of them are your boys or your neighbors' boys. We know you've been working hard. But we ask you to work even harder and to do even more work, so your boys and your neighbors' boys can come back home'" (94).

44. Ibid., 92.
45. "Mother's Tears for Her Five Heroic Sons."
46. Joshua Goldstein, citing Susan Griffin, put it this way: "For a grown man to cry implies 'not only the pain of all he had endured becoming in one moment no longer endurable but the shattering, at the same moment, of a sheltering, encircling notion of who he was, a strong man, a protector'" (Joshua S. Goldstein, *War and Gender: How Gender Shapes the War System and Vice Versa* [Cambridge: Cambridge University Press, 2001], 268; Susan Griffin, *A Chorus of Stones: The Private Life of War* (New York: Anchor, 1992), 49. One advertisement suggested that even children might show more composure than women, but perhaps only if the child were a boy. The National Biscuit Company ran an ad entitled "Man of the Family," which showed a son comforting his mother: "He was only four, . . . but somehow he knew, somehow he understood the loneliness and misery I felt. For as I sat there worrying and wondering if his Daddy was safe, he came over and stood by me. Then he put his hand on my arm and whispered: Don't worry mother . . . don't worry . . . I'll take care of you till Daddy comes home." The message seemed to be that if a son is to be a proxy father—if he is to *act like* his dad—he must be a pillar of strength (National Biscuit Company, war bond ad, "Man of the Family," 1944).
47. "Sailor's Death Fatal to Father," *New York Times*, 8 January 1945; "2 Hutson Family Deaths: Don's Brother Killed in Action, Father Dies Day News Comes," *New York Times*, 24 September 1943 (the father was in a sanitarium at the time).
48. Katherine I. Miller, "My Father and His Father: An Analysis of World War II Correspondence," *Journal of Family Communication* 8 (April 2008): 148–65.
49. "2d Son Inducted, Father Dies," *New York Times*, 6 November 1943.
50. "Brother Killed, Enlists: Gloversville Youth Is Urged by Father to Join Navy," *New York Times*, 19 September 1942; "Avenges Sons in Marines; Father, 54, Carries on in Corps for Two Killed in Pacific," *New York Times*, 30 August 1943.
51. Sullivan, "I Lost Five Sons," 94.
52. General Electric ad, "Man of War," *Time*, 16 March 1942.

CHAPTER FIVE

1. "The War in Europe Is Ended! Surrender Is Unconditional"; "V-E Will Be Proclaimed Today"; "Our Troops on Okinawa Gain," *New York Times*, 8 May 1945.

2. "Japan Surrenders, End of War! Emperor Accepts Allied Rule"; "M'Arthur Supreme Commander"; "Our Manpower Curbs Voided," *New York Times*, 15 August 1945. For some families, the news of the surrender was bittersweet. On the same day that Japan submitted its letter of surrender, it was reported that the USS *Indianapolis* was sunk in the Philippine Sea. (The ship was torpedoed on July 30, 1945.) Every crewman aboard—1,196 in all—were said to be dead, wounded, or missing. Ultimately, only 316 survived. They were rescued after drifting for four and a half days in the ocean. (Naval Historical Center, Department of the Navy, "The Sinking of the USS *Indianapolis*," online at http://www.history.navy.mil/faqs/faq30-1.htm [accessed 28 May 2008]). Weeks before, the *Indianapolis* had delivered components of the atomic bomb that was eventually dropped on Hiroshima. The announcement of the sinking came only a few minutes before the president announced the Japanese surrender ("Cruiser Sunk, 1,196 Casualties; Took Atom Bomb Cargo to Guam," *New York Times*, 15 August 1945). Two and half weeks later, the articles of surrender were formally signed on the USS *Missouri* in Tokyo Bay ("Japan Surrenders to Allies; Signs Rigid Terms on Warship; Truman Sets Today as V-J Day," *New York Times*, 2 September 1945).

3. Geoffrey C. Ward and Ken Burns, *The War: An Intimate History, 1941–1945* (New York: Knopf, 2007), 403, 416–21; Frank S. Adams, "Millions Rejoice in City Celebration: Night Crowds Overrun Times Square After Orderly Day—Many War Plants Close," *New York Times*, 9 May 1945.

4. Frank S. Adams, "Germany Surrenders: New Yorkers Massed Under Symbol of Liberty; Wild Crowds Greet News in City While Others Pray," *New York Times*, 8 May 1945; Arthur Krock, "President Roosevelt Is Dead; Truman to Continue Policies; 9th Crosses Elbe, Nears Berlin," *New York Times*, 13 April 1945. The *Times* also reported that telephone exchanges were busy: "Perhaps the best index to New York's reception of the news was to be found in the strain it placed on the city's communication and transportation systems. When the flash reached them, millions of persons reached for their telephones either to seek confirmation or to pass the glad tidings to friends or relatives. . . . Between 8: A.M. and noon, a record 1,163,470 calls were handled by the [New York Telephone Company] and it appeared last evening that the all-time high mark for a single day . . . probably had been surpassed" (Adams, "Germany Surrenders"). People understood, too, that the war was not necessarily over for the soldiers who had fought in Europe. Some battle-hardened veterans of the European campaign were scheduled to be shipped to the Far East. See, for example, Alex Kershaw, *The Bedford Boys: One American Town's Ultimate D-Day Sacrifice* (New York: Da Capo Press, 2003), 218.

5. Ward and Burns, *The War*, 416; see also 413–15.

6. Alexander Feinberg, "All City 'Lets Go': Hundreds of Thousands Roar Joy After Victory Flash Is Received, Times Sq. Is Jammed," *New York Times*, 15 August 1945.

7. Ibid. Elliott Roosevelt was a general in the army.

8. Ward and Burns, *The War*, 419 (Katharine Phillips).

9. Doris J. Winiker to Walter Winiker, 16 August 1945, in *Since You Went Away: World War II Letters from American Women on the Homefront*, ed. Judy Barrett Litoff and David C. Smith (Lawrence: University Press of Kansas, 1991), 268.

10. Ward and Burns, *The War*, 418.

11. "Army Plan Telling Just How a Soldier Will Be Demobilized," *New York Times*, 11 May 1945.

12. Thousands of soldiers were surveyed and asked "to identify the factors they considered most important in the decision about whom to let out first" (H. Peyton Young, *Equity: In Theory and Practice* [Princeton, NJ: Princeton University Press, 1994], 23).

13. In-service time and overseas time reported in Robert Goralski, *World War II Almanac, 1931–1945: A Political and Military Record* (New York: Bonanza Books, 1984), 422.

14. Hanson W. Baldwin, "Discharge 'Gripes'; Combat Men See Discrimination in System of Allotting Points," *New York Times*, 4 July 1945. The lieutenant's complaint was said to be "echoed by many soldiers."

15. Young, *Equity*, 24–25. It was the soldiers who, when asked to suggest "additional criteria that they considered to be important," first proposed that "exposure to combat" be included. This factor had not been in the first survey, which only sampled men stationed in the United States. When soldiers overseas were asked what they thought, the credit value of combat came to the fore.

16. Another by-product of the point system was that the "seasoned soldiers" left first. Secretary of War Robert P. Patterson was reported to say, "In the Air Corps the discharge of skilled mechanics on points grounded most of our planes last winter" ("Point Dismissals Called Army Blow," *New York Times*, 3 October 1946).

17. Kevin Coyne, *Marching Home: To War and Back with the Men of One American Town* (New York: Viking, 2003), 213. The reunions at seaports could draw large crowds because the arrival times of ships from overseas were often posted in the newspaper. See, for example, "Arrivals of Troops," *New York Times*, 3 December 1945; Ward and Burns, *The War*, 422 (Glenn Frazier).

18. Ward and Burns, *The War*, 422 (Sam Hynes).

19. Marjorie Haselton to Richard Haselton, 15 August 1945, in Litoff and Smith, *Since You Went Away*, 276–77. On the positive feelings about the men and women who helped win World War II, see Tom Brokaw, *The Greatest Generation* (New York: Random House, 1998).

20. Corporal Walter Slatoff, "We Soldiers Dream of Our Tomorrows: A First-Hand Report of the Mood and Mind of the Typical G.I. in Germany," *New York Times*, 14 October 1945.

21. Coyne, *Marching Home*, 206.

22. Brokaw, *Greatest Generation*, 187 (recollection of Martha Settle Putney). Black entertainer Lena Horne recalled that when she sang for the troops, she sometimes was asked to give two performances—one for whites and another for blacks. At one of her performances for black soldiers, German POWs were given privileged seats in the front rows (Emily Yellin, *Our Mothers' War: American Women at Home and at the Front during World War II* [New York: Free Press, 2004], 218–20).

23. Juan Williams, *My Soul Looks Back in Wonder: Voices of the Civil Rights Experience* (New York: AARP/Sterling, 2004), 43 (David Dinkins). Dinkins would go on to become New York City's first black mayor (1990–1993).

24. C. Madeleine Dixon, "Father Takes a Hand," *Parents Magazine*, April 1946.

25. James T. Patterson, *Brown v. Board of Education: A Civil Rights Milestone and Its Troubled Legacy* (New York: Oxford University Press, 2001), 1. In one March 1943 poll, 43 percent of black enlisted men said they thought they would have more rights and privileges after the war, compared to 38 percent who said they thought their rights and privileges would be the same, and 6 percent who thought they would be less.

Only 24 percent of white enlisted men, matched by education, region of origin, and branch of service, thought they would have more rights and privileges. See Samuel A. Stouffer, Edward A. Suchman, Leland C. DeVinney, Shirley A. Star, and Robin M. Williams Jr., *The American Soldier: Adjustment During Army Life* (Princeton, NJ: Princeton University Press, 1949; repr., New York: John Wiley, 1965), 1:514. The authors of the study cautioned, "It is possible, of course, that among some Negroes the optimism may have been more apparent than real, in so far as it may have reflected a bargaining psychology which made them reluctant to admit they believed that anything other than improvement could occur."

26. Christopher Paul Moore, *Fighting for America: Black Soldiers—The Unsung Heroes of World War II* (New York: Ballantine Books, 2005), 30; Maggi M. Morehouse, *Fighting the Jim Crow Army: Black Men and Women Remember World War II* (Lanham, MD: Rowman and Littlefield, 2000), 9–11.

27. Coyne, *Marching Home*, 206.

28. Williams, *My Soul Looks Back*, 60 (Jerome Smith). Believing that things had really changed, the youngster tried later to do the same thing, but was admonished—and told by the bus driver that he would be slapped. An elderly black woman, who was on the bus and provided verbal protection, said to him when they got off, "Never stop doing what you're doing. Never stop taking that sign down." When the child grew up and entered college, he became a civil rights activist.

29. Raymond Arsenault, *Freedom Riders: 1961 and the Struggle for Racial Justice* (New York: Oxford University Press, 2006), 34.

30. Steve Estes, *I Am a Man: Race, Manhood, and the Civil Rights Movement* (Chapel Hill, NC: University of North Carolina Press, 2005), 36. Some felt that black soldiers were safer if they were not in uniform. One black G.I. "recalled that his father brought his civilian clothes to the train station so he would not have to risk wearing his uniform home" (Renee C. Romano, *Race Mixing: Black-White Marriage in Postwar America* [Cambridge, MA: Harvard University Press, 2003], 27).

31. Arsenault, *Freedom Riders*, 34.

32. Frank [artist's last name, written in bottom right corner of cartoon], "Welcome Home!" *Chicago Defender*, 26 October 1946; Oliver W. Harrington, cartoon, Library of Congress, "African-American Odyssey: A Quest for Full Citizenship," ("The Civil Rights Era: Land Where Our Fathers Died"), online at http://www.loc.gov/exhibits/odyssey/archive/09/0928001r.jpg (accessed August 2, 2006). Oliver W. Harrington's work appeared in a number of newspapers. See *Dark Laughter: The Satiric Art of Oliver W. Harrington*, from the Walter O. Evans Collection of African-American Art, edited, with an introduction, by M. Thomas Inge (Jackson, MS: University Press of Mississippi, 1993). Founded in 1905, the Chicago Defender is a newspaper sponsored by members of the black community and read primarily by African Americans. See *Chicago Defender*, "About Us," online at http://www.chicagodefender.com/article-1369-about-us.html (accessed 5 October 2010).

33. Suzanne Mettler, *Soldier Citizens: The G.I. Bill and the Making of the Greatest Generation* (New York: Oxford University Press, 2005).

34. Moore, *Fighting for America*, 321.

35. "Tells Plight of Negro Veterans," *Chicago Defender*, 28 September 1946. The retired officer, who saw combat in Europe, was Winthrop Rockefeller, son of John D. Rockefeller Jr. His remarks were made at the annual conference of the National Urban League.

36. Richard E. Goldsberry, "New Dormitories 'For White Only,'" *Chicago Defender*, 27 April 1946.

37. R. B. Goldsberry, "Negro Veterans Not Wanted in Evanston Dorms," *Chicago Defender*, 13 July 1946.

38. Charles A. Davis, "Schools Bar Negro Vets," *Chicago Defender*, 27 March 1948. Said the author of the article, "To the Negro serviceman and women of Illinois who served during the war, there was no race when volunteers were frantically sought to stem the Nazi advance in the Battle of the Bulge, or when blood was begged for at $10 a pint unsegregated for the casualties of Leyte and Ryukus. Race came back as the crisis passed."

39. Williams, *My Soul Looks Back*, 41, 42 (Vernon Jarrett). The housing in question was Airport Homes, which originally had been constructed during the war. The director of the Chicago Housing Authority had "established a rule of first come, first served for war veterans, regardless of creed or color." Jarrett recalled how his grandfather—"a teenage runaway slave during the Civil War"—would insist that he and his brother "read the *Chicago Defender* out loud from cover to cover." After his grandfather died, Jarrett said, he learned that his grandfather could not read. Jarrett began writing for the *Defender* in 1946.

40. David Halberstam, "Forward: The Transforming Moment," in Williams, *My Soul Looks Back*, xvii–xxiii; Moore, *Fighting for America*, 322.

41. Estes, *I Am a Man*, 36.

42. For a study of the reaction of white southerners to challenges to the color line in postwar America and a sense of what white children were forced to witness and sometimes be a part of, see Jason Sokol, *There Goes My Everything: White Southerners in the Age of Civil Rights, 1945–1975* (New York: Knopf, 2006).

43. Williams, *My Soul Looks Back*, 20–21 (Jesse Epps). Jesse Epps grew up to be a labor official who participated in the 1968 Memphis sanitation workers' strike, which "came to be known as the 'I Am a Man' campaign, and drew the attention of Martin Luther King, Jr., for his last, fateful journey" (19).

44. Arsenault, *Freedom Riders*, 22–39, 533–34. The rides, which presaged the famous "freedom rides" of 1961, were referred to as the *Journey of Reconciliation*. The black volunteers were Dennis Banks, Andrew Johnson, Conrad Lynn, Wallace Nelson, Bayard Rustin, Eugene Stanley, William Worthy, and Nathan Wright. The white volunteers were Louis Adams, Ernest Bromley, Joseph Felmet, George Houser, Homer Jack, Jim Peck, Worth Randle, and Igal Roodenko. The Morgan in *Morgan v. Commonwealth of Virginia* was Irene Morgan, a twenty-seven-year-old mother and bomb-plant worker, who, on her way home to her husband and two children, refused to give up her seat to a white passenger on an interstate bus in 1944. Doing so would have required her to stand for some length of time. She was "dragged . . . out of the bus" and put in jail, while being charged with both violating Virginia's Jim Crow transit law and resisting arrest. The NAACP represented Morgan in her appeal up to the U.S. Supreme Court, which ruled in favor of the plaintiff (11–20).

45. Ibid., 47.

46. Ibid., 48–49.

47. President Harry Truman, "Executive Order 9981: Desegregation of the Armed Forces," Truman Presidential Museum and Library, online at http://www.truman library.org/9981.htm (accessed 24 June 2008).

48. "Defender Editor Hails Truman's Historic Orders," *Chicago Defender*, 31 July 31, 1948.

49. Morehouse, *Fighting the Jim Crow Army*, 212.

50. John Y. Tateishi, "Memories from behind Barbed Wire," in *Last Witnesses: Reflections of the Wartime Internment of Japanese Americans*, ed. Erica Harth, 129–38 (New York:

Palgrave Macmillan, 2001), 137; Chizu Omori, "The Life and Times of *Rabbit in the Moon*," in Harth, *Last Witnesses*, 224.

51. Donna K. Nagata, "Echoes from Generation to Generation," in Harth, *Last Witnesses*, 63.

52. Stephen S. Fugita and Marilyn Fernandez, *Altered Lives, Enduring Community: Japanese Americans Remember Their World War II Incarceration* (Seattle: University of Washington Press, 2004), 107 (Frank Yamasaki).

53. Chiye Tomihiro, "Minidoka," in *And Justice For All: An Oral History of the Japanese American Detention Camps*, ed. John Tateishi, 239–41 (New York: Random House, 1984), 240.

54. Fugita and Fernandez, *Altered Lives, Enduring Community*, 111 (Louise Kashino). The husband, Shiro Kashino, was court-martialed in 1945 for trying to break up a fight between a fellow serviceman and the military police. Years later, as the facts of the case became clear, the judge advocate general (JAG) set aside the conviction. By this time, Kashino had passed away. In a footnote to his decision, the JAG wrote, "Your husband was an American hero—and that is how he should be remembered" (William Y. Thompson, "The Last Battle of Shiro Kashino," extracted from the *Miami Herald*, 6 March 1998, online at http://www.javadc.org/kashino.htm (accessed 21 July 2006).

55. Brokaw, *Greatest Generation*, 354 (Daniel Inouye). The 442nd was the 442nd Regimental Combat Team, an all-Japanese unit. Inouye would go on to become a member of the U.S. House of Representatives and later a U.S. Senator representing the state of Hawaii.

56. Victor G. and Brett de Bary Nee, *Longtime Californ': A Documentary Study of an American Chinatown* (New York: Pantheon, 1973), 154 (Charlie Leong).

57. Iris Chang, *The Chinese in America: A Narrative History* (New York: Viking, 2003), 228.

58. K. Scott Wong, "War Comes to Chinatown: Social Transformation and the Chinese of California," in *The Way We Really Were: The Golden State in the Second Great War*, ed. Roger W. Lotchin, 164–85 (Urbana: University of Illinois Press, 2000), 175, 177, 179, 181, 182.

59. Diana Mei Lin Mark and Ginger Chih, *A Place Called Chinese America* (Dubuque, IA: Kendall Hunt, 1982), 100; cited in Wong, "War Comes to Chinatown," 182.

60. Reed Ueda, "The Changing Path to Citizenship: Ethnicity and Naturalization during World War II," in *The War in American Culture: Society and Consciousness During World War II*, ed. Lewis A. Erenberg and Susan E. Hirsch, 202–16 (Chicago: University of Chicago Press, 1996), 202. Nancy Carnevale has pointed out that "the issue of whether or not immigrants and ethnics themselves embraced an American identity during the war . . . remains debatable. The sharp rise in naturalization rates of white ethnics during the war years, for example, can be seen as indicative of a desire to appear loyal to one's country of residence during a time of international crisis especially when the appearance of disloyalty could have potentially dire consequences. This is in marked contrast to the more sanguine interpretation that equates rising naturalization rates with the desire for assimilation. For Italian Americans, becoming a citizen was the only way to avoid designation as an enemy alien, and Italian-American community leaders attempted to facilitate the naturalization process for just this reason." See Nancy C. Carnevale, "'No Italian Spoken for the Duration of the War': Language, Italian-American Identity, and Cultural Pluralism in the World War II Years," *Journal of American Ethnic History* 22 (Spring 2003): 6.

CHAPTER SIX

1. Pennsylvania Railroad ad, *Time*, 30 July 1945.
2. Worthington Air Conditioning ad, *Time*, 23 April 1945.
3. Nash Motor Company ad, *Time*, 2 April 1945.
4. Nash Motor Company ad, *Time*, 1 January 1945 (ellipses in original). Another Nash ad relied on a similar kind of narrative but focused on an infantryman. "But I know when I go home . . . I'll go home sure [that] no kids of mine will ever spend *their* Christmases in jungles, in foxholes, or on beachheads. When I go home, I want it understood the victories we've won . . . the peace we have secured . . . will be meaningless to us unless all our strength, all our power to destroy can be the power to create" (*Life*, 8 January 1945 [ellipses in original]).
5. War bond ad, "Are You My Daddy?" *New York Times*, 19 June 1944. This and other war bond ads cited herein are drawn from the Ad*Access Project at Duke University, online at http://library.duke.edu/digitalcollections/adaccess/.
6. Whitman Chocolates ad, *Time*, 15 October 1945.
7. *The Fighting Sullivans*, the 1944 film about the five Sullivan brothers who were killed when the USS *Juneau* went down, devotes only a few minutes to the sea battle. The film was made, in part, to advance a patriotic view of the war and encourage enlistments. Hollywood films about D-Day—even those made fairly recently—may earnestly try to convey what happened on June 6, 1944, but they do not come close to capturing the carnage on the beaches. *Saving Private Ryan* (1998), for example, which chronicled the invasion and the battles in Europe that followed, was applauded by the critics for its vividness. Said one review, "*Saving Private Ryan* opens with a 30-minute cinematic tour de force that is without a doubt one of the finest half-hours ever committed to film. This sequence, a soldier's-eye view of the D-Day invasion of Normandy, is brilliant not only in terms of technique but in the depth of viewer reaction it generates. It is certainly the most violent, gory, visceral depiction of war that I have ever witnessed on screen." See James Berardinelli, "*Saving Private Ryan*: A Film Review," online at http://movie-reviews.colossus.net/movies/s/saving.html (accessed 14 April 2006). But how "gory" was it? Anyone who stormed the beaches could testify that the film, despite its best intentions, still offered only a sanitized picture of what happened that day. The same may be said of the ten-hour television miniseries, *The Pacific*, which first aired in 2010. *The Pacific* was expressly created to show the horrors of war. Steven Spielberg, one of the executive producers (with Tom Hanks and Gary Goetzman), set out to create a film that would come closer to representing the combat stories that he had been told: "My uncle and my dad were telling me how hellacious the war was, and it just wasn't jibing with what was coming out of Hollywood. Missing were the grind and harshness that the ground troops on the islands experienced." Although *The Pacific* may be the best film rendition of combat to date, its ten episodes still do not—and could not—fully capture what it truly meant to be in battle (Neil Genzlinger, "No Enchanted Evenings in This Pacific Warfare," *New York Times*, 7 March 2010). Two nonfiction works that tried to describe the horrors of war are Paul Fussell, *Wartime: Understanding and Behavior in the Second World War* (New York: Oxford University Press, 1989); and Joshua S. Goldstein, *War and Gender: How Gender Shapes the War System and Vice Versa* (Cambridge: Cambridge University Press, 2001), esp. 253–55. These, too, could only approximate the horrors.
8. As Jean Bethke Elshtain related in her book, *Women and War* (Chicago: University of Chicago Press, 1987), "War seduces us in part because we continue to locate our-

selves inside its prototypical emblems and identities. Men fight as avatars of a nation's sanctioned violence" (3).

9. Fussell, *Wartime*, 145–46.

10. J. M. Smith to his wife, 22 February 1942, in *War Letters: Extraordinary Correspondence from American Wars*, ed. Andrew Carroll (New York: Scribner, 2001), 193; Eugene Lawton to his father and mother, 31 August 1944, in ibid., 236. Sergeant Smith, father of two daughters (one born while he was gone), was captured by the Japanese and killed. In all likelihood, he died when he and thousands of other American soldiers were forced to march more than sixty miles to a prisoner of war camp. Staff Sergeant Lawton died in action in the Battle of the Bulge.

11. Richard King to his parents, 8 September 1945, in ibid., 301, 302, 304. Private First Class King apparently had sent a Japanese saber to his parents. Upon receiving it, they wrote to ask how he got it. "You asked how I got the Jap saber," he wrote back. "On June 8th, we were cleaning our caves. I was first scout on patrol, and moving down a valley of vines and coral. My second scout yelled to duck, and I turned around and ducked. A Jap officer had the saber just ready to chop my head off. I knocked it out of his hands, and bayoneted him. That's the story. Look at the nicks on the blade where my bayonet hit" (303).

12. Fussell, *Wartime*, 151, 270, 277, 285; Goldstein, *War and Gender*, 253–57 (on the nature of battle), 309 (on soldiers calling out to their mothers). Eugene B. Sledge talked of "the most repulsive thing [he] ever saw an American do in the war": a marine officer urinating into the mouth of a Japanese corpse (Eugene B. Sledge, *With the Old Breed at Peleliu and Okinawa* [Novato, CA: Presidio Press, 1981], 199, cited in Fussell, *Wartime*, 293. He also was horrified by soldiers who yanked gold teeth out of the mouths of the enemy, and recalled an instance when someone in his unit killed a defenseless woman. "You son of bitch," Sledge yelled at the soldier. "They didn't send us out here to kill old women." See Studs Terkel, *"The Good War": An Oral History of World War Two* (New York: Pantheon Books, 1984), 60–61 (E. B. [Sledgehammer] Sledge). As for acts of omission, soldiers grieved over not being able to save comrades who were stranded in "no man's land" or who drowned (e.g., on D-Day), and wondered if they could have done more. Some did not fire their weapons as often as they were trained to, or did not fire at all, for fear of killing other human beings. Not doing so may have cost the lives of others in their unit—not an easy thing to forget. See S. L. A. Marshall, *Men Against Fire* (New York: William Morrow, 1947), 77–78, cited in Elshtain, *Women and War*, 207. Some veterans simply felt awkward about how they performed compared to others. Reflecting on his wartime experiences, one father admitted that "physically [he] couldn't compete with a lot of the men doing the fighting." Of small stature, he judged himself ill equipped for the challenges of battle. Erika Chance, "Father's Perception of Self and First-Born Child," in *Father Relations of War-Born Children: The Effect of Postwar Adjustment of Fathers on the Behavior and Personality of First Children Born While the Fathers Were at War*, ed. Lois Meek Stolz, 75–105 (Stanford, CA: Stanford University Press, 1954), 97 (Mr. Marston, war-separated father). The interviewer for the project described the father as "a man of unusually small stature."

13. World War II Media Data Base, "Casualties in World War II," online at http://www.worldwar2database.com/html/frame5.html (accessed 13 April 2006); U.S. Census Bureau, "Fact for Features (Special Edition): Dedication of National World War II Memorial," online at http://www.census.gov/Press-Release/www/releases/archives/facts_for_features_special_editions/001747.html (accessed 2 July 2008).

14. Catherine Mackenzie, "When Father Comes Home," *New York Times Magazine*, 26 August 1945.

15. On "battle fatigue" as a euphemism, see Fussell, *Wartime*, 147. According to the U.S. Department of Veterans Affairs, "Posttraumatic Stress Disorder, or PTSD, is a psychiatric disorder that can occur following the experience or witnessing of life-threatening events such as military combat, natural disasters, terrorist incidents, serious accidents, or violent personal assaults like rape. Most survivors of trauma return to normal given a little time. However, some people will have stress reactions that do not go away on their own, or may even get worse over time. These individuals may develop PTSD. People who suffer from PTSD often relive the experience through nightmares and flashbacks, have difficulty sleeping, and feel detached or estranged, and these symptoms can be severe enough and last long enough to significantly impair the person's daily life." PTSD was only seriously researched after the Vietnam War. However, "written accounts of similar symptoms . . . go back to ancient times, and there is clear documentation in the historical medical literature starting with the Civil War, when a PTSD-like disorder was known as 'Da Costa's Syndrome.' " See U.S. Department of Veterans Affairs, "What Is Posttraumatic Stress Disorder?" online at http://www.ncptsd.va.gov/facts/general/fs_what_is_ptsd.html (accessed 13 April 2006).

16. The movie, made in 1990, is about an actual B-17, christened the "Memphis Belle," that was the first to complete twenty-five combat missions, after which it was sent back to tour the United States to help sell war bonds (National Museum of the United States Air Force, "Boeing B-17F-10-BO: *Memphis Belle*," online at http://www.wpafb.af.mil/museum/research/bombers/b2-20d.htm [accessed 13 April 2006]).

17. Tom Mathews, *Our Fathers' War: Growing Up in the Shadow of the Greatest Generation* (New York: Broadway Books, 2005), esp. 35–61.

18. 10th Mountain Division Association, "Chronology of the 10th Mountain Division," online at http://www.10thmtndivassoc.org/chronology.pdf (accessed 13 April 2006).

19. Mathews, *Our Fathers' War*, 2–4, 10.

20. Ibid., 25.

21. Ibid., 268–69. *Our Fathers' War* includes several stories of fathers whose lives were haunted by their experiences in the war. Having witnessed the effect that the war had on his dad, Mathews set out to interview other sons of World War II fathers, and in some cases the fathers themselves. "The more sons and fathers I talked to, the more I felt a small shock of recognition. Maybe this wasn't just about me? . . . The real question for a son was not, 'What did you do in the war, Daddy?' It was, 'What did the war do to you?' " (29, 32).

22. Gerald F. Linderman, *The World within War: America's Combat Experience in World War II* (Cambridge, MA: Harvard University Press, 1997), 1. Linderman focused on combat-hardened army infantrymen and marine riflemen. He reported, "In numerous theaters, fighting men comprised 10 percent, or less, of the full military complement. Infantrymen, constituting 14 percent of American troops overseas, suffered 70 percent of the casualties."

23. Fussell, *Wartime*, 282–83.

24. Corporal Walter Slatoff, "We Soldiers Dream of Our Tomorrows: A First-Hand Report of the Mood and Mind of the Typical G.I. in Germany," *New York Times*, 14 October 1945.

25. Terkel, *"Good War,"* 57 (E. B. [Sledgehammer] Sledge).

26. Linderman, *World within War*, 362 (Betty Hutchinson; Jack Short).

27. Peggy Robbins, "What Shall I Tell Him? A Mother's Honest Search for Answers to Her Small Son's Questions About His Father's Part in the War," *Parents Magazine*, April 1944.

28. T. McKean Downs, "When a Sailor Comes Home," *Hygeia*, May 1945. For accounts of World War II combat veterans later connecting with sons who fought in Vietnam, see Michael Takiff, *Brave Men, Gentle Heroes: American Fathers and Sons in World War II and Vietnam* (New York: William Morrow, 2003).

29. Adam Adkins, "Secret War: The Navajo Code Talkers in World War II," *New Mexico Historical Review* 72 (October 1997): 319–47. Although the contribution of the code talkers to the war effort is now widely known, they were not the only Native Americans who were in uniform. Indeed, "the percentage of Native American participation in relation to their total population was higher than any other American ethnic group represented in World War II, including Anglo-Americans, and this ratio was also higher for some categories involving the number of wounded and killed." See William C. Meadows, *The Comanche Code Talkers of World War II* (Austin: University of Texas Press, 2002), 39.

30. The fabrication of one's combat record is common and, as Jerry Lembcke explained, sociologically understandable: "War is a rite of passage in this society [and many others]. To paraphrase Nietzsche, war is to men what childbirth is to women. The society demands an account of the men it sends to war. It's always the same question: Did you see combat? And the only right answer is 'yes.' 'No' will end the conversation. No one wants to hear experiences of the veteran who did not see combat. No one wants to hear the stories of the men who spent a year as clerk-typists, motor pool specialists, mail clerks, or cooks" (*The Spitting Image: Myth, Memory, and the Legacy of Vietnam* [New York: New York University Press, 1998], 116). How a record is fabricated and by whom depends on the circumstance. For German soldiers and their families, deception was of another sort. Because of the silence initially surrounding the Holocaust, children in Germany consciously steered clear of asking their fathers what they did in the war. See Eviatar Zerubavel, *The Elephant in the Room: Silence and Denial in Everyday Life* (New York: Oxford University Press, 2006), 7.

31. Cynthia Rice Nathan, "Servicemen Face Discharge with Hope and Fear," *Family* 26 (March 1945): 91–97.

32. Alfred Schutz, "The Homecomer," *American Journal of Sociology* 50 (December 1945), 363–76. Reprinted in Alfred Schutz, *Collected Papers II: Studies in Social Theory*, ed. Arvid Broderson (The Hague, Netherlands: Martinus Nijhoff, 1964), 118.

33. John Ibson, "Masculinity Under Fire: *Life's* Presentation of Camaraderie and Homoeroticism Before, During, and After the Second World War," in *Looking at Life Magazine*, ed., Erika Doss, 179–99 (Washington, DC: Smithsonian Institute Press, 2001), 191. On romantic attachments between men during the nineteenth century, see E. Anthony Rotundo, *American Manhood: Transformations in Masculinity from the Revolution to the Modern Era* (New York: Basic Books, 1993).

34. John D'Emilio and Estelle B. Freedman, *Intimate Matters: A History of Sexuality in America* (Chicago: University of Chicago Press, 1988), 289.

35. Allan Berube, *Coming Out Under Fire: The History of Gay Men and Women in World War Two* (New York: Free Press, 1990), 228–29, 244, 249.

36. John Costello, *Virtue Under Fire: How World War II Changed Our Social and Sexual Attitudes* (Boston: Little, Brown, 1985), 119.

37. Ernest W. Burgess, "The Effect of War on the American Family," *American Journal of Sociology* 48 (November 1942): 343–52. See also Ernest W. Mowrer, "War and Family

Solidarity and Stability," *Annals of the American Academy of Political and Social Sciences* 229 (September 1943): 100–106; Henry L. Zucker, "Working Parents and Latchkey Children, *Annals of the American Academy of Political and Social Science* 236 (November 1944): 43–50. For an alternative assessment, see Charlotte Towle, "The Effect of War on Children," *Social Service Review* 17 (June 1943): 144–58, who reported, "Perhaps all one can say is that the full import of war for adolescents is as yet unknown. Predictions are dark, though some observations note decline or at least no increase in delinquency as well as individual instances of improved behavior" (152).

38. H. J. Locke, "Family Behavior in Wartime," *Sociology and Social Research* 27 (March/April 1943): 277–84.

39. See Ray E. Baber, "Marriage and the Family After the War," *Annals of the American Academy of Political and Social Science* 229 (September 1943): 164–75; Edward McDonagh and Louise McDonagh, "War Anxieties of Soldiers and Their Wives," *Marriage and the Family* 24 (December 1945): 195–200; Winfred Overholser, "Effects of War on the Family," *Journal of Home Economics* 35 (September 1943): 393–95; Esther E. Twente, "The Impact of the War upon the Husband-Wife Relationships in the Rural Family," *Family* 24 (October 1943): 226–31.

40. Reuben Hill, "The Returning Father and His Family," *Marriage and Family Living* 7 (May 1945): 32–33. Hill also authored a major study on the war's effect on families; see Reuben Hill, *Families Under Stress: Adjustment to the Crisis of War Separation and Reunion* (New York: Harper and Brothers, 1949).

41. Winifred Rand, Mary E. Sweeny, and E. Lee Vincent, *Growth and Development of the Young Child* (Philadelphia, PA: W. B. Saunders, 1930; 2nd ed., 1934; 3rd ed., 1940). This was a popular prewar textbook that leaned toward a feminist perspective. In the first edition, the authors argued, "The signs of the times indicate that the patriarchal type of family must be and is being greatly modified. . . . The educational advantages open to women have widened their vision and opened up many paths of work hitherto unknown to them. Women are today in business and professions as never before. . . . Many interesting questions arise out of this modern condition of the earning woman. . . . If she is her husband's partner in carrying the financial burden may he not be her partner in some of the home duties and share with her in the care of the children?" (1st ed., 1930, 23). In the third edition, they went on to say, "If in addition to being a house wife [a woman] carries on a business or profession, is it not fair that the husband become something of . . . [a] house husband?" (3rd ed., 1940, 364). Although the authors offered a minority view, they were not the only ones who spoke out against gender inequality in the early twentieth century. For other examples, see Ralph LaRossa, *The Modernization of Fatherhood: A Social and Political History* (Chicago: University of Chicago Press, 1997).

42. Rand, Sweeny, and Vincent, *Growth and Development of the Young Child* (4th ed., 1946), 32.

43. Edith Sokol to Victor Speert, 9 November 1945, in Judy Barrett Litoff and David C. Smith, eds., *Since You Went Away: World War II Letters from American Women on the Homefront.* (Lawrence: University Press of Kansas, 1991), 157.

44. "Mothers Protest Day Nursery Cuts," *New York Times*, 3 February 1948; Catherine Mackenzie, "Need for Good Day-Care Centers Not Ended by Peace, Study Shows," *New York Times*, 24 April 1947. Critics suggested that the drive to keep public day care centers open was communist inspired. See Walter MacDonald, "Reds Dupe Well-Meaning Citizens in Drive for Child Care Funds," *New York World-Telegram*, 24 February 1948. Highlighting the article, the editor said, "Why did the state withdraw

its funds from the child care center program. Who is agitating to have state support restored and the program expanded? This is the first article of a series by Walter MacDonald, World-Telegram staff writer, describing the history of this controversial program and the Leftist influences among those backing it."

45. Rachel Ann Elder, "Traditional and Developmental Conceptions of Fatherhood," *Marriage and Family Living* 11 (Summer 1949): 106.

46. Hill, *Families Under Stress*, 85.

47. Coleman R. Griffith, "The Psychological Adjustments of the Returned Serviceman and their Families," *Journal of Home Economics* 36 (September 1944): 386. Newspaper and magazine articles also addressed what families could anticipate when the men came back. "The returning husband and father is bound to encounter various kinds of home situations which are new to him," noted one. "In many instances there will be a baby or small child whom he may never have seen or seen very little. He is glad that he has a child and he may unwittingly expect his child to be just as glad that he has a father." Another spoke of the "readjustments for the children, in getting acquainted with their fathers, and for the mother, who has been carrying a double load." Yet another advised mothers to "let the children be the first to hear the big news of the father's return, to have some of the fun of telling everybody, and share in the shopping and unpacking and other preparations." Moms also were counseled that children, upon seeing their dads, might "get shy and 'frozen,'" or "burst into tears from sheer excitement," or "act as though they didn't care and just turn away to play with some toy" (Virginia M. Moore, "When Father Comes Marching Home," *Parents Magazine*, January 1945; Catherine Mackenzie, "Fathers Home from War," *New York Times Magazine*, 4 February 1945; Mackenzie, "When Father Comes Home").

48. John F. Cuber, "Family Readjustment of Veterans," *Marriage and Family Living* 7 (Spring 1945): 28–30. The study found, too, that becoming a civilian could mean a loss in social status. "I *was* somebody in the Air Corps," said one man. "Now I'm one of the common herd. Nobody has called me 'sir' in five weeks. . . . What worries me most is the fact that [my wife] Jane may have fallen in love as much with my [lieutenant or captain] bars as with me. I fear that much of the romance may have collapsed when I took off the uniform. She doesn't know it and wouldn't admit it if she did, but I know that she thinks less of me than she did. And as my inglorious future unfolds she may have a very hard time accepting the mediocrity which she ultimately will get" (29).

49. Frederic March received an Oscar for his portrayal of the father. Harold Russell, who played a young man whose hands were blown off in an explosion on a navy ship, received one, too. As it so happens, Russell was, in fact, a veteran who had lost his limbs in a military training accident. Some of the most poignant scenes in *The Best Years of Our Lives* are those between Russell and Cathy O'Donnell, who portrayed the double amputee's fiancée. A central question: Would a fiancée be willing to marry a man who, prior to the war, had been the star quarterback on the high school football team but who, after the war, needed assistance in getting ready for bed at night? (In the film, the answer was yes.)

50. Lois Meek Stolz et al., *Father Relations of War-Born Children: The Effect of Postwar Adjustment of Fathers on the Behavior and Personality of First Children Born While the Fathers Were at War* (Stanford, CA: Stanford University Press, 1954; repr., New York: Greenwood Press, 1968), 1–26, 316–26, 68–69 (Mr. Burgman). The other members of the research team, in order of their appearance on the title page, included Edith M.

Dowley, Erika Chance, Nancy Guy Stevenson, Margaret Siler Faust, Laverne C. Johnson, William Langdon Faust, Alberta Engvall, Leonard Ullmann, Joyce Marian Ryder, and D. Bob Gowin. Some of the fathers in the control group served in the military but were *not* absent during the first year of their first-born child's life. Pseudonyms or case numbers were used throughout the study.

51. Ibid., 70, 71 (Mr. Soule; Mr. Mathews; Mr. Irwin). In contrast, men who had not been separated from their children because of the war would talk of being fairly close to their children. At least, this is the comparison that the investigators strove to make. For example: "I've always been rather fond of babies. Cathy was a great thrill. She was very cute. . . . She was always responsive. Always liked to be with people and she was aware of them. . . . I'm not only reconciled to having two girls but I consider myself lucky that it panned out so well. Strictly from the parents' point of view, I think it's probably a lot easier to start with girls than boys. . . . Oh yes, they were planned. We wanted two right close together, then some more later on. . . . We think they're pretty wonderful kids. I think we're very lucky. . . . I couldn't honestly say there's any difference in Cathy's attitude toward me or my wife. I'm good for certain things, and mother's good for certain things. . . . I'm inclined to be more sentimental with her, and to baby her more than her mother does" (Mr. Moffett). Although *Father Relations of War-Born Children* tended to focus on how war-separated fathers could be estranged from their children who were born while they were away, this problem did not necessarily occur in all families. Reported one child in a 1948 "My Pop's Tops" contest, "My Pop's tops because he was a brave soldier. He didn't see me until I was three years old yet he is just as good to me as if he knew me all my life" ("That's My Pop!" *Reader's Digest*, September 1948).

52. Stolz et al., *Father Relations of War-Born Children*, 39, 40 (Mr. Bryan). This father experienced a range of emotions when he returned. At one point in his interview, he said, "Within a few days I realized the moment I had been anticipating for three years: I was face to face with my baby, my daughter" (39). At another point he reported, "It was a great shock when I came back from the war to find [my daughter] so aggressive. I'd gotten snapshots of her but I hadn't realized she was so aggressive. I had pictured her quite different—more like my ideal of little girls" (43).

53. Ibid., 95 (Mr. Wagner).

54. Ibid., 36 (Case E9, Case E17).

55. Ibid., 42.

56. Ibid., 41 (Mr. Weiss).

57. Ibid., 42, 43 (Mr. Statler; Mr. Bryan; Mr. Wolf; Mr. Weiss).

58. Ibid., 44 (Mr. Wycoff). Tom Mathews's dad (discussed earlier in the chapter) reduced his military approach to child rearing to "four basic rules of manhood": "Don't cry, don't bitch, don't bother me when I'm busy, and never pretend to be sick." Said his son, "The word he used for the last dereliction was 'malingering,' an Army term" (Mathews, *Our Fathers' War*, 14).

59. Stolz et al., *Father Relations of War-Born Children*, 37 (Case E17).

60. Ibid., 141 (Mrs. Osborne).

61. R. L. (woman) to Rose Franzblau, 19 August 1949, box 27, Rose Franzblau Papers, Columbia University. As far as I know, Franzblau did not respond to the mother's request for help. There is no indication of a response in the files.

62. Sally C. Clarke, "Advance Report of Final Divorce Statistics, 1989 and 1960," *Monthly Vital Statistics Report* 43 (March 22, 1995): 1–7.

CHAPTER SEVEN

1. For a history of the ebb and flow of these three themes, see Ralph LaRossa, *The Modernization of Fatherhood: A Social and Political History* (Chicago: University of Chicago Press, 1997).

2. Edward L. Kain, *The Myth of Family Decline: Understanding Families in a World of Rapid Social Change* (Lexington, MA: Lexington Books, 1990), 89 (table 6-3); *U.S. Working Women: A Databook* (Washington, DC: U.S. Department of Labor, Bureau of Labor Statistics, 1977), 17 (chart 4). For example, in 1950 the labor force participation rates, in percentages, for Japanese American, African American, Chinese American, European American, Filipina American, Chicana, and American Indian women were 41.6, 37.4, 33.7, 28.1, 28.0, 21.9, and 17.0. See Teresa Amott and Julie Matthaei, *Race, Gender, and Work: A Multicultural Economic History of Women in the United States*, rev. ed. (Boston, MA: South End Press, 1996), 412 (table C-1). The names for the groups are those used by the authors. The authors also noted that "European American and African American women include Latinas classified as white or black. . . . Rates for Asian Americans include Hawaii. . . . Data for Chicanas . . . are for whites, in five southeastern states only, with Spanish surnames or of Spanish origin respectively" (412).

3. Elizabeth B. Hurlock, "A New Role for Fathers," *Today's Health*, January 1950; Willard D. Lewis, "When Daddy Comes Home," *Parents Magazine*, May 1950; J. George Frederick, "What Does Daddy Do?" *Parents Magazine*, November 1950.

4. James H. S. Bossard, "Father's Occupation," *New York Times Magazine*, 23 November 1952.

5. "A Man's Place Is in the Home . . . It Wasn't Always," *McCall's*, May 1954. The article also related, "Caring for three lively children—Ricky, 6, Chris, 4, and Susie, 2—makes tremendous demands on Carol Richtscheidt. But Ed is a cheerful working partner to her, helps with the children and housework whenever he can, gives everything he has to make his family happy. In return they give him all the love and affection a husband and father could hope for" (32).

6. David R. Mace, "Fathers Are Parents Too," *Woman's Home Companion*, June 1953. Mace was a professor of Human Relations at Drew University. To lend substance to the notion expressed in the article that "no matter how good a mother you are, your children will miss something vital unless their father is a real and important person in their lives," the magazine's editor inserted the following about Mace and his family: "The whole family—the Maces have two children—love to spend vacations camping in a trailer both in this country and in Europe" (9).

7. Ethel Kawin, "For Father's Only," *Parents Magazine*, September 1934.

8. L. C. Moore, "For Fathers Only," *Parents Magazine*, March 1933 (my italics). On the rhetoric used in history-of-fatherhood narratives, see LaRossa, *Modernization of Fatherhood*; Ralph LaRossa, "Stories and Relationships," *Journal of Social and Personal Relationships* 12 (November 1995): 553–58; Ralph LaRossa, "Mythologizing Fatherhood," *NCFR Report: Newsletter of the National Council on Family Relations* 54 (Spring 2009): F3, F4, F6.

9. Catherine Mackenzie, "Father's Share," *New York Times Magazine*, 29 May 1949. Mackenzie was reporting on an essay entitled "Fathers Are Necessary," published in the Association for Family Living newsletter.

10. Lloyd W. Rowland, "Father's Role," *New York Times Magazine*, 31 July 1949; Andrew Takas, "What Children Need from Dad," *Parents Magazine*, May 1953.

11. Kenneth Robb, "Today's Father," *Today's Health*, June 1955. Michael Kimmel contended that in the fifties "virtually all [hobbies] were celebrated because they could bring dad and son [and arguably also dad and daughter] together in a project that was theirs alone." Michael Kimmel, *Manhood in America: A Cultural History* (New York: Free Press, 1996), 247. James Gilbert observed that handyman advice books were very popular in the fifties and that the magazine, *The Family Handyman*, was expressly intended "to promote 'togetherness.' " It was aimed at women as well as men (James Gilbert, *Men in the Middle: Searching for Masculinity in the 1950s* [Chicago: University of Chicago Press, 2005], 153).

12. Mary and Lawrence K. Frank, "Dads, Juniors and Toys," *New York Times Magazine*, 4 December 1949. "And, according to the rules set down by cartoons, Daddy will play with the train," the article went on to say. A notable exception to the assumption of affluence is the memoir of a father who, contemplating whether he was "denying his children the companionship they craved," wondered about "a few other fathers . . . who can't buy expensive dolls and scooters for their children, but more than make up for this in the time and thought they give to them. One man I know always has a trinket when I meet him on the train. Nothing expensive—a balloon or a geegaw from the ten-cent store—but it tells the child his father has remembered him" (Henry Lee, "Have Fathers Neglected Their Jobs?" *Coronet*, March 1951).

13. Rowland, "Father's Role," 27.

14. Rita B. Marshall, "Father's in the Kitchen," *Parents Magazine*, June 1951.

15. Katherine Clifford, "Weekend Off . . . for Mother," *Parents Magazine*, November 1949.

16. Ibid.

17. Ruth Wall, "Let Daddy Take Over," *Parents Magazine*, June 1951.

18. *Webster's College Dictionary* (New York: Random House, 1991), 100. The contribution of fathers has been called *babysitting* at other times, too, and the use of the term has been a subject of debate. See Ralph LaRossa and Maureen Mulligan LaRossa, *Transition to Parenthood: How Infants Change Families* (Beverly Hills, CA: Sage, 1981); Safer Child, Inc., "Fatherhood and Men's Issues," online at http://www.saferchild .org/fatherhood.htm (accessed 27 April 2006).

19. Edward Streeter, "Have Fathers Changed?" *New York Times Magazine*, 9 May 1954.

20. The Korean War began in 1950. A cease fire was signed in 1953. More about the Korean War appears in chapters 8 and 13.

21. Ralph LaRossa, Charles Jaret, Malati Gadgil, and G. Robert Wynn, "The Changing Culture of Fatherhood in Comic Strip Families: A Six-Decade Analysis," *Journal of Marriage and the Family* 62 (May 2000), 375–87. The 1950–54 period is compared to the 1945–49 and 1955–59 periods. To be "incompetent," a father figure or mother figure had to "behave in a way that could be classified as ignorant, inadequate, incapable, ineffectual, inefficient, inept, stupid, unable, unfit, or weak" (380). The "Snookums" strip appeared in the *Atlanta Journal and Constitution*, 18 June 1950.

22. Museum of Broadcast Communications, "*Father Knows Best*: U.S. Domestic Comedy," online at http://www.museum.tv/archives/etv/F/htmlF/fatherknows/fatherknows .htm (accessed 27 December 2006). See also Nina C. Leibman, *Living Room Lectures: The Fifties in Film and Television* (Austin: University of Texas Press, 1995), 7–8, 22; "Who Remembers Papa?" *Saturday Review of Literature*, July–December 1951. The actor Robert Young played Jim Anderson in both the radio (1949–53) and television (1954–63) versions of *Father Knows Best*. In a 1950 article that he wrote about his real-life family, and where he comes across as a man of wisdom in the home, he

said, "It seems to me that the fact that I'm an actor has had little effect on our girls. They're delighted to see any movie I'm *not* in; frequently, they get too nervous if I am in it, especially if anything tragic befalls me. . . . [But] they got a boot out of my radio program . . . in which I'm always wrong" (Robert Young, as told to Jane Morris, "We Have Four Daughters," *Parents Magazine*, July 1950). In a 1950 radio episode of *The Adventures of Ozzie and Harriet*, Ozzie says to his son, Ricky, "You're probably too young to grasp this but . . . a man's home is his castle, and the husband and father is the Master of the house. In other words, I'm the boss around here." Ricky replies, "I know you are, pop," which prompts Ozzie to ask, "You do? How did you know?" Ricky then delivers the punch line: "Mom *said* you were the boss . . . and what mom says, goes" (quoted in Gilbert, *Men in the Middle*, 135.

23. TV.com, "Lucy Goes to the Hospital" (Episode 56, Season Number 2, 19 January 1953), online at http://www.tv.com/i-love-lucy/lucy-goes-to-the-hospital/episode/15136/recap.html (accessed 27 December 2006). This widely anticipated episode was watched by more than forty million people. See also Judy Kutulas, " 'Do I Look Like a Chick?' Men, Women, and Babies on Sitcom Maternity Shows," *American Studies* 39 (Summer 1998), 13–32; Judith Walzer Leavitt, *Make Room for Daddy: The Journey from Waiting Room to Birthing Room* (Chapel Hill: University of North Carolina Press, 2009), 1–5. During its television run, from 1954 to 1960 (its last new-show season), the tone of *Father Knows Best* changed. Robert Young's character was transformed from buffoon to Super Dad; see "Father Knows Best: Robert Young Proves a TV Dad Doesn't Have to Be Stupid," *TV Guide*, 16–22 June 1956. (To exemplify the change, the question mark at the end of the title was eliminated.) In contrast to the television series of the early 1950s, the television series of the late 1950s tended to portray fathers in positive terms. These included, along with *Father Knows Best* (which did not become popular until the late 1950s), *Leave It to Beaver* (1957), *The Donna Reed Show* (1958), *The Rifleman* (1958), and *Bonanza* (1959). See Ralph LaRossa, "The Culture of Fatherhood in the Fifties: A Closer Look," *Journal of Family History* 29 (January 2004): 47–70; and Leibman, *Living Room Lectures*. See chapter 10 for more about these shows.

24. On the plurality of masculinities and femininities, see See R. W. Connell, *Masculinities* (Berkeley and Los Angeles: University of California Press, 1995; 2nd ed., 2005).

25. O. Spurgeon English, M.D., and Constance J. Foster, *Fathers Are Parents, Too: A Constructive Guide to Successful Fatherhood* (New York: G. P. Putnam's Sons, 1951). English and Foster inferred that "under the pressure of serving as breadwinner, [the father] has often lost sight of any other goal or purpose in life. . . . Many men are finding the responsibilities of the masculine world more than they can manage." Mothers, on the other hand, were accused of "emasculating" men and of placing "the prestige and value of a career above the normal emotional satisfactions of homemaking and motherhood" (ix–x). Others also complained about how fathers were being presented in the media. "The American father [as portrayed in comic strips and on radio and television] is a miserable, chinless half-wit. He is ignorant, incompetent and immature and has barely enough mechanical skills to tie his own shoes" (John Crosby, [untitled], *New York Herald Tribune*, 7 June 1954, cited in "Role of Father in the Home," *America*, 19 June 1954).

26. See the following by O. Spurgeon English, M.D., and Constance J. Foster: "How to Be a Good Father," *Parents Magazine*, June 1950; "Father's Changing Role," *Parents Magazine*, October 1951; "What's Happening to Fathers?" *Better Homes and Gardens*, April 1952; and "How Good a Family Man Is Your Husband?" *Parents Magazine*, September 1952.

27. O. Spurgeon English, M.D., and Constance J. Foster, *A Guide to Successful Fatherhood* (Chicago: Science Research Associates, 1954), 2. English and Foster also said, "In the ideal modern household no one is 'boss.' Father and Mother share responsibility, although each is responsible for particular areas. Mother has much more to say about her child's education than formerly. She participates in decisions about money. She and Father agree on rules and how they should be carried out. Although earning the family income is mostly Father's responsibility and running the home mostly Mother's, Father doesn't scorn dishdrying or feeding the baby occasionally or changing a diaper as 'woman's work' and therefore outside his province" (19). On the next page is a drawing of an apron-dressed father bathing his infant son, while his daughter looks on. "Children need to feel that Father is a competent pinch hitter for Mother," the caption reads (20).

28. Kimmel, *Manhood in America*, 118–19.

29. LaRossa, *Modernization of Fatherhood*.

30. A similar kind of tirade against mothers had appeared also during the war years. "The mealy look of men today is the result of momism," said Philip Wylie in *Generation of Vipers* (New York: Rinehart, 1942), 197.

31. On the impact of World War II on the father-as-male-role-model theme, see Joseph H. Pleck, "American Fathering in Historical Perspective," in *Changing Men: New Directions in Research on Men and Masculinity*, ed. Michael S. Kimmel, 83–97 (Newbury Park, CA: Sage, 1987). On the impact of the Cold War on masculinity and fatherhood, see Elaine Tyler May, *Homeward Bound: American Families in the Cold War Era* (New York: Basic Books, 1988). On the "crisis in masculinity" in the fifties in general, see Steven Cohan, *Masked Men: Masculinity and the Movies in the Fifties* (Bloomington: Indiana University Press, 1997); Robert J. Corber, *Homosexuality in Cold War America: Resistance and the Crisis of Masculinity* (Durham, NC: Duke University Press, 1997); Gilbert, *Men in the Middle*; Kimmel, *Manhood in America*.

32. Andre Fontaine, "Are We Staking Our Future on a Crop of Sissies?" *Better Homes and Gardens*, December 1950 (my italics). The definition of a "sissy" used in the essay was attributed to Dr. Luther E. Woodward, a "psychologist and co-ordinator of the New York State Mental Health Commission."

33. Walter Neisser and Edith Neisser, "Making the Grade as Dad," *Rotarian*, June 1951. The list was said to be adapted from *Making the Grade as Dad*, a pamphlet published by the Public Affairs Committee in New York.

34. G. B. (woman) to Rose Franzblau, 11 March 1954, box 113, Rose Franzblau Papers, Columbia University (hereafter cited as RFP).

35. A. J. G. (woman) to Rose Franzblau, 2 May 1954, box 113, RFP. For a history of the term *sissy*, see E. Anthony Rotundo, *American Manhood: Transformations in Masculinity from the Revolution to the Modern Era* (New York: Basic Books, 1993), 273. According to Rotundo, the use of the term to refer to a man or boy did not appear in the *Oxford English Dictionary* until the 1890s. See also Kimmel, *Manhood in America*, 100; Peter N. Stearns, *American Cool: Constructing a Twentieth-Century Emotional Style* (New York: New York University Press, 1994), 33. In *The Feminine Mystique* (New York: W. W. Norton, 1963), Betty Friedan talked at length about the attack against mothers in the fifties and the unsubstantiated claim that, as a result of their "overprotectiveness," boys in America were becoming more effeminate and prone to homosexuality.

36. John D'Emilio and Estelle B. Freedman, *Intimate Matters: A History of Sexuality in America* (Chicago: University of Chicago Press, 1988), 288–89. See also John D'Emilio,

Sexual Politics, Sexual Communities: The Making of a Homosexual Minority in the United States, 1940–1970 (Chicago: University of Chicago Press, 1983).

37. Alfred C. Kinsey, Wardell B. Pomeroy, and Clyde E. Martin, *Sexual Behavior in the Human Male* (Philadelphia, PA: W. B. Saunders, 1948).

38. Robert J. Corber, *In the Name of National Security: Hitchcock, Homophobia, and the Political Construction of Gender in Postwar America* (Durham, NC: Duke University Press, 1993), 8–9.

39. Robert J. Corber, "Cold War Masculinities," in *Men and Masculinities: A Social, Cultural, and Historical Encyclopedia*, ed. Michael Kimmel and Amy Aronson (Santa Barbara, CA: ABC CLIO, 2004), 162–65.

40. Central also to understanding the cultural climate at the time is to appreciate the degree to which U.S. officials were actively involved in firing from government jobs workers who were perceived to be gay, justifying their actions on the belief that homosexuals were a threat to national security. As related by the historians John D'Emilio and Estelle B. Freedman in *Intimate Matters*, "In June 1950, the Senate authorized a formal inquiry into the employment of 'homosexuals and other moral perverts' in government. The report that the Senate released in December painted a threatening picture of gay civil servants. The committee alleged that homosexuals lacked 'emotional stability' and that their 'moral fiber' had been weakened by sexual indulgence. Homosexuality took on the form of a contagious disease imperiling the health of anyone who came near it. Even one 'sex pervert in a Government agency,' the committee warned, 'tends to have a corrosive influence upon his fellow employees.' . . . The response to the panic over homosexuals in government was immediate and far-reaching. Dismissals from civilian posts increased twelvefold over the pre-1950 rate. . . . The armed forces sharply stepped up its purges of homosexual men and women from the ranks. . . . The labeling of homosexuals as moral perverts and national security risks, along with the repressive policies of the federal government, encouraged local police forces across the country to harass them with impunity. Throughout the 1950s, and well into the 1960s, gay men and lesbians suffered from unpredictable, brutal crackdowns. Arrests were substantial in many cities" (292–94).

41. Benjamin Spock, *The Common Sense Book of Baby and Child Care* (New York: Duell, Sloan, and Pearce, 1946); Robert S. Pickett, "Benjamin Spock and the Spock Papers at Syracuse University," *Syracuse University Library Associates Courier* 22 (Fall 1987): 3–22; see also Benjamin Spock and Mary Morgan, *Spock on Spock: A Memoir of Growing Up with the Century* (New York: Pantheon Books, 1989); Julia Grant, *Raising Baby by the Book: The Education of American Mothers* (New Haven, CT: Yale University Press, 1998), 220. In writing the book, Spock received considerable assistance from Jane Cheney Spock, his first wife. The book was formally dedicated "To Jane," but her contribution to the overall work was not acknowledged. In later years, however, it was. See Benjamin Spock, *Baby and Child Care*, 4th ed. (New York: Hawthorne Books, 1976), v; Pickett, "Benjamin Spock and the Spock Papers," 10–11.

42. Grant, *Raising Baby by the Book*, 220; James T. Patterson, *Grand Expectations: The United States, 1945–1974* (New York: Oxford University Press, 1996), 362; Pickett, "Benjamin Spock and the Spock Papers," 15; Spock and Morgan, *Spock on Spock*, 135. After his book was published, Spock received a number of invitations to write articles and other books and to endorse baby products of one kind or another. Initially, he declined these offers. As time went on, however, he agreed. One reason was money. Although the publisher earned a considerable amount from the sales of *Baby and*

Child Care, Spock did not. Unfamiliar with book contracts and not realizing how popular his manual would be, he had signed a contract that gave him only a meager share of the profits. In January 1954, the *Ladies Home Journal* approached him to ask if he would be interested in writing a monthly column dealing with questions on child rearing. "Because of the tremendous and continuing success of your book, I am sure that many mothers must write you because they want some particular subject covered at more length," wrote one of the editors. "It seems to us . . . that [your mail] might be a most fruitful source for a continuing column in the *Journal.*" In his letter of response, Spock said, "I have had many requests since my book came out to write articles on a regular basis," but "I have emphatically turned them down." He explained that he found writing so time-consuming that it made him "an unacceptable family member." (Spock, at the time, was a married father with two children.) But *now* he had to admit that he needed the money, and thus if the magazine would agree to his writing an "informal" column, one "flexible in length and free as far as subject were concerned," he would be "interested." The magazine signed off on Spock's conditions and so began a series of columns under the banner, "Dr. Spock Talks with Mothers." See Peter Briggs (at *Ladies Home Journal*) to Benjamin Spock, 12 January 1954, box 2, BSP, Syracuse University (hereafter cited as BSP); Benjamin Spock to Peter Briggs, 22 January 1954, box 2, BSP. See also Eric Pace, "Benjamin Spock, World's Pediatrician Dies at 94," *New York Times,* 17 March, 1998. Spock agreed to do the column because he needed, in his words, "additional income" for a "situation in the family." "For a number of years," he said in his autobiography, "I made only about five thousand dollars a year on the book, though it was selling at a phenomenal rate" (Spock and Morgan, *Spock on Spock,* 137). Spock also was not sure, at least in the beginning, whether he would ever recover from his failure to negotiate a better contract with his publisher. "If I had been an experienced author and sensible business man six years ago I would have caught the significance of every remark and pinned [Donald] Geddes [Pocket Books editor] down by the time the contract appeared. Unfortunately, this is my only book with the possible exception of a textbook in my old age" (Benjamin Spock to Charles Duell [at Duell, Sloan and Pearce, Publishers] 7 May 1949, box 1, BSP). *Baby and Child Care* has been revised repeatedly and is one of the best-selling books of all time. Spock, who died in 1998 at the age of 94, ultimately became a millionaire from both the book and other professional activities stemming from its success.

43. The discussion that follows is based, in part, on LaRossa, "The Culture of Fatherhood in the Fifties."

44. In the "Letter," Spock apologized to the parents of daughters for referring to the baby throughout the book as a "him." He said he did so because he wanted to avoid having to repeatedly say "her or him." (He also thought that referring to the child as "it" was inappropriate: "Parents would rather have their baby called by the wrong sex than be called 'it.'") He added: "Why can't I call the baby 'her' in at least half the book? I needed 'her' to refer to the mother." Spock, *Baby and Child Care,* 2. The correspondence between Spock and his publisher also indicates that Spock viewed his audience as primarily mothers. In one letter, published several years after the first edition came out, Spock talked of how "mothers" were likely to discuss the book among themselves, and of how he had thought about paying for an ad to promote the book on Mother's Day (Benjamin Spock to Charles Duell, 7 May 1949, box 1, BSP.

45. Spock, *Baby and Child Care,* 1946 edition, 15–16.

46. Ibid., 254, 255.
47. Ibid., 489, 490.
48. Ibid., 492.
49. Ibid., 491.
50. Spock's psychoanalytic orientation and training were an important influence on the warnings and prescriptions in *Baby and Child Care*. See Spock and Morgan, *Spock on Spock*, 130; also Grant, *Raising Baby by the Book*, 219–20; Charles E. Strickland and Andrew M. Ambrose, "The Baby Boom, Prosperity, and the Changing Worlds of Children, 1945–1963," in *American Childhood: A Research Guide and Historical Handbook*, ed. Joseph M. Hawes and N. Ray Hiner, 533–85 (Westport, CT: Greenwood Press, 1985), 540.
51. Spock, Baby and Child Care, 1946 edition, 481, 482.
52. The gender breakdown and pronoun pattern in the Spock letters is reported in Grant, *Raising Baby by the Book*, 237–39. Grant's reference to the women's use of *we* is particularly interesting. In a study of fatherhood in early twentieth-century America, parents' letters to Angelo Patri (high school principal, syndicated columnist, radio host, and child-rearing book author) were carefully examined for pronoun and possessive patterns. The analysis revealed that mothers often used the pronoun *we* and the possessive *our* when talking about their children, but the extent to which they did so was correlated with the focal child's gender and age. Mothers were significantly more likely to refer to their children in *we* and *our* terms, when the focal child was a girl. They were also more likely to speak in the plural when the child was older. See LaRossa, *Modernization of Fatherhood*, 163–65; Ralph LaRossa and Donald C. Reitzes, "Continuity and Change in Middle Class Fatherhood, 1926–1939: The Culture-Conduct Connection," *Journal of Marriage and the Family* 55 (May 1993): 455–68.
53. D. and R. H. (woman) to Benjamin Spock, 12 August 1954, box 2, BSP (the mother signed the letter "D. and R. H" to convey that she wrote on behalf of her husband, too); W. S. B. (woman) to Benjamin Spock, 19 July 1954, box 2, BSP; O. M. P. (woman) to Benjamin Spock, n.d. (probably July 1954), box 2, BSP; G. P. S. (woman) to Benjamin Spock, 20 August 1954, box 2, BSP (my italics throughout).
54. Benjamin Spock to E. A., 29 April 1954, box 2, BSP; E. A. (man) to Benjamin Spock, 2 May 1954, box 2, BSP. Interesting, too, is the letter from a life insurance agent who wrote, "I have seen one of your pocket books of *Baby and Child Care* . . . and would like to get a few dozen of those books to hand out to mothers in my business" (R. C. C. [man] to Benjamin Spock, 24 May 1954, box 2, BSP). Although *Baby and Child Care* was written more for mothers than for fathers, Spock did acknowledge a role for men when it came to children, and fathers may have been more willing to write him because he did not depict men as incompetent. Although Spock did not ridicule dads in the book, others indirectly did, and in at least one case Spock approved of the ridicule. A *Parents Magazine* article entitled "The Care and Feeding of Spock-marked Fathers," infantilized fathers by taking passages from *Baby and Child Care* and rephrasing them so they referred to men. For example, Spock opened the section called "Preparing for the Baby," with the words, "You know more than you think you do." (This was intended to encourage parents to follow their own gut feelings when it came to child rearing. It is an ironic opening, since Spock goes on for hundreds of pages telling parents what they might *not* know.) Spock then went on to say: "Soon you're going to have a baby. Maybe you have him already. . . . Lately, you have been listening more carefully to your friends and relatives when they talked about bringing up a child." The same passage, rewritten for the *Parents Magazine* article, said,

"You know more than you think you do. Soon you're going to have a husband. Maybe you have him already. . . . Lately, you've been listening more carefully to your friends and relatives when they talked about handling a husband." The author of the article said that he sent a copy of the manuscript to Spock. "Here's an ingenious article which will help all wives with the nurture and care of husbands. Dr. Spock himself approved its publication—with a hearty laugh. The author is the father of five thoroughly Spock-marked children" (Dan Gillmor, "The Care and Feeding of Spock-marked Fathers," *Parents Magazine*, June 1954; Spock, *Baby and Child Care*, 1946, 3).

55. R. A. G. (woman) to Benjamin Spock, 25 June 1954, box 2, BSP.

56. LaRossa, *Modernization of Fatherhood*. See also Terry Strathman, "From the Quotidian to the Utopian: Childrearing Literature in America, 1926–1946," *Berkeley Journal of Sociology* (annual) 29 (1984): 1–34. For a discussion how such a "pick and choose" strategy applies not just to reading child-rearing lore but to reading cultural objects in general, see Janice Radway, *Reading the Romance: Women, Patriarchy, and Popular Culture* (Chapel Hill: University of North Carolina Press, 1984); Wendy Simonds, *Women and Self-Help Culture: Reading Between the Lines* (New Brunswick, NJ: Rutgers University Press, 1992); Ann Swidler, "Culture in Action: Symbols and Strategies," *American Sociological Review* 51 (April 1986): 273–86.

CHAPTER EIGHT

1. The baby boom began in 1946 and is generally considered to have ended in 1964. In 1946, 3.4 million babies were born in the United States, a 20 percent increase over the year before. In 1947, the numbers jumped again, to 3.8 million. Throughout the 1950s, 4 million babies, on average, were born each year (James T. Patterson, *Grand Expectations: The United States, 1945–1974* [New York: Oxford University Press, 1996], 77).

2. Ibid., 78–81; see also Steven Mintz and Susan Kellogg, *Domestic Revolutions: A Social History of American Family Life* (New York: Free Press, 1988), 177–202; Elaine Tyler May, *Homeward Bound: American Families in the Cold War Era* (New York: Basic Books, 1988), xiii–xvii.

3. M. G. (woman) to Rose Franzblau, 15 July 1949, box 27, Rose Franzblau Papers, Columbia University (hereafter cited as RFP). M. T. H. (woman) to Rose Franzblau, 9 April 1954, box 114, RFP.

4. Benjamin Spock, *The Common Sense Book of Baby and Child Care* (New York: Duell, Sloan, and Pearce, 1946), 15–16. On the culture vs. the conduct of fatherhood, see Ralph LaRossa, "Fatherhood and Social Change," *Family Relations* 37 (October 1988): 451–57; Ralph LaRossa, *The Modernization of Fatherhood: A Social and Political History* (Chicago: University of Chicago Press, 1997).

5. Ruth Davis, "Cum Laude for Dad and Baby Too," *American Home*, April 1948; Catherine Mackenzie, "Schools for Fathers," *New York Times Magazine*, 4 January 1948; "School for Expectant Fathers," *Hygeia* 27 (October 1949): 690–91; LaRossa, *Modernization of Fatherhood*, 84–85. Although men were taking the classes, the assumption was that their job was to "help" mothers. "Men, it seems, are anxious to learn the details of baby care, but want it clearly understood that they have no intention of taking Mother's place. Most say, however, they will be glad to pinch-hit on occasion. Actually, lessons show Dad that babies *are* approachable so he'll not be timid about getting acquainted." Also, it was implied that an involved father was a patriotic father. "The basic purpose of this course in parenthood is to promote better family

relations, and to make men realize that the strength of the nation lies in its sound, healthy families. 'Better parents mean better babies, and better babies mean better citizens,' explains one instructor. 'Fathers can perhaps do more than anyone else to help establish that harmony in everyday living which is so important to family life' " (Davis, "Cum Laude for Dad and Baby Too," 28.

6. Lois Meek Stolz et al. (see chap. 6, n. 50), *Father Relations of War-Born Children: The Effect of Postwar Adjustment of Fathers on the Behavior and Personality of First Children Born While the Fathers Were at War* (Stanford, CA: Stanford University Press, 1954; repr., New York: Greenwood Press, 1968).

7. Ruth Jacobson Tasch, "The Role of the Father in the Family," *Journal of Experimental Education* 20 (June 1952), 334. Asked to rank "problems" of parenthood, the men ranked "routines" as number one (340). This did not necessarily mean that the men shunned routine child care. In another study, related to Tasch's, mothers were asked the same question. They ranked "routines" as number two. First on the list, for the mothers, was a child's "personality." See Arthur T. Jersild, Ella S. Woodyard, and Charlotte del Solar, in collaboration with Ernest G. Osborne and Robert C. Challman, *Joys and Problems of Child Rearing* (New York: Teachers College, Columbia University, 1949). Tasch also found, as have later researchers, that father reports and mother reports could differ, and that ideally both men's and women's perceptions should be considered. See Ruth J. Tasch, "Interpersonal Perceptions of Fathers and Mothers," *Journal of Genetic Psychology* 87 (September 1955): 59–65; Ralph LaRossa and Donald C. Reitzes, "Gendered Perceptions of Father Involvement in Early 20th Century America," *Journal of Marriage and the Family* 57 (February 1995): 223–29.

8. Tasch, "Role of the Father in the Family," 342, 358.

9. Ibid., 359. In her dissertation, Tasch reported on the range of fathers she interviewed. Of the eighty-five, twenty were born in America and had parents who were born in America; forty-seven were born in America to parents who were from another country; and eighteen were born in another country. The countries she listed were Ireland, Scotland, Germany, China, Czechoslovakia, Bulgaria, Russia, Italy, Poland, France, and Canada (Ruth J. Tasch, "The Role of the Father in the Family: Fathers' Expressed Attitudes and Opinions with Regard to Their Role in Family Life and the Responsibilities, Satisfactions, and Perplexities Which Fatherhood Entails" (PhD diss., Columbia University, 1950), 14.

10. For a detailed description of the study, see Robert R. Sears, Eleanor E. Maccoby, and Harry Levin, *Patterns of Child Rearing* (Evanston, IL: Row, Peterson, 1957). I discuss the questions pertaining to the women's (and men's) lives in the early 1950s, when the focal child was in kindergarten, in chapter 9.

11. Sears, Maccoby, and Levin, *Patterns of Child Rearing*. The quantitative data are housed at the Murray Research Center of the Harvard-MIT Data Center and are cataloged as Robert R. Sears, Eleanor E. Maccoby, and Harry Levin, "Patterns of Child Rearing, 1951–52" (Log Number 235). The data are used are used with the permission of the center. The categories and findings are based on a statistical analysis of the standardized survey responses. The first code sheet included only six categories. The third and fifth categories (the "between" categories) were apparently added in the course of coding. Rather than force the mothers' responses into preexisting categories, the coders modified the coding scheme to accommodate the responses, which speaks well for the research team's conscientiousness. Inter-coder agreement was said to be high.

12. Ibid., 44. In the sample, 7 percent of the mothers never worked; 30 percent worked before marriage, but not after; 43 percent worked after marriage but not since the

focal child was born; and 17 percent worked at least part time since the focal child was born. In 3 percent of the cases, the work history of the mother could not be ascertained.

13. The transcripts of the interviews are housed at the Murray Research Center of the Harvard-MIT Data Center and are used with the permission of the center. These data also are cataloged as Robert R. Sears, Eleanor E. Maccoby, and Harry Levin, "Patterns of Child Rearing, 1951–52" (Log Number 235). My analysis of the interviews is based on 76 cases (38 where the focal child was a girl and 38 where the focal child was a boy) that I randomly chose from the 379 cases that were archived. In quoting from the transcripts, I have tried to remain faithful to the punctuation that the researchers used. Exceptions include my being consistent in the length of dashes, even if the researchers were inconsistent. Also, ellipses without brackets denote ellipses in the original transcript, while bracketed ellipses denote instances where I have omitted or skipped over sentences that were in the original transcript. For the sake of clarity, I have made stylistic changes to some of the renderings of the transcripts. The questions posed by the interviewers are not in quotation marks, so as to separate them from the women's responses. The questions are either verbatim or paraphrased. This transcript excerpt is from Mother 36, (page) 2, Sears, Maccoby, and Levin, "Patterns of Child Rearing" (PCR) interview, Murray Research Center (MRC), Harvard-MIT Data Center (hereafter cited as Sears et al., PCR interview).

14. Mother 435, 1, Sears et al., PCR interview. A third mother said, "Not very much," when asked about how much her husband contributed. Change diapers? "Never." Feed her or give her a bath? "Never" (Mother 522, 1). A fourth commented that her husband did "nothing," and offered as a reason, "He's not a father that does diapers or does . . . no, he never did anything . . ." (Mother 684, 1).

15. Mother 10, 1, Sears et al., PCR interview; Mother 57, 1.

16. Mother 451, 1, Sears et al., PCR interview.

17. Among them were the following: "He is kind of afraid of little babies" (Mother 105, 1, Sears et al., PCR interview). "He was just a bit leery of [picking up the baby the first few days]" (Mother 113, 1). "He's kind of shy around babies" (Mother 226, 1).

18. Mother 244, 1, Sears et al., PCR interview.

19. Mother 138, 1–2, 32, Sears et al., PCR interview.

20. Suzanne Mettler, *Soldier Citizens: The G.I. Bill and the Making of the Greatest Generation* (New York: Oxford University Press, 2005).

21. Mother 24, 1, Sears et al., PCR interview.

22. Mother 324, 1, Sears et al., PCR interview.

23. Mother 145, 1, Sears et al., PCR interview.

24. Mother 149, 1, Sears et al., PCR interview.

25. Mother 513, 1, Sears et al., PCR interview. Others in the subsample who "helped" a fair amount included the husbands of Mothers 32, 239, 607, and 672.

26. Mother 205, 1, Sears et al., PCR interview. In a second family, the baby daughter picked up the mother's "low-lying infection" and "developed diarrhea"; as a result, the baby "was ill for a good two months" and "required a great deal of care." How much did your husband do? "Just as much as he could. He did quite a bit at night. He'd always give her—sometimes he'd give her her five o'clock bath, then a little meal, and her bottle and put her to bed while I was taking care of the oldest child." Did he do all the routine things like changing diapers and bathing? "Yes, although he never felt completely at ease" (Mother 307, 1, 2–3).

27. Mother 4, 1–2, Sears et al., PCR interview.

28. Mother 217, 1–2, Sears et al., PCR interview.
29. Mother 46, 1–2, Sears et al., PCR interview.
30. Mother 337, 2, Sears et al., PCR interview.
31. Mother 661, 1–2, Sears et al., PCR interview. Another woman talked about the fact that her husband sometimes was able to come home in the middle of the day, and he would feed the baby then. She also noted that the two of them had a business and worked together at home, and that he would contribute while she was occupied with the business. "If we were both home, and I was busy with something, he would certainly take the baby and get him ready" (Mother 660, 1–2).
32. Mother 614, 1, Sears et al., PCR interview.
33. Mother 428, 1, Sears et al., PCR interview.
34. Mother 623, 1, Sears et al., PCR interview.
35. Mother 443, 25, Sears et al., PCR interview.
36. When an armistice was signed, both sides declared they had won. See David Halberstam, *The Coldest Winter: America and the Korean War* (New York: Hyperion, 2007), 4. Halberstam's book is an overview of the politics of the war and the military strategy that was employed.
37. "U.S. Service and Casualties in Major Wars and Conflicts," *New York Times Almanac* (New York: Penguin, 2003), 150. Approximately 415,000 South Koreans were killed; about 429,000 were wounded. Deaths among the North Koreans and Chinese are estimated to be roughly 1.5 million (Halberstam, *Coldest Winter*, 4).
38. Halberstam, *Coldest Winter*, 52.
39. The U.S. government's main rationale for coming to South Korea's defense was to fight the spread of Communism and deter the use of nuclear weapons (Spencer C. Tucker, "Why Study the Korean War?" *Organization of American Historians Magazine of History* 14 [Spring 2000]: 3–9).
40. Ibid.
41. The threat of nuclear war and the anxieties it generated are well documented. The family bomb shelters, the hide-under-your-desk school exercises, the photographs and films of mushroom clouds were all constant reminders of "what if . . .?" For a history of family life during the Cold War, see May, *Homeward Bound*. May began her book by telling the story of a couple who spent their honeymoon in a backyard bomb shelter (reported in "Their Sheltered Life," *Life*, 10 August 1959).
42. "Father Rejects Dead Sons' Medals; Calls Truman Unfit to Confer Them," *New York Times*, 12 January 1952. According to the Pentagon, this was the first time the Medal of Honor had ever been turned down. Nonetheless, the soldiers were entered in the rolls. An army spokesman said, "The medal was not awarded to the father. . . . It was awarded to the son in death." The father said he did not believe in awards. "Boys are dying by the thousands. . . . Perhaps some receiving awards for their gallantry did not measure up to some whose deeds went unnoticed." About two weeks after this incident, Truman wrote a letter to his adult daughter, Margaret, who had just spent the weekend with her parents. Thinking perhaps about the reactions of Americans to unpopular decisions he had made, he said to her: "Great men and women are assayed in future generations. Your dad will never be reckoned among the great but you can be sure he did his level best and gave all he had to his country" (Harry S. Truman to Margaret Truman, 28 January 1952, cited in Evan Jones, "From Father to Child: Philosophy, Etc.," *New York Times*, 15 June 1958).
43. Tucker, "Why Study the Korean War?" The dustjacket of Halberstam's *The Coldest Winter* calls the Korean War "the black hole of modern American history."

44. Ruth Wall, "Let Daddy Take Over," *Parents Magazine*, June 1951. Men with children served in the Korean War but, as a class, they were not routinely drafted. Their exemption from compulsory military service was the subject of some debate. Fatherhood as a basis for deferment was lifted in the summer of 1953 ("Drafting Fathers," *New York Times*, 18 July 1953). Said the *Times*, "No more deferments for draftable young men who become fathers after August 25 . . . is certainly as it should be, and probably as it should have been for some time past. It is no picnic to go to war leaving a wife and child behind. But it is no picnic to go to war under any conditions. And seeing some chaps taking advantage of the fatherhood exemption can be a dispiriting sight to those who are answering the call in good faith."

45. Paul Harvey, "What Are Fathers Made Of?" *Parents Magazine*, October 1950. One naval officer spoke of being called to active duty in the Korean War just a few years after he had returned from World War II (Lieutenant Leslie E. This, "Remember Me? I'm Your Dad," *Parents Magazine*, March 1952). The first time he was sent overseas, he and his wife had two young girls who, in his words, were "too young to have established a real comradeship with their dad." The absence of a close connection hurt. He recalled stepping off the train after being away for a year and seeing his three-year-old daughter clinging to his wife's skirt. "Mother," the girl asked, "who is that man?" It was at that moment, the father said, that he "decided something must be done to make Daddy a real person." The *something* became the letters that he and his children exchanged while he was gone. Through the letters, he felt he had kept "an absentee daddy alive." The effect of military service on families in the early 1950s also came to the attention of Benjamin Spock. In 1954, a California woman penned a letter to Spock to ask him to "please write an article concerning *Fathers* that haven't shared every new thing their children learn and who just don't know how to go about gaining their love—or understanding their ways and means of learning and accomplishing new things." She added, "There are thousands of us young services [sic] wives who *are torn between husband and child. Please do something!*" The woman explained that she and her husband were married in August 1951 but were separated in October when he was sent overseas for two years. During that time, she lived with her parents and gave birth to a daughter. When her husband came home, the baby was eighteen months old and had grown accustomed to having her mother's undivided attention. "She resented her father because I spent so much time with him that I had always spent with her," she said. At the time the woman wrote, her husband was again "on duty at sea," and would be "returning next month" (R. A. G. (woman) to Benjamin Spock, 25 June 1954, box 2, Benjamin Spock Papers, Syracuse University.

46. Milton J. E. Senn and Claire Hartford, eds., *The Firstborn: Experiences of Eight American Families* (Cambridge, MA: Harvard University Press, 1968). Though the authors did gather information about men's involvement in infant care, they also said, "On the whole, . . . the fathers' participation was limited because of their work, their reluctance to become involved, and their expectations that the study primarily involved the mother and child" (21).

47. Ibid., 417.

48. Ibid., 237, 240.

49. Ibid., 492, 502.

50. The California study was carried out by Robert R. Sears, Lucy Rau, and Richard Alpert, and titled "Identification and Child Rearing, 1958." All interviews took place in the Stanford University Village School during the summer session of 1958. The

transcripts, upon which I draw in the sections to follow, are housed at the Murray Research Center (hereafter MRC) of the Harvard-MIT Data Center (Log Number 578) and are used with the permission of the center. My analysis of the interviews is based on forty cases (the entire sample), which involved separate interviews with husbands and wives. (Fathers were interviewed once. Mothers generally were interviewed twice; some, with the addition of a pilot or makeup interview, were queried three times.) As with the New England mother study that Sears had headed up, each respondent was asked a series of questions about a focal child, who was in kindergarten when the interviews were conducted. At the beginning of the interview, the questions dealt with the birth of the child and who was involved in the child's early care. Later in the interview, the couples were asked how they presently cared for and socialized the focal child. Thus, one part of the interview describes the family's life in the early 1950s. The other part, which I discuss in chapter 12, describes the family's life in the late 1950s. In quoting from the transcripts, I have tried to remain faithful to the punctuation that the researchers used. Exceptions include my being consistent in the length of dashes, even if the researchers were inconsistent. Also, ellipses without brackets denote ellipses in the original transcript, while ellipses within brackets denote instances where I have omitted or skipped over sentences that were in the original transcript. For a detailed description of the study, see Robert R. Sears, Lucy Rau, and Richard Alpert, *Identification and Child Rearing* (Stanford, CA: Stanford University Press, 1965).

51. Research shows that both men and women sometimes inflate their personal contributions to child care. On the egocentric or credit-taking bias, by gender, in prior times, see LaRossa, *Modernization of Fatherhood*; 82–83, 237; LaRossa and Reitzes, "Gendered Perceptions of Father Involvement in Early 20th Century America."

52. Father 40, (page) 3, Sears, Rau, and Alpert, "Identification and Child Rearing" (ICR) interview, MRC, Harvard-MIT Data Center (hereafter cited as Sears et al., ICR interview). The questions posed by the interviews are not in quotation marks, so as to separate them from the men's and women's responses. The questions are either verbatim or paraphrased.

53. The categories and findings are based on a statistical analysis of the standardized survey responses, used here with the permission of the Murray Research Center. The code sheet included only eight categories from the start.

54. Father 8, 1, 3–4, Sears et al., ICR interview.

55. Father 10, 2, Sears et al., ICR interview; Mother 10, first interview, 4.

56. Mother 21, first interview, 4, Sears et al., ICR interview.

57. Father 14, 2, Sears et al., ICR interview; Mother 14, pilot interview, 8.

58. Father 20, 2–3, Sears et al., ICR interview; Mother 20, makeup interview, 2. Other fathers who were in the military around the time the focal child was born included Fathers 11, 19, 22, 32, 34, 35, 41, 43, and 45. Father 42 appeared to have served in World War II.

59. Father 5, 2 (my italics), Sears et al., ICR interview; Mother 5, first interview, 6.

60. Father 23, 2, Sears et al., ICR interview; Mother 23, first interview, 4. This particular father was in graduate school and was working on his thesis when his son was born. Yet another father admitted that he was not present much either during the focal child's infancy ("I'd see [the baby] at the most, maybe thirty minutes a day"), and offered little explanation, other than to say that he "wasn't at home." (The interviewer did not ask him why.) During the wife's interview, however, it was revealed that the family was living on a "very isolated ranch in Arizona" when the baby arrived and

that her husband "was tied up six days a week" for "sometimes 18 hours a day." The mother said that her husband "never did have time" to care for the baby (Father 39, 2; Mother 39, 3).

61. Father 40, 2–3, Sears et al., ICR interview; Mother 40, first interview, 4. Another mother said that her husband "was very busy" and provided more "moral support" than anything else. "I mean, I don't think he ever got involved in changing her diapers or anything like that. And I nursed her, so he certainly never got up in the night." The father, however, said that while his baby daughter was breastfed for the first three months, he recalled feeding her about once a day. "We took turns," he insisted (Father 28, 3; Mother 28, first interview, 3, 4). In one case a father and mother offered conflicting perceptions, but the direction of their recall was *reversed*. The mother said that she and her husband "took turns on the feedings," while the father confessed that he fed the baby only occasionally ("it was a casual thing rather than a regular schedule"). Both, however, agreed that, on the whole, the father did (he said) "very little" or (she said) "didn't help [. . .] very much" (Father 33, 2; Mother 33, first interview, 3).

62. Father 25, 3, Sears et al., ICR interview; Mother 25, first interview, 4.

63. Father 41, 5, Sears et al., ICR interview; Mother 41, first interview, 3.

64. Father 37, 2, 3, Sears et al., ICR interview; Mother 37, first interview, 3.

65. Father 16, 2, 3, Sears et al., ICR interview; Mother 16, first interview, 3.

66. Father 30, 1–2, 3, Sears et al., ICR interview; Mother 30, first interview, 3.

67. Father 38, 3, Sears et al., ICR interview; Mother 38, first interview, 3–4.

CHAPTER NINE

1. Inflation also was accompanied by a wave of labor strikes, as workers strove to deal with higher prices. Although throughout the war there had been a number of strikes (many "directed against decisions of the War Labor Board"), the period between January and June of 1946 "marked what the U.S. Bureau of Labor Statistics called 'the most concentrated period of labor-management strife in the country's history.' " Jeremy Brecher, *Strike!* rev. ed. (Cambridge, MA: South End Press, 1997), 242, 246.

2. Ron Marzlock, "I Have Often Walked," *Queens Chronicle* (New York), 20 June 1996.

3. Rosalyn Baxandall and Elizabeth Ewen, *Picture Windows: How the Suburbs Happened* (New York: Basic Books, 2000), 80. The history of the Seabees can be traced to World War II. "After the 7 December 1941 Japanese attack on Pearl Harbor and the United States entry into the war, the use of civilian labor in war zones became impractical. Under international law civilians were not permitted to resist enemy military attack. Resistance meant summary execution as guerrillas. . . . On 5 January 1942, [Rear Admiral Ben Moreell] gained authority from the Bureau of Navigation to recruit men from the construction trades for assignment to a Naval Construction Regiment composed of three Naval Construction Battalions. . . . Moreell personally furnished them with their official motto: *Construimus, Batuimus*—'We Build, We Fight.' " (Department of the Navy, Naval Historical Center, "Seabee History: Formation of the Seabees and World War II," online at http://www.history.navy.mil/faqs/faq67-3.htm (accessed 27 April 2006).

4. Baxandall and Ewen, *Picture Windows*, 122. Levitt came up with name Levittown, which dismayed some residents. His response: "Levitt and Sons as owners and developers are the only people with the right to name this community as they see fit." He also said, "I wanted the name as a kind of monument to my family. And, by gosh, I wasn't going to brook any interference" (144). For an official history of Levittown,

see Levittown Historical Society, "A Brief History: Levittown USA," online at http://www.levittownhistoricalsociety.org/history.htm (accessed 27 April 2006).

5. "Housing: Up from the Potato Fields," *Time*, 3 July 1950, 68, 69.

6. Bruce Lambert, "At 50, Levittown Contends with Its Legacy of Bias," *New York Times*, 28 December 1997.

7. *Newsday*, 12 March 1949, cited in Baxandall and Ewen, *Picture Windows*, 175, 176; capitals in original. One of the demonstrations against segregation in subsidized housing immediately after the war is chronicled in Oakland Museum of California, "Picture This, World War II/Post War Era: 1940–1950s (Protest: War Vets)," online at http://www.museumca.org/picturethis/4_10.html (accessed 27 April 2006). See also Andrew Wiese, *Places of Their Own: African American Suburbanization in the Twentieth Century* (Chicago: University of Chicago Press, 2004), 125–29.

8. "President Roosevelt's Message to Congress on the State of the Union," *New York Times*, 7 January 1941. The speech also inspired the illustrator Norman Rockwell to create a series of paintings in 1943 on the "Four Freedoms" theme. The paintings "served as the centerpiece of a massive U.S. war bond drive and were put into service to help explain the war's aims" (National Archives, "Powers of Persuasion: Poster Art from World War II," online at http://www.archives.gov/exhibits/powers_of_persuasion/four_freedoms/four_freedoms.html (accessed 26 December 2006).

9. James W. Loewen, *Sundown Towns: A Hidden Dimension of Racism in America* (New York: New Press, 2005), 10. Towns where African Americans (or Chinese Americans, Jewish Americans, etc.) were not allowed to live were "often called 'sundown towns,' owing to the signs that many of them formerly sported at their corporate limits, which said 'Nigger, Don't Let the Sun Go Down on You in _____'" (3). Whites who had blacks as guests in their suburban homes could face recrimination. Levitt evicted two white families in 1950 "because they had invited black children to spend some summer afternoons playing with their children." (Baxandall and Ewen, *Picture Windows*, 177).

10. Kenneth T. Jackson, *Crabgrass Frontier: The Suburbanization of the United States* (New York: Oxford University Press, 1985), 241. In 1957, a black husband and wife, William and Daisy Myer, purchased a home for $12,150 in the Dogwood Hollow section of the suburban community of Levittown, Pennsylvania. Mr. Myer was a veteran of World War II. The couple had three children. Within days after the Myers moved in "a mob variously estimated between two-hundred and six-hundred adults and juveniles converged on Dogwood Hollow out of curiosity or malice. Close to midnight someone punctuated the shouting and jeering by throwing a rock which shattered the picture window of the beleaguered dwelling" (Marvin Bressler, "The Myers' Case: An Instance of Successful Racial Invasion," *Social Problems* 8 [Fall 1960]: 126–42).

11. Wiese, *Places of Their Own*, 114, 124.

12. "Housing: Up from the Potato Fields," 68, 69.

13. Some were concerned that the children of the suburbs were too "homogenized" by age. "The families of the New Suburbia consist typically of a young couple with one or two children, or perhaps one child and another on the way. The child living here sees no elderly people, no teen-agers. . . . In one new Eastern suburb with a population of 30,000 there is no high school. There is not yet any *need* for a high school. One may wonder how these young children, lacking many of the normal associations, will ever fit into a high school" (Sidonie M. Gruenberg, "Homogenized Children of the New Suburbia," *New York Times Magazine*, 19 September 1954).

14. "Housing: Up from the Potato Fields," 69.

15. Peter Bacon Hales, "Building Levittown: A Rudimentary Primer," online at http://tigger.uic.edu/~pbhales/Levittown/building.html (accessed 29 April 2006).

16. Lewis Mumford, "Rebirth of the Family," *House Beautiful*, December 1952 (my italics). This article was derived from a book, published a decade earlier, before Mumford could see the full effects of postwar suburbanization. See Lewis Mumford, *Faith for Living* (London: Secker and Warburg, 1941). In the book, Mumford said, "The family's basic need is for space; garden space and house space. Space for living: commodious rooms, well equipped for rest, relaxation, conversation, social intercourse, space for infants to toddle in and for runabout children to romp in; space for solitude as well as for sociability" (186–87). The same statement appears in the article. For his views on suburbanization, see Lewis Mumford, *The City in History: Its Origins, Its Transformations, Its Prospects* (New York: Harcourt, Brace, 1961).

17. Herbert J. Gans, *The Levittowners: Ways of Life and Politics in a New Suburban Community* (New York: Pantheon, 1967), 409; Harvey M. Choldin, *Cities and Suburbs: An Introduction to Urban Sociology* (New York: McGraw-Hill, 1985), 393; italics in original. Gans's account was based on a participant-observation study of Levittown, Pennsylvania in the late 1950s and early 1960s.

18. Gans, *Levittowners*, 221, 223; my italics.

19. Sebastian de Grazia, *Of Time, Work, and Leisure* (Garden City, NY: Doubleday/Anchor, 1962), 419 (table 1), 457 (chart A). This does not mean, of course, that there were no men whose away-from-home time was considerably longer.

20. Gans, *Levittowners* , 221.

21. "Housing: Up from the Potato Fields," 69.

22. Edgar M. Hoover and Raymond Vernon, *Anatomy of a Metropolis* (Cambridge, MA: Harvard University Press, 1959).

23. William M. Dobriner, *Class in Suburbia* (Englewood Cliffs, NJ: Prentice-Hall, 1963), 17.

24. During the postwar era, experts discussed the relationship between suburbanization and family life. At a 1955 conference, a professor of education at Columbia University said that suburban living "might present 'cause for concern' " and that there could be "serious consequences" for sons in particular. "There is no society in the world which isolates the to-be-man from the world of men to the extent that [sic] does Suburbia" ("Commuting Imperils Home Life in Suburbs, Teachers Are Told," *New York Times*, 19 March 1955). In 1960, as suburbs became even more commonplace, panelists on a radio program, "Life in Suburbia," tried to offer solace to men by telling them "it wasn't the amount of time fathers spent at home but the way they spent it that was important to creating a happy home." The implication was that quality could make up for a lack of quantity. The panelists also said that the moments sitting on a train or bus could be turned into a learning experience. "Fathers should take the opportunity at such times to discuss with other fathers the problems that arise with their children" ("Suburban Fathers Get Panel's Advice," *New York Times*, 3 January 1960). The fact that people *feared* the effects of suburbanization does not necessarily mean that suburbanization had a debilitating effect. The empirical evidence indicates that suburbanization did not generally reduce the amount of time that men spent with their families and that, in fact, suburban living may have encouraged more father-child interaction.

25. Robert R. Sears, Eleanor E. Maccoby, and Harry Levin, *Patterns of Child Rearing* (Evanston, IL: Row, Peterson, 1957). These are the same mothers who provided information about their husbands' contributions to infant care. Now they were referring to the focal children not when they were only a few months old but when they

were of kindergarten age. In quoting from the transcripts, I have tried to remain faithful to the punctuation that the researchers used. Exceptions include my being consistent in the length of dashes, even if the researchers were inconsistent. Also, ellipses without brackets denote ellipses in the original transcript, while bracketed ellipses denote instances where I have omitted or skipped over sentences that were in the original transcript. For the sake of clarity, I have made stylistic changes to some of the renderings of the transcripts. The questions posed by the interviewers are not in quotation marks, so as to separate them from the women's responses. The questions are either verbatim or paraphrased. In an open-ended interview, when queried about the husband's current relationship with the focal child, each mother was asked, "What happens when your husband comes home from work and [the focal child] is here?" or, simply, "What happens when [your husband] comes home at night?" See, for example, Mother 128, (page) 25, Mother 145, (page)18, Sears, Maccoby, and Levin, "Patterns of Child Rearing" (PCR) interview, Murray Research Center (MRC), Harvard-MIT Data Center (hereafter cited as Sears et al., PCR interview). Each mother was also asked, "What kinds of things do [your husband and the focal child] do together?" "How much does your husband do these days in connection with taking care of her or him?" See, for example, Mother 443, 24–25. In a standardized survey, each mother was also asked, "Nature of affectional bond, father to [focal] child?" (range of answers: extremely warm, loving, plays with child for fun, enjoys doing things for child, [. . .] loves child, warm toward him [or her], enjoys being with, but with less intensity than 1, [. . .] not much warmth, matter-of-fact, not demonstrative [. . .]); and "Amount of coldness and lack of affection between [father] and [focal child]?" (range of answers: always happy to see each other, lots of affection shown by both [. . .] moderate attachment between the two, do some things together, [. . .] act coldly toward each other, do very little together [. . .]). The methodology for the study was described in chapter 8.

26. See, for example, Mother 149, 22, Sears et al., PCR interview; Mother 537, 21–22; Mother 685, 18.

27. Mother 441, 32, Sears et al., PCR interview.

28. In the standardized survey, each mother was asked, "How much does father do these days in connection with taking care of [the focal child]?" (range of answers: none, relatively little, moderate amount, quite a bit).

29. Theodore B. Johannis Jr., "Participation by Fathers, Mothers, and Teenage Sons and Daughters in Selected Child Care and Control Activity," *Coordinator* 6 (September 1957): 31–32.

30. Ibid., 31, 32.

31. Ibid., 31. A companion article, based on the same study, reported that the division of household tasks—that is, housework—was a lot more traditional. For example, only a small percentage of fathers made the beds (3.5), cleaned and dusted (5.3), ironed (1.9), or did the wash (4.9) (Theodore B. Johannis Jr., "Participation by Fathers, Mothers, Teenage Sons and Daughters in Selected Household Tasks," *Coordinator* 6 [December 1957]: 61–62).

32. An exception would include the father who was said to be away often; he had little to do with his children and was not greeted at the door. Said the mother, referring to her daughter: "She doesn't rush to kiss him when he comes home or anything like that" (Mother 441, 32, Sears et al., PCR interview). Another example of non-observance was provided by a woman who, when asked what happened when her husband came home from work, said simply, "Oh, usually no reaction at all." She

initially implied that the reason was that her husband came home "fairly early, four or four-thirty." (He was a teacher.) But then she added, "It is not the same in this family as I have noticed in others, where the father comes home at six and the children are all washed and scrubbed and ready to greet him, and they romp all over him when he comes in." She did mention that because her husband got home early "he does see the children a great deal more than a man who gets home at six and is tired and has to sit down to eat." The father's after-work time with the children apparently was largely confined to the late afternoon, because he spent little time with them after dinner. "After dinner, except in the summer time," the mother reported, "the children go directly to bed. After they are excused from the table, they say good night, and that's that." She did say that she or her husband would tuck the children in and hear their prayers, while the other did the dishes, and that her husband often would read the children a bedtime story. "If [my husband] puts them to bed, they ask him for a story, but if I put them to bed, they don't even ask me for a story. I'm around all day, and it's not the same. It's a treat for him, and he takes the time to tell them a story" (Mother 661, 26–27).

33. Mother 703, 39. Sears et al., PCR interview.

34. Mother 703, 39–40, Sears et al., PCR interview. The mother also talked about the children's antics during dinner and how she and her husband dealt with issues of fairness. "Course we have quite a rumpus some nights at the supper table. I have a set of dishes that has one dark blue plate and if I'm quick enough to think about it, I try not to put the blue plate on the table. There are some nights when it gets on the table and the first one that spies it, then they all yell, 'Well I want the blue plate, so and so had the blue plate last night.' So we have a circus. So then we tried to set it down so [one child] has it tonight, [another child] has it tomorrow night, [the third child] has it the next night. Then try to remember from one night to the next who had it" (40).

35. The mothers were asked, "Does father ever stay with child when the mother is out?" The answers were arrayed on an eight-point scale, ranging from "practically never and mother indicates that father feels it is not his job, [or] doesn't want to do it" to "frequently." Missing cases are excluded from the results reported here.

36. Mother 32, 19, Sears et al., PCR interview.

37. Mother 623, 37, Sears et al., PCR interview. The transcript does read as follows: "it has been quite a connotation when [my husband] comes home." The mother may have said *commotion*. But she may also have been referring to the *significance* of her husband's arrival. I have reproduced the transcript as is.

38. Mother 105, 23, 24, Sears et al., PCR interview.

39. Mother 529, 29–30, Sears et al., PCR interview. After supper, she said, the father plays with his son "until he goes to bed." Also, said the mother, "He's right with him, he'll read him a story, one of his favorite stories, or he has homework now and he'll give him a piece of paper and he'll write the alphabet or the numbers down" (30).

40. Mother 205, 17, Sears et al., PCR interview.

41. Mother 729, 27, Sears et al., PCR interview.

42. Mother 50, 19, Sears et al., PCR interview.

43. A. C. Nielsen figures, reported in Cobbett Steinberg, *TV Facts* (New York: Facts on File Publications, 1985), 86.

44. In *Patterns of Child Rearing*, Sears et al. reported that 92 percent of the families owned TV sets (288). But the survey responses indicated between 87 and 88 percent owned a set and that between 1 and 2 percent "didn't own, but lived where there [was] one."

45. Baxandall and Ewen, *Picture Windows*, 134. Levitt arranged to buy four thousand TVs from the Admiral Corporation and had them installed in the living rooms of the new homes. The house-with-TV package became available in 1950, which meant that some of the older houses in Levittown had no TVs. The imbalance had the effect of encouraging interactions *across* households. "Families who bought televisions became popular with their TV-hungry neighbors; watching television became a block activity" (146).

46. Eleanor E. Maccoby, "Television: Its Impact on School Children," *Public Opinion Quarterly* 15 (Fall 1951): 421–44. It is fascinating to see what people's reactions to television were at the historical moment that it was being introduced, given that they did not necessarily know how popular the medium would become and the directions it would take. After addressing the "psychological implications" of the study's findings (e.g., could TV become "addictive," could it interfere with the "practice of real-life skills"?), the author concluded, "It is not the intention of the present discussion to view the advent of television with alarm. Many of the questions which have been raised are matters of degree: the part television plays in a child's life is probably not qualitatively different from that of the movies and other mass media, and in many ways TV probably plays a role similar to that of the fairy stories and fantasy play which have been part of children's lives since our earliest records of man. It appears likely, however, that TV has changed the quantitative impact of certain forms of fantasy to the point that it is pertinent to inquire into the long-range effects such a change will have" (443–44). Besides being asked whether they had a TV in their homes, the New England mothers were also asked, "How many hours does [the focal child] spend *looking* at TV per day?" The mothers' responses follow: no time (0.3 percent), a half hour or less (6.3 percent), more than a half hour to an hour (24.5 percent), more than an hour to an hour and a half (16.9 percent), more than an hour and a half to two hours (23.0 percent), more than two hours to two-and-a-half hours (3.4 percent), more than two-and-a-half hours (14.5 percent). In 11.1 percent of the cases, data were missing. Watching TV also was a very common activity among adults. One 1957 survey reported that 57 percent of the respondents had watched television "yesterday." No other activity came close to TV watching, in terms of frequency: 38 percent said they visited with friends or relatives the previous day, 33 percent said they worked around the yard and in the garden, 27 percent read magazines, 18 percent read books. (de Grazia, *Of Time, Work, and Leisure*, 441 [table 8]).

47. V. D. (woman) to Rose Franzblau, 26 April 1954, box 113, Rose Franzblau Papers, Columbia University (hereafter cited as RFP).

48. Maccoby, "Television," 422.

49. Mother 647, 9, Sears et al., PCR interview. Other nonbuyers also had to deal with the fact that their children could go to friends' houses and watch television: "She [the focal child] only sees TV once in a while when she visits the neighbor. We refuse to buy one ourselves. [. . .]" (Mother 653, 9–10.)

50. Mother 331, 14, Sears et al., PCR interview. The mother was asked whether the children accepted the one-hour rule. "Yes, they do. They pick out the shows each day they want the most to see, and if you tell them something and are nice about it, and use persuasion I think that they will accept it and go along with you. I have found that true."

51. Mother 658, 15, Sears et al., PCR interview. The mother conceded that their daughter was allowed to watch TV on Sunday "between five and six when she watched *Zoo*

Parade and *Super Circus*, [but] there is no talk about it." She also said, "The other kids talk about *Cisco Kid* and the other things, but she has never asked to see them, and I would like to keep it that way."

52. Fathers who came home when *The Howdy Doody Show* was on the air faced stiff competition for their children's attention. The title character was a marionette whose friends were an assortment of colorful characters—some human, some not. The stars of the show included rancher Buffalo Bob Smith and clown Clarabelle (both human), and Doodyville mayor Phineas T. Bluster and multiple-animal-hybrid Flubadub (both puppets), among others (Museum of Broadcast Communications, "The Howdy Doody Show: U.S. Children's Program, online at http://www.museum.tv/archives/etv/H/htmlH/howdydoodys/howdydoodys.htm [accessed 21 July 2008]).

53. Mother 138, 30, Sears et al., PCR interview. Another mother reported: "Nothing [happens when he comes home from work], she's watching television. (laughs). She ignores him. The little one, the three-year-old is the only one [of the three children] that prefers him to the television. But, other occasions when she's not [watching television], why, she says, 'Hi, daddy, it's good to see you,' and she often will run up and put her arms around him and give him a hug and he's glad to see her." Sometimes the focal child and father watched westerns together (Mother 607, 28, 29).

54. Mother 451, 46, Sears et al., PCR interview. Said another mother: "Well, it's usually during a television program [when my husband gets home]. Of course, [the focal child] usually runs up and kisses him but then goes back to his program" (Mother 679, 22).

55. Mother 614, 27, Sears et al., PCR interview.

56. Mother 448, 23, Sears et al., PCR interview. The mother said the focal child liked it when his father told him "stories about when he [presumably the father] was young and things like that."

57. Z. (woman) to Rose Franzblau, 16 April 1954, box 114, RFP.

58. C. E. C. (woman) to Rose Franzblau, 1 March 1954, box 114, RFP.

59. The letter writer, a fourteen-year-old girl, said of her father: "He is domineering and nervous. [. . .] We can't tell him anything. His way goes" (E. W. [woman] to Rose Franzblau, undated 1952, box 35, RFP).

60. Mother 610, 20, Sears et al., PCR interview. Another mother said, "Well, sometimes my husband gets peeved about that—she's usually so engrossed in television, that she doesn't notice as a rule [that he is home from work], but if television isn't on, and there is nothing that has her interest, she'll hug and kiss him, but usually she ignores him, and he gets edgy about that. The little one [three years old] rushes right up him, and she doesn't. She's very reserved in her affections" (Mother 28, 34).

61. Although a number of men engaged in routine child care throughout the week, some men were more likely to do so on Saturdays and Sundays. For example, when one mother was asked whether her husband "helped" to get the focal child dressed or prepare the child's meals, she said, "He would be more apt to do that on a Saturday or Sunday morning" (Mother 149, 23, Sears et al., PCR interview. Another, asked the same question, said, "He does that on Saturdays, and holidays occasionally" (Mother 324, 31).

62. Mother 149, 22, Sears et al., PCR interview.

63. Mother 443, 24–25, Sears et al., PCR interview. The mother also reported, "If she is ill, he is perfectly willing to help take care of her and if she wakes up during the night, which she doesn't do often, but she does do it if she is not feeling too well, he will

get up and take her into the bathroom. He does as many things as he possibly can for her. He is really a second mother. He is wonderful to her" (25).

64. Mother 113, 27, Sears et al., PCR interview.

65. Mother 623, 36, 37, Sears et al., PCR interview. The mother happened to remark that her husband called every day from work to talk to the children and that he had taught them things that she felt she could not. "I mean there is a real comradery there that can't be broken or altered."

66. Little League, "History of Little League," online at http://www.littleleague.org/Learn_ More/About_Our_Organization/historyandmission.htm (accessed 29 May 2009).

67. Lance and Robin Van Auken, *Play Ball: The Story of Little League Baseball* (University Park: Pennsylvania State University Press, 2001), 47, 51, 203.

68. Ibid., 203–8; Little League, "Little League Chronology," online at http://www.little league.org/Learn_More/About_Our_Organization/historyandmission/chronology .htm (accessed 29 May 2009). Little League Baseball is today played in more than a hundred countries (Choldin, *Cities and Suburbs*, 360–61).

69. Edward A. Connell, "Little League Baseball Praised," *New York Times*, 12 September 1952.

70. Arthur Daley, "30,000 Little Big Leaguers," *American Magazine*, April 1951; Arthur Daley, "The Little League Is Big Time," *New York Times Magazine*, 25 May 1952; The Little League regulations in 1951 stipulated that "girls [were] not eligible under any conditions." Kathryn "Tubby" Massar tucked her hair under her cap during baseball tryouts in 1950 and was selected to become a member of a team, at which point she announced that she was a girl. She was allowed to play that year and said she probably would have played in 1951 as well, except for the stipulation in the 1951 Little League rule book. Her father told her she "couldn't play because of the new rule and said, 'Look what you've started!'" In 1974, after a court battle, the Little League organization was ordered to allow girls to participate (Van Auken, *Play Ball*, 145, 147, 154–56).

71. Milton Bracker, "Little Leaguers' Parents Need Relief as Children Play it Cool," *New York Times*, 26 August 1959.

72. The "my-dad-wasn't-there" stories could be central to a baby boomer's insistence that he was a different kind of father—someone who was *physically present* at his young children's games. On the stories that men tell about their fathers and the role that the stories play in the politics of parental identities, see Ralph LaRossa, "Stories and Relationships," *Journal of Social and Personal Relationships* 12 (November 1995): 553–58; Ralph LaRossa, *The Modernization of Fatherhood: A Social and Political History* (Chicago: University of Chicago Press, 1997).

73. The following discussion is drawn, in part, from Ralph LaRossa, "'Until the Ball Glows in the Twilight': Fatherhood, Baseball, and the Game of Playing Catch," in *Situated Fathering: A Focus on Physical and Social Spaces*, ed. William Marsiglio, Kevin Roy, and Greer Litton Fox, 141–61 (Lanham, MD: Rowman and Littlefield, 2005).

74. A review of references to the game of playing catch over much of the twentieth century revealed that a yard or, more specifically, a *backyard*, was mentioned more than any other single location as the place where the game has been or should be played.

75. "To know a boy you must play with him" (Edgar A. Guest, "My Job as a Father," *American Magazine*, August 1922).

76. A skilled player's arm operates like a catapult to hurl the ball. A whip of the wrist can provide additional spin and speed. The connotation of "throwing like a girl" is

almost always negative. The denotation is harder to pin down. (What does "throwing like a girl" look like?) The negative label often appears to be associated with an arm motion that *stops* just as the ball is released, as opposed to allowing the arm to *continue downward*, while finely timing the ball's release.

77. Alan Hart, "The Man Who Made It Christmas One Day in May," *Times Union*, 24 December 2002, online at http://web.lexis-nexis.com (accessed 31 October 2002).

78. Michael Messner, "Ah, Ya Throw Like a Girl!" *M: Gentle Men for Gender Justice* 11 (Winter 1983–84): 21–22. Playing catch also provided an opportunity for a father and child to bond. Said one author, writing about the "1955 Model Dad": "A reticent father, unable to talk his son's language, nevertheless develops companionship with the boy merely by tossing a ball in the yard in the few minutes before supper. Father and son may rarely speak, but an ease with one another results from their game of catch" (Kenneth Robb, "Today's Father," *Today's Health*, June 1955).

79. Lesley Kennedy, "Having a Ball with Dad," *Rocky Mountain News*, 12 June 2003. Online at http://web.lexis-nexis.com/universe/printdoc (accessed 31 October 2003).

80. Donald Hall, *Fathers Playing Catch with Sons* (New York: North Point Press, 1985). Hall's book probably has done more to promote the *culture* of the game of catch than any other text. Other authors who have written about the game often reference (and revere) the book. The lead chapter, "Fathers Playing Catch with Sons," originally was a 1974 article (in *Playboy* magazine), but it is the 1985 book that has become synonymous with the game's sacralization.

81. George B. Leonard Jr., "These Five Are Family," *Look*, 15 March 1960. On the "pursuit of perfect childhood" in the postwar era, see Steven Mintz, *Huck's Raft: A History of American Childhood* (Cambridge, MA: Harvard University Press, 2004). On the scheduled activities of children in contemporary society, see Annette Lareau, *Unequal Childhoods: Class, Race, and Family Life* (Berkeley and Los Angeles: University of California Press, 2003).

CHAPTER TEN

1. *Leave It to Beaver*, "Beaver's Hero," 9 April 1959, epguides.com and TV.com, "*Leave It to Beaver*: A Titles and Air Dates Guide," online at http://epguides.com/LeaveItto Beaver/ (accessed 31 July 2008). *Leave It to Beaver* was created by Joe Connelly and Bob Mosher, who were both fathers. Beaver and Wally were inspired by Connelly's eight- and fourteen-year-old sons, Rick and Jay ("Joe Connelly, 85, a Creator of 'Leave It to Beaver' on Television," *New York Times*, 17 February 2003). In the first season, Beaver was said to be seven; Wally, twelve. Since "Beaver's Hero" was broadcast a year and a half after the series began, I added a year to each of the children's ages. See Tim Brooks and Earle Marsh, *The Complete Directory to Prime Time Network TV Shows, 1946–Present*, 4th ed. (New York: Ballantine Books, 1988), 441.

2. "Did you kill anybody?" was "an inevitable question" for a son to ask his dad, said a writer for the *New York Times* in 1959. "A knowledge and understanding of what his father did in the war can be important to a child in many ways. Boys at an age at which hero worship for their fathers is natural and good find pleasure and pride in knowing what daddy did. Seeing the uniforms and the ribbons, looking at the snapshots and the yellowed clippings, hearing the stories of successes and frustrations can bring combat out of the realm of something seen on television into the reality of life as it affects people, real people, their own fathers" (Dorothy Barclay, "A Child Asks 'What's War?'" *New York Times Magazine*, 8 November 1959). Note the author's assumption that only boys would be interested in asking the question and that the

fathers who served in the military would have been in combat. The reference to "the war" appears to mean World War II. The Korean War was not mentioned.

3. In *Honey I'm Home! Sitcoms: Selling the American Dream* (New York: Grove Weidenfeld, 1992), Gerard Jones briefly summarized the same episode and saw Ward's answer as transformative: "Thus the violent past was symbolically put away; the day of the manly hero had yielded to the day of the builder, the planner, the quiet team player" (125). Another interpretation would be not that a "softer" kind of masculinity was supplanting a "harder" kind, but that simultaneous multiple masculinities were being acknowledged. The "manly hero" was not eradicated, for he was—and continues to be—valued in America. Other kinds of masculinity, however, were placed alongside it. I would say, too, that if any of the versions could be considered hegemonic, it was that of the "manly hero," for it was the basis of comparison throughout the episode. On multiple masculinities and the social construction of hegemonic masculinity, see R. W. Connell, *Masculinities* (Berkeley and Los Angeles: University of California Press, 1995; 2nd ed., 2005).

4. Christopher Paul Moore, *Fighting for America: Black Soldiers—The Unsung Heroes of World War II* (New York: Ballantine Books, 2005), 326, 327.

5. Ibid., 329.

6. A. C. Nielsen figures, reported in Cobbett Steinberg, *TV Facts* (New York: Facts on File Publications, 1985), 86.

7. The following discussion on television and fatherhood is drawn, in part, from Ralph LaRossa, "The Culture of Fatherhood in the Fifties: A Closer Look," *Journal of Family History* 29 (January 2004): 47–70.

8. Muriel G. Cantor, "Prime-Time Fathers: A Study in Continuity and Change," *Critical Studies in Mass Communication* 7 (1990): 279.

9. Jessica Weiss, *To Have and To Hold: Marriage, the Baby Boom, and Social Change* (Chicago: University of Chicago Press), 83.

10. Brooks and Marsh, *Complete Directory to Prime Time Network TV Shows*, 15–16, 213, 257–258, 441.

11. Ibid., 963–66; Steinberg, *TV Facts*. Daniel Scott Smith has made this point with respect to *Ozzie and Harriet*, noting that it "was never among the most popular" programs when it was broadcast ("Recent Change and the Periodization of American Family History," *Journal of Family History* 20 (Fall 1995): 329–46).

12. To put the ratings for *Father Knows Best* in a historical perspective, the *New York Times* reported that, in the 1957–58 season, *Leave It to Beaver* had a rating of 19.6, which meant that 8.2 million households watched the show. In the 1999–2002 season, *The Sopranos* had a rating of 6.8, which translated into 7.3 million households (Bill Carter, "Calibrating the Next Step for 'The Sopranos,'" *New York Times*, 7 October 2002).

13. Diana C. Reep and Faye H. Dambrot, "TV Parents: Fathers (and now Mothers) Know Best," *Journal of Popular Culture* 28 (1994): 13–23.

14. One fifties' Web site spotlights only these four shows on its "TV Families of the Fifties" page (www.fiftiesweb.com/families.htm).

15. David Halberstam, *The Fifties* (New York: Villard Books, 1993), 514.

16. Stephanie Coontz, *The Way We Never Were: American Families and the Nostalgia Trap* (New York: Basic Books, 1992).

17. Including shows that debuted in the fall of 1960 may seem a stretch, since they were on the air for only a few months before the fifties, as defined here (1945–60), ended. We should bear in mind, however, that these shows were conceptualized in the midst of the fifties and thus reflect the television industry's mindset at the time.

18. Brooks and Marsh, *Complete Directory to Prime Time Network TV Shows*, 664. The same point can be made for other westerns that showcased fathers. When Lorne Greene, the father on *Bonanza*, died, it was said that his TV character "became a worldwide image of firm but gentle fatherhood" (Associated Press Report, "Actor Lorne Greene Dies at 72, Starred as Father in TV's 'Bonanza,'" *Atlanta Journal and Constitution*, 12 September 1987).

19. Many of the most popular shows in the late fifties were westerns. Brooks and Marsh, *Complete Directory to Prime Time Network TV Shows*; Ella Taylor, *Prime-Time Families* (Berkeley and Los Angeles: University of California Press, 1989), 33.

20. There is a Web site devoted to chronicling single TV fathers (www.tvdads.com).

21. Brooks and Marsh, *Complete Directory to Prime Time Network TV Shows*, 543, 56, 97.

22. Ibid., 184.

23. Taylor, *Prime-Time Families*, 26; see also 40.

24. Elizabeth and Joseph Pleck contended, "Both white working-class fathers in sitcoms, such as Stuart Erwin in 'The Trouble with Father,' and their middle-class counterparts, Jim Anderson, Ward Cleaver, and Ozzie Nelson, were portrayed as bumblers. These men were often manipulated by their wives, who had an intuitive and empathic understanding of the best course" (Elizabeth H. Pleck and Joseph H. Pleck, "Fatherhood Ideals in the United States," in *The Role of the Father in Child Development*, ed. Michael E. Lamb, 33–48 [New York: John Wiley and Sons, 1997], 43). Lynn Spigel took a similar position in *Make Room for TV: Television and the Family Ideal in Postwar America* (Chicago: University of Chicago Press, 1992), 64. Others disagree (see following endnote).

25. Cantor, "Prime-Time Fathers"; Lynda M. Glennon and Richard Butsch, "The Family as Portrayed on Television, 1946–1978," in *Television and Behavior: Ten Years of Scientific Progress and Implications for the Eighties*, vol. 2, *Technical Reviews*, ed. David Pearl, Lorraine Bouthilet, and Joyce Lazar (Rockville, MD: National Institutes of Health, U.S. Department of Health and Human Services), 264–71; Lisa Heilbronn, "Breadwinners and Loafers: Images of Masculinity in 1950s Situation Comedy," *masculinities* 2 (Fall 1994): 60–70; Nina C. Leibman, *Living Room Lectures: The Fifties Family in Film and Television* (Austin: University of Texas Press,1995); Elaine Tyler May, *Homeward Bound: American Families in the Cold War Era* (New York: Basic Books, 1988), 129; Steven Mintz and Susan Kellogg, *Domestic Revolutions: A Social History of American Family Life* (New York: Free Press, 1988), 190–93.

26. Glennon and Butsch, "The Family as Portrayed on Television"; Cantor, "Prime-Time Fathers"; May, *Homeward Bound*, 129; Mintz and Kellogg, *Domestic Revolutions*, 190–93.

27. Mary Beth Haralovich, "Sitcoms and Suburbs: Positioning the 1950s Homemaker," *Quarterly Review of Film and Video* 11 (May 1989): 61–83.

28. Glennon and Butsch, "The Family as Portrayed on Television," 265.

29. Cantor, "Prime-Time Fathers," 280. Also: "In 1955 the Family Service Association presented Robert Young—Superdad Jim Anderson on Father Knows Best—a plaque for his Constructive Portrayal of American Family Life" (Mark Crotty, "Murphy Would Probably Also Win the Election—The Effect of Television as Related to the Portrayal of the Family in Situation Comedies," *Journal of Popular Culture* 29 [Winter 1995]: 1–15).

30. "Who Remembers Papa?" *Saturday Review of Literature*, July/December 1951; Morton Hunt, "The Decline and Fall of the American Father," *Cosmopolitan*, April 1955, 20–25.

31. "Father Knows Best: Robert Young Proves a TV Dad Doesn't Have to Be Stupid," *TV Guide*, June 16–22, 1956.

32. Glennon and Butsch, "The Family as Portrayed on Television" 267. It is important to note as well that domestic comedies broadcast in the late fifties (versus those broadcast before) were more likely to elevate fathers at the expense of mothers. Nina Leibman's careful analysis of the narrative patterns in *The Adventures of Ozzie and Harriet, Father Knows Best, Leave It to Beaver, The Donna Reed Show*, and *My Three Sons*, with particular emphasis on the middle three, revealed that "the fictional dads were always available, and were much more desired than the mother in their ability to resolve family crises. . . . The centralization of [these] fathers and the father-filial bond resulted in a consequent denigration of the status of the mother. . . . They [June Cleaver and Donna Stone] *seemed* to be crucial to the emotional needs of their children, just as these series *seemed* to be comedies. Only with a closer reading and the benefit of . . . years of hindsight does it become clear that visibility does not render the television mothers important any more than the laugh track renders the domestic melodrama a comedy." In the main, the shows were "characterized by their consistent thematic emphasis on patriarchy" (Leibman, *Living Room Lectures*, 252, 253, 256, 259). James Gilbert examined in depth *The Adventures of Ozzie and Harriet* and illustrated how Ozzie was repeatedly portrayed as an incompetent dad—a striking contrast to how the fathers in *Father Knows Best, Leave It to Beaver*, and *The Donna Reed Show* were portrayed. See *Men in the Middle: Searching for Masculinity in the 1950s* (Chicago: University of Chicago Press, 2005).

33. Halberstam, *The Fifties*, 514; Coontz, *The Way We Never Were*, 29.

34. Jay Fultz, *In Search of Donna Reed* (Iowa City: University of Iowa Press, 1998), 129.

35. Moore, *Fighting for America*, 328–29.

36. Murray A. Straus, Richard J. Gelles, and Suzanne K. Steinmetz, *Behind Closed Doors: Violence in the American Family*. (New York: Anchor/Doubleday, 1980), 34, 62.

37. Linda Gordon, *Heroes of Their Own Lives: The Politics and History of Family Violence* (New York: Viking Penguin, 1988), 23.

38. On marriage and divorce trends in the early and mid–twentieth century, see Andrew J. Cherlin, *Marriage, Divorce, Remarriage* (Cambridge, MA: Harvard University Press, 1981. On the culture of marriage and divorce in the 1950s, see Karla B. Hackstaff, *Marriage in a Culture of Divorce* (Philadelphia, PA: Temple University Press, 1999). On the "violence, terror, or simply grinding misery that only occasionally came to light" in the postwar era, see Coontz, *The Way We Never Were*, 35.

39. There were other avenues by which therapeutic professionals were made aware of abuse in the home. Linda Gordon found evidence of family violence in the case records of Boston-area social work agencies from 1880 to 1960 (Gordon, *Heroes of their Own Lives*). The plight of victims of family violence in the 1920s and 1930s is also revealed in the letters written to the U.S. Children's Bureau and to the syndicated columnist and child-rearing book author, Angelo Patri. See Ralph LaRossa, *The Modernization of Fatherhood: A Social and Political History* (Chicago: University of Chicago Press, 1997).

40. C. B. (woman) to Rose Franzblau, undated, November 1953, box 40, Rose Franzblau Papers, Columbia University (hereafter cited as RFP).

41. On the "cycle of violence" in abusive relationships, see Leonore E. Walker, *The Battered Women Syndrome* (New York: Springer, 1984); see also Jane H. Wolf-Smith and Ralph LaRossa, "After He Hits Her," *Family Relations* 41 (July 1992): 324–29.

42. L. G. (woman) to Rose Franzblau, 9 March 1954, box 114, RFP. One woman, the mother of two sons, said that her husband would beat her when she was pregnant. In a postscript, she offered, "Maybe! we got married to[o] young. He was 20 yrs. old and I was 16" (J. C. M. [woman] to Rose Franzblau, 6 May 1954, box 114, RFP.

43. L. R. (woman) to Rose Franzblau, 13 April 1953, box 40, RFP. "I have been threatening to leave him for some time at least until the children are grown [besides the twelve-year-old daughter, the couple had a nine-and-a-half-year-old son], but my mother and sister advised me against such [unintelligible word]. I don't know what to do."

44. P. M. (woman) to Rose Franzblau, 2 August 1951, box 31, RFP.

45. Ibid.

46. On the rise of Freudian ideas in the United States after World War II, see Rachel Devlin, *Relative Intimacy: Fathers, Adolescent Daughters, and Postwar American Culture* (Chapel Hill: University of North Carolina Press, 2005).

47. M. G. (woman) to Rose Franzblau, 15 August 1953, box 40, RFP.

48. J. F. (woman) to Rose Franzblau, 9 February 1959, box 62, RFP.

49. M. H. (woman) to Rose Franzblau, 23 January 1959, box 62, RFP. Before giving her name and address at the bottom of the letter, the twelve-year-old signed herself "CONFUSED." There is no record of a reply.

CHAPTER ELEVEN

1. John Ketwig, . . . *And a Hard Rain Fell: A GI's True Story of the War in Vietnam*. (Naperville, IL: Sourcebooks, 2002), xvi–xvii.

2. Civil rights leader and U.S. Congressman John Lewis said that 1955 "was a watershed year not just for [him] but for the movement as well." He elaborated: "Actually, no one was using the term 'movement' quite yet, but they would be before the year was out. . . . Things were truly beginning to 'move,' both for bad and good. Lines were starting to be drawn, and blood was beginning to spill" (John Lewis, *Walking with the Wind: A Memoir of the Movement* [New York: Simon and Schuster, 1998], 46).

3. Ibid.

4. In her memoir of the events leading up to and surrounding the murder of her son, Mamie Till-Mobley referred to the aunt and uncle as Aunt Lizzy and Papa Mose (Mamie Till-Mobley and Christopher Benson, *Death of Innocence: The Story of the Hate Crime That Changed America* [New York: Ballantine Books, 2003]).

5. Davis W. Houck, "Killing Emmett," *Rhetoric and Public Affairs* (Summer 2005): 225–62. Houck discussed the newspaper coverage of the murder.

6. Till-Mobley and Benson, *Death of Innocence*, 122.

7. William Bradford Huie, "The Shocking Story of Approved Killing in Mississippi," *Look*, 24 January 1956; Public Broadcasting System, "The Murder of Emmett Till," online at http://www.pbs.org/wgbh/amex/till/ (accessed 9 May 2006).

8. Juan Williams, *Eyes on the Prize: America's Civil Rights Years, 1954–1965* (New York: Viking Penguin, 1987) 52. Forty years after the verdict, one of the jurors insisted still that the body found in the Tallahatchie was not Till's. The claim circulated at the time, and repeated by the juror long after the fact, was that the NAACP had planted the corpse to try to stir up a "racial tornado." See Richard Rubin, "The Ghosts of Emmett Till," *New York Times Magazine*, 31 July 2005. (All interviews were conducted in 1995.) What happened in the Emmett Till case was not unusual. For years, whites who murdered blacks were rarely punished—or even prosecuted. See, for example, Herbert Shapiro, *White Violence and Black Response: From Reconstruction to Montgomery* (Amherst: University of Massachusetts Press, 1988).

9. Till-Mobley and Benson, *Death of Innocence*, 202. Till-Mobley also questioned the charges against Louis Till: "With the revelation about Louis, I began to hear from his army friends. The unit he served in was an all-black unit made up mostly of fellows from the Chicago area, so it was not hard for them to locate me. Louis's friends told me they thought he had gotten set up. First, they didn't think Louis was capable of doing what he was accused of doing. Second, there was a larger problem that black soldiers were dealing with. It was a problem that had followed them overseas from the United States. [My brother-in-law] talked about it too. He had served in Europe and recalled how black soldiers would get roused at three in the morning. Military police would look over the black soldiers in formation. The MPs would bring in local women who would point out someone in the line. . . . Black soldiers who got pointed out at three in the morning were always taken away. They were not brought back" (203).

10. Houck, "Killing Emmett," 225, 246.

11 Till-Mobley and Benson, *Death of Innocence*, 145, 212; Huie, "Shocking Story."

12. Houck, "Killing Emmett," 246. Carolyn Bryant, the star witness for the defense and the woman whom Emmett Till had allegedly offended, was praised by the press for her beauty.

13. Ibid, 247; see also Till-Mobley and Benson, *Death of Innocence*, 163.

14. For a discussion of the social interactions involved in people's "presentation of self," see Erving Goffman, *The Presentation of Self in Everyday Life* (New York: Double-day/Anchor, 1959). For a discussion of how parents can use their children as props in order to gather credit for themselves, see Ralph LaRossa and Maureen Mulligan LaRossa, *Transition to Parenthood: How Infants Change Families* (Beverly Hills, CA: Sage, 1981). A member of the men's defense team, interviewed in 1995, said that Milam's military service record convinced him that Milam was a "good man." He also said that he felt Milam deserved consideration as a father. "Now I don't say I felt like he was a man I wanted to know and be with every day. But I felt like he was honest. I felt like he was—could be counted on to do things and look after his family. I never changed my mind about that. . . . I don't dismiss him in every respect because he made one mistake—bad mistake, but his children are still—he's still entitled to work and feed his children" (Rubin, "Ghosts of Emmett Till.")

15. Public Broadcasting System, "People & Events: Mamie Till Mobley (1921–2003)," online at http://www.pbs.org/wgbh/amex/till/peopleevents/p_parents.html (accessed 9 May 2006).

16. Public Broadcasting System, "People & Events: The Impact of Emmett Till's Murder," online at http://www.pbs.org/wgbh/amex/till/peopleevents/e_impact.html (accessed 9 May 2006).

17. *Supposedly* is an intentional qualification. This description of what happened when Emmett Till was rounded up and later murdered is based on Bryant's and Millam's account, as reported in Huie, "Shocking Story." Moses and Elizabeth Wright, according to other accounts, did try to intervene on the night the killers came to their door. See, for example, Houck, "Killing Emmett," 227. What happened after Emmett Till was kidnapped is open to dispute. Mamie Till-Mobley, for one, questioned the sequence of events that Huie reported. "The tale that unfolded in the *Look* article was horrible," she said. One example she cited: "Oh, God, if Huie had only looked at the photograph of Emmett's body, he would have known that Emmett was in no condition to stand at the riverbank and talk back" (Till-Mobley and Benson, *Death of Innocence*, 212, 213). For an analysis of how Mamie Till-Mobley was portrayed during

and after the trial and of how the social meaning of motherhood was connected to race and gender, see Ruth Feldstein, "'I Wanted the World to See': Race, Gender, and Constructions of Motherhood in the Death of Emmett Till," in *Not June Cleaver: Women and Gender in Postwar America, 1945–1960,* ed. Joanne Meyerowitz (Philadelphia, PA: Temple University Press, 1994), 263–303.

18. Stanford University, The Martin Luther King Jr. Research and Education Institute, "People and Events: Moses and Elizabeth Wright," online at http://www.pbs.org/wgbh/amex/till/peopleevents/p_wrights.html (accessed 10 May 2006).

19. Lewis, *Walking with the Wind,* 47. Black children in the fifties learned about the Emmett Till case from newspapers, as well as from their families and friends. "We read about these horrifying events, and others, in Negro newspapers like the *Pittsburgh Courier,*" recalled one woman who was a teenager at the time of the murder. Not every newspaper offered a sympathetic take on the case, the woman noted. "The *Charlotte Observer,* which was supposed to be a liberal or moderate newspaper, condemned the NAACP, saying it was just as bad as the Ku Klux Klan in raising 'racial' issues about [the] murder." See Tananarive Due and Patricia Stephens Due, *Freedom in the Family: A Mother-Daughter Memoir of the Fight for Civil Rights* (New York: Ballantine Books, 2003), 40, 158. Children also saw Emmett Till as not only a victim but also a hero—with whom they could identify in a variety of ways. A man who was only three at the time was moved by Till's wanting to wear his dead father's ring. "Like Emmett Till," he reminisced, "my earliest idol was my father" (Christopher Paul Moore, *Fighting for America: Black Soldiers—The Unsung Heroes of World War II* (New York: Ballantine Books, 2005), 326. Finally, Emmett Till's murder inspired a generation of children to get involved in the civil rights movement. "It put fire in you," said one man, who was twelve at the time. Wilma King, *African American Childhoods: Historical Perspectives from Slavery to Civil Rights* (New York: Palgrave/Macmillan, 2005), 164.

20. Parks was not the first person to actively protest against segregated seating on public transportation. Several similar demonstrations occurred between 1944 and 1955. Parks, however, has become the most celebrated of the demonstrators. See Barry Schwartz, "Collective Forgetting and the Symbolic Power of Oneness: The Strange Apotheosis of Rosa Parks," *Social Psychology Quarterly* 72 (June 2009): 124–42.

21. Taylor Branch, *Parting the Waters: America in the King Years, 1954–63* (New York: Simon and Schuster, 1988), 128–37; Clayborne Carson, "To Walk in Dignity: The Montgomery Bus Boycott," *OAH Magazine of History* 19 (January 2005): 13–15.

22. Stanford University, The Martin Luther King Jr. Research and Education Institute, "*Browder v. Gale,*" online at http://www.stanford.edu/group/King/index.htm (accessed 9 May 2006).

23. Stanford University, The Martin Luther King Jr. Research and Education Institute, "Rosa Parks (1913–2005)," online at http://www.stanford.edu/group/King/index.htm (accessed 9 May 2006).

24. Branch, *Parting the Waters,* 149.

25. Ibid., 145, 151.

26. Ibid., 159, 160, 161.

27. Ibid., 162.

28. Martin Luther King Center for Nonviolent Social Change, "Chronology of Dr. Martin Luther King, Jr.," online at http://www.thekingcenter.org/mlk/chronology.html (accessed 15 May 2006).

29. Branch, *Parting the Waters,* 197–98.

30. Due and Due, *Freedom in the Family,* 45; Polk County Public Schools, Florida, "Activi-

ties for the Tallahassee Bus Boycott of 1956–58," online at http://www.polk-fl.net/
tah/Lessons/f-6-3.htm (accessed 15 May 2006); "Passive Resistance Spreading?" *Chicago Defender*, 2 June 1956.

31. Lewis, *Walking with the Wind*, 49.

32. Branch, *Parting the Waters*, 175–76 (my italics).

33. Lewis, *Walking with the Wind*, 116, 47. Earlier in his book, Lewis summed up his parents' attitude about people who had run-ins with the law: "As far as my parents were concerned, anyone who was arrested for any reason was 'riffraff,' and that was that. 'Decent' black folks stayed out of trouble. It was that simple" (44).

34. Due and Due, *Freedom in the Family*, 48–50.

35. Ibid., 48–52. The father preferred to refer to himself as Daddy Marion. He was not the women's biological father but their stepfather (10). Daddy Marion was a principal in the Palm Beach County school system and "was chastised by superiors . . . for not controlling his children" (72).

36. Ibid., 73.

37. Ibid.

38. Ibid., 52.

39. Gary M. Pomerantz, *Where Peachtree Meets Sweet Auburn: A Saga of Race and Family* (New York: Scribner, 1996), 279.

40. *Brown v. Board of Education*, 347 U.S. 483 (1954); Charles J. Ogletree Jr., *All Deliberate Speed: Reflections on the First Half Century of "Brown v. Board of Education"* (New York: W. W. Norton, 2004), 9–10.

41. *Brown v. Board of Education*, 349 U.S. 294 (1955); Ogletree, *All Deliberate Speed*, 10–11.

42. Adam Fairclough, *Better Day Coming: Blacks and Equality, 1890–2000* (New York: Viking Penguin, 2001), 225, 221, 222.

43. Cameron McWhirter, " 'Uptown Klan,' Remnant of Racist History," *Atlanta Journal and Constitution*, 11 July 2004. The observer was the newspaper editor, Hodding Carter. "Whatever the rhetoric," Carter explained, "this was a vicious group. They were, to the core, unyielding racists."

44. The Brown case joined five different cases, the first of which, *Briggs v. Elliot*, dated back to 1947 (Ogletree Jr., *All Deliberate Speed*, 4–6). The five cases were not the first to try to end school desegregation. "As early as 1849, African Americans filed suit against the educational system that mandated racial segregation, in the case of *Roberts vs. City of Boston*" (Brown Foundation, "Brown v. Board of Education: About the Case," online at http://brownvboard.org/summary/ [accessed 18 May 2006]). The thirteen plaintiffs, in alphabetical order, were Darlene Brown, Oliver Brown, Lena Carper, Sadie Emmanuel, Marguerite Emmerson, Shirla Fleming, Zelma Henderson, Shirley Hodison, Maude Lawton, Alma Lewis, Iona Richardson, Vivian Scales, and Lucinda Todd (Brown Foundation for Educational Equity, Excellence and Research, "Kansas Plaintiffs in This Landmark Case," online at http://brownvboard.org/trvlexbt/pnl10/pnl10.htm [accessed May 18, 2006); see also James T. Patterson, *Brown v. Board of Education: A Civil Rights Milestone and Its Troubled Legacy* [New York: Oxford University Press, 2001], 27–35).

45. KTWU/Channel 11, Topeka, Kansas, "Black/White & Brown: *Brown versus the Board of Education of Topeka*" (transcript of program, 3 May 2004), online at http://brownvboard.org/video/blackwhitebrown/ (accessed 18 May 2006).

46. Due and Due, *Freedom in the Family*, 15.

47. Lewis, *Walking with the Wind*, 44.

48. Pomerantz, *Where Peachtree Meets Sweet Auburn*, 240. One man, who grew up in

the South and was six years old when the decision was handed down, said it would be a slight exaggeration to say [he] clearly remember[ed]" *Brown*. "I was about to complete second grade, and like every other little colored child in the state of North Carolina, I was in a racially segregated school at the time." He added: "Even at six though, I was keenly aware of segregation and what it meant" (William B. Harvey, "Part I—Life as a Brown Baby," in William B. Harvey and Adia M. Harvey, "A Bi-Generational Narrative on the Brown vs. Board Decision," *Negro Educational Review* 56 (January 2005): 43–49.

49. Fairclough, *Better Day Coming*, 219. A 1955 Gallup poll reported that while 82 percent of southern blacks approved of racial integration on trains and buses, only 53 percent of southern blacks approved of *Brown* (see Kara Miles Turner, "Both Victors and Victims: Prince Edward County, Virginia, the NAACP, and *Brown*," *Virginia Law Review* 90 (October 2004): 1667–91. Some blacks thought that a segregated school did not necessarily mean that black children were worse off; they might actually be better off than going to an integrated school where they would be subject to racism on a daily basis. Others were proud of what they felt all-black schools could achieve (Patterson, *Brown v. Board of Education*, 42–43).

50. Steve Estes, *I Am a Man! Race, Manhood, and the Civil Rights Movement* (Chapel Hill: University of North Carolina Press, 2005), 41, 45. For a detailed analysis of how whites in the south responded to *Brown v. Board of Education* and other advances in the civil rights movement, see Jason Sokol, *There Goes My Everything: White Southerners in the Age of Civil Rights, 1945–1975* (New York: Knopf, 2006).

51. Reported in "The Diehards of Dixie," *Chicago Defender*, 17 March 1956. "Most white southerners," according to Jason Sokol, "identified neither with the civil rights movement, nor with its violent resisters. They were fearful, silent, and often inert" (*There Goes My Everything*, 4).

52. *Congressional Record*, 84th Cong., 2nd sess., 12 March 1956, 4460–61. In the same editorial, the *Chicago Defender* charged that the manifesto was a declaration of treason. The members of Congress who signed the statement, the editorial board said, "have irrevocably pledged themselves to the overthrow of the highest judicial body in the land. This, as we see it, is the same as the advocation of the overthrow of the government by violence, if necessary, and that is treason" ("Declaration of Treason," *Chicago Defender*, 24 March 1956).

53. Fairclough, *Better Day Coming*, 222–23. For a chronology of events in Prince Edward County, see Turner, "Both Victors and Victims." Lampooning the Southern states, the *Chicago Defender* published a cartoon that depicted two children, one white and one black. The white child is labeled "South" and is shown feeding "public school" food to an excited dog. Turning to the black child, he says, "Ah'll throw it away befo' ah giv' *you* any!" ("All White or None," *Chicago Defender*, 4 February 1956).

54. Pomerantz, *Where Peachtree Meets Sweet Auburn*, 223.

55. McWhirter, "'Uptown Klan.'"

56. David Halberstam, "*Brown v. Board of Education*: What It Means to Every American," *Parade*, 18 April 2004.

57. *Congressional Record*, 84th Cong., 2nd sess., 12 March 1956, 4460–61. On the perception of segregationists that the black civil rights movement was, in the main, Communist inspired, see Branch, *Parting the Waters*, 181–82, 209–10; Patterson, *Brown v. Board of Education*, 97; Sokol, *There Goes My Everything*, 85–86.

58. Ernie Suggs, "Old Fighter Faces New Battle: Co-Founder of SCLC Takes Helm of Group," *Atlanta Journal and Constitution*, 25 December 2003. Fred Shuttlesworth

was founder of the Alabama Christian Movement for Human Rights (ACMHR) and an early member of the Southern Christian Leadership Conference (SCLC). See also Marjorie L. White, "Phillips High School: Can It Be a National Historic Landmark?" *Birmingham Historical Society Newsletter*, February 2006. (This article originally appeared as a "Commentary" in the *Birmingham News*, 22 January 2006.)

59. King, *African American Childhoods*, 158. The nine students, who in 1999 were awarded Congressional Gold Medals, were Minniejean Brown, Melba Patillo, Gloria Ray, Ernest Green, Thelma Mothershed, Elizabeth Eckford, Terrence Roberts, Jefferson Thomas, and Carlotta Walls.

60. Ibid. Writing pseudonymous letters to the newspapers, the father of Arkansas Governor Faubus accused his son of being a racist (Branch, *Parting the Waters*, 223).

61. Daisy Bates, *The Long Shadow of Little Rock: A Memoir* (New York: David McKay, 1962), 73, 102–3, 113–60. Daisy Gatson Bates, with her husband L. C. Bates, published the *Arkansas State Press* and served as a mediator and advocate for the students and their families. She also was the president of the state conference of the NAACP. When the teacher of one of the Little Rock nine asked if anyone wanted to attend Central High School, the youngster raised her hand. "I thought about all those times I'd gone past Central High, wanting to see inside" (Melba Patillo Beals, *Warriors Don't Cry: The Searing Memoir of the Battle to Integrate Little Rock's Central High* [New York: Simon Pulse, 1994; abridged ed., 2007], 19).

62. Juan Williams, *My Soul Looks Back in Wonder: Voices of the Civil Rights Experience* (New York: AARP/Sterling, 2004), 65. Not every white southerner perpetrated or condoned violence. Only a fraction did. Yet, though many southerners did not openly advocate violence, they did not necessarily intercede to prevent it. A white male student, who befriended Melba Patillo Beals during the Little Rock crisis, said his father "had been forced to contribute money to the Citizens Council" to keep the family business alive. The young man tried to offer a sympathetic portrait of his dad, despite the father's racist attitudes: "He isn't for race mixing, but he also isn't for beating up anybody's children" (Pattillo Beals, *Warriors Don't Cry* 193).

63. "U.S. Maps War on Terrorism," *Chicago Defender*, 15 November 1958.

64. Melissa Fay Greene, *The Temple Bombing* (New York: Fawcett Columbine, 1996), 5.

65. Ibid., 1–2, 8.

66. Ibid., 6–7.

67. Alexander S. Leidholdt, *Standing Before the Shouting Mob: Lenoir Chambers and Virginia's Massive Resistance to Public School Integration* (Tuscaloosa: University of Alabama Press, 1997), 13, 101, 128.

68. Due and Due, *Freedom in the Family*, 82.

69. "If You're a Man, Granpa—How Come They Call You 'Boy'?" *Chicago Defender*, 7 July 1956.

70. Moore, *Fighting for America*, 327–28. The nephew thought that black parents "who lived in the North" might be more likely to shield their children.

71. "What Country Are We in Now, Mom?" *Chicago Defender*, 26 August 1956.

CHAPTER TWELVE

1. John Hancock Life Insurance Company ad, "How Good a Father Are You?" *Time*, 8 April 1946. The ad also underscored the importance of fathers being good economic providers.

2. Ralph LaRossa, *The Modernization of Fatherhood: A Social and Political History* (Chicago: University of Chicago Press, 1997).

3. L. A. (woman) to Benjamin Spock, 20 June 1956, box 3, Benjamin Spock Papers, Syracuse University (hereafter cited as BSP.). Other examples: A Michigan woman wrote to Spock to say, "With thousands of other couples we signed up as users of your 'Baby-Bible' long ago. Your advice is so realistic, sensible, and 'down-to-earth,' and has helped me through many a dilemma." The writer identified herself as a mother with four children who felt she was "completely unprepared for the joys, tantrums, and challenges of motherhood" (S. K. [woman] to Benjamin Spock, 5 December 1955, box 3, BSP). Less exuberant but equally appreciative, a New York father thanked Spock for his continued assistance (they had corresponded before) and then promptly asked for advice on what to do about his five-year-old boy's "anger and hostility" tantrums. When "punished," the son's "response" was to yell, "When I grow up I'll kill you" (D. D. [man] to Benjamin Spock, 11 December 1957, box 3, BSP). Spock also attracted *super* admirers. One New York mother regularly corresponded with Spock, telling him how "wonderful and charming" she thought he was and advising him not to "worry about [his] book being 'bossy.'" She told him, "If you have learned (and through you, we have learned) that children like to be disciplined, led and directed, it is also true that parents like to be told what to do. In fact, parents are downright *thankful* to be told what to do!" H. I. (woman) to Benjamin Spock, 30 August 1957, box 2, BSP. Spock received mail from outside the United States as well, and some writers expressed concern that *Baby and Child Care* was not as widely available as they felt it should be. See, for example, B. D. ([British] woman) to Benjamin Spock, 3 March 1955, box 2; and N. T. ([Vietnamese] woman) to Benjamin Spock, 29 July 1956, box 3, BSP. Not everyone was caught up in the craze. After Spock moved from the University of Pittsburgh to Case Western Reserve University in 1955, his patient load consisted mainly of low-income African American women who, in his words, "[did]n't seem to expect or to want medical advice on infant feeding, weaning, toilet training, sleeping arrangements, sleep problems." He confessed to a colleague (the Cornell University child psychologist Urie Bronfenbrenner), "I keep saying to the students that it's wonderful there still are parents with complete confidence in their own beliefs and traditions, but I must say that it leaves a physician who has gotten his gratification from rescuing anxious parents feeling out of work and unwanted." Benjamin Spock to Urie Bronfenbrenner, 10 December 1957, box 3, BSP.

4. L. A. (woman) to Benjamin Spock, 20 June 1956, box 3, BSP.

5. "Please write to fathers too," a Detroit women beseeched Spock. "If my husband thought it really important, he might help more, but I can't argue with him all the time about it" (W. K. [woman] to Benjamin Spock, 17 July 1957, box 3, BSP. The writer began her message, "I am writing this at the request of a young mother who borrows my [*Ladies Home Journal*] solely for the purpose of reading your articles on Child Training." In a postscript, the woman said the mother wasn't too strong, tired easily, and needed the assistance of her husband who, in the mother's words, was "full of fun and still a boy at heart."

6. The following discussion on *Baby and Child Care* is based, in part, on Ralph LaRossa, "The Culture of Fatherhood in the Fifties: A Closer Look," *Journal of Family History* 29 (January 2004): 47–70.

7. Spock, *The Common Sense Book of Baby and Child Care*, 2nd ed. (New York: Duell, Sloan, and Pearce, 1957), 1, 15–18.

8. Ibid., 314–16.

9. Ibid., 357–59.

10. Specifically, Spock said, "A father who realizes that his young son sometimes has unconscious feelings of resentment and fear toward him does not help the boy by trying to be too gentle and permissive with him or by pretending that he, the father, doesn't really love his wife very much. In fact, if a boy was convinced that his father was afraid to be a strong man, a firm father, and a normally possessive husband, the boy would sense that he himself was having his mother too much to himself and would feel really guilty and frightened. And he would miss the inspiration of a manly father, which he must have in order to develop his own manliness and courage" (ibid., 360).

11. The term *reify* (which derives from the Latin term for "thing") is used here in the way that Peter L. Berger and Thomas Luckmann suggested it be used. Instead of viewing any *perceived* differences between fatherhood and motherhood as social constructions (i.e., products of convention, subject to cross-cultural, historical, and situational circumstance), Spock seemed to be inclining toward the view that the differences were "something else than human products—such as facts of nature, results of cosmic laws, or manifestations of divine will." That is, he was leaning toward treating them not as "reality" (with quotes) but as reality (without quotes). See Peter Berger and Thomas L. Luckmann, *The Social Construction of Reality: A Treatise in the Sociology of Knowledge* (Garden City, NY: Doubleday/Anchor, 1966), 89. In feminist theoretical terms, the second edition of *Baby and Child Care*, more so than the first, *essentialized* gender. On gender essentialism vs. gender as a social construction, see Candace West and Don H. Zimmerman, "Doing Gender," *Gender and Society* 1 (June 1987): 125–51.

12. U.S. Children's Bureau, *Infant Care* (Washington, DC: U.S. Department of Labor, 1914, 1921, 1929, 1931 [1935 printing], 1942, 1945, 1951). The content analysis of *Infant Care* in the years before the war is reported in LaRossa, *Modernization of Fatherhood*, 41–56. Even though the 1942 and 1945 versions of *Infant Care* were directed to fathers as well as mothers, it still remained a traditional text. The care of a sick baby in the home, for example, was considered "the mother's responsibility" from the start, and it continued to be viewed that way later on, even with the changes made to other sections of the manual. For a history of the Children's Bureau, see Molly Ladd-Taylor, *Raising a Baby the Government Way: Mothers' Letters to the Children's Bureau, 1915–1932* (New Brunswick, NJ: Rutgers University Press, 1986); Nancy Pottishman Weiss, "Save the Children: A History of the Children's Bureau, 1903–1919," (PhD diss., University of California, Los Angeles, 1974). The earlier shift in attitudes was apparent as well to outside observers. Said one journalist, "The effort to get father back in the family (harmoniously) has been going on for years. Ten years that we know of. Looking over a file of these columns, we find the subject coming up repeatedly over that period. . . . Signs of the times over ten years have included the revision of texts on infant care to stress father's interest in development, his enjoyment of the baby, as well as his help in changing, bathing and feeding" (Catherine Mackenzie, "When Father's Help," *New York Times Magazine*, 29 August 1948).

13. U.S. Children's Bureau, *Infant Care* (1955).

14. Ralph LaRossa, Charles Jaret, Malati Gadgil, and G. Robert Wynn, "The Changing Culture of Fatherhood in Comic Strip Families: A Six-Decade Analysis," *Journal of Marriage and Family* 62 (May 2000): 375–87. To be "nurturant and supportive" a character had to be "verbally or physically expressing affection toward a child, serving or caring for a child, verbally encouraging a child, or comforting a child or inquiring about the child's feelings and thoughts." A second analysis added "praising

a child for a completed task or activity or for a job well done, listening to a child's problem, or purposefully teaching a child" (380). A related study, which looked at the same set of comic strips but examined housework and other variables, discovered further evidence of a conservative shift. Higher levels of "patriarchal gender dispari- ties" were found in the late 1950s than in either the late 1940s or early 1950s (or at any other time covered in the project). See Ralph LaRossa, Charles Jaret, Malati Gadgil, and G. Robert Wynn, "Gender Disparities in Mother's Day and Father's Day Comic Strips: A 55 Year History," *Sex Roles* 44 (June 2001): 693–718.

15. Stella Bruzzi, *Bringing Up Daddy: Fatherhood and Masculinity in Post-War Hollywood* (London: British Film Institute, 2005), 38–39. For another analysis of films at this time, see Steven Cohan, *Masked Men: Masculinity and the Movies in the Fifties* (Bloom- ington: Indiana University Press, 1997).

16. Candice Leonard, "Illusions of Change: An Analysis of the Fatherhood Discourse in *Parents Magazine*, 1929–1994" (PhD diss., University of New Hampshire, 1996), 37; Maxine P. Atkinson and Stephen P. Blackwelder, "Fathering in the 20th Century," *Journal of Marriage and Family*, 55 (November 1993): 975–86. Atkinson and Black- welder reported that the ratio of articles referencing nurturant fathering to those referencing economic providing was 1.3 in 1955, compared to 2.5 in 1945 (981). Although much evidence shows that the culture of fatherhood in the late fifties was more traditional than it was in the early fifties, I do not want to give the impres- sion that the difference between the early and late fifties was unequivocal. There is evidence of cultural traditionalization in the early fifties too, providing support for the proposition that the shift was gradual. A good example is what happened to a popular college-level textbook, *Growth and Development of the Young Child*. Before and immediately after the war, the textbook took a fairly progressive stand on issues of gender, but it reversed itself in the early 1950s, becoming more traditional. The 1946 edition said that "the signs of the times indicate that the patriarchal type of family must be and is being greatly modified." It also raised the question, "Is there any reason why [the father] should not help in the care of the sick child if his wife is carrying as heavy a work program as he is. 'H. W.' (housewife) are the initials one finds on records indicating that a woman is staying at home caring for her home. If in addition to being a housewife she carries on a business or profession, is it not fair that the husband become something of an 'H.H.' (house husband)?" The 1953 edition (with a set of new authors on board) eliminated any and all references to "patriarchy" and "househusbands" and talked little, if at all, about the importance of a "fair" division of labor in the home. (The 1958 edition continued on a traditional track.) See Winifred Rand, Mary E. Sweeny, and E. Lee Vincent, *Growth and Develop- ment of the Young Child*, 4th ed. (Philadelphia, PA: W. B. Saunders, 1946), 25, 33; Winifred Rand, Mary E. Sweeny, and E. Lee Vincent, *Growth and Development of the Young Child*, revised by Marian E. Breckenridge and Margaret Nesbitt Murphy, 5th ed. (Philadelphia, PA: W. B. Saunders, 1953); Marian E. Breckenridge and Margaret Nes- bitt Murphy, *Rand, Sweeny, and Vincent's Growth and Development of the Young Child*, 6th ed. (Philadelphia, PA: W. B. Saunders, 1958).

17. An article in *Today's Health* in 1955 reported, "A recent survey of 300 young hus- bands disclosed that nine in ten did not know just what their place in the family was; one in three complained he had no place at all." The author assured readers that the "role of the father . . . [was] not fundamentally different from what it has always been." He then cast his vote in favor of tradition. "Generally speaking, in a two- parent home the man best serves as breadwinner. Only a father can be detached

enough from home to mirror the great world outside. A father has the best chance to set an example of manliness for his son, to be a model of the adult male for his daughter. And because of his link between the world and home, Father can be the most effective teacher of honesty, self-conscience, humor and sportsmanship. When reduced to these essentials, it can be seen that modern fathers have greater opportunity to fulfill their classic role than ever before. Every indication is that they're doing a good job of it, too" (Kenneth Robb, "Today's Father," *Today's Health*, June 1955). Michael Kimmel has made the point that, while a crisis of masculinity may have seemed to people in the late fifties to be "new," in actuality "bygone days" were also "weighted down with their own gendered anxieties" (262). Similar "crises" erupted at the turn of the twentieth century, at the height of the Great Depression, and in the immediate wake of World War II. See Michael Kimmel, *Manhood in America: A Cultural History* (New York: Free Press, 1996), 261.

18. Margaret Mead, "Job of the Children's Mother's Husband," *New York Times Magazine*, 10 May 1959.

19. Bruno Bettelheim, "Fathers Shouldn't Try to Be Mothers," *Parents Magazine*, October 1956.

20. Mead, "Job of the Children's Mother's Husband."

21. Arthur M. Schlesinger Jr., *The Politics of Hope* (New York: Houghton Mifflin, 1962), 244, 246.

22. Ibid., 237, 238. On the inconsistencies in prescriptive texts in the fifties, see Joanne Meyerowitz, "Beyond the Feminine Mystique: A Reassessment of Postwar Mass Culture, 1946–1958," in *Not June Cleaver: Women and Gender in Postwar America, 1945–1960*, ed. Joanne Meyerowitz (Philadelphia, PA: Temple University Press, 1994), 229–62; see also LaRossa, "The Culture of Fatherhood in the Fifties."

23. In one of his books, *The Natural Superiority of Women* (New York: Macmillan, 1952), Ashley Montagu argued that women were innately superior to men. He also thought, however, that women should stay home with their children—a position that angered feminists.

24. B. L. (woman) to Ashley Montagu, 31 December 1957, box 115, Rose Franzblau Papers, Columbia University (hereafter cited as RFP). This letter and the others are among the Franzblau papers in a folder marked "American Husbands." Montagu appeared on the *Arlene Francis Show*. It is not clear why the files from this particular show are stored with the Franzblau papers.

25. M. D. (woman) to Ashley Montagu, no date (probably December 1957), box 115, RFP.

26. M. Y. (woman) to Ashley Montagu, 31 December 1957, box 115, RFP.

27. A. S. (woman) to Arlene Francis, no date (probably December 1957), box 115, RFP. This letter was addressed to the host of the show rather than to Montagu.

28. E. B. (woman) to Ashley Montagu, no date (probably December 1957), box 115, RFP. Some women wrote about housework. "Do American husbands do too much house work on week ends and should they also do the dusting?" (B. A. [woman] to Ashley Montagu, 30 December 1957, box 115, RFP). This writer also recounted an observation: "Recently, while waiting at a bus stop I saw two young husbands walking to their cars. Their arms were loaded with groceries. While they were waiting for the light to change I heard one ask the other, 'After you're through with the super market which other chore do you detest?' The answer was 'I hate them all, but dusting is the devil's own invention.'" Another woman asked, "I would like to know what you think about American husbands who do the family grocery shopping?" (B. W.

[woman] to Ashley Montagu, 30 December 1957, box 115, RFP. A third inquired, "My husband was brought up in the 'old school' type home in which his father was concerned only with earning a living and did not lift a finger in the house. My husband earns more and works less hard—so don't you think he should help out around the house a little?" (E. S. [woman] to Ashley Montagu, 30 December 1957, box 115, RFP.

29. P. D. (woman) to Ashley Montagu, no date (probably December 1957), box 115, RFP. The woman added: "I believe that the husband should 'wear the pants' in the wedded home and also rule the home and family and I was wondering if you thought the same." Another woman talked about a judge who had concluded that the "tragedy of the American teenager" was due the fact that America had become "a nation of matriarchs." His solution: "Put father back as the head of the family" (E. L. R. [woman] to Ashley Montagu, 30 December 1957, box 115, RFP. She may have been referring to a judge in New York City who, in an article in *America* in 1958, was reported to have been impressed with Italy's low juvenile delinquency rate and was told by an Italian official that what made the difference was that "the young people of Italy respect authority." His solution (repeated): "Put father back at the head of the family" ("Put Father Back," *America*, 15 March 1958), 682. In yet another take on the American condition, a woman who listened to Ashley Montagu decided not to ask a question but to state her own beliefs on men. She was not exactly positive. "I understand you're going to speak on American husbands as your next topic. [Montagu apparently discussed the topic more than once on the show.] May I pass on a few words[?] Since my husband is in the Air Force we get a very good look at the American husbands and wives and just what they're made of. On the whole our husbands are irresponsible, immature and expect to be waited on and everything done for them in the home. They come home and stay a few hours not lifting a finger with the children or the housework. They go into a torment when their shirts aren't done just so and if we forget to bring the dry cleaning away one day late. . . . Husbands don't remember anniversaries, birthdays or anything it seems to the wife that's important to her. But I guess I will admit the old saying. 'You can't live with them and can't do without them' is true" (W. F. [woman] to Ashley Montagu, 30 December 1957, box 115, RFP.

30. M. P. (man) to Ashley Montagu, no date (probably December 1957), box 115, RFP.

31. For a detailed description of the study, see Robert R. Sears, Lucy Rau, and Richard Alpert, *Identification and Child Rearing* (Stanford, CA: Stanford University Press, 1965). The transcripts of the interviews, upon which I draw in the sections to follow, are housed at the Murray Research Center of the Harvard-MIT Data Center (Log Number 578) and are used with the permission of the center. As before, in quoting from the transcripts, I have tried to remain faithful to the researchers' punctuation. Exceptions include my being consistent in the length of dashes, even if the researchers were inconsistent. Also, ellipses without brackets denote ellipses in the original transcript, while ellipses with brackets denote instances where I have omitted or skipped over sentences that were in the original transcript.

32. Father 44, 23; Mother 44, second interview, 1, pilot interview, 49, Sears, Rau, and Alpert, ICR interview, MRC, Harvard-MIT Data Center (hereafter cited as Sears et al., ICR interview).

33. Some of what the wife said could also be construed as support for a traditional philosophy: "Well uh, the house is more or less my property." The father's "help with the children" came down to seeing them for a brief time in the morning before he left for work and for generally no more than an hour at night when he returned. "I

come home in the evening and then I like to read the newspaper, and then we eat. And after dinner, I sometimes play with them for half an hour or an hour and sometimes spend—very rarely on occasion, spend the whole evening with them, and then put—sometimes put them to bed. I put them to bed maybe a third of the time. And they like that." The father also reported that he "used to" read to his children, but had not done so "in the last couple of months." The mother did say that now that they had a new baby, the father "usually help[ed]" her get the children to bed" (Father 5, 19, 27; Mother 5, first interview, 24, Sears et al., ICR interview. At the time of the interview, the baby was six weeks old.

34. Father 25, 26; Mother 25, second interview, 4, Sears et al., ICR interview.

35. Said the mother, "In our family it's . . . the father who earns the money and the mother takes care of the house" (Father 9, 12; Mother 9, second interview, 2, Sears et al., ICR interview).

36. Ralph LaRossa, "The Culture and Conduct of Fatherhood in America, 1800 to 1960," *Japanese Journal of Family Sociology* 19 (October 2007): 87–98.

37. Marvin E. Olsen, "Distribution of Family Responsibilities and Social Stratification," *Marriage and Family Living* 22 (February 1960): 60–65.

38. In a time-diary study, subjects are given a special calendar and asked what was being done and by whom at certain times of the day. Time-diary methodology is one of the best ways to gather information on the division of labor in the home, because of the concrete nature of the questions. The Nebraska study did not employ a time-diary methodology. For an excellent example of time-diary methodology in social research, see Suzanne M. Bianchi, John P. Robinson, and Melissa A. Milkie, *Changing Rhythms of American Family Life* (New York: Russell Sage Foundation, 2006).

39. Olsen, "Distribution of Family Responsibilities and Social Stratification," 62 A similar measurement issue emerges when we examine an investigation of 104 married couples in southwestern Los Angeles who were interviewed in 1957. Husbands and wives were interviewed conjointly about their respective spousal roles and "asked to report what they believed were the most important role components, the usual functions or actions subsumed or implied by each role." The child-rearing roles that the couples identified for a wife were "helps the children grow by being their friend, teacher, and guide"; "serves as the model for women for her children"; and "cares for the children's everyday needs." The corresponding roles identified for a husband were "helps the children grow by being their friend, teacher, and guide"; "serves as a model of men for his children"; and "does his wife's work around the house if his help is needed." The kinds of things a husband might do to "help" included caring for the children if his wife was ill. (The corresponding "helping" role for a wife was "she helps earn the living when her husband needs her help or when the family needs more money." The husband, in turn, was expected to be "the breadwinner.") Similar to the other project discussed, this investigation is a study of culture rather than conduct. We get a sense that the couples *believed* that men should be substitute caregivers, but we do not know how the men *behaved* (Nathan Hurvitz, "The Components of Marital Roles," *Sociology and Social Research* 45 (1961): 301–9).

40. For a description of these two California studies, see John A. Clausen, *American Lives: Looking Back at the Children of the Great Depression* (Berkeley and Los Angeles: University of California Press, 1993).

41. Jessica Weiss, *To Have and to Hold: Marriage, the Baby Boom, and Social Change* (Chicago: University of Chicago Press, 2000), 94, 100. Only thirteen of the women in the subsample "criticized their husbands' lack of involvement in childrearing" (99).

42. Sears, Rau, and Alpert, *Identification and Child Rearing*, 265, 274, 275, 280. Another point worth making: When the couples' focus was on the kindergartner's infant care (five years before), their answers were sometimes perfunctory. When the focus shifted to their current situation, the couples offered more detailed accounts. Interviewers also were more open to allowing the fathers and mothers to elaborate about men's *play* activities with their kindergarten-age children.

43. As was done when evaluating the men's level of infant care, the division of kindergartner care was assessed by coders working with the original team of researchers. The coders read the interview transcripts and content-analyzed the couple's answers to the questions. Also, as with infant care, the men's contribution to child care was broken down into categories (six rather than eight). Judging the level of the "father's interaction with [the] child," the coders grouped the men as follows: little interaction (5 percent); between little and friendly interaction (17.5 percent); friendly interaction (42.5 percent); just above friendly interaction (12.5 percent); two steps above friendly interaction but not enough to be categorized as maximal (15 percent); and maximal interaction (7.5 percent). Friendly interaction included having "friendly interchanges with [the] child every day, either at breakfast or in late afternoon, slightly more [than lower category] interaction on weekends, [and having] one or two things [the] father and child do together fairly regularly." Maximal interaction meant "[the] father [was] home a great deal, [made] great effort to be with [the] child in an active way, definitely arrange[d] to spend time alone with [the] child, and [evidence of] many specific things father and child enjoy doing together." Thus, three-fourths of the men had, at the very least, friendly-level interactions with their kindergartners, and one-fifth were maximally involved or close to maximally involved. Interaction was defined as "the amount of time father and child spend in direct interaction with other, doing things and going places together, [as well as] father helping in care of [the] child, etc." However, the nature of the questions appeared to limit the amount of attention given to men's contribution to child care work. The coders also evaluated the degree to which the mothers were "satisfied" with their husbands' child care. On a nine-point scale, all but seven of the forty mothers were scored at the top third of the scale, indicating high satisfaction or close to it. (The categories and findings are based on a statistical analysis of the standardized survey responses, used here with the permission of the Murray Research Center.)

44. Andrew J. Cherlin, *Marriage, Divorce, and Remarriage* (Cambridge, MA: Harvard University Press, 1981), 6. The number of births rose briefly again in the early 1960s. See James T. Patterson, *Grand Expectations: The United States, 1945–1977* (New York: Oxford University Press, 1996), 311. For a history of the ideology of "separate spheres," see Barbara Welter, "The Cult of True Womanhood: 1820–1860," *American Quarterly* 18 (Summer 1966): 151–74.

45. Linda J. Waite, "Working Wives, 1940–1960," *American Sociological Review* 41 (February 1976): 65–80.

46. Patterson, *Grand Expectations*, 80; William M. Tuttle Jr., *"Daddy's Gone to War": The Second World War in the Lives of America's Children* (New York: Oxford University Press, 1993), 248.

CHAPTER THIRTEEN

1. Theodore H. White, *The Making of the President, 1960* (New York: Atheneum, 1961), 350.

2. Kennedy, in particular, claimed there was a missile gap. Eisenhower, defending his administration's policies, insisted there was not. With the benefit of new spy satellites, it was determined in 1961 that Russia had nowhere near the number of warheads that the United States had (Tim Weiner, "Robert McNamara, Architect of Futile War, Dies," *New York Times*, 7 July 2009).

3. A survey in 1956 and 1960 asked a sample of Americans, "During the last few years, do you think our chances of staying out of war have been getting better, getting worse, or stayed the same?" In 1956, 12.6 percent said the chances were getting worse. In 1960, the number jumped to 36.2 percent. In both years, the stayed-the-same answers were virtually identical: 41.1 percent and 41.3 percent. Clearly, the possibility of another full-scale war was on the minds of many voters during the 1960 presidential election (Philip E. Converse, Jeane D. Dotson, Wendy J. Hoag, and William H. McGee III, *American Social Attitudes Data Sourcebook, 1947–1978* [Cambridge, MA: Harvard University Press, 1980], 421).

4. Michael Kimmel, *Manhood in America: A Cultural History* (New York: Free Press, 1996); E. Anthony Rotundo, *American Manhood: Transformations in Masculinity from the Revolution to the Modern Era* (New York: Basic Books, 1993).

5. Jeffrey Montez De Oca, "'As Our Muscles Get Softer, Our Missile Race Becomes Harder': Cultural Citizenship and the 'Muscle Gap,'" *Journal of Historical Sociology* 18 (September 2005): 145–72; see also Robert L. Griswold, "'The Flabby American,' the Body, and the Cold War," in *A Shared Experience: Men, Women, and the History of Gender*, ed. Laura McCall and Donald Yacovone (New York: New York University Press, 1998), 323–48. On backyard bomb shelters, see Elaine Tyler May, *Homeward Bound: American Families in the Cold War Era* (New York: Basic Books, 1988).

6. Alec M. Gallup and Frank Newport, eds., *The Gallup Poll: Public Opinion 2005* (Lanham, MD: Rowman and Littlefield, 2006).

7. In March 1960, public opinion polls indicated "a high degree of anti-Catholic feeling," but one polling organization (Louis Harris and Associates) reported that "there does not appear to be enough . . . to have any deleterious effect on the outcome of the primary" (W. H. Lawrence, "The Democrats: Kennedy's Hope," *New York Times*, 20 March 1960). Anti-Catholic feeling, however, probably posed a greater risk for Kennedy in the general election. On the other side of the coin, and working in Kennedy's favor, was the fact that his support among Catholics was "unusually high" (Jeff Manza and Clem Brooks, "The Religious Factor in U.S. Presidential Elections, 1960–1992," *American Journal of Sociology* 103 [July 1997]: 38–81).

8. Nielsen Wire, "Highest Rated Presidential Debates: 1960 to Present" (Complete Nielsen Ratings Page), online at http://blog.nielsen.com/nielsenwire/media_entertainment/top-ten-presidential-debates-1960-to-present/ (accessed July 31, 2009).

9. White, *Making of the President*, 289.

10. David Halberstam, *The Fifties* (New York: Random House, 1993), 731.

11. White, *Making of the President, 1960*, 288, 289, 291. Kennedy was not actually as physically vigorous as he made himself out to be. He suffered from severe back pain, among other ailments, but was able to conceal his poor health through medication. Robert Dallek, "The Medical Ordeals of JFK," *The Atlantic* (December 2002): 49–61; Robert Dallek, *An Unfinished Life: John F. Kennedy, 1917–1963* (Boston: Little, Brown, 2003); Robert D. Dean, "Masculinity as Ideology: John F. Kennedy and the Domestic Politics of Foreign Policy," *Diplomatic History* (Winter 1998): 29–62.

12. K. A. Cuordileone, "'Politics in an Age of Anxiety': Cold War Political Culture and

the Crisis in American Masculinity, 1949–1960," *Journal of American History* 87 (September 2000): 515–545; Stephen J. Whitfield, *The Culture of the Cold War* (Baltimore, MD: Johns Hopkins University Press, 1991), 209.

13. Toward the end of his term, Eisenhower, too, tried to strike what he thought was a proper balance between being "a man of war" and being "a man of peace." Halberstam, *The Fifties*, 705.

14. Russell Baker, "Nixon Risks War, Kennedy Charges," *New York Times*, 11 October 1960. The war that Kennedy was talking about in this instance was the possibility of an armed clash with Communist China over two Taiwanese islands in the South China Sea which were being bombarded. A week before the election, in answer to a specific set of questions from the *New York Times*, Nixon said he thought "nuclear weapons 'would inevitably be employed' in any general war against the Soviet Union." Hanson W. Baldwin, "Nixon Calls Atom Bombing 'Inevitable' in a Major War," *New York Times*, 30 October 1960.

15. John F. Kennedy Presidential Library and Museum, "JFK in History: John F. Kennedy and PT 109," online at http://www.jfklibrary.org/Historical+Resources/JFK+in+History/John+F.+Kennedy+and+PT109+Page+2.htm (accessed 27 June 2009). One of Kennedy's campaign ads specifically focused on his military service. Museum of the Moving Image, "The Living Room Candidate: Presidential Campaign Commercials, 1952–2008; 1960 Kennedy vs. Nixon," http://www.livingroomcandidate.org/commercials/1960 (accessed 27 June 2009). The actor Henry Fonda was the narrator. A crewman on Kennedy's PT boat testified to Kennedy's courage.

16. Austin C. Wehrwein, "Survey Shows Kennedy is Favored in Wisconsin," *New York Times*, 1 April 1980 (my italics).

17. "Evolution of a President," *New York Times Magazine*, 6 November 1960 (capitalization in original).

18. John Lewis, *Walking with the Wind: A Memoir of the Movement* (New York: Simon and Schuster, 1998), 121.

19. White, *Making of the President*, 323.

20. Taylor Branch, *Parting the Waters: America in the King Years, 1954–63* (New York: Simon and Schuster, 1988), 351–378. Martin Luther King Sr. was replying to the musician and civil rights activist, Harry Belafonte, who was endeavoring to explain to the elder King why it was inappropriate for Martin Luther King Jr. to endorse Kennedy. Said Belafonte, "I don't think Martin should ever be put in the position of becoming an advocate for any candidate." King Sr. told Belafonte, "You are too young for these things" (369). See Lewis, *Walking with the Wind*, 121.

21. Douglas Cater, "Are We Picking a Whirling Dervish?" *New York Times Magazine*, 16 October 1960; "Kennedy Steps Up Attacks on Nixon," *New York Times*, 16 October 1960. One may wonder, if the baby-kissing ritual was a "prerequisite" of American politics, why did it take Kennedy so long to get around to it?

22. Joseph A. Loftus, "Kennedy Campaign to Open In Hawaii, with Alaska Next," *New York Times*, 22July 1960.

23. "Kennedy Skips Campaign Lunch to Vote on Aged-Care Measure," *New York Times*, 30 August 1960.

24. "Kennedy Dazzles Women on Tours," *New York Times*, 2 October 1960 (capitalization in original).

25. Donald Janson, "Kennedy's Wife Charms Voters," *New York Times*, 11 March 1960.

26. "Mrs. Kennedy Learned Politics by 'Osmosis,'" *New York Times*, 15 July 1960.

27. "He Has a Habit of Victory: John Fitzgerald Kennedy," *New York Times*, 14 July 1960.
28. Dallek, *An Unfinished Life*, 253.
29. "Kennedy Starts Tour of Alaska," *New York Times*, 4 September 1960.
30. Martha Weinman, "Now 'Dr. Spock' Goes to the White House," *New York Times Magazine*, 4 December 1960.
31. "Kennedy Dazzles Women on Tours."
32. Anna L. Harvey, *Votes without Leverage: Women in American Electoral Politics, 1920–1970* (Cambridge, UK: Cambridge University Press, 1998), 213.
33. Like JFK, Jacqueline Kennedy was a popular figure during the Presidential primaries. "Isn't she lovely?" said one woman at a Wisconsin campaign stop. "Gorgeous," said another. "Kennedy's Wife Charms Voters," *New York Times*. Nixon's wife, Patricia Ryan Nixon, also could be seen out on the stump. Her press reviews, however, were more contained. "Many of the guests, who included women of both political parties, seemed impressed by Mrs. Nixon's efficiency and coolness," reported the *New York Times*, after a visit she made to New York. "Mrs. Nixon Limns a Homey Picture," *New York Times*, 29 September 1960. Another factor—also connected to fatherhood—that may have contributed to the outcome of election was Jacqueline Kennedy's pregnancy, which meant that JFK was not only the parent of a photogenic daughter but also an expectant dad. In the early days of the campaign, Kennedy made little mention of Jacqueline Kennedy's condition. As the campaign progressed, however, he brought it up—and was asked about it—more. "My wife is going to have a boy in November," JFK noted one morning at a campaign stop, after alluding to the pregnancy a few days before. At his next stop a reporter asked, "How do you know it's going to be a boy?" Kennedy impishly answered, "My wife told me," prompting laughter among the press (White, *Making of the President*, 256). Kennedy's standing as a father may also have been boosted by the fact that in May 1960 the National Father's Day Committee named his younger brother, Robert F. Kennedy, "Father of the Year." At the time, he was the youngest father to receive the award. (RFK also was the father of seven children.) JFK would be awarded the same title in 1963 and was the first president of the United States to be named by the organization. Eisenhower received the award in 1943, long before he became president. Eisenhower's younger brother, Milton S. Eisenhower, was honored in 1958. See *Father's Day: 75th Anniversary Commemorative, 1910–1985* (New York: Father's Day Committee, 1985), 48; see also "Father of the Year Named: Robert F. Kennedy, 34, Youngest to be Given the Honor," *New York Times*, 17 May 1960.
34. "Mrs. Kennedy Has a Boy After a Dash to the Hospital," *New York Times*, 25 November 1960; "Kennedy Child Is First for a President-Elect," *New York Times*, 26 November 1960. Only two children, to date, have been born to a sitting president—the daughters of Grover Cleveland, in 1893 and 1895. The second daughter, named Esther, was the only child ever to be delivered *in* the White House.
35. "Kennedy Brings Caroline News," *New York Times*, 26 November 1960. During the pregnancy, Jacqueline Kennedy had prepared Caroline for the new baby's arrival. As to when she might have first brought the topic up with her, it had been reported during the campaign that she "had followed Dr. Benjamin Spock's advice not to tell her . . . too soon" (Bess Furman, "Broadcasts Set by Mrs. Kennedy," *New York Times*, 20 September 1960).
36. Jacqueline Kennedy had a miscarriage in 1955 and gave birth to a stillborn child

in 1956. To safeguard the pregnancy, she was advised by her physician to limit her activities. Questions from the press about her condition thus were probably also prompted by genuine concern. See Michael O'Brien, *John F. Kennedy: A Biography* (New York: St. Martin's Press, 2005), 500, 777.

37. Ibid., 341, 775.
38. W. H. Lawrence, "Nation Exhorted: Inaugural Says U.S. Will 'Pay Any Price' to Keep Freedom," *New York Times*, 21 January 1961; Anthony Lewis, Presidential Diary: Kennedy's Day Is Long, Exhilarating and Occasionally Tedious," *New York Times*, 21 January 1961.
39. " 'New House' Enthuses Kennedy's Daughter," *New York Times*, 21 January 1961.
40. "It Was a Long, but Proud Day for the Wife of the New President," *New York Times*, 21 January 1961; Doris Kearns Goodwin, *The Fitzgeralds and the Kennedys* (New York: Simon and Schuster, 1987), 940–42.
41. *Inaugural Addresses of the Presidents of the United States from George Washington, 1789, to John F. Kennedy, 1961* (Washington, DC: United States Government Printing Office, 1961), 268. 269.
42. Ibid., 267.

EPILOGUE

1. It is hard to imagine that war would not have such an effect. As Joshua S. Goldstein noted in *War and Gender: How Gender Shapes the War System and Vice Versa* (Cambridge: Cambridge University Press, 2001), "War's influence shadows all of our lives" (410).
2. Dorothy Barclay, "A Child Asks 'What's War?' " *New York Times Magazine*, 8 November 1959. The author also made the point that "far more fathers of this generation were directly involved in war activity than were the fathers of the Nineteen Twenties [in the wake of World War I]."
3. Benjamin Spock, *The Common Sense Book of Baby and Child Care*, 2nd ed. (New York: Duell, Sloan, and Pearce, 1957), 270, 271.
4. Miriam Selchen, "What Are Fathers For?" *Parents Magazine*, June 1957.
5. Ralph LaRossa, "The Culture of Fatherhood in the Fifties: A Closer Look," *Journal of Family History* 29 (January 2004), 47–70.
6. "A Grateful Army Presents Uniform Like Dad's to Child," *New York Times*, 5 February 1960.
7. Howard Schuman and Jacqueline Scott, "Generations and Collective Memories," *American Sociological Review* 54 (June 1989): 359–81. The authors indicated that "judgment [was] necessary in creating . . . [the] categories." For example, "Even a well demarcated 'event' such as World War II consisted of a complex series of more specific events (the attack on Pearl Harbor, the invasion of North Africa, the surrender of Germany, etc.), and the placement of these under the label 'World War II' is an act of conceptualization" (364).
8. Howard Schuman and Willard L. Rogers, "Cohorts, Chronology, and Collective Memories," *Public Opinion Quarterly* 68 (Summer 2004): 217–54. In 2000, the researchers expanded the question to ask about "the past 70 years," to give the events and changes that were mentioned in the 1985 survey the chance to be mentioned again by the new cohort of respondents.
9. Ibid, 222.
10. Schuman and Rogers, "Cohorts, Chronology, and Collective Memories." The classic

statement on generational effects and people's memories was made by Karl Mannheim in "The Problem of Generations," in *Essays on the Sociology of Knowledge*, ed. Paul Kecskemeti (1928; repr., London: Routledge and Kegan Paul, 1952), 276–320. Mannheim proposed the ages from seventeen to twenty-five to be the critical period. Schuman and Rogers expanded the definition to between the ages of twelve and twenty-nine. "We do not have enough events to determine the boundaries more confidently," they said. "Indeed, both boundaries and peaks are likely to vary somewhat for different types of events and different sociocultural settings" (252). For other works on World War II in collective memory, see Francesca Cappelletto, ed., *Memory and World War II: An Ethnographic Approach* (Oxford: Berg, 2005); Kenneth D. Rose, *Myth and the Greatest Generation: A Social History of Americans in World War II* (New York: Routledge, 2008); Susan Rubin Suleiman, ed., *Crises of Memory and the Second World War* (Cambridge, MA: Harvard University Press, 2006); Michael Takiff, *Brave Men, Gentle Heroes: America's Fathers and Sons in World War II and Vietnam* (New York: William Morrow, 2003); Marianna Torgovnick, *The War Complex: World War II in Our Time* (Chicago: University of Chicago Press, 2005).

11. Schuman and Scott, "Generations and Collective Memories," 373.

12. Ibid., 374.

13. More than 58,000 U.S. soldiers were killed in the Vietnam War, with the death toll being highest between 1967 and 1969. More than 49,000 of those who died were between the ages of seventeen and twenty-five. More than 25,000 were under twenty-one (The National Archives, "Statistical Information about Casualties of the Vietnam War," online at http://www.archives.gov/research/vietnam-war/casualty-statistics.html [accessed 28 September 2009]).

14. Schuman and Scott, "Generations and Collective Memories," 372–75.

15. On social mindsets and how they are constructed, see Eviatar Zerubavel, *Social Mindsets: An Invitation to Cognitive Sociology* (Cambridge, MA: Harvard University Press, 1997).

16. Defense Prisoner of War/Missing Personnel Office (DPMO), U.S. Defense Technical Information Center (DTIC)," World War II Accounting History," online at http://www.dtic.mil/dpmo/worldwarII/worldwar_history.htm (accessed 18 September 2009). Of these, 32,610 were in the Navy; 20,557 were in the Air Corps; 17,081 were in the Army; 3,114 were in the Marines; and 851 were classified as "other." The last category includes civilians.

17. Elisabeth Bumiller, "Seizing a Last Chance to Find Lost G.I.'s as WWII Memories Fade," *New York Times*, 6 September 2009.

18. The younger brother of Joseph Huba, an air corps pilot who crashed in the Burmese jungle and whose remains have never been located, spoke of the grief that his family has had to live with: "My poor mother would say, 'If they could just find him so I could bury him—I don't want the birds picking on his body'" (Nina Bernstein, "Still Trying to Bring Their Fallen Heroes Home," *New York Times*, 3 February 2008). The next-of-kin of William Bernice Clark, who participated in the D-Day assault and was unaccounted for afterward, refused to accept that he had perished. "There was no proof, no body," said a cousin, now seventy-nine. Years later, Private Clark's identification tag ("dog tag") was discovered in the sand and ceremoniously returned to his next of kin. Having the relic allowed the family to achieve some semblance of closure. Remarked the cousin, "This feels like an ending" (Kristin M. Hall, "Soldier's Dog Tag Back 63 Years Later," *Atlanta Journal and Constitution*, 7 June 2007).